THE ATTACK
ON
THE
LIBERTY

*The Untold Story of Israel's Deadly
1967 Assault on a U.S. Spy Ship*

James Scott

Simon & Schuster
NEW YORK LONDON TORONTO SYDNEY

Simon & Schuster
1230 Avenue of the Americas
New York, NY 10020

First Simon & Schuster hardcover edition June 2009

SIMON & SCHUSTER and colophon are registered trademarks
of Simon & Schuster, Inc.

For information about special discounts for bulk purchases,
please contact Simon & Schuster Special Sales at
1-866-506-1949 or business@simonandschuster.com.

The Simon & Schuster Speakers Bureau can bring authors
to your live event. For more information or to book an event,
contact the Simon & Schuster Speakers Bureau at
1-866-248-3049 or visit our website at www.simonspeakers.com.

Designed by Paul Dippolito

Manufactured in the United States of America

1   3   5   7   9   10   8   6   4   2

Library of Congress Cataloging-in-Publication Data is available.

ISBN: 978-1-4165-5482-0

For my father, John Scott, who lived to tell about it.
And in memory of the thirty-four, who didn't.

William B. Allenbaugh
Philip McC. Armstrong, Jr.
Gary R. Blanchard
Allen M. Blue
Francis Brown
Ronnie J. Campbell
Jerry L. Converse
Robert B. Eisenberg
Jerry L. Goss
Curtis A. Graves
Lawrence P. Hayden
Warren E. Hersey
Alan Higgins
Carl L. Hoar
Richard W. Keene, Jr.
James L. Lenau
Raymond E. Linn
James M. Lupton
Duane R. Marggraf
David W. Marlborough
Anthony P. Mendle
Carl C. Nygren
James C. Pierce
Jack L. Raper
Edward E. Rehmeyer, III
David Skolak
John C. Smith, Jr.
Melvin D. Smith
John C. Spicher
Alexander N. Thompson, Jr.
Thomas R. Thornton
Philippe C. Tiedtke
Stephen S. Toth
Frederick J. Walton

Oh, hear us when we cry to Thee,
For those in peril on the sea!

—NAVY HYMN

THE ATTACK ON THE LIBERTY

PROLOGUE

I know what a slaughterhouse looks like. That's what this was.
—PETTY OFFICER 3RD CLASS GARY BRUMMETT

Captain William L. McGonagle mustered his men.

On June 8, 1997, the skipper gathered with his remaining crew in front of grave #1817 in section 34 of Arlington National Cemetery. Beneath the single granite headstone rested the unidentified remains of six of McGonagle's men. Eight others lay in individual graves amid manicured lawns and rolling hills of the nation's military cemetery on the banks of the Potomac River.

McGonagle had commanded the U.S.S. *Liberty,* a spy ship the Israelis strafed and torpedoed in what the *Washington Post* later described as "one of the most bloody and bizarre peacetime encounters in U.S. naval history." On this humid morning—the thirtieth anniversary of that dreadful day—McGonagle finally was ready to speak.

This marked the first time in decades some of these men had seen their reclusive captain. He had shied away from interviews and the controversy that still dogged the *Liberty* years after metal cutters reduced it to scrap in a Baltimore shipyard. Now seventy-one, McGonagle took stock of his men through Coke-bottle glasses. His sandy hair was gray and thinning, his trademark tan faded. The Medal of Honor, the nation's highest award for heroism, dangled from his neck.

His silence over the years mirrored his style as captain. He rarely mingled with his men. Even in his downtime on board the *Liberty,*

1

he had retreated alone to the officers' wardroom to watch Doris Day movies. McGonagle's reserved demeanor stemmed in part from his biblical reverence for Navy regulations. He drilled his sailors daily and demanded swabbed decks and sparkling latrines. His men nicknamed him "Shep"—a reference to a loyal dog in a country song, but a fitting description.

The captain greeted his crew among the gravestones with a slow drawl and a nasal accent that reflected his Kansas roots. His family had weathered the Dust Bowl and the Great Depression, ultimately migrating to Southern California, where his father had traded in a job as a sharecropper for one as a janitor. McGonagle got his first toothbrush when he was twelve, his first pair of shoes at fourteen. When a Navy recruiter showed up at his high school near the end of World War II, he skipped a chemistry exam to enlist.

McGonagle's refusal to talk about the *Liberty* made some of his men hate him. But his efforts to suppress the attack that left two-thirds of his sailors dead or wounded failed. The *Liberty* festered inside him, much like the piece of shrapnel lodged for decades between his ribs. Then one day the twisted piece of metal popped out and snagged on his washcloth in the shower. He doubled over in agony when he yanked it out.

Dressed in starched Navy whites, McGonagle was dying. Within months, doctors would remove a portion of his cancerous left lung, leaving him mostly wheelchair bound. In twenty-two months, a team of six horses would deliver McGonagle's flag-draped remains to a hilltop grave overlooking the spot where he now stood. This would be his last chance to address his men about what had happened that sunny afternoon three decades earlier in the eastern Mediterranean.

He didn't disappoint them.

On June 8, 1967, the Israeli Air Force and Navy pounded the *Liberty* as the ship trolled alone in international waters off the coast of the Gaza Strip, eavesdropping on the war between Israel and its Arab neighbors. The attack killed thirty-four American sailors and injured 171 others in the most deadly assault on an American ship since the U.S.S. *Indianapolis* was torpedoed in the waning days of World War II.

The specter of the *Liberty* has haunted the U.S. Navy and intelligence community for decades. The underlying question the attack raised in 1967 still resonates: How do politics and diplomacy impact battlefield decisions? In the case of the *Liberty,* the White House, afraid of offending Israel's domestic backers at a time when it needed support for its Vietnam policy, looked the other way. Likewise, Congress failed to formally investigate the attack or hold public hearings. No one was ever punished.

Vital lessons went unheeded, including the flawed logic of sending unarmed spy ships alone into hostile waters with only the American flag for protection. Seven months after the attack on the *Liberty,* communist North Korea seized the spy ship U.S.S. *Pueblo* in international waters, resulting in what some analysts argue was the worst intelligence breach in modern history.

The attack on the *Liberty* began when Israeli fighter jets hammered the ship with rockets and cannons. Napalm turned the deck into a 3,000-degree inferno. Torpedo boats soon followed, ripping a hole thirty-nine feet wide and twenty-four feet tall in the ship's steel skin. The approximately hour-long attack spared no one. Stretcher bearers were shot, sailors burned, liferafts sunk.

Armor-piercing bullets zinged through the ship's bulkheads and shattered coffee mugs, lodged in navigation books, and rolled about on the deck floors. Investigators later counted 821 shell holes, some created with American-made munitions used by Israeli forces. "There wasn't any place that was safe," one of the officers later recalled. "If it was your day to get hit, you were going to get hit."

For nearly seventeen hours, McGonagle and his men fought to save the ship. The injured and dying crowded the mess deck, where corpsmen converted lunch tables to gurneys. Transfusions were given arm to arm. Uninjured sailors learned to stitch up wounds. The ship's lone doctor performed surgery by the light of a battle lantern.

On the bridge, McGonagle, suffering a concussion, his leg peppered with shrapnel, steered the *Liberty* out to sea as it spewed classified documents and oil from the torpedoed hole. With the navigation system largely destroyed, McGonagle studied the ship's wake and ordered turns of the rudder. That evening, he steered by the stars. Crewmen on the bow aimed signal lights skyward, hoping to alert American rescue planes and helicopters to the *Liberty*'s position. None came.

Halfway around the world, the unknowing American public celebrated Israel's stunning victory over its Arab neighbors in what later became known as the Six-Day War—a welcome reprieve from the grind of the Vietnam War and race riots that left American cities in flames. Israel apologized within hours of the attack, blaming it on a series of tactical blunders that culminated in its forces mistakenly concluding that the *Liberty* was an Egyptian horse and troop transport ship. The White House eagerly accepted the apology.

The Navy barred its investigators from traveling to Israel to interview pilots and torpedo boat skippers. The inquiry lasted just eight days—less time than it took to bury some of the dead. The Navy's top-secret final report proved a muddled mess with typos, misspellings, and contradictory findings.

The declassified summary released to the press on June 28, 1967, concluded that the attack by Israeli forces was most likely an accident, but it also ruled that it had insufficient information to determine reasons for the assault. The investigation seemed engineered to protect Israel, stating that witnesses reported that the *Liberty*'s flag might have been difficult to see, even though that statement contradicted the testimony of every officer and crewmember aboard the ship.

Chief of Naval Operations Admiral David McDonald seethed when he read the findings prepared for the public. The report left him "with the feeling that we're trying our best to excuse the attackers." "Were I a parent of one of the deceased this release would burn me up," he wrote in an angry handwritten memo. "I myself do not subscribe to it."

The media didn't either. The *Washington Post* slammed the Navy's investigation as "not good enough." The *Chicago Tribune* proclaimed it generated "more fog and unanswered questions than clarification." "Did the attackers, in fact, know that the *Liberty* was an American ship?" asked the *Evening Star,* another Washington daily. "It seems to us they must have known."

Deaf ears greeted the handful of congressmen who rallied for action.

"Whatever is the reason for the attack, it was an act of high piracy," declared Representative Craig Hosmer of California on the floor of the House. "Those responsible should be court-martialed on charges of murder, amongst other counts."

"I can't tolerate for one minute that this was an accident," Senator Bourke Hickenlooper of Iowa told fellow members of the Senate Foreign Relations Committee. "I can't accept these explanations that so glibly come out of Tel Aviv."

"How could this be treated so lightly in this the greatest Capitol in all the world?" asked Representative Thomas Abernethy of Mississippi. "The world has been standing by looking at us now for days since the *Liberty* was pounced upon. What do we do? What do we say?"

The United States said nothing.

Neither did McGonagle.

For the men gathered in Arlington, the *Liberty* had become an albatross. Some crewmembers battled through years of physical therapy and surgeries. Emotional trauma drove others to alcoholism and divorce court. One crewmember, who nearly drowned in the ship's flooded bowels, still woke up some nights under his bed, banging on the bottom of the box spring, pleading for someone to let him out.

McGonagle also couldn't let go. He refused to throw out notes that detailed with clinical precision how each of his men died: "Blast injury to brain," "Multiple bullet and shrapnel wounds," "Basal skull fracture." He also clung to copies of the letters he wrote to the wives and parents of the dead, letters he wept over as he composed them in a hotel room in Malta days after the attack.

Over the years, many of President Lyndon Johnson's former advisers—including the directors of the CIA, NSA, and State Department—acknowledged what many in the intelligence community secretly believed for years: the attack was no accident. But McGonagle would not live long enough to learn some of the darker secrets, including how senior American officials had contemplated sinking his ship at sea to block reporters from photographing the damage and sparking public outrage against Israel.

Still, McGonagle remained silent. He refused to join the *Liberty*'s survivors association, whose members begged Congress to investigate the attack. When asked to attend the 1987 reunion marking the attack's twenty-year anniversary, he drafted a six-page letter to one of his former chief petty officers, telling him that the association might not like what he had to say. The implication was not lost on the sailors. Their captain, who had steered the men to safety using only the North Star, had abandoned them.

One of his officers wrote him hate mail.

In Arlington that June morning, surrounded by a sea of white tombstones, McGonagle had reached the end of a personal journey. For years he had wrestled with his responsibility to protect his men and his oath to serve the Navy, which had plucked him from the poverty of the Coachella Valley date fields and declared him a hero.

Unbeknownst to his men, McGonagle had quietly conducted his own inquiry. He hammered out letters over the years to the Navy, the State Department, and the National Archives, demanding files on the attack. He pored through records from the Navy's court of inquiry and sifted through yellowed memos, diaries, and telegrams at the Lyndon Baines Johnson Library and Museum in Texas.

His questions were many. Why were the fighter jets that had been sent to help the *Liberty* suddenly recalled? Why did it take almost seventeen hours for help to arrive? If he was a hero the nation was to be proud of, why had President Johnson shunned him, refusing to present his Medal of Honor at the White House, as is customary?

McGonagle also examined Israel's story. He questioned how pilots and torpedo boat commanders from one of the world's top militaries confused the *Liberty* with an aged Egyptian transport ship a fraction of its size. Why didn't the Israelis fire warning shots across the bow or try to stop the *Liberty* before torpedoing it? How had the attackers on a clear afternoon failed to spot the American flag or freshly painted hull markings in an assault that raged for approximately an hour?

After all these years, McGonagle now had something to say.

The eager teenage boys who had scrubbed decks and chipped paint had turned gray and soft bellied. Some had grown children and spouses in tow, all crowded among the headstones. A warm breeze rustled the trees as McGonagle clutched the podium. Old Shep, their wayward captain, had returned.

"For many years I had wanted to believe that the attack on the *Liberty* was pure error. It appears to me that it was not a pure case of mistaken identity," McGonagle told his men. "I think that it's about time that the state of Israel and the United States government provide the crewmembers of the Liberty, and the rest of the American people, the facts of what happened."

CHAPTER 1

I got my orders today! They weren't anything like what I put in for. I got a ship, the USS Liberty.

—ENSIGN JOHN SCOTT, LETTER TO HIS PARENTS

Commander William McGonagle paced the bridge of the U.S.S. *Liberty* dressed only in his boxer shorts, white T-shirt, and slippers. The skipper, who normally refused to be seen out of full uniform, felt anxious this Wednesday morning. It was 4:30 A.M. on May 24, 1967, and the skipper could see little through the darkness that settled over the Ivory Coast port. McGonagle ordered the officers and crew awakened. The ship's loudspeaker soon crackled: "Reveille! Reveille! All hands heave out and trice up." Exhausted officers, many of whom had just gone to bed after a late-night party, stumbled out of staterooms, tucking in shirts, fastening belts, and tying shoelaces to prepare for the unexpected sea duty. The main lights in the passageways flickered on and the corridors filled with voices of tired sailors en route to duty stations. McGonagle directed his officers to prepare for departure. The skipper usually would be asleep in his stateroom at this hour, but a new set of orders had rolled off the ship's teletype approximately forty-five minutes earlier, demanding the *Liberty* immediately set sail. In his haste to obey, McGonagle didn't feel he had time to dress.

The *Liberty*, squeezed between two ships at the end of a concrete pier in Abidjan, now buzzed. Down in the engine room, sailors stoked the ship's boilers. Cooks in the mess deck and wardroom brewed coffee

9

by the gallon for the nearly three hundred officers and crewmembers. Deckhands outside in the humid African morning secured the shore boats and readied mooring lines. The *Liberty* had arrived in Abidjan on a rainy morning just forty-eight hours earlier, its first port of call in a planned four-month cruise along the west coast of Africa. McGonagle had intended to spend a few days loading crates of vegetables, fruits, and provisions before steaming on to Angola, Liberia, and Gabon. Many of the crewmembers, restless after three weeks at sea, had hit the bars, beaches, and even a bowling alley. Others enjoyed a three-hour safari in the embassy's propeller-driven DC-3, which buzzed over elephants, water buffalo, and local villages. The *Liberty*'s change of orders had come so quickly that many of the men still downed beers in Abidjan's bars. The skipper dispatched one of his officers in the ship's pickup truck to gather them. The sun would be up soon: McGonagle needed to move.

The *Liberty*'s new orders—four sentences on a single sheet of paper—provided little detail about the upcoming mission. The orders directed McGonagle to steam north to Spain, load extra equipment and men, and depart for the Egyptian coast in the eastern Mediterranean and await further instructions. The headlines of the world's newspapers foreshadowed the ship's new assignment. Even on board the *Liberty* as it crossed the Atlantic, the teletype spit out abbreviated bulletins that tracked the growing tension in the Middle East. A week earlier Egypt had expelled United Nations peacekeepers from the Sinai Peninsula, the vast desert that separates most of Egypt from Israel. As many as a hundred thousand Egyptian troops, tanks, and artillery amassed along the Jewish state's border. Less than thirty-six hours earlier, as sailors had spilled down the *Liberty*'s gangway in Abidjan, Egypt had announced a blockade of the Strait of Tiran, a narrow waterway that connects Israel to the Red Sea. Closure of the strait restricted Israel's oil imports and cut off its trade markets in Asia and Africa. War appeared imminent.

The skipper's haste this morning reflected the pressure he had felt since the *Liberty* sailed from its home port of Norfolk, Virginia, on May 2. McGonagle's career was flatlining—and he knew it. Many of his peers commanded destroyers, led fighter wings, and worked policy problems for the Navy's senior officers at the Pentagon. The *Liberty* in contrast ranked as the latest in a series of mediocre assignments that had dogged the forty-one-year-old skipper. McGonagle had spent the past thirteen months inching his ship along the African coast, patrolling an obscure frontier of the Cold War. Prior to his command of the *Liberty,* he had taught naval science at the University of Idaho. McGonagle spent much of his career at sea on tug and salvage vessels, a mundane job that had taught him the limits of what a ship could endure. He had towed target rafts for gunnery practice and raised sunken vessels off Guam after Typhoon Karen wrecked the island in 1962. A highlight of his career was a commendation letter the governor of American Samoa sent after McGonagle salvaged a Japanese tuna boat that had burned and sunk in the Pago Pago harbor.

McGonagle lacked the U.S. Naval Academy pedigree or family legacy that assured others entrance into the Navy's aristocracy. Rather than hone his seafaring skills as a midshipman on the banks of the Severn River, McGonagle had earned his commission through the Naval Reserve Officers Training Corps program at the University of Southern California. Marine sergeants had barked at him at 5:30 each morning as he cranked out push-ups and ran mile after mile. He learned to wear a uniform and march to and from class. The Navy's fifty-dollar monthly stipend, he found, afforded him little more to eat than oatmeal. McGonagle's first test of his training came soon after graduation when he served as a gunnery officer in the Korean War, hammering shore batteries with 40-mm cannons from the deck of the minesweeper U.S.S. *Kite.* He participated in the defense of Pusan and the amphibious landings at Inchon and Wonsan, earning the Korean Service Medal with six battle stars. McGonagle would later recall the chaos he witnessed when two nearby ships struck mines. The explosion hurled sailors into the water. The stunned young officer watched as both ships sank in minutes.

Now, on the bridge of the *Liberty,* as he shouted orders in his boxers and T-shirt, McGonagle recognized that his career hinged on the success of this next mission. Twice the Navy had passed him over for promotion to the rank of captain. If the Navy didn't promote him soon, McGonagle knew he would be forced to retire as the Navy thinned its ranks to allow what it perceived as more talented officers to advance. For the married father of three that would mean the end of a career he had fought for since the afternoon he had enlisted more than two decades earlier. The *Liberty*'s officers sensed his frustration. Though he was twice the age of many on board, McGonagle remained an imposing figure. His lean six-foot-one-inch athletic frame hinted at the speed and agility of a onetime high school football star and team captain. The Coachella Valley Lions Club had honored him in 1943 as the school's most inspirational and outstanding player. He had even played left guard in 1945 during the brief period he spent at the University of Redlands—the team went undefeated that year—before he transferred to USC.

McGonagle's disposition proved equally intimidating. His slow Kansas drawl disguised a rigid demeanor that reflected his World War II–era training. He ordered his officers to wear hats at all times and forbade them to dress in the Navy's white short uniform, an uncomfortable restriction in Africa's tropical climate. The skipper rarely fraternized with his men. When many of the officers gathered in the wardroom after meals to smoke cigarettes and drink coffee, McGonagle often retreated to his stateroom to write letters and read. McGonagle took command of the *Liberty* seriously and set high expectations for his crew. He drilled his men almost daily to test firefighting, damage control, and gunnery skills. The skipper greeted his crew's foul-ups with a scorching temper that one officer described in a letter as "the wrath of the old man." McGonagle's career pressure only exacerbated his outbursts and sparked him to micromanage his men. He demanded to review all of the *Liberty*'s incoming and outgoing messages. He woke sleeping sailors in the middle of the night to chew them out over petty errors. A minor infraction left one junior officer confined to quarters for meals.

Ensign Patrick O'Malley had suffered the sting of McGonagle's temper only days earlier. The *Liberty*'s mission marked the first assignment at sea for the twenty-two-year-old Minneapolis native, the ship's most junior officer. The assistant operations officer and ship's secretary, who

had barely had time to unpack his footlocker before the *Liberty* sailed
out of port, fumbled basic tasks, reflecting his inexperience. When
one of O'Malley's men lost an important message regarding quarterly
tests for promotions, O'Malley dashed off a message requesting the
Navy personnel office transmit another copy. McGonagle exploded.
The skipper summoned O'Malley to the bridge over the loudspeaker.
The young officer arrived to find McGonagle perched in his chair. He
wore dark sunglasses and a cigar dangled from his mouth. McGonagle
plucked out the cigar, blew a plume of smoke, then waved the cigar in
front of O'Malley. "My career is at stake here," the skipper barked. "If
there is another mistake like this, this cigar is going to light the cannon
that is going to blow your career to smithereens. You're a smart kid. Is
that clear?"

Tied up alongside the Abidjan pier, the *Liberty* appeared unremark-
able. It was painted a standard Navy gray with its name freshly stenciled in black across the stern and its hull numbers in white on either
side of the bow. The superstructure that contained the bridge and officer staterooms towered four stories above the center of the main deck.
A single stack belched dark smoke from the bunker fuel oil the *Liberty*
burned in its boilers. When the ship was under way, the American flag
fluttered above the bridge from the tallest of the three masts. The *Liberty* stretched less than half the length of an aircraft carrier and lacked
the cannons of a battleship, for years the symbol of American naval
dominance. Compared to sleek destroyers, the greyhounds of the sea,
the *Liberty* wheezed over waves at a top speed of only eighteen knots,
or just under twenty-one miles per hour. Its undistinguished appearance camouflaged its mission: the *Liberty* was a spy ship.

Oregon shipbuilders hammered out the *Liberty* in just ten weeks
in the waning months of World War II. The 455-foot-long cargo ship,
originally christened the S.S. *Simmons Victory*, joined a fleet of more
than five hundred freighters punched out on assembly lines nationwide
to compensate for the losses caused by German submarines. These
cargo ships ferried everything from troops and bullets to food, fuel,
and toilet paper. The *Simmons Victory*, delivered in May 1945 to the

Maritime Commission, served only briefly in the Atlantic and Pacific in the final days of World War II but played a vital role in the Korean War. Between November 1950 and December 1952, the cargo ship chugged across the Pacific nine times to equip American troops fighting communist North Korea. Six years later, with the Korean War over, the *Simmons Victory* joined the National Defense Reserve Fleet and was mothballed in Washington's Puget Sound, its career seemingly over.

Halfway around the world, Soviet technicians transformed trawlers into spy ships, jammed with eavesdropping equipment and linguists trained to intercept American radio communications and radar signals. The fleet of as many as forty ships harassed American forces in the Mediterranean and off the coast of Southeast Asia. Others monitored America's overseas bases in Spain and Scotland. One ship patrolled off Guam and reported the takeoffs of B-52 bombers to North Vietnam. Soviet spy ships even prowled America's shores near major military bases, including the Charleston Naval Base in South Carolina and Florida's John F. Kennedy Space Center. The ships trolled just beyond America's three-mile territorial limit though still close enough that sunbathers on beaches could easily spot them. Occasionally trawlers trespassed into American waters, prompting the Navy to escort them back into international waters.

The Defense Department decided the United States would not be outflanked by the Soviets. The National Security Agency and the Navy developed a plan. American warships and planes for years had carried out similar spy missions. But warships were expensive to operate and were handicapped by various maritime treaties. Stationed off the coast of foreign nations, combat ships appeared provocative and made eavesdropping difficult. Fuel costs and flight-time restraints likewise handicapped airplanes. Cargo ships offered an ideal solution. The lumbering liners could troll for weeks in a single spot, intercepting radio broadcasts, phone calls, and radar transmissions twenty-four hours a day, a job one estimate showed would require as many as thirteen spy planes to duplicate. The conversion from a cargo ship to spy ship cost taxpayers approximately $3.1 million. Fueling, staffing, and operating each ship cost $2.5 million annually.

The Navy commissioned the U.S.S. *Oxford* in July 1961. The 11,500-

ton ship soon sailed for its first mission along the east coast of South America. Over the next few years, the Navy commissioned the U.S.S. *Georgetown,* U.S.S. *Jamestown,* and U.S.S. *Belmont.* The U.S.N.S. *Pvt. Jose F. Valdez* and U.S.N.S. *Sgt. Joseph E. Muller* joined the fleet, though civilians with the Military Sea Transportation Service largely operated both. The Navy classified its new fleet as "technical research ships" and developed a cover story: the vessels conducted scientific studies into electromagnetic propagation and advanced communications systems, including moon relay and satellite tracking. The Navy's policy, however, was "to discourage any public attention on these ships and their mission." Impressed by the success of the program, the Navy called the *Simmons Victory* back into service in February 1963.

Shipfitters with Oregon's Willamette Iron & Steel Corporation reengineered the *Simmons Victory* over the next two years, converting its cargo holds into secret rooms guarded by cipher locks. Technicians installed receivers designed to intercept radio communications and Morse code along with magnetic tape recorders. Electricians later affixed a satellite dish to the ship's stern that towered approximately thirty-five feet above the deck and bounced messages off the moon at a hundred words a minute back to NSA headquarters in the wooded suburbs of Washington. Forty-four other antennae aimed skyward, prompting one admiral to describe the ship as a "porcupine." On the frigid morning of December 30, 1964, the 13th Naval District Band launched into the National Anthem on the docks in Bremerton, Washington. The American flag rose up the mast as the ship's new executive officer set the first watch. The U.S.S. *Liberty*—named in honor of ten cities and towns with the same name—officially was born.

Like its namesakes, the *Liberty* functioned as a small town. Two Babcock & Wilcox boilers produced superheated steam that powered the turbines at up to 8,500 horsepower and generated the electricity to run the ship's lights, radios, and navigation system. A desalination plant made ocean water drinkable and provided fresh water for showers, the galleys, and boilers. Walk-in freezers, refrigerators, and pantries carried frozen steaks, chickens, and canned hams. The main griddle was so large that the cooks coated their arms in Crisco to protect against popping grease when flipping burgers near the back. The *Liberty* boasted a small infirmary along with a doctor and two medical corpsmen for emergencies. A post office sold George Washington stamps for a nickel while pricier airmail stamps cost eight cents. The ship's barber buzzed heads in his one-stool shop and a small store sold everything from razor blades and toothpaste to underwear, radios, and cigarettes.

Sailors checked out Louis L'Amour, Zane Grey, and Ray Bradbury paperbacks in the ship's library and leafed through issues of *Reader's Digest* and *Life* magazine when not at work. Some of the enlisted men used the quiet space to cram for high school equivalency exams while others piled in on Sunday mornings for a nondenominational worship service. Men built and raced model cars in the hobby shop while the ship's collection of woodworking tools allowed McGonagle's predecessor to handcraft the African mahogany rails that adorned the bridge. Other crewmembers lifted weights, played hearts in the berthing spaces, or fished for red snapper and sharks off the stern when anchored. The ship's soda fountain offered ice cream after dinner, and in the evenings sailors watched scratched Dean Martin, Rock Hudson, and Tyrone Power movies on 16-mm reels projected on curtains on the walls of the mess deck and wardroom.

A class system permeated the *Liberty*'s ranks. Nearly half the sailors worked for the Naval Security Group, the intelligence and cryptology command that reported to the National Security Agency. These crewmembers, dubbed "spooks," held top-secret clearances and bunked together in the rear of the ship. The spooks' clean fingernails and starched uniforms contrasted with the dirty dungarees and the smell of sweat and fuel oil clinging to members of the ship's company, often condescendingly referred to as "deck apes." Many among the ship's company felt that the spooks were arrogant, uninterested in the ship's drills, and received preferential treatment. The rear-berthing compartment was a smoother ride in rough seas and was just steps to the mess deck and ship's laundry. The spooks fueled the tension by playing practical jokes on gullible sailors, often warning them not to stray too close to the moon-relay dish on the stern or risk sterilization.

Unlike most Navy ships that steamed as part of a fleet, the *Liberty* and its sister spy ships sailed alone, often along remote and sometimes hostile shores. Though the government denied it for years, the spy ship *Muller* routinely fished refugees from the waters off Cuba. The *Liberty* operated off Africa, eavesdropping on the developing nations and scouting signs of Soviet penetration. The ship spent so much time there that the men decorated the wardroom walls with African masks and batiks. The *Liberty* had steamed up the Congo River on one mission, while crewmembers built houses at a leper colony on another. The terrain was so barren at times that tree stumps onshore served as the only navigational aids. The *Liberty* and its sister ships carried only four .50-caliber machine guns for defense, designed in case the ship ever needed to repel boarders. These Navy ships sailed under an American conviction, fueled by the nation's post–World War II status as a superpower, that no nation would dare attack a U.S. flagged vessel in international waters.

With the crewmembers all on board, fresh vegetables loaded, and the ship's truck secured on deck, the *Liberty* sailed at 7:30 A.M., clearing Abidjan's narrow Vridi Canal, separating the harbor from the ocean, in fifteen minutes. It had proven a difficult morning for many of the officers and crew. Some officers, who had attended an embassy party the night before, had stumbled back to the ship shortly before the orders arrived. Ensign John Scott had to escort the ship's chief engineer to bed, unfastening Lieutenant George Golden's sword and tunic to make sure he didn't choke in his sleep. Golden dozed through reveille. Scott fared little better. The early departure coupled with his headache meant he failed to mail his weekly letter to his parents. "I was too hung over to remember," Scott later confessed in a letter. "It was a bad morning for getting underway."

Lieutenant Commander Philip Armstrong, Jr., the ship's executive officer and second in command, chided the younger officers, many of whom nursed hangovers with cups of black coffee in the wardroom as the *Liberty* steamed north toward Spain at fifteen knots. The thirty-seven-year-old Armstrong, born in Detroit on Independence Day in 1929, managed the *Liberty*'s officers and enlisted sailors, oversaw the ship's administrative duties and executed McGonagle's orders. He was a much less imposing figure than McGonagle. Armstrong often hid his buzzed hair, which had begun to gray, beneath his khaki officer's hat. He stood just shy of six feet and was slender with a chiseled jaw and solid physique, despite his penchant for scotch. The executive officer wore glasses and chain-smoked cigarettes. The married father of five—three boys and two girls—was one of only three Naval Academy graduates on the *Liberty*.

Armstrong and McGonagle could not have been more different. Compared to the skipper, who applied a strict interpretation of Navy regulations, Armstrong was a cerebral leader and a keen appreciator of personalities. He recognized that not all decisions could be found in the pages of Navy manuals, that good governance involved creativity and an understanding of people's strengths and weaknesses. The executive officer observed, for example, that McGonagle's rigidity irritated many of the junior officers, who often suffered his outbursts. Armstrong refused to allow his men to criticize McGonagle in the skipper's absence, but would often do so himself. The younger officers realized that Armstrong did so not out of dislike or disrespect for the skipper, but to defuse the tension McGonagle created among the officers and crew. Armstrong's criticism let the men know that he appreciated the concern over McGonagle's leadership, but also prevented one of them from a career-damaging slip-up.

The executive officer had demonstrated his camaraderie with his men a year earlier. The Navy holds an initiation ceremony the first time a sailor crosses the equator. Veteran sailors called "shellbacks" shave the heads of the uninitiated "pollywogs." The pollywogs climb through an approximately thirty-foot chute made from a tarp and filled with rotting trash and food waste as sailors heckle and paddle them. Armstrong had never participated in a line-crossing ceremony despite his long career in the Navy. The shellbacks couldn't wait. For two weeks, cooks hoarded rotting food in a locked compartment as nervous sailors waited. The day before the ceremony, Armstrong met in secret with a dozen of his fellow pollywogs. Lieutenant j.g. Mac Watson recorded the meeting with a single line in his journal: "Formulated plan to capture garbage." The pollywogs broke into the locked compartment that night and seized the trash. Bag after bag of garbage soon dropped into the ocean as Armstrong secured his hero status.

Unlike the rigid McGonagle, Armstrong often bent regulations. The ship's supply officer discovered in a routine audit that the executive officer had used some of the *Liberty*'s money to buy personal power tools and carpeting for his Virginia Beach home. His close ties with some sailors at a repair shop back in a Norfolk had resulted in a taxpayer-funded paint job for his aged Plymouth, albeit battleship gray. His most serious infraction concerned his thirst for scotch. The Navy barred alcohol on ships, which meant *Liberty* sailors could go as long as a month without a drink. But not Armstrong. Ensign Scott discovered that when he first reported aboard the *Liberty* and knocked on the door of the executive officer's stateroom. A gravelly voice ordered him inside, where Scott found Armstrong at his desk and two other officers seated on a nearby couch. The Liberty's newest officer introduced himself.

"What's your pleasure?" Armstrong asked. "Scotch or bourbon?"

"Sir?"

"Scotch or bourbon?" he repeated.

Scott froze. The twenty-three-year-old was no prude but was stunned by Armstrong's offer. Scott recalled one of his instructors in Officer Candidate School ordering him to crank out extra push-ups as punishment for a hangover he had earned while on time off. He felt certain Armstrong's invitation was a test. Not until later did Scott learn this was how the executive officer welcomed all new officers aboard the *Liberty*. Scott considered his options when he noticed a couple of bottles that poked out of one of the drawers of Armstrong's desk. He glanced at the officers on the couch. Each one held a glass. One of the men raised his and shook it so the cubes rattled in the bottom. Armstrong motioned for Scott to decide.

"Scotch, please," he said. "Sir."

The executive officer fished a bottle of his favorite Johnnie Walker Black Label from the drawer, unscrewed the top, and poured a glass for the *Liberty*'s new ensign in what would become an afternoon ritual.

Armstrong mixed his Johnnie Walker with cold water from the fountain in the passageway outside his stateroom. Fearful that McGonagle might discover his afternoon cocktail hour, Armstrong later asked a favor of Scott, one of the *Liberty*'s engineers. With the help of a couple of shipfitters one afternoon, Scott pulled the water fountain away from the wall, removed the rear plate, and spliced a new waterline. The men cut a hole through the passageway bulkhead into the executive officer's stateroom with a blowtorch and ran the new cold water line into Armstrong's room just beneath his sink that produced only tepid water. A valve on the end controlled the flow. Armstrong never again would have to leave his stateroom to mix a cold drink.

Many of Armstrong's men looked past his flaws. The executive officer recognized that the majority of the *Liberty*'s sixteen officers were under thirty. The Navy was the first time many had been away from home. Armstrong invited some of them to his Virginia Beach home each week when the *Liberty* was in port, for dinner with his wife and children. He encouraged both officers and enlisted men to seek him out with problems. He graciously corrected errors and tried not to demean his men. Though Armstrong endeared himself to the younger sailors, some senior officers disapproved of his behavior. Lieutenant Commander Dave Lewis, who ran the National Security Agency's operation, had lived across the hall from Armstrong at the Naval Academy. Armstrong's drinking concerned Lewis. He also disliked the executive officer's habit of swiping the NSA's magnetic tapes to record music on the reel-to-reel recorder in his stateroom.

Despite Armstrong's flaws, McGonagle respected him. The skipper would deny years later that he knew Armstrong drank on board, though it was well-known among the officers and crew. McGonagle rated his second in command in his performance evaluations as "outstanding" and "exceptional," the two highest marks. Because Armstrong was a Naval Academy graduate—and would ascend the ranks faster—McGonagle likely would have been reserved with his criticism, but his evaluations appeared genuine. He singled out Armstrong's loyalty, cooperation, and imagination. He noted no weaknesses in Armstrong's evaluation and often recommended him for promotion, including in the evaluation he worked on as the *Liberty* steamed north toward Spain.

"LCDR Armstrong is self-confident and inspires confidence in his ability," McGonagle wrote in one report. "He is concerned with the welfare, personal and professional advancement of his subordinates and willingly assists them whenever possible." That confidence and willingness to assist would prove essential on this next mission.

CHAPTER 2

The circumstances surrounding the misrouting, loss and delays
of those messages constitute one of the most incredible failures of
communications in the history of the Department of Defense.

—HOUSE ARMED SERVICES
INVESTIGATING SUBCOMMITTEE

President Lyndon Johnson charted the latest headlines out of the Middle East that rattled off the Oval Office teletype machines in late May 1967. In the background, other news reports droned on three televisions next to his desk. The crisis between Israel and Egypt could not have come at a more inopportune time. The cost of the Vietnam War had soared to more than $2 billion a month. Casualties for May 1967 totaled 9,142, including 1,177 deaths. America lost 337 men in the third week of May alone—a new weekly record. The war had evolved into an obsession that poisoned the White House. "Vietnam was a fungus, slowly spreading its suffocating crust over the great plans of the president, both here and overseas," observed Jack Valenti, one of Johnson's closest advisers. "No matter what we turned our hands and minds to, there was Vietnam, its contagion infecting everything that it touched, and it seemed to touch everything."

America had ramped up its bombing campaign in the past two years in an attempt to force the North Vietnamese to surrender. The 25,000 sorties flown in 1965 more than quadrupled by 1967. During the same time period, the tonnage of bombs jumped from 63,000 to 226,000. American bombers choked the skies day and night, pounding bridges, railroads, power stations, and factories. Nearly a half-million American soldiers and Marines slogged through the damp jungles, battling over obscure strongholds with names such as Hill 861. To ferret out communist guerrillas, troops bulldozed villages and hamlets. Others torched fruit trees and rice granaries. The Pentagon spent $32 million on five million gallons of defoliants in 1967 alone, and increased the budget to about $50 million for the following year. Civilian casualties climbed into the thousands.

The ferocity of the American attacks repulsed national religious leaders and some members of Congress. The Reverend Dr. Martin Luther King, Jr., in an April speech at Manhattan's Riverside Church, ran through a litany of American atrocities and begged the president to end the war. "If America's soul becomes totally poisoned, part of the autopsy must read 'Vietnam,'" preached the Nobel Peace Prize winner. "I speak as a citizen of the world, for the world as it stands aghast at the path we have taken." Democratic senator George McGovern of South Dakota lashed out three weeks later on Capitol Hill at what he described as a "war without end." "We seem bent upon saving the Vietnamese from Ho Chi Minh even if we have to kill them and demolish their country to do it," he said in a speech on the Senate floor that grabbed national headlines. "I do not intend to remain silent in the face of what I regard as a policy of madness."

It was clear the president's policy had failed. In interrogations with captured North Vietnamese fighters and fishermen, the Central Intelligence Agency had determined in a string of reports released in May that twenty-seven months of American bombing had not weakened North Vietnam's strategy or morale. Its leadership remained "fanatically devoted." Even the popular mood, the spy agency concluded, comprised "resolute stoicism with a considerable reservoir of endurance still untapped." On May 23—the same day *Liberty* sailors strolled the wide boulevards of Abidjan—the CIA said that the United States might have to resort to extreme measures not seen since World War II if it wanted to win in Southeast Asia: "Short of a major invasion or nuclear attack, there is probably no level of air or naval action against

North Vietnam which Hanoi has determined in advance would be so intolerable that the war had to be stopped."

Vietnam had hit a stalemate.

The frustration that permeated the White House and Congress reflected the mounting tension and hostility of the American public. The first president to regularly employ a private polling company, the fifty-eight-year-old Johnson obsessed over public-approval polls. Over the past year, as the president paced the Oval Office, he had watched his approval numbers plummet from 61 percent in March 1966 to 48 percent in early May 1967. Beyond popularity, polls showed that nearly three out of four Americans doubted Johnson was telling them the truth about the war. The 1968 election loomed less than eighteen months away. Polls taken in the winter and spring showed that Republican candidates Richard Nixon and George Romney might tie or beat Johnson if the election were held then. It all came down to Vietnam.

The president and his senior advisers became magnets for criticism and anger, particularly Secretary of State Dean Rusk and Secretary of Defense Robert McNamara. The men outwardly projected a stoic front, but the increased hostility and ugliness of the antiwar campaign rattled them. The Georgia-born Rusk, who once joked that he looked more like Hoss Cartwright from the television western *Bonanza* than a statesman, found himself the target of protesters, some of whom on occasion hurled bags of cow's blood at him. During an April speech at Cornell University with his son in the audience, dozens of students suddenly jumped up and pulled on skull masks. The jarring scene left Rusk's wife in tears in the car afterward. The stress manifested into nightmares and a constant stomachache that left Rusk at times on his back on the living room floor in agony. The secretary of state propelled himself on a daily regimen of "aspirin, scotch, and four packs of Larks."

McNamara fared no better. Twice activists set fire to his Colorado vacation home. Once at Harvard several hundred angry students blocked his car and mobbed him, forcing the defense secretary to escape through the university's underground tunnels. When McNamara waited to board a plane in the Seattle airport in August 1966, a man spit on him and called him a "murderer." A similar event had happened over the Christmas holidays as McNamara and his wife dined in an Aspen restaurant. "Baby burner," a woman yelled at him. "You have blood on your hands!" McNamara's wife and son developed ulcers; his wife's even required surgery. To get through the night, McNamara began swallowing sleeping pills.

Even the president, shielded by Secret Service agents who increasingly restricted his public appearances, felt the sting of the public's growing hatred of the war. He watched as his frustrated aides defected to other jobs in Washington and beyond, and his plans for the Great Society stagnated. The war's fallout infiltrated the president's private life, dominating conversations with the first lady. At night, the president often lay awake. "The only difference between the Kennedy assassination and mine," he complained to friends, "is that I am alive and it has been more torturous." Lady Bird Johnson detailed the tensions in her diary. "Now is indeed 'the Valley of the Black Pig,'" she confessed, quoting a poem by William Butler Yeats. "A miasma of trouble hangs over everything."

The *Liberty* reached the Spanish port of Rota the morning of June 1 after a three-thousand-mile trip north from Abidjan that had taken eight days. The spy ship had averaged fifteen knots even after it suffered a boiler failure, followed by high winds and heavy seas that ripped life raft covers, toppled paint cans inside the deck locker, and coated the bow in salt. Conditions had improved the day before the *Liberty*'s arrival in Spain, allowing crews the first chance in a week to swab the decks with salt water. The *Liberty* reduced speed from seventeen knots to five knots as it approached the American naval station on the southern tip of Europe. A harbor pilot climbed aboard at 9:40 A.M. as two Navy tugboats pulled alongside to help guide the *Liberty* to pier 1, near the U.S.S. *Canopus*, a docked submarine tender. The *Liberty* secured anchor detail, doubled its mooring lines and set the in-port watch by 10:29 A.M.

Commander McGonagle had hoped to spend as little as five hours in Rota, time enough to pump 380,000 gallons of fuel and load food, personnel, and crypto records before steaming east toward the spy ship's assigned operating area twelve and a half miles off the Egyptian coast. Mechanical failures slowed the *Liberty*'s departure by a day as technicians repaired a faulty hydraulic line on the satellite dish and removed two antennae and a cable from one of the masts for repairs. Deck crews used the time to clean and rearrange the paint locker, stitch the damaged life raft covers, and remove the harbor pilot ladder for repairs after one of the tugs damaged it. Vice Admiral William Martin, the commander of the Sixth Fleet, planned a visit to the *Liberty* the next week. McGonagle ordered his executive officer and deck crew to inspect the ropes and pulleys that might be needed to high-line the admiral between ships. "I can just see us dunking him in the water," Ensign Dave Lucas wrote to his wife. "That would be a gas!"

Questions over the *Liberty*'s mission had intensified as the spy ship steamed up the African coast. Uncertainty evolved into apprehension after a rumor spread that astrologer and professed psychic Jeane Dixon had predicted America would lose a Navy ship that year. The celebrity psychic claimed in 1956 in an article published in *Parade* magazine that America would elect a Democrat as the president in the 1960 election and that he would die in office. Kennedy's assassination in 1963 cemented her pop culture status and earned her the nickname the "Seeress of Washington." Though Dixon never actually predicted the loss of a ship, rumor morphed into fact in conversations in the mess deck, wardroom, and berthing spaces. Even those uninterested in her alleged predictions still wondered what lay ahead. "Everybody is speculating as to where the ship is going exactly; what ports we'll visit, if any, and for how long we'll be in the Med.," Ensign John Scott wrote to his parents. "If you don't hear from me again before I return to Norfolk, it will be because we couldn't offload any mail and not because I'm lazy."

Marine Staff Sergeant Bryce Lockwood strode up the gangway in the June heat soon after the *Liberty* docked in Rota. Normally based in Germany with his wife and three children, the twenty-seven-year-old had been given temporary duty orders to Spain. The lanky Russian linguist had spent the past couple of weeks in the back of a spy plane, eavesdropping on the Soviet Navy as it performed its annual exercises in the North Sea. His hopes to return home to Germany ended with a knock on the barracks door in the middle of the night. He opened the door to find a Navy messenger with a new set of orders from the Joint

Chiefs of Staff. Lockwood tossed some uniforms in a sea bag and soon after sunrise marched to the end of the Rota pier to meet the *Liberty.* Five Arabic linguists joined him as he climbed aboard the spy ship, including two Marines and three NSA civilians.

Lockwood and the other new arrivals differed from the *Liberty*'s usual cadre of French and Portuguese linguists needed for missions off West Africa. The Middle East had become another beachhead in the Cold War. America supported Israel; the Soviets backed the Arab countries. Neither side wanted its proxy to lose if war broke out. The *Liberty*'s new linguists would allow the United States to intercept Egypt's air and defense communications. Intelligence indicated that a Soviet squadron of Tupolev Tu-95s, a long-range bomber and reconnaissance plane known as the Bear, operated out of Alexandria, Egypt. America wanted proof. Because the *Liberty*'s mission was directed solely against Egypt, the spy ship carried no Hebrew linguists, though one Arabic speaker had briefly studied Hebrew. U.S. spy missions against Israel, which used Athens-based airplanes, were so politically sensitive that the NSA classified its Hebrew speakers as "special Arabic" linguists.

The *Liberty* prepared to sail on the afternoon of June 2. McGonagle's new orders directed him to steam east along the North African coast and advised him to remain just beyond the territorial waters of nations such as Libya, Algeria, and Tunisia, a position that would allow the spooks to intercept communications en route. McGonagle was aware of the dangers. Though the *Liberty* was classified as a scientific research ship, its towering antennae revealed its true mission. As the skipper would later tell Navy investigators, the spy ship's unusual configuration had prompted some African navies to harass the *Liberty* on two of its four previous cruises. McGonagle ordered a five-section watch with two officers stationed on the bridge at most times. The log shows that at 1:22 P.M., the harbor pilot climbed aboard. Two Navy tugs helped guide the *Liberty* out of port. The harbor pilot departed at 1:58 P.M. and McGonagle assumed the conn, meaning he dictated the ship's speed and direction. The *Liberty* soon increased speed to seventeen knots.

Sailors crowded the deck as the ship slipped through the Strait of Gibraltar, the narrow waterway that separates Africa and Europe. The *Liberty* overtook three Soviet ships that steamed in a column at thirteen knots. Officers on the *Liberty* identified two of the ships as the *Semen Dezhnev* and the *Andrey Vilishksit* in a message to the Navy's London headquarters. One of the ships queried the *Liberty*'s identity with a signal light. McGonagle ordered a curt reply: "U.S. Navy ship." The winds created whitecaps in the entrance to the Mediterranean. Even at a distance of approximately six miles and with a late afternoon haze, sailors pointed to and snapped photos of the jagged Rock of Gibraltar rising 1,400 feet above the sea. The fabled Pillars of Hercules amazed even the seasoned McGonagle, who likely had only imagined them as a poor youth in the California date fields. One of the officers captured the skipper's fascination in a letter: "Shep was like a kid with a new toy when he saw the Rock."

President Johnson crawled into his four-poster bed around 11:45 P.M. on the evening of June 4. The commander in chief had weathered an intense couple of weeks as he strove to balance the demands of the Vietnam War with the Middle East crisis. America had set another tragic record in Southeast Asia in late May, with 2,929 American casualties in a single week, including 313 killed. Those numbers fueled the domestic hostility that greeted Johnson the previous night when he flew to New York to give a speech at a state Democratic Committee fund-raiser, accompanied by his wife and elder daughter. As the president arrived at the Americana Hotel, more than 1,400 antiwar demonstrators crowded the streets waving posters that depicted Johnson dressed as Adolf Hitler and saluting like a Nazi soldier beneath slogans that read "Wanted for Murder."

The scene could have been much worse. News reports had predicted as many as five thousand protesters might march outside the hotel near Times Square. Many Jewish organizations at the forefront of the antiwar movement opted not to protest, hoping to reduce pressure on the president as Israel sought America's support in its standoff with Egypt. The diminished pressure on the street did little to compensate for the stifling tension he found inside at the hundred-dollar-a-plate fund-raiser. Many of the 1,650 tuxedoed diners represented New York's influential Jewish community, all anxious to hear Johnson's views on the crisis on a night when he had planned a speech warning about the uncertain future of his welfare programs. The president, described by one aide as "part Jewish" because of his close ties with that community, found that his years of support did little to shield him from the demands to intervene in the Middle East.

Israel enjoyed its strongest relationship with the United States under Johnson. American presidents—both Republican and Democrat—historically had been cool toward the Jewish state. David Ben-Gurion, who would become Israel's first leader after it declared independence, waited in a Washington hotel for ten weeks in 1941–42 for a meeting with President Franklin Roosevelt that never materialized. President Harry Truman officially recognized Israel after its independence in 1948 but refused to sell the Jewish state weapons. After Israel seized the Sinai Peninsula and Gaza Strip in 1956 in response to Egypt's nationalization of the Suez Canal, President Dwight Eisenhower threatened to halt all foreign aid and eliminate private tax-deductible donations to Israel if it did not withdraw. President John Kennedy, one of the first presidents to grasp Israel's influence on domestic politics, strengthened relations and sold sophisticated surface-to-air missile batteries to Israel.

Johnson went further. Soon after Kennedy's assassination, he signaled his intentions. "You have lost a very great friend," Johnson confided to an Israeli diplomat, "but you have found a better one." The president's support stemmed from his religious upbringing in the dusty hill country of Texas. Family elders had preached that the destruction of Israel would trigger the apocalypse. "Take care of the Jews, God's chosen people," Johnson's grandfather scrawled in a family album. "Consider them your friends and help them any way you can." The president never forgot those teachings, as illustrated by a speech he gave to members of B'nai B'rith, a national Jewish organization. "Most, if not all of you, have very deep ties with the land and with the people of Israel, as I do, for my Christian faith sprang from yours," Johnson said. "The Bible stories are woven into my childhood memories as the gallant struggle of modern Jews to be free of persecution is also woven into our souls."

The president's fondness for Israel had as much to do with politics as biblical stories. The nation's six million Jews in 1967 accounted for only a fraction of the 200 million Americans, but Jews commanded a larger role in political life than the population figures might otherwise have indicated. Many American Jews monitored the issues, voted, and involved themselves in business organizations, labor unions, and civic groups. Others occupied important leadership roles in newspapers and in the television and motion picture industry. Jews donated and raised millions for political candidates, mostly Democrats. Many also lived in major cities in crucial political states, including New York, Newark, Boston, Philadelphia, Los Angeles, and Chicago. Candidates recognized that these large populations could determine the outcome of states that accounted for 169 of the 270 electoral votes required to win the White House.

Johnson surrounded himself in office with Jewish and pro-Israel advisers. The shrewd politician picked brothers Walt and Eugene Rostow to serve as his national security adviser and undersecretary of state for political affairs, respectively. The president chose Supreme Court justice Arthur Goldberg as ambassador to the United Nations, replacing him on the bench with Abe Fortas, another Israel supporter. John Roche, a former dean at Brandeis University, wrote many of Johnson's speeches. The president also relied on close Jewish friends for advice, including high-profile lawyers Ed Weisl and David Ginsburg, who often represented the Israeli Embassy. Johnson never missed a call from Democratic fund-raiser Abe Feinberg, because, as one senior aide noted, "it might mean another million dollars." United Artists Chairman Arthur Krim and his wife, Mathilde, a former gunrunner for early Zionist guerrillas, spent so many nights in the White House that Room 303 became the couple's regular quarters.

The United States under Johnson increased aid to the Jewish state. "No one who has an insider's view," noted Robert Komer of the National Security Council, "could contest the proposition that the US is 100% behind the security and wellbeing of Israel. We are Israel's chief supporters, bankers, direct and indirect arms purveyors, and ultimate guarantors." Israel's leaders welcomed the attention, believing that for years the State Department had favored the Arabs. The administration tallied that support in a report that revealed that America gave

Israel $134 million in economic aid between 1964 and 1966. America also sold tanks and combat aircraft on liberal credit terms, provided grants and loans, and funded another $8 million annually in scientific research, 25 percent of all money Israel spent each year on nonmilitary research. "Perhaps the best way to characterize US-Israeli relations in this period is to say that they are closer today than ever," the report concluded. "The breadth and depth of US help for Israel, even more than aid levels themselves, are impressive."

Despite Johnson's lavish support of Israel, many American Jews refused to back the Vietnam War, a source of frustration inside the administration as antiwar rallies increased and the president's popularity plummeted. Jews had become so prominent in the antiwar movement that it sparked a protest button: "You don't have to be Jewish to be against the war in Vietnam." Johnson, who viewed Vietnam and Israel as small countries threatened by Soviet-backed adversaries, struggled to understand that discontent. Jewish frustration over Vietnam served as a focus of a report for the president that analyzed public opinion. The report, which noted that many Jews worked as writers, teachers, and political and civil rights activists, discussed the possible threat to the president's 1968 reelection. "Viet Nam is a serious problem area," the report concluded. "If Viet Nam is favorably resolved before the elections, defections among Jews will be minimal; if Viet Nam persists, a special effort to hold the Jewish vote will be necessary."

Many Jews who protested the war in Southeast Asia now urged the president to use force if necessary to help Israel in its standoff with Egypt. Letters, telegrams, and petitions inundated government mailrooms. The State Department processed 17,440 letters during the four days between May 29 and June 1 in what analysts recognized was part of an organized campaign. The analysis showed that 95 percent of the writers supported Israel, 4.5 percent opposed American intervention, and only a half percent favored the Arabs. Pro-Israel demonstrators crowded the streets. An estimated 125,000 men, women, and children, including several concentration camp survivors, had rallied days earlier in New York City's Riverside Park, singing Israel's national anthem and demanding the United States intervene.

The president had worked to calm Israeli fears since Egypt closed the Strait of Tiran and mobilized its forces in the Sinai. Johnson assured Israeli diplomats that he would gather a multinational naval force to break the blockade. Progress had proven slow and Johnson feared the Jewish state would launch a preemptive strike, even though he and defense secretary Robert McNamara had informed Israel's foreign minister that American intelligence showed Egypt did not plan to attack. The president knew Israel had mobilized for war. Its military had called up thousands of reservists and requisitioned hundreds of buses, vans, and delivery trucks at an estimated cost of five hundred thousand dollars a day. Workers piled sandbags in window frames in Jerusalem as residents strung blackout curtains, stockpiled candles, and filled bathtubs with water. Trenches zigzagged across city parks and squares in the city of Elat on the Gulf of Aqaba. Medics converted hotel lobbies into hospitals in Tel Aviv as undertakers transformed movie theaters into makeshift morgues.

Despite Israel's preparations, Johnson still hoped to avert a war. The president diverged from his prepared remarks on welfare in his speech in New York to reiterate his commitment to peace in the Middle East, comments that drew loud applause. Abe Feinberg whispered to Johnson over dinner that Israel would hold back no longer. The Jewish state planned a preemptive strike. Johnson's efforts had apparently failed; now he waited. He tried to relax Sunday afternoon on the presidential yacht followed by a quiet dinner at the home of Justice Fortas. The president returned to the White House and retired for the evening at 11:45 P.M. The call came at 4:30 A.M. Johnson listened in silence to his national security adviser and asked few questions. He hung up at the end of the seven-minute conversation. Lady Bird asked what was the matter as he dropped back on his pillow. "We have a war on our hands."

At the National Security Agency's eighty-two-acre campus in Washington's Maryland suburbs, senior leaders worried over the outbreak of the war and what it might mean for the *Liberty*. Analysts at the clandestine agency had worked nonstop in recent days. With more than fourteen thousand employees and an estimated billion-dollar annual budget the NSA was designed for just such a crisis. The secretive nature of the organization—employees joked its initials stood for "No Such Agency"—camouflaged an operation that resembled a small city. The agency boasted a cafeteria that could feed more than a thousand, plus eight snack bars. An infirmary complete with operating rooms, x-ray equipment, and dental chairs could accommodate minor emergencies while employees enjoyed an on-site post office, barbershop, dry cleaner, and shoe repair. Workers could even cash checks and make deposits at a branch of the State Bank of Laurel, all without ever leaving the Marine-guarded gates.

The *Liberty*'s mission required it to steam as close as twelve and a half miles off Egypt and six and a half miles from Israel, a mission planned days before the war started, when America had a reasonable expectation of the ship's safety. NSA officials watched on the first day of the war as the Israeli pilots obliterated Egypt's air force. Israeli ground forces soon moved into the Sinai Peninsula. Intelligence leaders feared the *Liberty*'s proximity to the conflict might endanger it. The spy ship, which passed just sixteen miles off the Sicilian island of Pantelleria only hours before the war began, steamed east at full speed and expected to arrive off the coast of Egypt in as little as three days. Though the NSA recommended the *Liberty*'s missions, the agency had no authority to move the ship. The Navy assumed responsibility for its safety, and any orders from the NSA had to go through the Joint Chiefs of Staff.

America had faced a similar problem five years earlier during the Cuban Missile Crisis. The spy ship *Oxford* had trolled for months off Havana as it eavesdropped on the Soviet buildup. The mission proved vital. The *Oxford* sniffed out surface-to-air missile sites and sophisticated Soviet radars used to track and target airplanes. The Soviets had used such radars to shoot down an American spy plane over Siberia in May 1960. Tensions soon arose. Cuba deduced the *Oxford*'s mission from its elaborate antennae and harassed the spy ship with gunboats. Spooks down below listened as the Cuban military trained its fire-control radar on the *Oxford*. The United States feared the spy ship, which patrolled so close to shore that its sailors could see Havana's famed Morro Castle, might create a flashpoint for a larger conflict. Despite the intelligence boon the *Oxford* provided, authorities ordered the ship farther back into the Straits of Florida.

Richard Harvey and Eugene Sheck, who assigned and scheduled the NSA's spy ships and planes, remembered that decision from five years earlier. The same considerations now applied to the *Liberty*. No nation had ever attacked a spy ship, so the worries were not overt, particularly because the *Liberty* sailed in international waters. If the war in the Middle East warranted an order to the *Liberty* to pull back, the NSA would need to readjust the mission. The men phoned John Connell, the agency's liaison at the Joint Reconnaissance Center. Located in a secure area deep in the Pentagon, the center scheduled and managed military spy missions. Connell agreed with his colleagues. Hundreds of miles separated the *Liberty* from the rest of the Sixth Fleet. Connell conferred with his counterparts in the Pentagon only to discover that no one had any plan to move the *Liberty*.

The *Liberty* approached the Middle East as the rest of the Navy pulled back. Before the *Liberty* had reached Rota, Spain, the Navy ordered the Mediterranean-based Sixth Fleet to restrict air operations to at least one hundred miles from Egypt. Concerns increased when the war began and twenty Soviet warships and support vessels, joined by another eight to nine submarines, steamed in the eastern Mediterranean. The Navy ordered aircraft carriers to operate no closer than one hundred miles from Egypt, Israel, Lebanon, and Syria. Vice Admiral Martin warned the *Liberty* to remain alert, given Egypt's "unpredictability." The message, broadcast over a teletype circuit the *Liberty* no longer monitored, never reached the spy ship. Events would soon overshadow the Sixth Fleet's effort to determine why the *Liberty* failed to respond. "Maintain a high state of vigilance against attack or threat of attack," read the admiral's message, sent the second day of the war. "Report by flash precedence any threatening or suspicious actions directed against you or any diversion from schedule necessitated by external threat."

Chief of Naval Operations Admiral David McDonald reviewed his operational briefing notes on the morning of June 7, the third day of the war. The four-star admiral, the Navy's most senior officer, seized on the two-sentence reference at the bottom of the page to the *Liberty*'s mission a dozen miles off Egypt. McDonald scrawled his concern in the margin beneath it with a red pencil: "I don't know why we do something like this now?" He ordered his subordinates to remedy it and brief him on his return to the Pentagon from Annapolis no later than 2:30 P.M. Based on McDonald's concern, the Navy recommended that the Joint Chiefs of Staff order the *Liberty* to approach no closer than twenty miles from Egypt and fifteen miles from Israel. The memo that detailed the recommended change arrived in McDonald's office at 2:37 P.M., but the admiral did not read it until 6 P.M.

The minor adjustment failed to satisfy McDonald. The veteran admiral with a reputation for bluntness jotted a one-sentence response in the memo's bottom margin: "I wouldn't even let her go down that way now!" In a conversation with his executive assistant shortly before he left at 6:20 P.M., McDonald barked that the change was not enough. The admiral saw no reason for the *Liberty* to operate so close to a war zone. The potential risks outweighed the intelligence the United States might gain. Beyond the danger, McDonald worried about political fallout. Israel's success in the first few days of the war had prompted Egypt to accuse the United States of helping the Jewish state. The U.S. refuted Egypt's allegations before the United Nations when U.N. ambassador Arthur Goldberg assured the Security Council that no Navy ships sailed within "several hundred miles" of the conflict. The *Liberty*'s presence would make him a liar. McDonald demanded the spy ship steam no closer than one hundred miles from shore.

A senior officer in the Joint Reconnaissance Center phoned the Navy's London headquarters of its European and Middle East command with the new orders at 7:50 P.M. Later investigations by the Joint Chiefs of Staff and a subcommittee of the House Armed Services Committee would chronicle the incredible communications breakdown that evening that rendered this and other efforts to reach the ship futile. Bureaucratic bungling, delays, and misrouted messages—some sent all the way to the Philippines—meant the *Liberty* would not receive its new orders in time to change its location. Nearly six thousand miles away, the spy ship steamed through the darkness. The officer in the Joint Reconnaissance Center, with the phone pressed tight against his ear, relayed the desperate need to reach the *Liberty* before it sailed too close: "Time is getting short to where she will be in those limits." The lieutenant on the other end of the phone in London only confirmed the Pentagon's fears: "Looks to me like she's almost there."

CHAPTER 3

While we are not responsible for the safety of the vessel, we
cannot absolve ourselves totally from the considerations of safety.

—SECRET NSA MEMO

Shortly before 4 A.M. on Thursday, June 8, Ensign John Scott assumed deck watch on the *Liberty*'s bridge. Located in front of the smokestack, and rising several stories above the main deck, the bridge on the twenty-two-year-old ship was austere. A radarscope, plotting board, and writing desk lined the forward bulkhead, beneath five portholes that offered a view of the ship's bow and the sea ahead. The navigator's chart table sat against the portside bulkhead; directly opposite it on the starboard side was the quartermaster's desk. There sailors kept a running log of the ship's course, speed, and sightings of other vessels in a notebook that ultimately became the ship's log. In the center of the bridge stood the *Liberty*'s gyrocompass, engine order telegraph, and the helm. Two doors on either side led out to wings—each with signal lights and a compass—that provided an unobstructed view of the bow and stern. In a throwback to the *Liberty*'s World War II origins, the bridge and starboard wing offered voice tubes that allowed the deck officer to shout orders through a network of pipes to the engine room.

An uneasy quiet settled over the bridge this morning as Scott scanned the dark horizon with binoculars. The spy ship, after days of steaming east at seventeen knots, had slowed to ten knots as it neared

36

the Egyptian coast. A helmsman, quartermaster, and a couple of lookouts joined Scott on the bridge. Most of the other officers slept below in nearly a dozen staterooms. The chief petty officers bunked in a single compartment and the rest of the crew shared three cavernous berths, the largest able to sleep 135 men in bunks stacked three high. The *Liberty* required only a few sailors to run the engineering plant, guide the ship, and stand watch. Far below deck in the National Security Agency's hub, work continued at a frenetic pace despite the early hour. Behind locked doors, communications technicians eavesdropped on radio communications, intercepted Morse code messages, and sniffed out radar systems.

Scott normally found the morning watch a miserable assignment. To stay awake, the young officer downed cups of black coffee and counted rivets on the deck plates. If he was lucky, the *Liberty* might sail through a patch of phosphorescent algae that sparkled in the dark seas and occasionally illuminated porpoises that liked to swim in the ship's bow wake. A couple of times, he had even spotted whales. The most exciting event Scott had witnessed on watch happened on an earlier cruise in Africa. The radarman that night had reported fuzzy blips as the ship trolled the coastline, but a scan of the dark waters revealed nothing. A small fleet of fishermen in dugout canoes suddenly appeared in front of the *Liberty*. The fishermen lit torches to signal the spy ship, but it was too late. Scott could do little more than shout apologies as the lumbering *Liberty* sliced through their fishing lines.

On this morning—Scott's twenty-fourth birthday—the eastern Mediterranean was empty. A stream of merchant ships exiting the war zone had passed the *Liberty* in recent days, but that traffic had ended. The deck log shows that the *Liberty*'s last encounter with another ship had come at 2:30 P.M. the day before, when it sailed within fifteen hundred yards of the Greek merchant vessel *Ioannis Aspiotis*. The *Liberty*'s teletype had churned out daily updates on Israel's stunning success in the war. In three days, the Jewish state had obliterated Egypt's forces, seized much of the Sinai Peninsula, and reached the banks of the Suez Canal. On the Jordanian front, Israel had captured much of the West Bank, including the Old City of Jerusalem, Bethlehem, and Jericho. "All this the armed forces of Israel did alone," declared Yitzhak Rabin,

Israel's chief of staff, in comments widely distributed by the wire services. "Everyone fought like lions."

Though the *Liberty* sailed in international waters, the crew remained on edge. The proximity to the war zone magnified the sense of loneliness and isolation. The rest of the Sixth Fleet, with its aircraft carriers and destroyers, assembled approximately five hundred miles west off the southern coast of Crete. The potential danger prompted McGonagle to occasionally summon intelligence officers to the bridge to provide updates. The night before, as the *Liberty* skirted the Egyptian coast, the men had watched the Israelis bomb the Suez Canal. The fire and smoke had clouded the night sky. Scott scanned the horizon this morning in silence. It all felt so eerie. A war raged on shore yet on the bridge the normal sense of routine permeated. In a few moments, the cooks would arrive with the first batch of warm biscuits. Scott felt like Marlow headed up the river in Joseph Conrad's *Heart of Darkness*.

The early morning light illuminated the empty horizon as Scott glanced up at the mast at about 5 A.M., where he spotted the American flag fluttering in the breeze. Fifteen minutes later, a lone plane zipped high overhead. Scott trained his binoculars on the plane. It flew high, too high to discern any markings, but he noted that the plane had a double fuselage and twin engines. The flying boxcar, as it was commonly known, lazily circled the *Liberty* several times.

High above the *Liberty* in the cockpit of the Nord 2501 Noratlas reconnaissance plane, an Israeli observer stared down at the spy ship. The plane had been airborne since 4:10 A.M., patrolling Israel's coastline to detect ships beyond radar range. Other than the *Liberty*, the sea was largely empty. The recon plane dropped as low as three thousand feet and circled a half mile away to better study the foreign vessel. The observer radioed that he had found what looked like a destroyer seventy miles west of Gaza. The observer soon corrected his earlier report. He had spotted an American supply ship. From the cockpit, the observer noted the *Liberty*'s unique hull markings, GTR-5, which identified it as a general technical research ship. The flight engineer later recalled that the ship lacked cannons. "It was a gray color," he said. "Not too big, not too small, like a cargo ship."

Back on the *Liberty*'s bridge far below, Scott watched the unidentified plane circle in the clear skies. It was obvious from the plane's maneuvering—and sudden interest in the *Liberty*—that it was on a reconnaissance mission. Scott snapped four pictures with a 35-mm camera. He then watched as the plane banked and soon departed. Seaman Apprentice Dale Larkins, who was on watch with Scott, later sketched the plane in his journal. "It made 3 runs fore and 2 aft in a figure eight pattern," Larkins wrote. "It then crossed from port to starboard in front of the ship and flew over the horizon." Using the gyrocompass on the wing of the bridge, Scott shot a direction bearing. The officer consulted a map and noted the plane headed toward Tel Aviv. There was no doubt in Scott's mind that the plane was Israeli. The phone on the bridge rang moments later. One of the chief petty officers in the NSA research spaces below asked Scott if he had spotted any aircraft. The spooks must have detected the plane's communications, Scott thought.

"You're clairvoyant," Scott replied. "I just did."

"Did you happen to notice which way it went?" the chief petty officer asked.

"It flew over us, circled, and headed back towards Tel Aviv."

The *Liberty* had been detected.

Commander McGonagle risked nothing. Since the outbreak of the war several days earlier—and even as the *Liberty* remained approximately nine hundred miles from the Middle East—the rigid skipper ramped up the ship's alert level to Modified Condition of Readiness Three. The Navy jargon mandated that sailors retrieve boxes of ammunition from the ship's magazine and store them alongside the four machine guns. McGonagle demanded that sailors remove the gun covers unless heavy sea spray threatened to soak them. For safety reasons he ordered that the weapons remain unloaded. He stationed two sailors at the forward machine guns at all times and instructed lookouts to remain ready to man the guns aft of the bridge.

The skipper also ordered that the ship immediately sound the general quarters alarm if any unidentified aircraft appeared to approach the ship on a strafing, bombing, or torpedo run. Likewise, he declared that any boat racing toward the *Liberty* at twenty-five knots or faster should be considered hostile and should prompt a ringing of the general quarters alarm. "Maximum effort must be made to minimize personnel/material damage, safeguard the watertight integrity of the ship, and continue performance of primary mission," McGonagle wrote in a memo to his officers Monday. "It is better to set general quarters in doubtful cases than to be taken by surprise and be unable to fight."

A former gunnery officer during the Korean War, McGonagle recognized that even with the heightened alert, the spy ship remained virtually defenseless. The four Browning .50-caliber machine guns—capable of firing up to five hundred rounds a minute with an effective range of only about one mile—would prove worthless against fighter jets or agile torpedo boats. The gunner had to manually track targets with an open sight while another sailor loaded rounds. Even the ship's four-page gunnery doctrine declared the mounted guns' "primary function" was to repel boarders, not shoot down fighters. On the rare occasion that gunners had to target a plane, the ship's doctrine stated that estimating the altitude would come down to "guess work." Two days earlier, the edgy skipper had cabled a gentle reminder of the *Liberty*'s meager arsenal to his superiors. "Self defense capability limited to four .50 caliber machine guns and small arms."

McGonagle initiated a relentless drill schedule to prepare the crew. In the last three days, he had drilled his men almost daily for a surprise attack. The deck log shows he ordered a steering casualty drill at 10:59 A.M. Monday to test the officers' ability to guide the ship in case the *Liberty* lost rudder power. He followed that up with a general quarters drill at 1:02 P.M. to simulate an attack. Sailors raced to battle stations, dogged down hatches to create watertight compartments, and unrolled fire hoses. McGonagle ordered another general quarters drill Wednesday at 1:01 P.M. With the *Liberty* steaming so close to a war zone, the officers and crew expected more drills today. "With all the excitement, the Captain hasn't chewed my ass for anything in about a week," one of the officers wrote in a letter. "He's too busy with other matters."

Reveille sounded soon after daybreak, and hungry sailors streamed into the mess deck, chief petty officers' lounge, and the officers' wardroom. Executive Officer Lieutenant Commander Philip Armstrong, Jr., mustered the crew at approximately 7:45 A.M. as he did most mornings. Before him on the main deck, sailors lined up by department as the ship's officers reviewed morning reports. The Plan of the Day reflected the *Liberty*'s proximity to the conflict. Posted throughout the ship, the two-page memo advised sailors on how to respond to a chemical attack—slip on gas masks and report to decontamination stations— and how to distinguish between nerve, blister, and blood agents. If infected with deadly nerve gas, sailors were instructed to immediately inject themselves with atropine.

The corpsmen began sick call at approximately 8 A.M. in the *Liberty*'s six-bed infirmary, a routine that involved checking sore throats and earaches, and administering the occasional shot of penicillin to clear up a case of gonorrhea picked up in the last port. Days of heavy seas had coated much of the bow with salt spray. Crews prepared to scrape rust from the decks and paint. Down in the engine room, a check revealed the *Liberty* still had more than 650,000 gallons of fuel oil, burning an average of 360 gallons an hour. A faulty steam-line gasket troubled the engineering officer, a problem that would require the *Liberty* to operate off a single boiler while crews replaced the gasket. Research operators who scanned frequencies in the NSA's hub now found Hebrew domi- nated the airwaves as the Israelis controlled the skies.

The deck log shows that the *Liberty* crossed the hundred-fathom curve—the edge of the continental shelf—at 8:08 A.M. as it steamed toward its operating area twelve and a half miles off Egypt. Forty-one minutes later, the spy ship turned and sailed a southwesterly course parallel to the Egyptian coast. The *Liberty* slowed to five knots at 9:05 A.M., a speed that allowed the operators to zero in on communications. Twenty-five minutes later, bridge officers spotted a minaret rising above El Arish twenty miles away on the Sinai Peninsula. Navigators used the conspicuous landmark that towered above the date palms of the dusty Bedouin town to identify the *Liberty*'s precise location. In the empty desert, no other distinguishable features registered on the radar.

Thursday morning shaped up beautifully. The sun climbed high in the cloudless sky and a warm breeze blew across the decks. The *Liberty*'s weather log recorded calm seas, a seventy-four-degree water tempera- ture, and visibility of at least ten miles, though officers on the bridge could see farther. Crewmembers occasionally lined the rails to catch a glimpse of Egypt. The desert dunes peppered by palm groves seemed to roll right into the sea. Sailors wrestling with cabin fever after days of gray weather stretched out during break on beach chairs and towels to sunbathe. Many smoked cigarettes and swapped stories of girlfriends while wondering what Mediterranean ports the *Liberty* might visit.

Reconnaissance flights now regularly buzzed the *Liberty.* A single jet aircraft passed astern then circled the spy ship at 8:50 A.M. Two more jets returned at 10:30 A.M. and orbited the ship three times. Twenty-six minutes later a single aircraft at a high altitude again circled the *Liberty.* Crewmembers noted other reconnaissance flights at 11:26 A.M., 11:50 A.M., 12:20 P.M., and 12:45 P.M. Many of the men on deck believed that the planes, which at times buzzed the *Liberty* at low altitude, snapped photos of the spy ship. Beyond the reconnaissance flights, officers observed a propeller-driven patrol plane inspecting the El Arish coastline at an altitude of five hundred feet. The recon flights zoomed by with such regularity that when a plane failed to materialize as expected promptly at lunchtime, one of the radar men commented: "Where's our buddy?"

McGonagle remained on edge. Only a dozen miles separated the spy ship from the war zone. Soon after the *Liberty* turned to parallel the Egyptian coast, the skipper left the bridge and headed down to the NSA's research spaces. He passed through the cipher-lock door and arrived at the office of Dave Lewis, the *Liberty*'s senior intelligence officer. The thirty-six-year-old Lewis had spent the morning directing his men. With the *Liberty* now in earshot of the war, operators hustled to soak up communications to later beam back to the NSA. McGonagle closed the door behind him. "Would it affect your mission if we moved farther offshore?" he asked.

Lewis recognized that one of the *Liberty*'s functions was to pick up ultrahigh- and very-high-frequency radio communications, commonly used by battlefield commanders. Those communications worked best when the sender and receiver were within each other's line of sight, typically no more than twenty miles apart. If the *Liberty* sailed over the horizon, Lewis knew the curvature of the earth would diminish some of those capabilities. Many of the *Liberty*'s other functions, such as intercepting Morse code transmissions, would not be affected. Lewis leveled with the captain. "Yes," he answered. "We'd lose some line of sight."

The skipper considered his options. The *Liberty* had sailed more than five thousand miles in the past two weeks for the sole purpose of eavesdropping on the war. At the same time, McGonagle had to ensure the safety of nearly three hundred crewmembers. The skipper had no way of knowing that the day before, the chief of naval operations had frantically dashed off a memo to pull the ship farther from shore. That message ordering the *Liberty* to remain at least one hundred miles from the coast had yet to roll off the ship's teletype. As far as McGonagle knew, he was right where the Navy wanted him—within eyesight of the war.

The skipper also had no way of knowing that the Israeli reconnaissance plane that buzzed the ship at 5:15 A.M. had landed. The naval observer aboard that plane had reported the *Liberty*'s distinct hull markings during debriefing. An Israeli officer looked up the ship's identity and forwarded his findings to his navy's war room and naval intelligence. Israel knew not only that an American ship trolled off the coast of the Sinai Peninsula, but that it was the spy ship *Liberty*.

"Well, if it affects your mission," McGonagle told Lewis, "we won't move offshore."

McGonagle joined his officers on the forward deck during lunch to sunbathe. The forty-one-year-old skipper maintained a running competition with his men for the best tan, often bragging that no one could ever beat him. McGonagle slipped back into his khaki uniform and strode onto the bridge at 1:05 P.M. The *Liberty* had changed course at 11:32 A.M. and now steamed northwest at five knots, paralleling the Egyptian coast. The ship's weather log shows that the morning's clear skies, calm seas, and excellent visibility carried over into the afternoon. Reconnaissance flights continued to buzz the spy ship about every half hour. The sense of danger loomed, prompting the spooks to torch the previous month's key cards required to operate the crypto equipment. The *Liberty* advised that it now planned to destroy all excess materials daily given the "current situation and shallow water operating area."

The week's rigorous drill schedule prompted crewmembers to speculate that the skipper planned another that afternoon. Soon after lunch, many sailors gravitated toward battle stations in anticipation. McGonagle didn't disappoint. The skipper ordered a chemical warfare drill at 1:10 P.M. The public address system broadcast the now familiar order: "General quarters! General quarters! All hands man your battle stations." Sailors hustled to set up chemical decontamination centers in the ship's showers and practiced on the *Liberty*'s gunners and topside crew. Damage control teams sealed hatches to compartmentalize the ship and create watertight integrity. Firefighters unrolled hoses and broke out stretchers as medical corpsmen manned casualty collection centers. The gunners, once successfully processed through the mock decontamination center, raced to the *Liberty*'s four .50-caliber machine guns.

McGonagle monitored the drill from the bridge. His earlier concern over the *Liberty*'s proximity to the war zone returned. At the start of the drill, the skipper spotted a cloud of black smoke on the beach approximately fifteen to twenty miles west of El Arish and thirteen miles from the *Liberty*. Twenty minutes into the drill, the skipper noted another dark cloud about five to six miles east of El Arish. McGonagle estimated that the second cloud, which appeared smaller, was about twenty-five miles from the *Liberty*. The quartermaster recorded both in the ship's log. Thirty-eight minutes after the general quarters drill began, the skipper ended it. The crew's overall performance pleased him. Sailors successfully manned battle stations in three minutes, though the skipper was unhappy that it took nearly five minutes for the ship to set condition zebra, the highest state of battle readiness. With his slow drawl, he addressed his crew over the loudspeaker, singling out the column of black smoke onshore as a reminder of the *Liberty*'s perilous location.

The skipper's warning hung over the crew as the men returned to duty. Dale Larkins paused for a cigarette break at the filter maintenance shop before he resumed work on a high line used to transfer people between ships. The twenty-one-year-old Nebraskan, whose half-brother had been killed in the Korean War, remained ticked off as he snubbed out his cigarette. The deck department had to pull extra duty that night as punishment for someone scribbling on the partitions between bathroom stalls. Bryce Lockwood stood at his bunk in a rear berthing compartment, clutching several white T-shirts he had just picked up at the *Liberty*'s store. In his haste to pack his sea bag a week earlier, Lockwood had neglected to grab enough undershirts. Armed with an inkpad and Marine-issued rubber stamp, he pressed his name in the collars. Petty Officer 2nd Class Dennis Eikleberry, a twenty-year-old communications technician from Ohio, climbed the ladder to the *Liberty*'s fantail. After an all-night shift monitoring the war, he stared at the golden beaches nearby.

Ensign Scott, still tired from his morning watch, drifted into the wardroom in search of a cup of black coffee. The six-foot-four officer from North Carolina lugged his Polaroid Model 210 color camera, hoping to snap a few pictures that afternoon of the Egyptian coast. Several officers relaxed on the red couch and in metal chairs in the wood-paneled lounge, waiting for the skipper to drop in for his usual critique of the afternoon drill. The men wished Scott a happy birthday. Ensign Dave Lucas reclined nearby, a cup of coffee in one hand. The twenty-five-year-old West Virginian, who had missed the birth of his daughter five weeks earlier, had vowed to stop smoking on this cruise; otherwise he likely would have enjoyed a Marlboro from the half-full carton he kept in a drawer beneath his bunk. Dr. Richard Kiepfer, the ship's thirty-year-old physician, chatted nearby with George Golden, the *Liberty*'s chief engineer and one of the ship's few World War II veterans. Word passed over the public address system to stand clear as crews planned a routine test of the motor whaleboat engine.

McGonagle remained on the bridge. Rather than meet in the wardroom for his usual critique, the skipper planned to talk to his officers individually later in the afternoon, though he had failed to alert his men gathered below of the change. Lieutenant j.g. Lloyd Painter, a twenty-six-year-old intelligence officer from California, studied the radar at 1:55 P.M. Painter, who normally reviewed intelligence reports and helped determine spy targets, noted that the *Liberty* sailed seventeen and a half miles from shore, as much as five miles beyond the spy ship's closest assigned operating area. Painter asked the skipper if he should correct the ship's course. McGonagle checked the *Liberty*'s position. He sighted the minaret at El Arish, approximately twenty-five miles away. Lookouts stationed above the bridge interrupted the discussion. Two fighters zoomed toward the *Liberty*. McGonagle grabbed his binoculars and headed onto the starboard wing to investigate. Five to six miles out, the skipper spotted a fighter. The jet dropped to seven thousand feet as it raced on a parallel course toward the spy ship.

Others on the bridge, including Lieutenant Commander Armstrong, crowded around the portholes or joined the skipper on the wing. Lieutenant Jim O'Connor and Lieutenant Jim Ennes, Jr., both intelligence officers who had just finished watch, climbed the ladder to the flying bridge above for a better view. Another sailor grabbed a Nikon camera. Ensign Patrick O'Malley studied the radar. O'Malley, the ship's assistant operations officer, had just arrived on bridge to begin his shift as the junior officer of the deck. He spotted more activity on the radar screen. Three blips now appeared, closing in fast on the *Liberty*. O'Malley summoned Painter, who peered down at the green radar screen. The older officer recognized the attack formation. He yelled to McGonagle. "We've got three unidentified vessels, steady bearing, decreasing range, coming right at us." McGonagle remained focused on the approaching fighter, binoculars pressed to his eyes. Planes had reconned the *Liberty* all day. He had personally witnessed several of the flights. But this felt wrong. All wrong. The skipper turned to Painter. "You'd better call the forward gun mounts," he ordered. "I think they're going to attack."

Painter grabbed the sound-powered phone to alert the gunners to the jets. Through one of the forward portholes, he spied the men stationed at the mounted .50-caliber machine guns on either side of the forecastle. Painter knew the guns would prove powerless against a supersonic jetfighter. The planes traveled too fast for the gunners to manually sight them in the guns' limited one-mile range. Painter pressed the phone to his ear. Twice he tried to raise the gunners, but failed. His frustration mounted. The jets bore down on the ship. On the third try, Painter reached them. "Gun mounts 51 and 52." Painter watched as the fighters dropped out of the sky before he could complete his sentence. He had no time to warn the men—kids really, he would later say. The guntubs vanished in a cloud of smoke and metal, the sailors blown apart with such force that friends could identify one only by his St. Christopher necklace. The explosion happened so fast that Painter would later tell the investigating board that he couldn't determine whether the fighters hit the starboard or port gun first. He now stared at the charred machine guns, the phone still clutched in his hand.

The fighters zeroed in on the bridge, strafing the command hub with rockets and 30-mm cannons. The forward portholes exploded, sending glass and metal flying through the bridge. The quartermaster, who stood next to Painter, collapsed to the deck, bloodied with shrapnel wounds. O'Connor, on the flying bridge above, dove to the deck for safety as shrapnel ripped into his back. He tumbled down the ladder to the bridge below. Ennes, who had climbed up to the flying bridge with O'Connor, was blown against a rail. Shrapnel had broken his left femur about five inches above the knee. Blood soon soaked the left side of his uniform from dozens of shrapnel wounds as he hopped down the ladder. The skipper, who had raced in from the wing at the start of the attack, landed shoulder to shoulder with Ensign O'Malley against a rear bulkhead. Acrid smoke flooded the bridge. In the confusion, O'Malley heard someone shout general quarters. He repeated the call. The young officer turned to the skipper next to him and in a combination of shock and naïveté asked if McGonagle wanted him to sound general quarters. The skipper confirmed. O'Malley reached up and hit the alarm. But no one on the *Liberty* needed the alarm to alert him to the attack.

The officers and crew raced to battle stations as the jets—later identified as French-made Mirage fighters—banked and prepared for another attack. The fighters destroyed the *Liberty*'s machine guns, knocked out the antennae, and targeted the bridge to kill the officers and spark chaos among the crew. Shells smashed portholes, ripped gashes in sealed metal doors, and left basketball-sized craters on the bridge, deck, and smokestack. Dead and injured sailors, many of whom had been chipping paint seconds earlier, littered the decks. One sailor, with two and a half feet of his colon blown out by shrapnel, used his own blood to cool his burning skin. Even far belowdecks, explosive rounds and shrapnel zinged through bulkheads and ruptured vent pipes, lodged in bunks, and busted lights. The ship's internal communications, including the public address system and many of the sound-powered phone circuits, soon malfunctioned and fried. Runners darted through smoke-filled passages to relay orders to repair parties, firefighters, and the engine room as the jets crisscrossed the spy ship nearly every forty-five seconds.

McGonagle grabbed the engine order telegraph, a pedestal that stood in the center of the bridge that allowed him to order speed changes with a lever. Bells five decks below in the engine room would alert crews there to increase speed. The skipper threw the lever to flank speed, ordering maximum power. The *Liberty* had trolled all morning at five knots, or just under six miles per hour. Compared to a supersonic fighter, the spy ship essentially stood still, an easy target. One of the ship's two boilers was still offline. With only one boiler, McGonagle knew the *Liberty*'s maximum speed was only about eleven knots. To protect his crew and the ship, McGonagle needed maximum speed of eighteen knots. Even that was slow, but fighters would have a harder time targeting the *Liberty* at full speed; that speed also would allow him flexibility to execute evasive procedures, such as zigzagging. McGonagle shouted at his officers to broadcast an emergency message that the *Liberty* was under attack by unidentified fighters and needed immediate help.

Below the bridge on the port side, two fifty-five-gallon gasoline drums ignited. Fire raged on the deck and engulfed deflated life rafts stored nearby in a metal rack. Clouds of black smoke flooded the bridge. The only breathable air hovered eighteen inches above the deck. The skipper could deal with the smoke, but he feared the gasoline drums might explode. The only solution: jettison the barrels into the sea. However, flames blocked access to the quick-release lever on the portside. McGonagle recognized that someone would have to climb down to the deck and knock the drums overboard. He turned to his executive officer. Armstrong didn't hesitate. He darted out of the starboard side of the bridge and grabbed the ladder, but there was no protection from the fighters. The rocket and cannon fire, as McGonagle would later write to Armstrong's wife, had proven "overwhelmingly accurate and effective." A jet slipped out of the sky before Armstrong could reach the gasoline drums. The explosion threw him to the deck. The force broke three bones in his right leg and two in his left. He couldn't move, but he was alive.

O'Connor lay at the bottom of the ladder, where he had fallen from the flying bridge above. Shrapnel riddled his back. He had no feeling from the waist down. He couldn't stand up, much less fight. O'Connor realized that he had to get out of the way of his uninjured colleagues. He dragged himself across the metal deck, now covered in shards of glass and twisted metal, to the Combat Information Center, located through a door in the rear of the bridge. There he found other injured sailors. Shrapnel tore through the bulkheads. A spent round landed on the deck between him and another sailor. He stared at it. O'Connor had a wife and child back home in Virginia Beach. His son would celebrate his first birthday on Sunday, three days from now. His wife, Sandy, was three months pregnant with their second son. O'Connor watched blood pool around him on the deck. He felt he was going to die. Ensign O'Malley suddenly appeared before him. The young officer and ship's secretary noted the blood, but saw no injuries on O'Connor's chest. He gently felt along O'Connor's back and discovered two large holes. O'Connor instructed him to peel off his T-shirt and stuff it inside his wounds to slow the bleeding.

Lieutenant Stephen Toth stood in the door to the Combat Information Center, clutching a camera in one hand. The twenty-seven-year-old navigator told O'Malley he planned to climb to the flying bridge to photograph the fighters. The *Liberty* still did not know the nationality of the attackers and needed evidence. He wanted O'Malley to join him. The younger officer refused. O'Malley told Toth not to go, either, but the navigator was determined. Though normally quiet and reserved, Toth could be stubborn, often at inopportune times. His refusal to compromise had led him to divorce his beautiful Brazilian wife, whom he had married soon after graduating from the Naval Academy. She had wanted the couple to return to South America, where her family planned to set Toth up in business. Toth had refused. The son of a retired Navy captain with whom he struggled to communicate, Toth had likely felt his own family pressures. He had instead urged his new bride to stay with him in the United States. Neither would compromise. Hours after the divorce was finalized, the couple had checked into a Virginia Beach motel for one last night together.

O'Malley urged Toth one last time not to go up to the flying bridge.

It was suicide; he would be totally exposed to the rocket and cannon fire. Toth again refused. O'Malley would see the navigator only one more time. Later that afternoon, several stories below the flying bridge, O'Malley would zip Toth's remains inside a black body bag. O'Malley watched Toth turn and disappear toward the ladder, camera in hand. When he reached the top, Toth towered above the battered ship. If he looked toward the bow, the young officer would have seen the destroyed guntubs along with the bodies of his shipmates and the blood trails that stained the deck. He would have watched firefighters spraying the raging infernos. He would have witnessed stretcher bearers, already out of litters, using mattresses and blankets to haul the wounded below. Had Toth looked up, he would have seen the brilliant afternoon sun and the clear blue skies interrupted only by the smoke from the chaos below. He would have felt the warm Mediterranean sun on his face and a gentle breeze that on any other day would have been divine.

CHAPTER 4

Primary cause of death on some men was penetrating wounds of chest and lungs which made it impossible for them to breathe.

—DR. RICHARD KIEPFER, TESTIMONY BEFORE THE *LIBERTY* COURT OF INQUIRY

Ensign John Scott strode out of the wardroom with a cup of black coffee in one hand and his new Polaroid in the other when the first explosion rocked the ship. An announcement over the loudspeaker moments earlier had warned sailors to stand clear of the twenty-six-foot motor whaleboat suspended on a davit about ten feet above the starboard deck. Crews had planned a routine test of the whaleboat's engine. When the explosion occurred, Scott thought the maintenance crew had dropped the whaleboat to the deck below. After he heard the secondary explosions, Scott realized that the *Liberty* was under attack. He threw his coffee to the deck and sprinted to his battle station in Damage Control Central. He paused only long enough to toss his Polaroid camera onto the floor of his stateroom before he jumped down the ladder to the deck below, his arms sliding on the rails. Scott arrived inside his office before the general quarters alarm sounded.

Scott assumed that the Egyptians had shelled the *Liberty* with artillery from shore. The spy ship had sailed much of the morning within sight of land. But the staccato attacks followed by a brief lull and then resumption of fire meant it had to be fighter planes. One of the first messages from the bridge to damage control over the phones con-

51

firmed his suspicion. Rocket and cannon shells pounded the *Liberty* as the planes tag-teamed the defenseless ship. Even in the damage control office below deck, Scott heard the deafening crash of metal on metal as shells ripped holes in the ship's steel skin and echoed through the passageways. Fragments ricocheted off bulkheads inside compartments and littered the decks below.

Scott's job was to coordinate firefighters, organize stretcher bearers, and assess and respond to damage. He operated this vital function out of an austere office four decks below the bridge. Two phone talkers joined him, using sound-powered phones to relay messages to the bridge and to repair parties strategically stationed around the ship. To help navigate the complex maze of compartments, Scott kept the ship's blueprints spread out under glass on a table in the rear of the room. An inclinometer that measured the *Liberty*'s tilt in the water hung from the ceiling. If the ship were to flood, the inclinometer would gauge the ship's list and whether it might capsize. Crews of up to fifteen sailors manned three other repair lockers near the bow, stern, and engine room. Each locker held axes, firefighting hoses, and stretchers along with pumps used to dewater compartments.

Reports arrived of multiple fires on deck. The gasoline drums used to store fuel for the ship's truck and pumps had ignited on the port side, and the fire threatened to spread. Fighters also had hit the motor whaleboat that dangled above the starboard side. The blast set the fiberglass boat ablaze in its davits. Phone talkers also reported that the attackers had hit the bridge. Scott ordered crews from the forward repair locker topside to fight the fires. Men unrolled canvas-covered hoses and turned a valve, releasing a spray of seawater. The effort proved futile. With each pass of the jets, shrapnel punctured the hoses and sapped the pressure. The hoses were worthless, so the firefighters grabbed axes and shovels from the repair locker and tossed flaming debris and rubber over the side.

The situation worsened. Each time sailors charged onto the deck to rescue the wounded, more were hit by shrapnel. Scott ordered his men to travel through the ship's superstructure, using the safety of the internal passageways. Only go on deck, he instructed, between lulls in the attacks. He also ordered his men to leave the dead and grab only the wounded. A round tore through the bulkhead and hit the valve on a vent pipe directly over Scott's head. He looked up to find that the force had turned the valve upside down. The close hit triggered one of the phone talkers to panic. Scott watched as the man suddenly recited the Lord's Prayer. Scott raced over and grabbed the man by his shirt. He slapped him. "Get it together," Scott ordered. "There's time to pray later, but not now."

Down in the engine room, Chief Petty Officer Richard Brooks heard the bell ring out over the roar of the machinery. The thirty-one-year-old Yonkers, New York, native shot a glance at the engine order telegraph and saw that the skipper had thrown the lever to all ahead flank, signaling the need for full power. With each pass of the fighters, shrapnel ricocheted inside the cavernous engine room and dropped to the grated deck below. "Get me all the steam pressure," the machinist's mate barked into the voice tube to the boilermen. "I don't want to wait fifteen minutes. I want it all now."

The fighters first strafed the *Liberty* from bow to stern, targeting the bridge, machine guns, and antennae. With those destroyed or on fire, the attackers crisscrossed the spy ship to target the engine room, the *Liberty*'s heart. Boilers there converted water to steam that raced through metal veins and arteries, driving the two turbines and the screw. Beyond the propulsion system, generators transformed steam pressure to electricity to power everything from the lights and refrigerators to the ship's radios and spy equipment. If the pilots crippled the engine room, Brooks knew the *Liberty* would be dead in the water, an easy target for fighters or torpedo boats. The *Liberty* was particularly vulnerable because it was designed as a cargo ship. Warships such as destroyers had two engine rooms and two boiler rooms to increase survivability in an attack.

Thirteen years in the Navy had taught Brooks that the engine room was one of the most dangerous places on a ship. Pilots knew to aim just beneath a ship's smokestack, but that was only one component of the risk. Superheated steam, often at temperatures as high as 750 degrees, crisscrossed the *Liberty*'s engine room in asbestos-covered pipes. If shrapnel or a round punctured a major line, Brooks knew scalding steam could flood the room and broil the men alive. That had happened too often during World War II. Another risk centered on the deaerating tank, filled with thousands of gallons of superheated water, suspended high above the engine room. If it ruptured, scalding water would rain down on the sailors. The *Liberty*'s two boilers also sat like grenades on the engine room floor. If a rocket or torpedo split open the ship's side beneath the waterline, the rush of cold seawater likely would trigger the hot tanks to explode.

The engine room represented a critical weak spot for the ship. Most of the *Liberty*'s compartments were restricted to a single deck and guarded by watertight hatches. That allowed damage control crews to seal off flooded compartments in an attack. The engine room's towering boilers and uptakes, about as high as a five-story building, made it impossible to compartmentalize the cavernous space. If a torpedo hit the engine room, seawater could flood the rest of the ship in a matter of minutes, if not seconds. The steel frame of the ship's decks and compartments also served as the ship's skeleton. The absence of that frame around the engine room weakened the *Liberty*'s hull. If the engine room were to flood, the combination of the added weight of the water and weak structure likely would cause the ship to break in half.

Golden, the *Liberty*'s chief engineer, charged in from the wardroom moments after the attack began to find that Brooks had ordered crews to light the No. 2 boiler and increase steam pressure. Though Golden served as the department head, Brooks ran the engine room. Golden even griped that Brooks refused to let him do anything. The machinist mate had an encyclopedic knowledge of the *Liberty*'s equipment. With his thick New York accent, he often challenged his men to pick any valve and draw a sketch of it. If he couldn't find the valve, Brooks would stand that sailor's watch. Men pored over the boilers, turbines, and pumps to find obscure and hidden valves, but no one had yet stumped Brooks. That knowledge proved essential now as rounds and shrapnel pinballed inside the compartment, busting lights and tearing the insulation from the steam pipes. Smoke from the stack now poured through the skylight above and soot rained down. Through the chaos, Brooks continued to bark at his men.

Petty Officer Eikleberry slipped on his headphones and tuned the receiver's dials in search of the attackers' radio communication. He felt winded from his sprint from the *Liberty*'s fantail to the research spaces two decks below. Eikleberry had wandered up to the main deck after the general quarters drill for a glimpse of the Egyptian coast, hoping to spot one of the recon flights that had buzzed the ship throughout the morning. He had scanned the golden beaches and seen the dark smoke on the horizon when he heard the first rockets. He had looked up to see a fighter roar down the port side of the *Liberty* from bow to stern and then bank into the sky. Smoke had billowed up from the ship's bow and bridge. Eikleberry slid down the ladder to the deck below and dashed through a rear-berthing compartment, past the aft repair locker, through the mess deck, and down another ladder to his general quarters station in the bowels of the ship.

Senior research officers hovered over Eikleberry and other communications technicians as rounds blasted the side of the ship and ricocheted inside the compartment. If Eikleberry or another operator could intercept the pilot's radio communications, the men could identify the attacker's nationality based on whether the pilots spoke Arabic, Hebrew, or Russian. Eikleberry fingered the black dials on his receiver. The young operator, who had joined the Navy two months before his eighteenth birthday, couldn't believe the ship was under attack. This wasn't supposed to happen. Only the night before, Eikleberry had worked the 11 P.M. to 7 A.M. shift. Chief Petty Officer Melvin Smith had plopped down beside him in the middle of the night. Eikleberry asked his supervisor if he thought the men might get a ribbon for the mission. "No," Smith told him. "Nobody is supposed to know we're even here."

The attacks came in waves, about every minute. Far belowdecks in the radio room, the clash of rockets and cannons echoed. The repeated pings sounded to Eikleberry like marbles hurled against glass. The Navy had trained Eikleberry to work under extreme pressure. During his twenty-two weeks at communications school in Pensacola, his Marine instructor had screamed at him and the others to disrupt their concentration as the recruits hustled to copy code. Other instructors made recruits suddenly swap positions, flashed the lights, and threw metal trash cans down classroom aisles to simulate combat conditions. If the students stumbled, instructors ordered them to sprint to the base's main gate and ask the guard his name. The burly Marine often ordered the winded recruits to lean forward and smell the typewriters. "That's not ink," he barked at them, "but puke from the previous washout."

Eikleberry ignored the attack and tuned the dials on his receiver. He had to find the attackers' communications. The *Liberty*'s survival depended on it. Each time Eikleberry locked on to a frequency it dissolved into static as the pilots targeted the spy ship's forty-five antennae. Other operators perched at nearby receivers hollered out the same. Frustration soared. The men were trained to work under fire, but an equipment failure would paralyze them. Another petty officer directed Eikleberry to the antenna switchboard. There he could route antennae to specific receivers by plugging the cables into jacks, similar to a telephone switchboard. Other operators yelled positions and Eikleberry scrambled to find antennae. With each pass of the fighters, the *Liberty* lost more antennae. Eikleberry's options dwindled and the effort soon proved hopeless.

Dave Lewis, the head of the *Liberty*'s intelligence operation, ordered his men to destroy classified materials. If the attackers chose to seize the *Liberty* rather than sink it, the racks of crypto equipment, key cards, and manuals would not only reveal the ship's mission, but also expose America's intelligence capabilities. The loss of the equipment and the key cards would jeopardize American missions worldwide. Technicians had installed identical gear in the bowels of ships and planes that prowled the coasts of Vietnam, North Korea, and the Soviet Union. Even more than the equipment, Lewis worried about the coded key cards, which functioned like an ignition key for the crypto equipment. Without the punched cards, operators could not decipher incoming messages or encrypt outgoing ones. Men gathered the cards and torched them in wastebaskets. Smoke flooded the spaces.

Bryce Lockwood, who had been at his bunk in the rear of ship when the attack started, grabbed ditching bags. The canvas satchels, each with a drawstring at the top and a weight in the bottom, were designed so sailors could toss classified materials over the ship's rail. The bags would plummet to the sea floor, hopefully to a depth that made recovery impossible. With the ship's incinerator located behind the smoldering bridge—too dangerous a spot to reach as the fighters strafed the deck—the men loaded the bags. Lockwood darted into the voice transcription room and began to fill a bag with tapes of intercepted Egyptian communications. Lockwood filled one bag, set it aside, and grabbed another. He loaded the second bag, then a third. Lockwood and others soon discovered a problem: the loaded satchels were too heavy to haul up two decks to the rails. Likewise, the bulky bags would not fit through the narrow hatches now partially sealed.

Petty Officer 1st Class Jeff Carpenter, a twenty-five-year-old Michigan native, yanked on the drawers to Lloyd Painter's desk but found them locked. Carpenter scanned the compartment, but didn't see Painter. The men had been ordered to destroy everything and Carpenter interpreted that to mean even the papers sealed inside Painter's desk. The petty officer grabbed a sledgehammer. With a single upward swing, he knocked the metal top loose and disabled the lock, allowing him to fish out the documents. The crash of the sledgehammer on the desk reverberated through the compartment. Many of the sailors flinched and then turned to spot the source of the racket. Carpenter realized that his drastic action demonstrated to the others even more than the rockets that the attack was real. The pace of destruction increased. Two other sailors grabbed sledgehammers and wire cutters and began to destroy the crypto equipment. "No Arab is going to get this stuff," one of the men shouted. "Give me something else to break."

Even far below deck in the research spaces, the men could not escape the attack. Petty Officer 3rd Class Terry McFarland spotted "flickers of light" in his peripheral vision that he later learned were tracer rounds that had punched through the ship's hull. McFarland lowered his headphones and heard what sounded like a chain dragging back and forth beneath the ship, a sound he speculated was bullets fired at a downward angle that ricocheted along the hull. Petty Officer 1st Class Joe Lentini felt a rush of warm air blow past his left leg. The communications technician looked down and found his jeans split open and what resembled a five-inch surgical incision across his thigh. Petty Officer 1st Class Reginald "Red" Addington, who had been on the flying bridge at the start of the attack, now appeared in the research spaces. Shrapnel had broken his left foot and bloodied his knee and thigh as Addington announced the obvious. "Somebody's up there shootin' at us."

A few of the men panicked. Dave Lewis found one first-class petty officer paralyzed in a corner crying. The man had urinated on himself. Another young sailor dropped to the floor facedown, sobbing in front of Lockwood, who shot a glance at one of the other Marines stationed below deck. The Marine grinned at Lockwood, but he could tell it was a pained look. The men recognized the fear the kid experienced. Rather than kick the young sailor and yell at him to get up—his first instinct—Lockwood stepped over him and continued to work. Petty Officer 2nd Class Ronnie Campbell, a father of a three-year-old son with a daughter on the way, announced to his colleagues that he planned to write a letter to his wife. As men filled ditching bags, torched key cards, and smashed crypto equipment, Campbell plopped down in front of his typewriter. "Dear Eileen," he typed in a letter he would never finish. "You won't believe what's happening to us."

Dr. Richard Kiepfer arrived in the *Liberty*'s sick bay about the same time as the first of the injured. The towering lieutenant moments earlier had enjoyed a cup of coffee in the wardroom with the chief engineer. He had stepped into the passageway to chat with one of the stewards when he heard a jet buzz the ship, followed seconds later by the first explosion. The doctor thought one of the *Liberty*'s pressurized steam lines might have ruptured in the engine room. Someone in the wardroom even suggested the deck crew might have dropped the motor whaleboat onto the deck. The officers, who had waited for the skipper to join them for his postdrill meeting, peered out the portholes. Smoke billowed from the deck as more explosions followed. The doctor didn't wait. He darted onto the deck, where he spotted a fighter zoom from the starboard bow to the port-side stern. The jet unleashed its arsenal of rockets just as Kiepfer jumped through the hatch into the sick bay.

Located on the main deck near the rear of the ship, the *Liberty*'s infirmary was designed to handle only routine medical care. The ship's two corpsmen administered vaccines and passed out aspirin to ease backaches and Maalox to calm upset stomachs. A small examination room with a surgical table, sterilization equipment, and a pharmacy allowed the doctor, in a pinch, to perform minor procedures that required only local anesthetic and sutures. A case of appendicitis on a previous cruise had forced Kiepfer's predecessor to evacuate a sailor to a hospital in Senegal. The infirmary's main ward could accommodate only four sailors out of a crew of nearly three hundred. An adjoining room housed the ship's two-bed isolation unit, designed to quarantine contagious sailors. The doctor's office, where he reviewed medical charts and wrote letters to his cancer-stricken mother back home in New York, sat to the rear of the exam room.

The *Liberty*'s corpsmen had already arrived. The doctor dispatched the junior corpsman to the wardroom that served as the forward casualty collection station as the first injured sailors streamed into sick bay. The fighters continued to strafe the *Liberty,* though the outer bulkheads muffled the blasts. Kiepfer learned of the attack's violence from the severity of the shrapnel injuries he saw. Many of the bloodied men, who were working on deck when the attack started, arrived on stretchers and in the arms of friends. Kiepfer and Petty Officer 1st Class Tom Van Cleave began treatment. The doctor and the corpsman lifted the first sailor to the surgical table. Shrapnel had lodged in the seaman's chest and collapsed his lung. Blood and air filled the chest cavity and made it even more difficult for the sailor to breathe.

The men inserted an intravenous line in the sailor's arm and administered morphine to ease his pain and a dextrose and saline solution to fight shock. The doctor swabbed the sailor's chest with an alcohol rub to sterilize it. Kiepfer made an incision between his fifth and sixth rib. He carefully sliced through the sailor's skin, the subcutaneous fat and muscle, and then broke through the pleura, the thin tissue that lines the chest cavity. The doctor slid a clear plastic tube into the sailor's chest. He sutured the skin around it to keep air out and secure the tube. The doctor and the corpsman covered the wound with a sterile dressing. To remove the fluid and air trapped inside the sailor's chest, Kiepfer attached a foot-powered suction pump. He worked the suction pump and watched the air and blood drain from the tube. The ten-minute procedure improved the sailor's breathing.

The bridge summoned the doctor. Kiepfer passed through the crew's mess deck, where many of the wounded lay stretched out on tables. The doctor climbed the ladder to the deck above. Injured men flooded the wardroom and chief petty officers' lounge. When he reached the bridge moments later, Kiepfer discovered that the skipper was the only man still on his feet. McGonagle clutched the *Liberty*'s helm. The rest of the skipper's men had either been killed or injured. The doctor peered outside the bridge and spotted the navigator's remains on a deck below. There was little the doctor could do. He kneeled alongside injured men crouched in the rear of the bridge to inspect wounds and administer morphine. He promised to send stretcher bearers up to evacuate the men as soon as possible.

The doctor hopped down the ladder to the wardroom. Only a half hour had passed since he had sipped coffee and chatted with one of the stewards. The passageway that led to the wardroom circled the engine room's uptakes and created a loop. Injured men sat shoulder to shoulder around the full circumference. Kiepfer had worked nonstop since the attack began. He had treated the injured in sick bay followed by the men on the bridge. But only as he stared at the dozens of bloodied sailors that crowded the passageway did he realize the massive scope of the *Liberty*'s casualties. Shrapnel wounds, chest injuries, and broken bones: these injuries were far more severe than the *Liberty* was equipped to handle. Kiepfer was particularly overwhelmed considering he had only completed two years of a four-year surgical residency. He realized that his best course of action was to stabilize the injured and hope help arrived soon. The doctor maneuvered around the wounded past the wardroom to the chief petty officers' lounge.

Kiepfer found Petty Officer 3rd Class Sam Schulman, the *Liberty*'s junior corpsman, crouched over the ship's injured postal clerk at the lounge entrance. Petty Officer 2nd Class John Spicher had been hit by shrapnel in the chest and face as he fought a fire on deck. Men had dragged the thirty-year-old inside as he begged to know how bad his injuries looked. When Spicher, the father of an eighteen-month-old, wasn't passing out letters, he had earned extra cash stitching insignia on uniforms with his wife's sewing machine. Blood now soaked his uniform and face. The sailors around him would later recall Spicher's labored breathing. Schulman gave him morphine and then sliced open his throat to help him breathe. An injured sailor with his arm in a sling operated a foot-powered suction pump to remove the fluids from

Spicher's chest. Kiepfer asked if Schulman needed help, but the corpsman declined. Spicher became unconscious. Schulman performed mouth-to-mouth resuscitation, but it was no use. Spicher died.

The doctor returned to the sick bay. The injured filled the beds, including the two in the isolation room. Other wounded sailors crowded the floor. Kiepfer sutured a patient's wounds on the table just as a round tore through the ceiling and struck the surgical light. The explosion threw the doctor against the bulkhead and glass rained down on the patient. The surgical light absorbed much of the blast and the table protected his legs, but scalding shrapnel lacerated Kiepfer's exposed midsection. The skin on his abdomen burned from the shrapnel and he felt flashes of pain elsewhere in his body. Propped up against the bulkhead, the doctor could see that some shrapnel and glass also had hit the sailor on the table, but fortunately the light had shielded him from much of the blast. The doctor pushed himself off the bulkhead and returned to the table despite his pain. He dressed the patient's wounds with sterile bandages and finished his sutures.

Kiepfer stepped into his office to treat his own wounds. He had no gurney or bed so he stretched out on the metal deck. The doctor opened his shirt and surveyed the lacerations that crisscrossed his abdomen. The wounds were superficial—no organs or vital arteries had been hit—but that knowledge did little to ease his pain. Like any other patient, he felt the onset of shock. Kiepfer knew that the *Liberty* had no other doctor; care of the wounded fell to him and the two corpsmen. He had no choice but to push ahead. The doctor tore open several abdominal pads and pressed them against his stomach. He slipped on his life jacket and cinched it around him to hold the pads in place. Kiepfer emptied two ampoules of morphine into an insulin syringe and injected himself, careful to strike a balance between dulling his pain and passing out. He climbed to his feet and returned to work.

Petty Officer 2nd Class James Halman hustled to seal the four porthole covers along the port-side bulkhead of the *Liberty*'s radio room after the first rockets and cannons exploded. Another blast shook the ship, followed seconds later by the general quarters alarm. Smoke billowed from the bow and bridge and Halman heard sailors race through the narrow passageways armed only with battle helmets and life jackets. Halman and the other radiomen closed the last of the portholes as the skipper came on the loudspeaker and ordered operators to broadcast a distress call over the high-command network. The Navy's high-frequency radio network, monitored by every ship in the Sixth Fleet, served as the fastest way to call for help. Halman didn't hesitate. The twenty-two-year-old leapt to his station and grabbed the microphone. He squeezed the transmit button. "Any station this net," Halman called out at 1:58 P.M. "This is Rockstar."

Like scores of other sailors, Halman felt stunned by the surprise attack. Only moments earlier, he had wandered out on the deck to see the dark smoke on the horizon. Rather than spark concern, the proximity to the war zone had excited Halman and added a touch of adventure in the *Liberty*'s otherwise mundane routine. Unlike the spooks down below who listened to the tank commanders on the battlefield, Halman and the other radiomen managed the ship's radio network out of an office just above the main deck. The sailors hunted usable frequencies, established ship-to-ship and ship-to-shore communications, and monitored distress networks. Though not part of the job description, the radiomen also reviewed the Associated Press and United Press International wires and printed copies of the latest headlines that when mimeographed served as the *Liberty*'s daily newspaper.

Halman repeated his distress call as the fighters circled back and hit the *Liberty* again. The radiomen struggled to concentrate as shells pounded the ship and knocked out the antennae. Smoke flooded the radio room from a gasoline fire that burned outside on the deck. Napalm dropped from bombers on later attack runs blistered the paint on the interior bulkheads. The radiomen soon dropped to the deck and crawled beneath the desks to seek protection from the shrapnel and find air less saturated with smoke. Halman pulled the microphone under the desk with him so he could continue to broadcast the *Liberty*'s distress signal. He pressed the transmit button again and yelled into the microphone. "Any station this net, this is Rockstar," Halman called out. "We are under attack. Be advised we are under attack."

The U.S.S. *Saratoga* was steaming approximately five hundred miles west of the *Liberty* at the time fighters strafed the spy ship. The 76,000-ton aircraft carrier could carry as many as ninety aircraft and a crew of approximately five thousand sailors. It performed maneuvers south of Crete with the majority of the Sixth Fleet. The aircraft carrier U.S.S. *America* sailed nearby along with the cruiser U.S.S. *Little Rock,* which carried Vice Admiral William Martin, the commander of the Sixth Fleet. Halman's distress call crackled over the airwaves. The *Saratoga*'s radio operators, likely stunned by the emergency message over the high-command network, struggled to decipher Halman's distress call. Two minutes after Halman made his first call, the carrier responded. "Rockstar, this is Schematic," answered the carrier's operator. "You are garbled. Say again."

As shells rocked the *Liberty* and smoke poured into the radio room, Halman fingered the transmit button and repeated his distress call. "I say again. We are under attack," Halman shouted. "We are under attack."

The *Saratoga*'s message came back the same. "You are still garbled," the operator replied. "Say again."

"Schematic, this is Rockstar. We are under attack. We are under attack," Halman yelled. "Any station this net, this is Rockstar. We are under attack. Do you read me?"

Six minutes into the assault, the *Liberty*'s radiomen switched transmitters but still could not get a clear message out. Chief Petty Officer Wayne Smith darted down to the transmitter room on the main deck near the rear of the ship. There Smith discovered that the frequency dial was one kilocycle off. He adjusted it and the radio operators tried again. Problems persisted. Each time the planes strafed the ship, the radiomen found the frequency interrupted by a sound like feedback. The noise over the receivers was so loud that one of the men would later tell the Navy's investigating board that the sailors concluded the transmitters had malfunctioned. The men switched frequencies only to find the same feedback noise on all of them. Halman and the other radiomen concluded the attackers had jammed the *Liberty*'s communications. Only between attacks could the operators receive signals.

The radio log shows that at 2:08 P.M.—ten minutes into the assault—

Halman called for help again. The fighters by now had strafed the *Liberty* multiple times. Fires raged on deck and wounded sailors flooded the sick bay, wardroom, and mess deck. The chaotic and frightful reality aboard the ship reflected in Halman's desperate call for help. "Schematic, this is Rockstar," the radio operator called out. "We are under attack. We are under attack. We are under attack."

"Roger," the carrier's operator finally replied.

"Schematic, this is Rockstar," Halman radioed one minute later. "We are under attack and need immediate assistance."

"Roger," the carrier's operator answered. The *Saratoga*'s radioman asked the *Liberty* for an authentication code, a secret variable letter combination that ships use to verify the identity of others. Petty Officer 2nd Class Joseph Ward crouched next to Halman and fed him the authentication code from a book. The carrier's radioman responded five minutes later. "Authentication is correct," the operator replied. "I am standing by for further traffic."

Ensign Dave Lucas leaned over to grab his battle helmet and life jacket out of the starboard gear locker just outside the bridge when he felt a round zing past his head. He dropped to the deck as another explosion rocked the spy ship. Lucas crawled the last few feet into the bridge, his battle helmet still clutched in one hand. He pulled himself up and surveyed the wrecked command hub. He choked on the smoke and broken glass from the shattered portholes crunched beneath his feet. Blood made portions of the deck slippery. Lieutenant Jim O'Connor had dragged himself into the Combat Information Center just behind the bridge. Lucas spied Lieutenant Jim Ennes, Jr., stretched out in the back of the bridge, his left leg broken. Petty Officer 3rd Class Francis Brown, one of the ship's quartermasters, had taken control of the helm. In the center of the room, McGonagle barked orders at the phone talkers.

Lucas buckled his battle helmet just as another fighter strafed the bridge. He dropped to the deck for a second time. Shrapnel dug into his arms, back, and fingers. He grabbed his handkerchief and cinched it around the pinkie finger on his right hand. The gunnery officer's battle station was on the flying bridge above, but Lucas knew he wouldn't survive up there with the fighter attacks. Instead he hopped down the ladder to help with the injured in the wardroom. Below he witnessed several men carry the executive officer on a stretcher down the passageway. The normally gregarious Armstrong lay silent and the color had drained from his face. Lucas recognized the signs of shock. Ennes now lay on the deck outside the wardroom, his shattered leg now swollen. Inside the wardroom, Lucas found one of the ship's corpsmen busy with another half dozen casualties.

Several men gathered in a passageway to fight a fire on the port side near the gasoline drums. Lucas joined them. The fire had spread from the drums and consumed four life rafts on deck. The men unrolled a fire hose and cranked the valve, unleashing a stream of salt water. Others kicked burned debris and fuel overboard. Each time the fighters passed, the men ducked back inside the passageway. The explosions echoed inside the metal superstructure and rounds whistled through the corridor where the sailors crouched. Injured men littered the decks. Many of them had been chipping paint on deck or were in the forward spaces when the attackers first shelled the ship. The repair party soon ran out of stretchers so Lucas and the men grabbed several blankets from nearby staterooms and hauled the injured below. Lucas returned to the bridge, climbing the ladder inside the superstructure.

In the brief time he had left the bridge—he estimated it to be no more than fifteen minutes—the fighters had continued to pound the command hub. Unbeknownst to the men on the *Liberty*, a pair of French-made Super Mystère fighter-bombers armed with napalm had replaced the Mirage fighters that had run out of ammunition. A napalm canister had struck the ship and the jellied gasoline fire had flooded the bridge with smoke. McGonagle, nearly alone on the bridge when the canister hit, would later recall one of his most vivid memories of the attack was "firefly-like pieces of napalm flying around inside the pilot house." Lucas found the radar and gyrocompass inoperable. The magnetic compass spun wildly and much of the radio equipment was fried. No one had written in the quartermaster's notebook—a chronology of events used to create the deck log—since 1:55 P.M., minutes before the attack. The final entry in the blood-splattered log noted only that O'Malley had assumed the ship's conn. Lucas took control of the log.

The young officer and father of a five-week-old daughter (whom he had never met) stood in a bridge that was now nearly empty. The relentless attacks had killed or injured the navigator, executive officer, and the helmsman along with the off-going officer and junior officer of the deck. Francis Brown, one of the ship's quartermasters, had assumed the helm to guide the battered ship. Lucas spotted a lone phone talker stretched out on the deck in the chart room in the rear of the bridge, relaying the skipper's orders to damage control. McGonagle paced the center bridge, clutching in one hand a camera that he used to photograph the fighters. Blood soaked the skipper's right pant leg from a shrapnel wound in his upper thigh and he had burns on his right forearm. Lucas sensed McGonagle's relief that another officer had joined him on the bridge.

The fighters disappeared in the sky and an eerie calm settled over the battered *Liberty*. Was the attack over, Lucas wondered, or would the fighters rearm and return. Who were the attackers? The young officer, like many others, assumed the Egyptians had strafed the *Liberty*. Lucas stepped onto the starboard wing of the bridge. Firefighters pushed charred debris overboard on the deck below. The men had extinguished some of the fires and had others under control. Stretcher bearers and volunteers rescued the wounded and hauled them down to the wardroom and mess deck on mattresses and wrapped in blankets. On the deck lay several dead bodies that no one had time yet to recover. The young officer looked at his feet and realized that he stood on the American flag that minutes earlier had flown from the mast above. The fighters had shot it down.

The *Liberty*'s problems magnified. Just before the fighter attack Ensign Patrick O'Malley had spotted three unidentified blips on the green radar screen, zooming toward the spy ship. O'Malley had summoned Lloyd Painter, who had identified the blips as surface vessels and alerted the skipper. In the chaos of the attack that followed, no one had had time to investigate the earlier radar report. Men had fought fires, rescued the injured, and stoked the boilers as the unidentified vessels closed the distance. McGonagle now scanned the horizon with his binoculars. Fifteen miles off the starboard side, he spotted three torpedo boats in attack formation aimed right at the *Liberty*.

CHAPTER 5

You are authorized to use whatever force required to defend USS Liberty from further attacks.

—JOINT CHIEFS OF STAFF ORDER

At 2:24 P.M. McGonagle studied the three torpedo boats in the distance. The skipper could see that the boats traveled nearly thirty knots and in a wedge formation separated from one another by as little as one hundred and fifty yards. The center boat led the group in what McGonagle would later tell Navy investigators appeared to be a "torpedo launch attitude." The skipper recognized that the *Liberty,* even at top speed of eighteen knots, was defenseless against the high-speed boats, which closed to within five miles. If he turned the ship to starboard, McGonagle would provide the boats a larger target. If he turned toward port, the skipper risked grounding the *Liberty* on shoals or violating Egypt's territorial waters. The skipper had no option but to sail on the same northwesterly course farther out into the Mediterranean. He ordered the machine guns manned and a new American flag raised. One of the *Liberty*'s signalmen grabbed a holiday ensign—the ship's largest—and hoisted the seven-by-thirteen-foot flag up the mast at 2:26 P.M.

Dale Larkins climbed the ladder to the bridge, where he nearly collided with the skipper. Larkins had manned the machine guns aft of the bridge at the start of the attack before the fires from the deck below chased him and the other gunners away. He had climbed down to help fight the fires before he hustled back up to the bridge. McGonagle now ordered him to man the forward guns. When he reached the forecastle, Larkins stumbled over the bloodied remains of the gunners and phone talkers. One of the bodies, located next to the phone box, had been cut in half. The sailor's intestines draped over the forecastle and blood ran down the bulkhead to the deck below. Larkins reached the starboard guntub steps later and found one of the gunners slumped over with a basketball-sized hole in his back. The other gunner lay next to him in the tub, barely alive with a massive head wound and chest injuries. Larkins could hear the man's labored breathing.

Up on the bridge, McGonagle watched the sixty-two-ton torpedo boats slice through the waves toward the *Liberty*. When the boats closed to within two thousand yards, the skipper spotted a blue and white flag with a Star of David in the center. The attackers had not been Egyptian, but Israeli. The boats appeared to signal the spy ship, but the intermittent smoke from the *Liberty*'s fires blocked McGonagle's view. He could not read the signals nor could he respond to them. The fighters had destroyed the *Liberty*'s twenty-four-inch signal light, leaving only a handheld Aldis lamp approximately six inches in diameter, far too weak to penetrate the smoke. McGonagle and his signalmen—as later testimony would show—did not even try to use the smaller light. A signalman on the bridge instead raised handheld flags to communicate by semaphore. Fearing the attack might have been in error, McGonagle yelled for the gunners to hold fire.

On the forecastle, Larkins found that shrapnel had hit the machine gun and broken the chain of bullets. There were no spent shells in the guntub. The dead gunners, he realized, had never even had a chance to fire. Larkins stepped inside the guntub and removed the broken chain. He fished the single bullet from the chamber and fed a fresh chain of ammunition into the machine gun. Larkins spotted the torpedo boats zooming toward the spy ship in the distance. The boats turned and pulled back in what appeared to Larkins to be a torpedo run. He swiveled his machine gun and sighted the boats approximately a half to three-quarters of a mile off the starboard side. Larkins squeezed the trigger. A single round fired before the machine gun's top plate blew open. He inspected it and discovered shrapnel had damaged the latch in the air attack. Larkins couldn't close the plate. He realized the machine gun was worthless at the same time he heard McGonagle's order to cease fire.

The starboard machine gun just aft of the bridge started to fire. The flames and smoke from the motor whaleboat fire on the deck below blocked McGonagle's view of the machine gun. The skipper assumed one of the gunners had failed to hear the cease-fire order so he instructed Lucas to stop the gunner. The young officer darted out of the hatch and found the bridge's port machine gun vacant. The flames from the gasoline fire below on deck had forced the gunners to abandon the post. He ran down the walkway where he had a clear view of the starboard machine gun that McGonagle believed fired on the torpedo boats. Lucas was surprised to find the guntub empty. The gun barrel rested on the edge of the tub and flames from the motor whaleboat fire danced over the lip of the mount. Lucas realized that no one had fired on the torpedo boats. The flames had sparked the ammunition.

The torpedo boats zoomed toward the *Liberty* in attack formation. Any hope McGonagle had to stop the assault vanished. The torpedo boats—armed with 20-mm and 40-mm cannons along with .50-caliber machine guns—opened fire on the defenseless spy ship. The skipper shouted to take cover as rounds crashed into the bridge and passed through the open starboard hatch. The men dropped to the deck as the clash of metal on metal returned. McGonagle knew that the cannon and machine gun fire was the least of the *Liberty*'s concerns. Israel's French-made boats each carried up to two torpedoes that gunners had to manually aim. The cannon fire was designed to provide cover and create distractions so the boats could slip in close and unleash the torpedoes. The skipper ordered an alert passed to his crew. At 2:31 P.M. the ship's loudspeaker crackled. "Standby for a torpedo attack."

Nearly three hundred sailors now prepared for the unthinkable. Not since the waning days of World War II—and before many of the *Liberty*'s crewmembers were even born—had another nation torpedoed an American ship. For many of the *Liberty*'s men, the surreal circumstances of the surprise attack only magnified the shock of the skipper's warning. The *Liberty* had sailed peacefully that morning along the Egyptian coast. Men had sunbathed on the forward decks, shopped for T-shirts in the ship's store, and written letters home. That had all changed in just half an hour. Scores of sailors had either been killed or wounded. Fires burned on deck and a torpedo now zipped through the water. Throughout the 455-foot long ship, sailors readied themselves for the blast. There was nowhere to go, nowhere to hide. Men could only wait and pray.

Down in the engine room, George Golden ordered all nonessential men to grab life jackets, climb the ladders, and vacate the spaces. The chief engineer knew the ship would not survive a direct hit to the engine room. Golden and a small cadre of boilermen, machinist mates, and firemen would remain behind to operate the engineering plant. Over in the research spaces, Dennis Eikleberry tucked the bottom of his pants into his socks and buttoned up his shirt to protect as much skin as possible from flash burns. Eikleberry lay down on the deck with more than a dozen other sailors in his compartment as the room fell silent. Jeff Carpenter, in a compartment across the hall, chose not to see what was about to happen. He slipped off his glasses, inserted them in his shirt pocket, and pulled his battle helmet low over his head.

Even if he survived the blast, Ensign Scott knew, the ship would lose power. He fished his flashlight out of his desk drawer in Damage Control Central and ordered the phone talkers to brace themselves. He thought again that today was his twenty-fourth birthday. James Halman, who desperately had tried to alert the Sixth Fleet of the attack, dropped his microphone, stepped into the passageway, and lay down along with the other radiomen. If he died, Halman hoped his death would be swift. Over in the *Liberty*'s sick bay, Dr. Kiepfer realized that many of the injured had no way to protect themselves, so the towering doctor lay across the wounded. An injured sailor on a table in the mess deck below turned to Seaman George Wilson and told him he was scared. The sailor asked Wilson, injured and stretched out on a table beside him, to pray for them. "Praised be God," Wilson began as sailors on nearby tables joined him. "All are His servants, and all abide by His bidding!"

Up on the bridge at 2:34 P.M. McGonagle spotted a torpedo racing through the water. He would later tell Navy investigators that he watched the torpedo miss the *Liberty*'s stern by only twenty-five yards. Unbeknownst to the skipper, the Israelis had launched five torpedoes.

The *Liberty* had no time to take evasive maneuvers. McGonagle could only hope that a torpedo did not hit the engine room. One minute after the near miss, an explosion rocked the ship. One of the five had hit its target. Many of the sailors later would say the blast lifted the *Liberty* out of the water before it settled back down. The generators shut down, power went out, and the steering failed as the *Liberty* became dead in the water. McGonagle peered over the starboard side and saw oil and debris flood out into the sea. Darkness settled over the *Liberty* as the ship started to roll.

Eikleberry never heard the blast. Stretched out on the deck of the research space he reminded himself that the ladder that led to the deck above was nearby. The compartment where he lay was below the waterline. The torpedo's explosion bathed Eikleberry in a terrific heat. The blast lifted him off the deck and dropped him on his stomach; his gray-rimmed glasses fell to the floor. The overhead lights shattered and shards of scalding glass rained down. He felt the tiny pieces burn his back as he fumbled for his glasses in the dark. Smoke flooded the room. He slipped on his glasses and took stock of the damage. The torpedo had destroyed the bulkhead that separated the compartment from the passageway. Eikleberry could see straight into the room across the hall. Through the smoke, he saw fire and a red glow that provided the only light in the wrecked spaces. He heard debris crash down around him, but he did not see anyone else nor hear voices. Am I dead? he thought. Why is it so quiet? He then heard someone yell out. "Let's get the hell out of here."

Eikleberry crawled to his feet and took two steps over the remains of the bulkhead. The cold seawater already was up to his waist. He peered through the coordination room that once sat across the hall. The bulkhead that had separated that room from the adjoining communication room had vaporized. He stared at the torpedo hole. Water rushed inside the ship. It flowed fast, he thought, like a river. When Eikleberry reached the emergency hatch a few steps away, the water had risen to his neck. Sailors paddled around the ladder, urging one another to remain calm and patient as one by one the men scurried up.

The water continued to rise. Eikleberry's turn finally came. He locked on to the ladder and climbed. Men reached down from above, grabbed his arms, and pulled him through the hatch. He had made it out alive. A sailor handed him a life preserver out of a box as word passed to prepare to abandon ship.

Jeff Carpenter, who had been in the compartment across the hall from Eikleberry, flew across the room when the torpedo exploded. He landed on his back and wondered, like Eikleberry, if he was dead. The cold rush of seawater assured him he had survived. Daylight briefly filtered through the torpedo hole and illuminated the room before the ship rolled back to starboard and the majority of the hole dropped beneath the water. The water rose and Carpenter tried to stand up to escape but found his leg pinned beneath a desk. The water slipped over his head. He panicked and jerked his leg but still could not free it. Carpenter thought drowning might not be the worst way to die. He took a mouthful of seawater. He calmed down and realized he needed to fight. Carpenter began to twist his leg. Seconds later he freed it and popped to the surface. He heard someone yell for help as he paddled toward the emergency hatch.

When the torpedo exploded, Petty Officer 2nd Class Robert Schnell saw a ball of orange flame before a flying desk knocked him unconscious. The seawater woke him up. Darkness settled over the compartment and he could smell smoke and fuel oil. Schnell grabbed hold of the steam pipes that once crisscrossed the compartment and pulled himself along the ceiling toward the ladder. Like Eikleberry, he found a crowd of sailors anxious to escape. Crews had sealed the compartment's larger hatch when the general quarters alarm sounded, leaving only the scuttle open. To alleviate the jam, sailors needed to open the hatch. Schnell climbed out and learned that sailors had tried to open it, but had found the hatch jammed. The twenty-four-year-old former college halfback, who had played in the 1962 Junior Rose Bowl, grabbed a hammer. He pounded the latches loose and yanked the hatch open. Men flowed out of the flooded compartment. Schnell did the opposite. He turned, climbed back down, and searched for survivors.

The torpedo had reduced the research spaces to a clutter of broken radio receivers, filing cabinets, desks, and chairs that sloshed about in the seawater. The blast had toppled the bulkheads that once divided the cavernous space into rooms and offices. Electrical wires and steam pipes now sagged from the ceiling. Sparks rained down. The Mediterranean rushed through a gash that investigators would later measure at thirty-nine feet wide and twenty-four feet high. Most of the teardrop-shaped hole was below the waterline. The more the *Liberty* rolled toward starboard, the greater the torrent of seawater. The explosion had killed twenty-five sailors. Bodies and body parts now floated in the water along with classified papers, key cards, and intercept tapes. Voices cried out for help. Disoriented survivors struggled to navigate a safe path through the twisted debris and razor-sharp metal toward the faint light of the open hatch that served as a beacon in the dark.

Bryce Lockwood fumbled for an exit. The explosion blew the Marine's glasses off, singed his face, and ruptured his right eardrum. Knocked to the deck, Lockwood felt the cold seawater and thought of his wife, Lois, and his three young children, two girls and a boy. He recently had updated his insurance policy and passed power of attorney to his wife. Lockwood felt relief that his family would be all right if he didn't survive. The seawater covered his legs as he struggled to his feet. The emergency lights had failed, but he could see the hatch thanks to the light that filtered through the torpedo hole. Lockwood stumbled across a sailor trapped under a collapsed bulkhead near the ladder. The water level rose as Lockwood reached down and grabbed the sailor beneath his arms. He pulled on the man to free him. Water rose and the injured sailor choked. Another sailor dove down to free the sailor's leg and then others hoisted him through the hatch.

Lockwood spotted another injured sailor who floated toward the torpedo hole. He latched on to the man and turned back toward the ladder. Shrapnel had damaged the rail and fuel oil from ruptured tanks in the bowels of the ship made the rungs slippery. Lockwood struggled to climb as he held on to the injured sailor. Halfway up the ladder he grasped the damaged portion of the rail and dropped the sailor. The man floated back toward the torpedo hole as Lockwood dove down and chased after him. He grabbed the sailor and returned to the ladder. This time Lockwood slipped on the rungs and again dropped the injured man. His frustration mounted as he chased after the injured sailor for a third time. Goddammit, he thought. I've gotten this far with him. I'm not going to let him get away now.

But when he reached the top of the ladder, Lockwood looked up to find the hatch now sealed. The sailors above had assumed all of the survivors had crawled out and had closed the hatch. Lockwood was trapped as the water rose. He held on to the injured man with one hand and used his other to pound on the bottom of the hatch. No one came. Lockwood pounded again and shouted. The water continued to climb. The experience would prove so traumatic that years later Lockwood would wake at night beneath his bed, banging on the box springs and pleading for someone to let him out. The hatch popped open. The oil-soaked Marine stared up at Petty Officer 3rd Class Phillip Tourney, a damage control crewman who had come down to inspect the hatches. "Goddamn squids!" Lockwood shouted, using the Marine's derogatory term for sailors. "Run off and shut me in down here."

The torpedo's explosion threw Ensign Scott and the phone talkers to the deck in Damage Control Central. The safe door blew open, logbooks crashed to the floor, and the metal filing cabinet that had been bolted to the deck tumbled over. The room went dark and acrid smoke flooded the office. Scott's ears rang and throat burned, but he was alive. The torpedo had dodged damage control, but Scott judged from the force of the blast that it had not missed by much. He assumed that it had hit the research spaces forward of the bridge. Though he determined that the torpedo had missed the engine room, Scott knew the ship still might sink. The young officer felt the *Liberty* roll to the port side from the force of the explosion. The rush of seawater into the flooded spaces one deck below prompted the ship seconds later to roll back to starboard.

Scott fumbled in the dark for his flashlight on the floor beside him. He aimed it at the inclinometer suspended from the ceiling. He knew that the weight of the seawater that now flooded the torpedoed spaces could capsize the ship. If the *Liberty* capsized, he knew it would sink and likely before many of the men would have a chance to jump overboard. He felt the ship roll. The inclinometer jumped from two degrees to three then five. Stop, Scott thought. Stop now. Stop this shit. He didn't need the inclinometer to tell him the ship was rolling. He could feel the unsettling rise of the ship in the pit of his stomach. Through the smoke, he read the inclinometer as it climbed to six degrees, then seven, eight, and nine. "Come on, stop!" he now shouted. "Stop. Stop. Stop." The roll began to slow as the inclinometer ticked up to ten degrees, then eleven. The roll froze at twelve degrees. The *Liberty* groaned.

The young officer felt the injured ship begin to roll back toward port. The inclinometer dropped to eleven degrees and then ten before it finally stabilized at nine. The bridge called down to the repair party in the engine room and ordered the men there to take over for Damage Control Central. The skipper had assumed that the torpedo had killed Scott and his men. Scott ordered the phone talker to call the bridge. "Tell the captain we're still here," he said. "We're still running." Scott climbed to his feet and stumbled into the passageway to survey the damage and determine precisely where the torpedo had hit. Sailors must dog down the watertight hatches and seal off the flooded compartments. The ship could remain afloat only if damage control teams isolated the flooded spaces. The emergency lights illuminated the passageway. Through the smoke, Scott could see that the blast had forced the steel deck beneath his feet to crumple. Around his ankles, he felt cold water.

Scott ordered one of his men to race to the forward repair locker and recruit more sailors. He instructed the sailor to tell the others to retrieve mattresses to cover the holes in the deck and slow the flooding. He kneeled down and stuck his hand through a hole. When he pulled it out, Scott found it black with fuel oil. The fuel tanks had ruptured. Moments later the bridge passed a message to standby for the possibility of another torpedo attack. Scott had determined that with its watertight hatches secured the *Liberty* could remain afloat. But he knew another torpedo hit, regardless of where it struck, would sink the ship. He ordered the phone talkers to relay that message to the bridge. Scott instructed his men that if another torpedo hit to immediately abandon ship. Drop your equipment, he told them, grab your life preserver, and head up the ladder and overboard. That was the only way the men might survive.

When the torpedo exploded, Chief Petty Officer Brooks had plummeted from atop a catwalk in the engine room to the metal grate below. Asbestos insulation and soot rained down. The blast even vibrated one of the lights out of its socket. The *Liberty*'s generators died, leaving the engine room in darkness along with the rest of the ship. Communication with the bridge also failed. Sailors grabbed battle lanterns to read gauges. George Golden would later tell Navy investigators that 20-mm cannon shells and armor-piercing machine gun rounds fired from Israeli torpedo boats tore through the sides of the engine room. A boilerman would later find one bullet dug into an interior bulkhead. Men shouted that the research space had been torpedoed. Brooks looked up to spot wet sailors who had climbed out of the torpedoed spaces pass through the engine room en route to higher decks. He did not have time to dwell on it, but had to restore power. Brooks shouted to the electricians to hustle.

Scott bypassed the engine room and charged over to the research spaces to inspect the torpedo's damage. He arrived at the hatch to find Tourney, who had just pulled Lockwood from below. Seawater flooded the research spaces, leaving only about a foot of air near the top. The water continued to rise and the men had to seal the hatch again. The safety of the ship demanded it, but Scott felt reluctant. What if men were still alive below? If he sealed the hatch, Scott knew any survivors would die. The water continued to rise. He had precious minutes to decide. He ordered Tourney to give him his belt. Scott fished the belt through the loop on his waterproof flashlight and dunked it in the water below. Tourney grabbed a wrench and banged on the hatch. The men hoped that any survivors, disoriented in the darkness, would see the light and find the exit. Scott leaned over the hatch. He could hear the pop and fizzle of electrical equipment in the water below.

Robert Schnell had climbed out of the torpedoed spaces only to return to rescue injured sailors. In the minutes after the explosion, Schnell made several trips into the flooded compartment as the water level rose. He plucked Dave Lewis, his eardrums ruptured and eyelids seared shut with Navy paint, from the water, then returned again to help others. With each trip, the water deepened. Schnell shouted for survivors in the dark. Sparks fluttered around him as he picked his way through the tangle of desks, crypto equipment, and wires. He had seen bodies floating in the oily water and found pieces of others. Schnell found himself alone, unsure of how to get out. The water neared the top of the compartment. He heard a bang and saw a light. He pulled himself along the pipes and wires that ran along the ceiling. He emerged seconds later from the hatch, winded and covered in fuel oil. He assured Scott and Tourney that no one else was alive down there. The men sealed the hatch.

Up on the bridge, McGonagle focused on the attackers. Before the torpedo hit, the injured skipper had spotted an Israeli flag on one of the boats, but he wanted more evidence. He clutched the camera that he had used to take pictures of fighters and now trained it on the torpedo boats that zipped past the spy ship. The boats continued to fire 20- and 40-mm cannons and armor-piercing machine gun rounds at the *Liberty,* but no torpedoes. Bullets sliced through the bulkheads of the engine room, mess deck, and the bridge. Spent shells rolled around on deck. The skipper summoned Lucas onto the starboard wing. One of the torpedo boats passed five hundred yards off the starboard side, traveling in the opposite direction from the *Liberty.* At 2:40 P.M.—five minutes after the torpedo hit—the young officer spotted one of the torpedo boat's hull numbers painted in white on the dark bow: 206–17, though what he read as 17 actually was the letter Tet, the ninth letter in the Hebrew alphabet. Lucas relayed the information to McGonagle. "Log it," the skipper ordered. Lucas obeyed, jotting down the first entry in the ship's log since moments before the attack began.

McGonagle shouted to the men to take cover. Rounds and shrapnel tore through the walls and the open hatch on the starboard side. Francis Brown remained at the helm to guide the ship. Brown stepped back for protection but left one hand on the wheel. He gasped and dropped to the deck. Petty Officer 2nd Class Charles Cocnavitch, one of the *Liberty*'s radarmen, darted onto the bridge to pull Brown out of the way. Cocnavitch slipped on the blood that soaked the deck. Brown's eyes were open in an empty stare. He had been hit in the back of the head. Cocnavitch realized that Brown had died before he hit the deck. Ensign

Lucas, who had been two steps behind Brown, took the helm. Lucas found that neither the gyrocompass nor the rudder angle indicator worked. Most of the other navigational equipment also had failed and the ship now aimed north. The bridge switched control to the after-steering department, where crews could manually move the rudder.

If the *Liberty* were to sink, McGonagle recognized, it was not in deep enough water to guarantee that another nation might not be able to salvage the classified equipment and material. The skipper instead planned to ground the injured *Liberty* on nearby shoals. Despite his intention, word passed to prepare to abandon ship. Throughout the *Liberty,* sailors responded. Cocnavitch heard the order passed over the sound-powered phones in the radar room and filled weighted bags. In Damage Control Central, Scott torched confidential manuals and papers in his wastebasket. Petty Officer Halman burned the radio authentication codes. Dr. Kiepfer prepared to move the wounded. Lieutenant Painter climbed up a ladder toward deck to prepare the life rafts. Painter discovered someone had already dropped several over-board. Through the hatch, he watched in horror as one of the torpedo boats zoomed past and machine-gunned the rubber rafts. There was no way now to abandon ship.

The torpedo boats soon halted fire and loitered as much as eight hundred yards off the stern of the *Liberty.* McGonagle trained his bin-oculars on them. The men on the *Liberty* did not know whether the boats might attack again. At 3:03 P.M.—one hour and five minutes after the attack began—one of the torpedo boats zoomed toward the *Liberty.* A signalman grabbed the handheld Aldis lamp and repeatedly flashed "US Naval Ship." When the torpedo boat closed to a distance of five hundred yards, it turned astern and slowed. The boat signaled in English: "Do you need help?" McGonagle ordered a signalman to flash a negative reply. The torpedo boat signaled: "Do you want us to stand by?" The skipper again ordered the signalman to flash "No, thank you." The torpedo boat closed to within one hundred yards of the port side and flashed "good luck" before it zoomed two minutes later toward shore.

The torpedo boats had not yet disappeared over the horizon when a helicopter approached the *Liberty*'s portside, hovering at five hundred yards. A second helicopter followed a minute later. The helicopters circled the battered ship as close as a hundred yards. McGonagle noted the Star of David markings and read the hull numbers as either 04 or D4 and 08 or D8. The helicopters departed and the torpedo boats returned at 3:37 P.M., approaching the *Liberty*'s starboard side at high speed at a range of five miles. McGonagle also spotted two fighters. The bridge alerted the crew again to stand by for a possible attack. McGonagle ordered a signalman at 3:40 P.M. to hoist the international flag symbol for "Not Under Command," meaning the *Liberty* maneuvered with difficulty and advising the torpedo boats to remain clear. The fighters did not attack and the boats reversed course two minutes later, but periodically returned over the next hour and a quarter.

The threat of another attack loomed as *Liberty* crewmembers rescued the injured, fought the last of the fires, and treated the wounded. The torpedo had knocked out power along with much of the *Liberty*'s navigational systems and communications. Engineers hustled to restore power. Damage control crews, who had sealed the watertight hatches, systematically searched compartments for leaks and hammered wooden cones into shell holes to prevent flooding. At 3:19 P.M. the engine room restored power to the bridge, but the rudder still did not function. The log shows that crews steered manually from the rear of the ship as the *Liberty* steamed northward to clear the area at speeds varying from zero to eight knots. Four minutes after power returned to the bridge, the *Liberty* lost lube oil suction and again came dead in the water until engineers could restore oil pressure.

Radiomen reestablished communications at 3:55 P.M. The only functioning transmitter—one that previously had been designated for repairs—was down in the transmitter room on the main deck near the rear of the ship. The radiomen grabbed all the necessary gear and relocated below. McGonagle, now weak from blood loss, stretched out on the deck of the bridge to prevent blacking out. A sailor tied a tourniquet around his right thigh as the skipper dictated a message to the Sixth Fleet. An officer jotted it down on the back of a teletype printout of news headlines. "Request immediate assistance. Torpedo hit starboard midship. Flooding. List was stopped at nine degrees," the message shows McGonagle dictated. "Approximate casualties four dead, three seriously wounded, 50 wounded. Radar, fathometer and gyroscope inoperable. Will require navigational aid consisting of sea and air escort."

Two aircraft reconned the ship at 4:15 P.M. Torpedo boats returned at 4:33 P.M. The men on the bridge identified one of the hull numbers as 204. The log shows McGonagle confirmed his previous identification when he stated: "Boats are believed to be Israeli." The *Liberty* slowed from eight knots to five after the crew struggled to control the ship. The skipper determined that his course could be off by as much as thirty degrees in either direction. The ship's fathometer, which for a while only functioned on the hundred-fathom scale, revealed the *Liberty* entering shallow waters. The skipper feared the ship was off course and might ground. He ordered Lucas to recruit volunteers to prepare to drop the anchor. McGonagle decided to wait until nightfall when he could sight the North Star and determine the ship's position. He then changed his mind and at 5:04 P.M. reversed the *Liberty* for approximately twenty minutes into deeper water.

In the mess deck below, Armstrong struggled. The executive officer, who had been hit on deck as he tried to knock gasoline drums overboard, stretched out on a table, both legs broken by shrapnel. He clutched a bottle of Terry brandy, a Spanish label picked up in a Rota liquor store. The ship's second in command remained pale and weak though he joked with the sailors on neighboring tables to elevate morale. Officers and enlisted men alike stopped by to visit. Despite his injuries, Armstrong comforted his men. He assured them the worst was over. The *Liberty* and its crew would survive. The sailors who visited Armstrong felt confident that he too would survive, but the executive officer sensed otherwise. He slipped off his Naval Academy ring and handed it to his favorite steward. "Here," he said. "Give this to my wife." Moments later, Armstrong died.

Another helicopter approached the *Liberty* at 6:40 P.M. McGonagle identified it as Israeli and the quartermaster recorded the tail markings in the ship's log as SA 321-K and the fuselage number 06. The helicopter signaled that it wanted to land. McGonagle considered the request, but realized that the various antennae and other obstructions on deck made it impossible. He only risked an accident and more injuries. He waved the helicopter off. A package dropped to the *Liberty*'s deck. Sailors delivered it to the skipper on the bridge at 6:52 P.M. From a bag weighted with oranges, McGonagle fished out a business card belonging to Commander Ernest Castle, the American naval attaché in Tel Aviv. McGonagle flipped over the card. On the back, Castle had scrawled a three-word message that made many of the men question how the attaché had failed to spot the dead bodies, the blood streams, and carnage littered below: "HAVE YOU CASUALTIES?"

Miles above the *Liberty* in the back of a Navy spy plane, Petty Officer 2nd Class Michael Prostinak tuned the dials on his receiver in search of Israeli communications. The Hebrew linguist had lifted off from the Athens Air Base in an EC-121 that morning for an eight-hour mission over the Middle East to eavesdrop on the fourth day of the war. The U.S. Air Force Security Service, working in conjunction with the NSA, had established an intelligence-processing hub a year earlier at the international airport in the Athens suburbs. The main runway was all that separated the Olympic Airlines terminal from the Greek military base that housed the NSA's secret operation. In a compound protected by a double hurricane fence and guard patrols, American analysts reviewed intercepted communications of the war and tipped off Prostinak and other airborne spies about certain call signs, unit identities, and frequencies to monitor.

Before the war, the Navy and Air Force each flew about eight spy missions a month over the Middle East, soaking up radio communications and zeroing in on radar installations. That all changed on May 23, the same day the NSA decided to reassign the *Liberty* from West Africa to its patrol off Egypt. Since then the Navy and Air Force had flown missions daily. The Navy's missions even jumped to twice daily when the war began. Unlike the *Liberty,* which could troll for days or even weeks offshore, planes wasted time and fuel traveling to and from targets. To maximize intercept time, the NSA staggered missions. Air Force planes took off at approximately 5 A.M. and the Navy followed five hours later. The propeller-plane—dubbed the Willy Victor—served as the airborne equivalent of the *Liberty,* a plodding cargo plane that could fly approximately three hundred miles per hour with a range of more than four thousand miles when stripped down. Crews had installed so many antennae that its navigator remarked that it was a miracle it flew at all.

Strapped in the back with Prostinak sat an intelligence evaluator, intercept operators, and other Arabic and Hebrew linguists. A twenty-four-year-old West Virginia native, Prostinak had enlisted in the Navy right out of high school to earn money for college. During the Cuban Missile Crisis in October 1962, the Navy realized it lacked Spanish linguists. Prostinak, who had studied Spanish in high school, landed in language school and discovered that he picked up Spanish easily. A two-year posting in Puerto Rico helped him master it. When he reenlisted, Prostinak opted to study a third language. He thought Hebrew might prove a challenge. For more than six months, he studied under a Lebanese teacher at the NSA's secret language school in Maryland. He learned to read and write the distinctive Hebrew alphabet, memorized vocabulary, and translated Israeli newspaper articles.

Prostinak had had ample opportunity to exercise his Hebrew skills in recent days. Normally based in the Spanish city of Rota—the same spot the *Liberty* had docked to take on supplies—Prostinak and other members of his squadron had received emergency departure orders within hours of the start of the war. The men each packed a bag and climbed aboard the Willy Victor for the eight-hour flight to Greece, the temporary staging area for the Middle East missions. Soon after landing late that afternoon, the men hopped a shuttle to the Hotel Seville in the Athenian suburb of Iraklion. With a kitchen and bar open twenty-four hours, the hotel proved a natural fit for the spooks and aircrews, who routinely flew odd hours. Before the men had a chance to unpack, commanders summoned them back to the base to fly the first mission. When the sun rose the second day of the war, Prostinak listened over his headphones as Israeli pilots climbed into the skies for more combat.

The mission this afternoon marked the third in as many days. Like the *Liberty,* the spy planes remained over the Mediterranean and outside the territorial reach of Israel and Egypt. When the plane arrived at a point off the coast of the Egyptian city of Alexandria, the pilot banked to the northeast, paralleling the Egyptian and Israeli coasts at altitudes as low as ten thousand feet. After passing Tel Aviv, the pilot hooked north, flying as far as the Lebanese capital of Beirut. The pilots turned south and repeated the track until fuel ran low. The workstations Prostinak and other linguists used—shielded by security curtains—included radio receivers designed to intercept air and ground communications. A four-track tape recorder that logged the time and frequency of intercepts allowed the spooks to capture communications that might have an intelligence value.

Though his Hebrew lagged behind his Spanish skills, Prostinak had learned to pick up on key words, such as "tanks," "artillery," and "mortar fire." He eavesdropped on a frequency long enough to get a basic understanding. If it had potential intelligence value, he recorded it. If not, he tuned the dials. More than the language, Prostinak listened for the excitement in a voice that almost always indicated action. That's what grabbed his attention this afternoon as the Willy Victor roared along the Egyptian coast. The flurry of Hebrew made it impossible for Prostinak to discern whether he heard aircraft or ground forces. He could sense from the excitement that something was going on far below. He strained to listen and translate. He then heard something that shocked him. He flipped on the secure intercom to his supervisor. "Hey, Chief. I've got really odd activity," Prostinak called out as he hit the record button. "They mentioned an American flag."

Radiomen on the aircraft carrier *Saratoga* approximately five hundred miles west of the *Liberty* forwarded the spy ship's distress calls to the commander of the Sixth Fleet and the London headquarters of the Navy's European and Middle East command. With each call, the desperation intensified. At 2:35 P.M.—the exact moment the torpedo split open the side of the *Liberty*—the *Saratoga* broadcast the first details of the attack. "Following received from Rockstar. I am under attack. My posit 31.23N 33.25E," the carrier's message read. "I have been hit. Request immed assistance." *Saratoga* radiomen relayed another message two minutes later that foreshadowed the horror the *Liberty* now faced. "3 unidentified gunboats approaching vessel now." The carrier followed that message at 2:45 P.M. with the relay of a five-word distress call. "Under attack and hit badly." Nine minutes later, the carrier forwarded the first confirmation that the *Liberty* had been torpedoed. "Hit by torpedo starboard side. Listing badly. Need assistance immediately."

Vice Admiral William Martin, the commander of the Sixth Fleet, sailed on the cruiser *Little Rock* as the attack unfolded. The three-star admiral's flagship had joined the carriers *Saratoga* and *America* for maneuvers off of Crete. Soviet warships had harassed the fleet, prompting Martin the day before to warn a Russian destroyer to remain clear. Over the open airwaves, Martin heard the desperation in the voice of *Liberty*'s radioman. At 2:50 P.M.—fifteen minutes after the torpedo killed twenty-five sailors—the admiral ordered his carriers to turn into the wind. "*America* launch four armed A4's to proceed to 31–23N 33–25E to defend USS *Liberty* who is now under attack by gunboats," Martin instructed. "Provide fighter cover and tankers. Relieve on station. *Saratoga* launch four armed A1's ASAP same mission." The Sixth Fleet sent a message to the *Liberty* at 3:05 P.M. to assure the defenseless ship help would arrive soon. "Your flash traffic received. Sending aircraft to cover you. Surface units on the way."

On the bridge of the *America,* Captain Donald Engen chatted with NBC News reporter Robert Goralski. Engen's 77,000-ton carrier—completed less than three years earlier at a cost of $293 million—had become the temporary home for as many as thirty reporters from major television networks, wire services, and newspapers, all eager to cover the events of the Middle East war. When the Combat Information Center alerted Engen of the attack over the squawk box, the skipper ordered the reporter off the bridge. News of the attack had arrived at an inopportune time. Not only did reporters swarm the carrier, but the *America* also was in the middle of a nuclear weapons drill. The drill required sailors to bring nuclear weapons up the bomb elevators and simulate arming the planes. Not until the weapons could be safely stored belowdecks and planes rearmed with conventional munitions could the *America* launch, a process Engen estimated would take approximately one hour.

The *Saratoga*'s communications officer personally delivered the news of the attack to Captain Joseph Tully, Jr., on the bridge of that carrier soon after radiomen picked up the *Liberty*'s distress calls. Unlike the *America*, the *Saratoga* had a strike group ready within minutes. Tully would later write that he immediately turned into the wind and launched fighters only to have his superiors order him moments later to recall the fighters and wait for the *America*. Tully wrote that he instantly readied a second strike group. Commander Max Morris, the *Saratoga*'s navigator, who later would rise to the rank of rear admiral, confirmed Tully's account of the launch and recall in a letter to his former commanding officer. The *Saratoga*'s deck log does not reflect the launch, but does show that at 2:41 P.M. the carrier began a series of course and speed changes that could indicate flight activity.

Deck crews raced to prepare the fighters. The *Saratoga* had been ordered to launch A-1 Skyraiders, a propeller plane with a slow speed of only about 350 miles per hour but a range of three thousand miles. The *America* in contrast had been ordered to launch A-4 Skyhawks, a jet that flew nearly twice the speed of the A-1 and at an altitude of almost fifty thousand feet, but had a range of less than one thousand miles. Ordnance crews retrieved rockets and missiles from the magazines below. Intelligence officers briefed pilots on weather conditions and used maps of Egypt to highlight port facilities, antiaircraft batteries, and surface-to-air missile sites. The *Saratoga* messaged Martin at 3:22 P.M. that it planned to launch its four A-1s at 4 P.M. The *Saratoga*'s deck log shows that the carrier increased speed to twenty-five knots at 4:01 P.M. and started the launch sequence one minute later as fighters zoomed down the flight deck. The *America*'s deck log failed to record the launch, but Engen wrote in his memoir that planes lifted off soon after the *Saratoga*.

"We are on the way," the *America*'s flight leader announced over the departure frequency. "Who is the enemy?"

No one knew. The *Liberty* had not identified the nationality of the attackers in its distress calls. Many of the senior commanders, who had monitored the Soviet fleet for days off Crete, doubted the U.S.S.R. had done it but could not rule out Egypt. Because Egypt was allied with the Soviets, Navy commanders had to be careful. The officers wanted to protect the *Liberty* without provoking a larger confrontation with another country. Even the small number of planes launched was designed to signal that purpose. "Not too large and warlike," Engen later wrote in his memoir, "but still large enough to protect *Liberty*." Rear Admiral Lawrence Geis, commander of the Mediterranean's carrier strike force, repeated Martin's launch order at 3:16 P.M. and instructed pilots only to protect the ship. "Defense of USS *Liberty* means exactly that," Geis ordered. "Destroy or drive off any attackers who are clearly making attacks on *Liberty*. Remain over international waters. Defend yourself if attacked."

At 3:36 P.M., Martin issued combat orders for the pilots that again reflected his intention not to provoke a larger conflict: "Ensure pilots do not repeat do not fly overland." The admiral also ordered the *Saratoga* to relay a message to the *Liberty*, asking if the spy ship could identify the nationality of the attackers. Martin outlined more detailed rules of engagement in a message at 3:39 P.M. "You are authorized to use force including destruction as necessary to control the situation. Do not use more force than required. Do not pursue any unit towards land for reprisal purposes. Purpose of counterattack is to protect *Liberty* only," Martin's message stated. "Brief pilots that Egyptian territorial limit only 12 miles and *Liberty* right on edge. Do not fly between *Liberty* and shoreline except as required to carry out provisions."

Martin waited for his fighters to reach the *Liberty*. The *Saratoga* had estimated its propeller-driven Skyraiders would take approximately three hours to cover the distance to the battered spy ship. Martin had told his superiors that he expected the faster jets to arrive in half that time. Soon after the fighters left the carriers, a flash message from the American naval attaché in Tel Aviv rolled off the ship's teletype. "Israeli aircraft and MTB's [Motor Torpedo Boats] erroneously attacked U.S. ship," Commander Ernest Castle wrote in the 4:14 P.M. message. "IDF [Israel Defense Forces] helicopters in rescue operations. No other info. Israelis send abject apologies and request info of other US ships near war zone coasts." The admission that Israel had attacked the *Liberty* by mistake changed everything. The assault was over. Fighters were no longer needed. Martin ordered the mission aborted before the planes ever reached the *Liberty*: "Recall all strikes repeat recall all strikes."

An Israeli torpedo boat zooms past the *Liberty* during the attack. (NATIONAL ARCHIVES)

Firefighters extinguish the last of the blazes soon after the attack. (LLOYD PAINTER)

The forward machine gun tubs took direct fire during the air attack. (DENNIS EIKLEBERRY)

Blood from the dead gunners still stains the forecastle the morning after the attack. (DENNIS EIKLEBERRY)

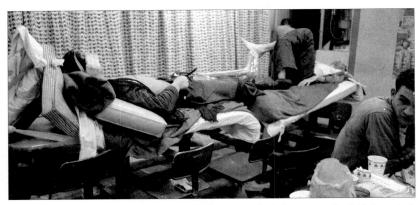

The *Liberty*'s medical staff converted the mess deck into a makeshift hospital, covering tables with mattresses to serve as beds. (NATIONAL ARCHIVES)

Shell holes riddle the bridge and smokestack. (DENNIS EIKLEBERRY)

Commander William McGonagle displays an armor-piercing machine gun round fired at the *Liberty* during the attack. Note the shell hole on the wall behind him. (NATIONAL SECURITY AGENCY)

Commander William McGonagle on the bridge at daybreak the morning after the attack. His right pant leg is gone, exposing his bloodstained leg. (FRANK MCINTURFF)

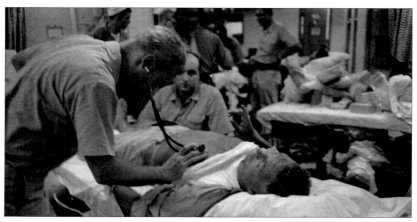

Dr. Peter Flynn, a surgeon from the aircraft carrier *America*, examines a patient on board the *Liberty* the morning after the attack. Dr. Richard Kiepfer, the *Liberty*'s only doctor, sits at the injured sailor's feet. (NATIONAL ARCHIVES)

President Lyndon Johnson and his advisers gather in the Situation Room the day of the attack. From left to right: Clark Clifford, Robert McNamara, McGeorge Bundy, Dean Rusk, Johnson (back to camera), Nicholas Katzenbach, Llewellyn Thompson, and Walt Rostow. (YOICHI OKAMOTO/ LYNDON B. JOHNSON LIBRARY)

Sailors race the injured off a helicopter on board the aircraft carrier *America* the day after the attack. (NATIONAL ARCHIVES)

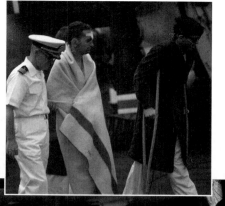

Injured *Liberty* crewmembers are escorted to a memorial service on the deck of the aircraft carrier *America* on June 10, 1967. (NATIONAL ARCHIVES)

President Johnson and his advisers gather in the Cabinet Room for a meeting of the Special Committee of the National Security Council the day after the attack. The *Liberty* is the focus of heated discussion. Clockwise from left: Robert McNamara, Clark Clifford, Harold Saunders, Walt Rostow, Vice President Hubert Humphrey, Joseph Clark, Francis Bator, Nicholas Katzenbach, Dean Rusk, Lyndon Johnson (both with back to the camera). (YOICHI OKAMOTO/LYNDON B. JOHNSON LIBRARY)

The *Liberty* arrives in Malta on June 14, 1967. Only the top of the torpedo hole is visible above the waterline. (NATIONAL ARCHIVES)

Men haul caskets on board the *Liberty* in Malta. (U. S. NAVY)

The full scope of the torpedo's damage is revealed as the ship sits on keel blocks in a Malta drydock. (DENNIS EIKLEBERRY)

Liberty Ensign Dave Lucas, center. (NATIONAL ARCHIVES)

Ensign John Scott inspects the shoring done by damage control crews to prevent the bulkhead from rupturing. (NATIONAL ARCHIVES)

Israeli Ambassador Yitzhak Rabin shakes hands with President Johnson at the door of the Oval Office. Rabin, who served as chief of staff during the Six-Day War, helped negotiate some of Israel's reparations for the attack on the *Liberty*. (YOICHI OKAMOTO/LYNDON B. JOHNSON LIBRARY)

Families greet the *Liberty* on its return to Virginia on July 29, 1967. (NATIONAL ARCHIVES)

CHAPTER 6

I just don't believe that it was an accident or trigger-happy local commanders. There was just too much of a sustained effort to disable and sink the Liberty.

—SECRETARY OF STATE DEAN RUSK

President Lyndon Johnson woke at about 7:45 A.M. Thursday morning, June 8. Normally an early riser, the president enjoyed a leisurely morning, eating his breakfast of creamed chip beef off a tray in his bedroom and washing it down with a cup of hot tea. Johnson had weathered a late night the evening before, working until nearly 10:30 when he finally sat down with the first lady for dinner of corned beef, potatoes, and cornbread muffins with butter and honey. He had followed the meal with two servings of chocolate pudding before retiring to the personal residence at 11:30. He chatted on the phone at midnight with close friend and Israel supporter Mathilde Krim.

The morning papers carried the latest news of the Middle East war. Israel now claimed victory in the Sinai Peninsula and announced that it had broken the blockade of the Strait of Tiran that triggered the conflict. Israeli pilots, whose average age was only twenty-three, had destroyed 441 Arab airplanes in strikes on twenty-five bases. Israeli forces had driven Egypt into retreat behind the Suez Canal and captured much of Jordan's territory along the West Bank of the Jordan River. Photos showed Israeli soldiers weeping and praying alongside the Wailing Wall in the Old City of Jerusalem.

Across the Potomac, Robert McNamara arrived at the Pentagon. Most mornings the defense secretary began early, riding his private elevator up from the basement parking garage to his third-floor office overlooking the dome of the Jefferson Memorial. Elsewhere, Secretary of State Dean Rusk prepared to testify this morning on the latest developments in the Middle East war before a closed-door session of the Senate Foreign Relations Committee.

In the wooded suburbs outside of Washington, guards at the National Security Agency screened employees arriving for work at the clandestine agency tucked away behind three barbed wire and electric fences. More than three hundred miles south of the capital in North Carolina, *Liberty* Ensign John Scott's mother drafted a letter, wishing her son a happy birthday. "You are getting so old that I have to strain to remember what went on 24 years ago," Ruth Scott wrote in her suburban Charlotte home. "We were so pleased with you, and have been ever since. You were the pride of the hospital nursery—the biggest, fattest, healthiest, most active baby in the lot!"

Unbeknownst to all of them, at that moment the *Liberty* struggled to survive.

At 9:11 A.M. Washington time—thirty-six minutes after the torpedo ripped open the side of the spy ship—the headquarters of America's European Command called the Pentagon with the news. The first reports relayed from the Sixth Fleet in the Mediterranean confirmed that the *Liberty* was under attack, had been torpedoed, and was listing badly. Early estimates put the spy ship approximately sixty to seventy miles from Egypt's Port Said. The Sixth Fleet commander had declared the attackers hostile and ordered fighters to defend the *Liberty*.

John Connell, the NSA's liaison officer to the Joint Reconnaissance Center, was chatting on the phone with his colleague Eugene Sheck back at NSA headquarters in Maryland when a Pentagon staffer darted in with the news. "The *Liberty*'s been torpedoed."

"What?" Connell asked, interrupting his call. "What the hell is going on?"

"The *Liberty*'s been torpedoed," repeated the officer.

"By whom?"

No one knew.

"Did you hear that?" Connell asked his counterpart on the phone back at NSA.

"If I got you straight, the ship's been torpedoed," Sheck answered. "My God!"

"That's right, start telling people, get up to the top right away."

"The top" meant the ninth floor of the NSA's headquarters, which housed the offices of the spy agency's director and his senior lieutenants. Moments after word of the attack arrived, Director Lieutenant General Marshall Carter and Deputy Director Louis Tordella gathered to determine the best plan of action. The first priority after the safety of the crew was to find out who had attacked the *Liberty.* Carter fired off a top-secret telegram to intelligence commands at 9:28 A.M.—thirteen minutes after he learned of the attack—ordering an immediate review of all recent intercepts. "USS *Liberty* has been reportedly torpedoed by unknown source in Med near 32N 33E," Carter wrote. "Request examine all communications for possible reaction/reflections and report accordingly."

Next the men focused on classified materials. Early reports showed the spy ship barely more than a dozen miles off the Sinai Peninsula. Charts the men consulted revealed the water was at most 240 feet deep. At that shallow depth, it would be easy for the Egyptians, Soviets, or any other nation to salvage the *Liberty*'s records and top-secret equipment. That bounty would immediately expose the *Liberty*'s mission and reveal that the United States had the capability to intercept and decipher VHF and UHF radio frequencies, common frequencies used for government and military communications. If the *Liberty* sank, America needed immediately to secure the site where the spy ship went down so divers could recover the equipment.

With each passing minute, the magnitude of the situation increased as fears mounted in Washington over the possibility that the Soviets had torpedoed the *Liberty.* The situation could no longer be handled solely by the Defense Department. Thirty-eight minutes after the first report reached Washington, National Security Adviser Walt Rostow dialed the president. Johnson had remained in the White House residence since he woke, though his daily planner shows that his leisurely morning had evolved into a typically hectic day. By the time Rostow phoned to inform him of the attack, the president already had checked in with his chief of staff between calls to four senators, the attorney general, and his defense and press secretaries.

Rostow followed up his phone call one minute later with a memo outlining the basic facts of the attack. Details remained scarce. "We have a flash report from the Joint Reconnaissance Center indicating that a U.S. elint (electronics intelligence) ship, the *Liberty,* has been torpedoed in the Mediterranean," the national security adviser wrote. "The ship is located 60–100 miles north of Egypt. Reconnaissance aircraft are out from the 6th fleet. We have no knowledge of the submarine or surface vessel which committed this act. We shall keep you informed."

The president phoned Robert McNamara ten minutes later, presumably about the *Liberty,* though no record of this conversation has surfaced. The attack was no doubt concerning, but absent more information, the president soon turned his attention back to politicking. "Get me in twenty minutes how many states I have been in since I became President," he barked to his secretary in a call on his private line. With five minutes to spare, the president's staff provided a rundown, showing that he had visited every state except Alabama, Mississippi, and North and South Dakota.

By 10:15 A.M., the latest report on the *Liberty* to reach Washington showed that carriers had launched eight fighter planes—four A-4's and four A-1's—to protect the *Liberty.* The United States still did not know who had torpedoed the ship. Reports indicated that the crippled ship faced serious trouble. Rostow shot off another memo to the president, this one only a single line: "The *Liberty* is listing badly to starboard."

At the same time, Deputy Undersecretary of State for Political Affairs Foy Kohler called the Soviet Embassy in Washington and informed one of its senior diplomats that the United States had an "urgent message." America could not risk an unnecessary confrontation with the communist power in the Middle East. Soviet naval forces had shadowed the Sixth Fleet for days in the Mediterranean. No doubt, commanders had watched the carriers turn into the wind and launch fighters. "An American ship, the USS *Liberty,* was torpedoed a few hours ago off Port Said," Kohler told Minister-Counselor Yuri Tcherniakov, according to a memo of the conversation. "We are not sure of the exact location where the incident took place. It is an auxiliary ship." Kohler told the Soviet diplomat that the United States had launched eight fighters "to investigate." "We wanted the Soviet Government to know that this was the purpose and the only purpose of those aircraft approaching in that direction."

Nearly six thousand miles away in Tel Aviv, the Israeli Foreign Liaison Office sent a car for American Naval Attaché Ernest Castle, the only time that happened during his tenure in Tel Aviv. The senior of America's two naval attachés, the forty-one-year-old Castle was a professional intelligence officer who had spent the past two years working out of the embassy alongside attachés from the other services. Lieutenant Colonel Michael Bloch told Castle upon arrival that Israeli pilots and torpedo boats had erroneously attacked an American ship, possibly a Navy vessel. Bloch apologized for the attack and asked if America had any other ships near the war zone. Castle fired off a six-sentence flash telegram—the highest priority available—to more than a dozen recipients, including the White House, Pentagon, State Department, and the Sixth Fleet.

At 11 A.M.—fifteen minutes after Castle's message arrived in the Pentagon's National Military Command Center—an unsigned memo on White House stationery shows it had reached the administration. "Our Defense Attaché in Tel Aviv has informed us that the attack on the USS *Liberty* was a mistaken action of Israeli boats," the memo stated. "The Israelis have helicopters en route to the ship for the purpose of facilitating rescue survivors. Tel Aviv message appears to be apology for mistaken action."

The president ordered a four-sentence message sent over the hotline—the telegraphic link connecting Washington and the Kremlin—to inform Soviet premier Alexei Kosygin of Israel's admission. More importantly, the president assured Kosygin that American fighters had been ordered only to investigate the attack. He asked Kosygin to relay his message to Egypt. Records show operators transmitted the message at 11:17 A.M. and it reached the Kremlin seven minutes later.

To reinforce the message, Kohler again called the Soviet Embassy. He told Tcherniakov in an 11 A.M. call that the United States now knew that Israel had attacked the *Liberty*. Kohler reiterated his earlier message that American fighters zooming to the scene were "in connection with the vessel and not for any other purpose."

At 11:04 A.M. the president departed the White House residence and made a brief stop in the Oval Office. Press Secretary George Christian and his deputy accompanied him. Two minutes later, the president arrived in the Situation Room. Maps plastered the walls and black ashtrays nearly filled to the rim with cigarette butts sat in the center of the wooden conference table in the basement command center. Around the table this morning sat the president's senior advisers: McNamara, Rusk, Rostow, Chairman of the President's Foreign Intelligence Advisory Board Clark Clifford, special consultant McGeorge Bundy, Undersecretary of State Nicholas Katzenbach, and Llewellyn Thompson, Jr., America's ambassador to the Soviet Union, who was in Washington at the time. The men had been summoned when word arrived of the attack. Johnson perched at the head of the table. A white phone sat in front of him.

Tensions soared. Rusk's calendar shows that the advisers had gathered as early as 10:40 A.M.—nearly half an hour before the president arrived—and pored over maps of the region and debated possible scenarios. Absent facts, the men had speculated that the attackers could have been the Egyptians or possibly the Soviets. Egypt was fuming over its loss to Israel. The *Liberty*'s location off the Sinai Peninsula, coupled with Egypt's hostility toward the United States over its support of the Jewish state, made an attack by the Arab nation a real possibility. The men on the *Liberty* originally suspected Egypt. The potential ramifications of a Soviet assault overshadowed one by Egypt. The communist power had backed the Arab states in the war and was likely frustrated by the devastating battlefield losses. While many of the president's advisers doubted the Soviets would go so far as to attack an American ship, the scenario could not be ruled out. America simply didn't know. "You tend to look at a worst case," recalled Katzenbach. "If you don't know, you say, 'Well what if.' "

When the men learned moments later that the Israelis had attacked the *Liberty*, tensions eased. The fear of a confrontation with the Soviets or a retaliatory attack by a rogue Russian proxy vanished. The administration could handle the attack diplomatically without the threat of war. The Navy could stand down. At approximately 11:25 A.M.—midway through the president's thirty-nine-minute meeting in the Situation Room—the order went out to recall the fighters, though Vice Admiral Martin had already done so about forty-five minutes earlier.

New questions soon arose. Israel claimed that its forces had attacked in error. But how could its exceptional military, which had nearly wiped out its Arab neighbors in only four days, make such a colossal blunder? The attack occurred in the middle of the afternoon, not at night when visibility would be more difficult. Knowing Soviet ships sailed in the area, why would the Israelis be so reckless as to torpedo an unidentified ship? None of it made any sense.

"We were baffled," Clifford later wrote in his memoir, *Counsel to the President.* "From the beginning, there was skepticism and disbelief about the Israeli version of events. We had enormous respect for Israeli intelligence, and it was difficult to believe the *Liberty* had been attacked by mistake. Every conceivable theory was advanced that morning. It became clear that from the sketchy information available we could not figure out what had happened."

Some American officials, even as the ship still struggled, urged the White House to downplay the attack. "Israelis do not intend [to] give any publicity to incident," wrote Walworth Barbour, America's ambassador to Israel at 11:10 A.M. as the president met with his advisers. "Urge strongly that we too avoid publicity. If it is US flag vessel its proximity to scene [of] conflict could feed Arab suspicions of US-Israel collusion." Barbour wasn't alone. Thirty-five minutes later, America's ambassador to Egypt, Richard Nolte, sent a telegram urging that the United States quickly come up with a cover story to explain the *Liberty.* "We had better get our story on torpedoing of USS *Liberty* out fast and it had better be good."

Israel's attack would soon trigger the unimaginable. The *Liberty*—now riddled with cannon blasts, its decks soaked in blood, and its starboard side ripped open by a torpedo—evolved in a matter of hours from a top-secret intelligence asset to a domestic political liability. That became clear to NSA deputy director Louis Tordella in a phone conversation with Captain Merriwell Vineyard at the Pentagon's Joint Reconnaissance Center. Vineyard confessed that to shield Israel, some people in Washington wanted the spy ship sunk. The proposal outraged

Tordella, who described it in a secret memo for the record. "Captain Vineyard had mentioned during this conversation that consideration was then being given by some unnamed Washington authorities to sink the *Liberty* in order that newspaper men would be unable to photograph her and thus inflame public opinion against the Israelis," he wrote. "I made an impolite comment about that idea."

White House Press Secretary George Christian took the podium at 11:18 A.M. for his morning briefing. Reporters for major newspapers and television networks camped out daily in the West Lobby, working out of small alcoves in the nearby pressroom and returning to home bureaus only long enough to pick up paychecks. The reporters spent so much time in the White House that some napped regularly in the lobby's sofas and chairs, prompting Christian to describe it as a "genteel flophouse."

Each morning and afternoon, the press secretary briefed reporters on the day's news and fielded questions. Many of the sessions had become intense and adversarial, particularly as the nation grew dissatisfied with the war in Vietnam and suspected that the White House was hiding information. Presidential adviser Jack Valenti compared the briefings to the Madrid bullring with reporters, like picadors, aiming "barbed questions" at the press secretary. Christian once likened it to being a "prisoner in the dock."

Christian, a fifth-generation Texas native, tangled skillfully with the press. A former reporter and editor, he had served as Texas governor John Connally's press secretary before President Johnson lured him to Washington. Christian made no mention of the *Liberty*—now smoldering in the Mediterranean—or the emergency meeting under way in the Situation Room. He started his briefing with the announcement that the president of Malawi would arrive in about an hour. Johnson would meet privately with the African leader then the two would have lunch. Christian then announced that the president had nominated thirty-eight Navy captains for promotion to rear admiral and passed out a list of names.

The reporters were suspicious. Many had heard that Secretary of State Dean Rusk had suddenly excused himself from testifying before the Senate Foreign Relations Committee and had left Capitol Hill for an urgent meeting at the White House. The press smelled a story. After Christian opened up the briefing for questions, one of the reporters asked if Rusk was in the White House.

"Yes," the press secretary replied.

"Seeing the President?"

"Yes."

A reporter noted that Senator Wayne Morse had told journalists on Capitol Hill that the secretary of state was called a way for an "emergency meeting." "Is that true?"

Christian conceded only that Rusk was in the White House.

"There is some grumbling on the Committee that he gave them short shrift and left suddenly," a reporter pressed. "That is the same question phrased a bit differently."

"The Secretary is here in the White House seeing the President."

"Can you say anything more?"

"No, I cannot."

A reporter questioned whether the meeting involved the afternoon session of the United Nations Security Council. Christian again cut off the reporter. "I can't say any more," he answered. "The Secretary of State has been over here frequently in the past few days."

"Are you aware of any emergency?" one of the reporters asked.

"I am not going to comment on it."

The press returned to Rusk's sudden departure from Capitol Hill moments later. "This is the first time that the Secretary of State has broken off an engagement on the Hill to come down here," a reporter asked. "You can't give us any help on this situation?"

"No."

"Do you think you might be able to later?"

"We will have to see how things progress during the day."

The reporters continued to press for answers. Would Christian release the president's morning schedule? Was Secretary of Defense Robert McNamara also with the president? Was the meeting in the

Situation Room? Would Rusk field questions with reporters before returning to Capitol Hill?

Christian blocked or deferred the questions throughout the seventeen-minute briefing. The transcript shows the mounting frustration of the reporters, who asked probing questions with the hope of exposing any weakness in Christian's stoic defense. The reporters soon grew exasperated. "Are there any new developments in the Middle East you can tell us about at this time?"

"No."

"Can we look for any news developments here today?"

"There is always a possibility," Christian replied.

Across the river at the Pentagon, senior officers from the Navy and Joint Chiefs of Staff filed into Secretary McNamara's third-floor office soon after reports arrived of the attack on the *Liberty*. Deputy Secretary of Defense Cyrus Vance, McNamara's top aide, and Pentagon chief spokesman Phil Goulding joined the meeting. The defense secretary normally perched behind his massive desk, which had once belonged to General John Pershing. Four different colored telephones lined the desk behind him—the white phone a direct link to the president—and a walk-in vault in the office's south end allowed McNamara to easily store classified documents.

Since he learned of the attack, the defense secretary had spent much of his time on the phone with NSA director Lieutenant General Marshall Carter and senior officers at the Naval Security Group. McNamara demanded to know the *Liberty*'s mission, the breakdown of its crew, and how many civilians it carried. Gathered with his advisers, McNamara understood enough to recognize the challenge the Pentagon now faced. An American spy ship had been torpedoed on a covert mission in the eastern Mediterranean. It would be a matter of hours—maybe less—before news leaked to the press either in the United States or overseas. The Pentagon had to determine how to tell the American people what its ship was doing and why so many of its sailors had been killed and injured.

Goulding argued that the United States should tell the truth. The

Pentagon did not have to discuss the ship's capabilities, but it at least should acknowledge that the *Liberty* was an intelligence ship. It was hardly more than an official secret, anyway. Besides, the ship's mission no doubt would leak to the press soon enough. By admitting it up front, the Pentagon could derail future accusations of a cover-up. "We should take the public affairs initiative, leveling with our people from the beginning," Goulding urged. "The government need not permit the press to force it into a classified point-by-point discussion of the operations of the ship. We will merely identify it as an intelligence collector and insist that all details of its functions are classified."

Others gathered this morning argued the opposite. Labeling it an intelligence ship meant the press would brandish it a "spy ship." Israel and Egypt would be angered to learn that the United States had been eavesdropping on radio communications during the war even though the *Liberty* had sailed in international waters. The admission that the *Liberty* and others like her were spy ships also would endanger the entire seaborne intelligence program. Leaders of foreign countries that normally allowed these ships in port for supplies and fuel might now face domestic political opposition and pressure from rival communist countries to refuse them.

McNamara listened to the opposing opinions of his senior aides before bowing to security and diplomacy concerns. The Pentagon would describe the *Liberty* simply as a technical research ship, its official cover story. To explain its presence in the Middle East, defense officials developed a hasty story: the *Liberty*'s mission was to relay communications stemming from the evacuation of Americans from the region. Goulding scrawled two short paragraphs describing the *Liberty* and its cover story. A preliminary casualty report soon arrived in the Pentagon along with Israel's apology. Goulding added two more brief paragraphs. The White House and State Department approved the release shortly before noon.

Even as the Pentagon prepared to alert the American public of the attack, its senior leaders moved to shut down the flow of news. With dozens of reporters aboard ships in the Mediterranean to cover the Middle East war, Pentagon leaders did not want to risk the possibility that a field commander might puncture the *Liberty*'s carefully crafted cover story. Deputy Secretary Vance called the commander of the Navy's European and Middle Eastern forces and issued a strict order that was broadcast to the Sixth Fleet: "Vance states that all news releases on *Liberty* affair will be made repeat will be made at Washington level. No releases to be made on ships."

Shortly before noon, Goulding walked down to the Pentagon's second-floor pressroom, clutching the six-sentence release. Like his White House counterpart, Goulding was a former journalist, having served nearly two decades as a Washington and Pentagon correspondent for the *Plain Dealer* of Cleveland. He understood the frenetic pace reporters worked at when on a story. Rather than call them into the Pentagon's press studio, he took the news to the pressroom, where reporters sat hunched over typewriters. Inside the cluttered room, Goulding told the reporters he had an announcement. The first official word about the *Liberty* was about to break. He read the release.

"A U.S. Navy technical research ship, the USS *Liberty* (AGTR-5), was attacked about 9 A.M. (EDT) today approximately 15 miles north of the Sinai Peninsula in international waters of the Mediterranean Sea. The *Liberty* departed Rota, Spain, June 2nd and arrived at her position this morning to assure communications between U.S. Government posts in the Middle East and to assist in relaying information concerning the evacuation of American dependents and other American citizens from the countries of the Middle East," Goulding read. "The United States Government has been informed by the Israeli government that the attack was made in error by Israeli forces, and an apology has been received from Tel Aviv. Initial reports of casualties are 4 dead and 53 wounded. The *Liberty* is steaming north from the area at a speed of 8 knots to meet U.S. forces moving to her aid. It is reported she is in no danger of sinking."

Reporters rallied with questions, many banging out responses on typewriters. "What attacked it?" one asked.

"It was attacked by motor torpedo boat or boats, and aircraft," replied Goulding.

"Was it hit by torpedoes?"

"The report we have indicates at least one torpedo hit."

"Did she fire back?" a reporter pressed.

"She is armed only with four .50-caliber machine guns," Goulding answered. "I don't have information on whether she fired back."

"Were her colors up?" someone asked.

"Yes, of course."

CHAPTER 7

You can come out of your hole now. Israel has saved you from decisive action.

—CONSTITUENT TELEGRAM TO PRESIDENT JOHNSON

Dean Rusk fumed over the attack on the *Liberty* as he departed the Situation Room and returned to his office at the State Department. Rusk found it inconceivable that Israeli forces had attacked in error. The assault occurred on a clear afternoon and involved fighters and torpedo boats in what appeared to be a well-coordinated strike. How could trained military forces fail to recognize the *Liberty* as an American ship during such a sustained attack?

Beyond the death and injuries of American sailors, the veteran statesman recognized that the United States had barely defused a potentially explosive scenario. What if the Israelis had attacked a Soviet ship? The communist power had watched for days as the Israelis clobbered the Arab states it backed and eradicated Soviet influence in the Middle East. The U.S.S.R. might have used an attack as a reason to enter the war and accomplish what the Arabs had failed. The United States, bogged down in Vietnam, would have had no option but to intervene.

Arriving at the State Department's Foggy Bottom headquarters, Rusk summoned Israeli ambassador Avraham Harman to his seventh-floor office. A Norman Rockwell watercolor painting of Lyndon Johnson adorned the wall behind the secretary's desk, inscribed by the president: "To Dean Rusk, my wise counselor."

The Israeli ambassador appeared in Rusk's office at 11:55 A.M. Like Rusk, Harman was a career statesman. Born in London to a rabbi and a Hebrew language teacher, Harman believed deeply in Zionism. He had earned a law degree from Oxford and worked for Zionist causes in London before immigrating to Palestine in his early twenties. Soon after Israel's independence, Harman entered the fledgling nation's foreign service. He served as Israel's first consul general in Montreal in 1949 and then joined Israel's delegation to the United Nations the following year. During the mid-1950s, he served as Israel's consul general in New York. After a brief assignment in Jerusalem, Harman returned to Washington as ambassador in 1959.

Rusk told Harman that afternoon that he had just spoken to the president, who had ordered him to "express in very strong terms" the American government's shock over the attack. Four American sailors had been killed and another fifty-three injured, according to the latest reports. The *Liberty* also was badly listing. Rusk wanted Harman to convey to Israeli prime minister Levi Eshkol America's anger and disbelief that Israel's military made such a mistake. "We consider it amazing that GOI [Government of Israel] motor torpedo commander could be unable to identify a U.S. naval vessel," Rusk barked. "We want GOI to issue very explicit instructions in this regard to Israeli naval commanders for we cannot accept attacks on our vessels on high seas."

"Well, there must be some mistake," Harman protested. "We would never—"

Rusk refused to let up. The United States appreciated Israel's prompt notification of the attack, which the secretary of state noted "may have avoided very serious consequences in many respects." Rusk reemphasized the American government's disbelief and frustration over the attack.

Harman told Rusk he didn't know anything about the attack other than the few details shared with him by one of the undersecretaries of state shortly before the meeting. But he assured the secretary of state that he would inform the Israeli government immediately of American concerns and expressed his sorrow for the attack and fatalities. "The implication was clear," Harman later telegrammed to the Foreign Ministry in Jerusalem. "Had the United States Government been uncertain as to the source of the attack, the situation would have been far worse."

Moments after Harman left, Rusk phoned the president. He then called Arthur Goldberg, America's ambassador to the United Nations. Rusk instructed Goldberg to confront Israeli foreign minister Abba Eban in New York. "Hit him hard on this attack," Rusk ordered during the 12:51 P.M. phone call. "If Israeli torpedo boats are attacking international shipping in international waters that is very dangerous business; if they were to hit a Soviet vessel that is extremely explosive."

Rusk's disbelief that Israeli forces attacked in error contrasted sharply with the first public statements of some members of Congress, many of whom appeared quick to forgive the Jewish state as the first bulletins appeared on the radio and in the afternoon newspapers. At about the same time Rusk met with the Israeli ambassador, Senator Jacob Javits took the Senate floor and asked his colleagues not to hastily judge Israel. The New York Republican had long served as a staunch supporter of Israel. The son of Jewish immigrants from Ukraine and Palestine, and raised in the Lower East Side's tight-knit Jewish community, Javits viewed Israel as an "anchor and bastion" of democracy in the Middle East. Javits had taken his son to Israel nearly five years earlier to celebrate his bar mitzvah there.

Javits told his fellow senators that the "tragic error" saddened him. The attack no doubt resulted from the stress under which Israeli pilots and Navy commanders had fought in recent days, though the senator conceded that fact alone did not excuse the near-sinking of an American ship. "The Government of Israel has already stated that this was an erroneous attack by Israel forces. The Government of Israel has apologized. I am sure that it will do everything that one would expect by way of compensation and other appropriate measures," Javits said. "The incident is one of those tragic fallouts of the dreadful situation in the Middle East, and the terrible pressure placed on pilots and naval people in that area."

On the opposite side of Capitol Hill, Representative Roman Pucinski echoed Javits's views. Soon after the House met at noon, the Illinois

Democrat from Chicago's Polish community—and known to friends simply as "Pooch"—cautioned his colleagues not to rush judgment and jeopardize America's close relationship with Israel. "It was with heavy heart that we learned a little while ago of the tragic mistake which occurred in the Mediterranean when an Israeli ship mistakenly attacked an American ship and killed four boys and injured and wounded 53 others," Pucinski said. "These are the tragic consequences of armed conflict. Such mistakes happen frequently in Vietnam. It would be my hope that this tragic mistake will not obscure the traditional friendship we in the United States have with the people of Israel."

The lawmakers' speeches set the tone for the rest of Congress. No one publicly demanded answers, questioned how Israeli pilots and torpedo boat skippers could have made such an incredible blunder, or called for an investigation or public hearings. The *Congressional Record* shows that only three other lawmakers mentioned the *Liberty* during the four hours and nine minutes the Senate met that afternoon. In each case, the senators referenced the attack only as a brief afterthought buried in longer speeches dedicated to the Middle East crisis. None of them challenged Israel's assertion that its forces attacked in error. The *Liberty* was not mentioned again during the six hours and twenty-five minutes that the House met.

Lawmakers failed to appreciate the gravity of the attack. But even in the coming days, as casualty figures climbed and the curious circumstances surrounding the assault emerged, the record shows that most elected leaders remained largely quiet. Those lawmakers who challenged Israel's explanation for the attack did so behind the closed doors of committee meetings and in hushed tones in the cloakrooms and dining rooms of Capitol Hill. The torpedoing of the *Liberty* did little to dampen the pro-Israel fervor that pervaded Congress.

More than two dozen lawmakers in both the Senate and House— many from states with large Jewish populations, such as New York, New Jersey, and Connecticut—took the floor the day of the attack to applaud Israel for its stunning war effort. Others rallied for emergency economic aid, urged America to reinforce its commitment to the Jewish state, and argued that Israel should be allowed to keep the territories it captured in recent days. One senator even inserted Abba Eban's

June 6 speech before the U.N. Security Council into the *Congressio-nal Record*. But the laudatory speeches came even as American sailors aboard the *Liberty* struggled to put out fires, stop bleeding, and prevent the ship from sinking.

The president and his advisers anxiously awaited the start of an afternoon rally by American Jews in Lafayette Park—directly across Pennsylvania Avenue from the White House—to urge increased American support for Israel. Many Jews had grown frustrated with the administration's han-dling of the war. A State Department spokesman the day the fighting began claimed in a press briefing that the United States was "neutral in thought, word, and deed." Many had interpreted that to mean that the United States had abandoned Israel just as the war began. In a stinging editorial, the *New York Times* blasted the comment as "grotesque."

John Roche, often called Johnson's "intellectual-in-residence," had questioned whether the president had control of his own State Depart-ment following the blunder. He urged the president to not even bother trying to appease Arab countries, but to focus on maintaining domestic Jewish support. "I was appalled to realize that there is real underground sentiment for kissing some Arab backsides. This is, in my judgment, worse than unprincipled—it is stupid," Roche wrote in an eyes-only memo to the president. "The net consequence of trying to 'sweet-talk' the Arabs is that they have contempt for us—and we alienate Jewish support in the United States."

Despite a desperate effort by the White House to assuage Jewish concerns, the political damage had been done. Aides worried that the afternoon rally would evolve into a political fiasco. Mathilde Krim, a loyal supporter of Israel and frequent White House guest, captured that fear in a desperate warning relayed to National Security Adviser Walt Rostow the day before. "There are reports of very strong anti-American feelings in Israel—that the Israelis feel they have won the war not with the U.S., but despite the U.S.," Krim reported. "There is great danger that the Jewish rally, to be held tomorrow in Lafayette Square here, will be an anti-Johnson, rather than a pro-Israel, demonstration."

The president, already under fire from American Jews for his Vietnam policies, did not need the image of thousands of protesters camped out across the street from the White House beamed into the homes of Americans nationwide on the evening news. Aides scrambled to prevent such a controversy. FBI director J. Edgar Hoover cabled a report to the Situation Room two days earlier that various New Jersey synagogues had chartered an unknown number of buses to depart New York's Port Authority Bus Terminal for Washington at 8 A.M. Closer to the rally, the White House received news that more than four hundred buses had been chartered from the New York area alone with more planned to depart New Jersey, Baltimore, and Philadelphia.

The planned rally reflected the surging pro-Israel sentiment that had swept much of the country as Jews and gentiles alike celebrated Israel's stunning success. "There never was an issue," observed McGeorge Bundy, "where public opinion was more in accord as to who were the good guys and who were the bad guys." Americans showed that support by donating millions of dollars to Israel since the war's outbreak. A lunch fund-raiser at the Waldorf-Astoria in New York netted $1 million a minute during a fifteen-minute period the day the war started. Donors pledged another $2.5 million at a fund-raiser that evening in Chicago, while congregants of a Washington temple pledged $1 million following a worship service only days later.

Many of the donations came from wealthy individuals and families. The publisher of the *Philadelphia Inquirer* donated $1 million and the chairman of Revlon gave $500,000. Robert T. Stevens, the former secretary of the Army, contributed $250,000 while fifty Boston families contributed a combined $2.5 million. Many others sold cars, real estate, and cashed in life insurance policies. A gas station owner signed over the deeds to his two stations and youths collected spare change in cans at subway entrances. In Denver, a thirteen-year-old made headlines after he donated the $500 he had received in gifts for his bar mitzvah.

The president and his advisers were not immune to the swelling pro-Israel support. Letters, telegrams, and petitions poured into the State Department, White House, and congressional offices. Between June 2 and 6, the State Department processed 17,445 letters related to the Middle East crisis. "Pro-Israeli letters now represent 98 per cent of the total. About 2 per cent of the mail is from persons opposed to American intervention in the Middle East, and there are only a handful of pro-Arab letters," stated a memo to Rusk. "Emotional content of the mail remains high."

The day of the rally the State Department mailroom would process another 9,470 letters and telegrams—nearly double the amount received just the day before—with 99 percent of the mail favoring Israel. Letter writers included mayors and state legislators. Towns and cities nationwide passed resolutions urging American support for Israel and forwarded them to Washington, including cities such as Miami Beach and Beverly Hills and small towns like Ramapo, New York. Many of the resolutions and letters predicted apocalyptic scenarios for Israel if America failed to intervene.

"There should be absolutely no doubt where the U.S. stands concerning the present conflict in the Middle East," the mayor of North Las Vegas cabled the president. "The very existence of Israel as a nation is threatened and our country can not stand by and see this courageous country lost to nations bent on its utter destruction."

Illinois congregants of the West Suburban Temple Har Zion in River Forest sent a petition calling for the United States to supply troops and equipment to Israel. "As an elected official we place our trust in you in the prevention of the genocide of 2,500,000 innocent people," the accompanying letter stated. "Action must be taken at once."

"The entire world will be affected by the fate of Israel," wrote an administrator with New York City's board of education, who begged the president to intercede on Israel's behalf. "To withhold aid now would be a crime against humanity. Let us not be guilty of needless human slaughter."

The increased pressure to support Israel from the public and his aides only frustrated the president. That frustration was evident when aides Larry Levinson and Ben Wattenberg suggested in a memo that the president send a message to the afternoon rally, expressing his support for Israel. The president exploded on Levinson soon after in a hallway confrontation outside the Oval Office that left the aide "shaken to the marrow." "You Zionist dupe!" the president shouted, raising his right fist. "Why can't you see I'm doing all I can for Israel. That's what you should be telling people when they ask for a message from the President for their rally."

On the eve of the rally, senior White House advisers called leaders of the Jewish community to assure them of the president's commitment to Israel and urge them to pass along that message to the Jewish community. Vice President Hubert Humphrey even met with the leaders of twenty-one national Jewish organizations the day of the rally, emphasizing the president's "quiet diplomacy." Washington lawyer David Ginsburg, a friend of the president and a powerful leader in the Jewish community, scored the biggest victory: the opportunity to edit and rewrite the main speech to be read during the rally. When Ginsburg finished, he assured the White House that everything was "under control." The theme of the speech: "solidarity with Israel." Two hours before the rally began, the president's advisers passed him a copy of the speech. The potential crisis appeared defused.

Busloads of American Jews arrived in the park early that afternoon. Despite the administration's efforts, the president still drew scorn from some of the estimated thirty thousand demonstrators. One woman, whose granddaughter was in Israel, described the president to a reporter as a *lemmischka,* someone with no backbone. That residual hostility soon dissipated when at 3:20 P.M. one of the rally organizers climbed on a platform and announced that Egypt had accepted a cease-fire. The crowd roared. Thousands sang the "Hatikvah," Israel's national anthem. The sudden emotional outpouring even moved reporters covering the event. "We were all Jews in the park," observed columnist Mary McGrory of the *Evening Star.* "Instant Israelization was occurring all over."

Children strung flags and banners from the park's statues. Others gathered in circles and danced the *hora,* a traditional Jewish folk dance. A group of rabbis sang "Next Year in Jerusalem" on the platform and danced to the backdrop of guitars, harmonicas, and accordions. "Moses led us out of the land of Egypt, now Moshe Dayan has led us back," declared one man, referring to Israel's defense minister. "Praise to almighty God." Several congressmen and senators joined the crowd as nearly three hundred police and park officers patrolled to make sure no fighting erupted between Israel's exuberant supporters and the two hundred pro-Arab demonstrators who marched across the street. "Look at this crowd," declared one man in a yarmulke. "We have so many friends. I never knew we had so many friends."

McNamara and Vance met that afternoon for a regular briefing with reporters in the defense secretary's private dining room. The two hosted a background briefing every Thursday for the Pentagon's beat reporters. The informal meetings allowed journalists, who normally received information through the filter of a spokesperson, to directly question top leaders about the week's news. The Pentagon considered the briefings on the record but barred reporters from using direct quotations. Journalists had to attribute all information to "defense officials." The Pentagon retained transcripts of each briefing and, in keeping with the ground rules, omitted the names of all speakers.

Defense officials considered scratching the background briefing this afternoon, knowing that reporters would press for details on the *Liberty*, details that hours later still remained scarce. But fearing that the press might misinterpret the cancellation, Pentagon officials opted to go forward with it. As expected, the attack soon became the focus of the afternoon session. The casualty figures had climbed since spokesman Phil Goulding's briefing in the pressroom only hours earlier. The latest reports now listed ten killed and as many as seventy-five wounded, up to fifteen critically. The transcript shows that reporters appeared more interested in the *Liberty*'s mission, capabilities, and location on the war's sideline than the casualty figures.

"Can you tell us why that ship was needed there?" a reporter asked soon after the briefing began.

The defense leaders fell back on the Pentagon's flimsy excuse concocted that morning: the *Liberty* served as a relay to offset the communications overload associated with pulling Americans out of the war zone. "We have evacuated literally thousands of individuals from certain Middle Eastern countries in the last several days, and there's been a tremendous amount of extra communications traffic as a result," officials said. "It's just driving us insane to read it, as a matter of fact."

"About how many have we evacuated?"

"About seventeen thousand," officials replied. "A fantastic movement of American personnel."

"How many are left to go?"

"It depends on a country-by-country basis."

Questions soon returned to the spy ship's location as journalists searched for details to explain the *Liberty*'s proximity to a war zone. Most recognized that the *Liberty* skirted the edge of Egyptian and Israeli territorial waters. "Is there a technical reason that this communications ship had to be fifteen miles off the Sinai Peninsula?"

"I honestly can't answer your question. I just don't know enough about the communications problem to know exactly where it has to be," answered an official. "There are technical reasons, technical factors, that dictate its location. It uses the moon as a passive reflector, and it's positioned in relation to that to get maximum amplification or relay capability."

A reporter then asked a question that exposed a fatal flaw in the cover story, a flaw that would haunt the Defense Department for weeks. If the *Liberty*'s mission was to serve as a benign communications relay—as the government publicly declared only hours earlier— then surely the Pentagon alerted the Egyptian and Israeli governments of its presence. That seemed only prudent given the ship's proximity to the fighting. McNamara and Vance stammered. "I can't answer that question either," officials conceded. "I just don't know."

The briefing then shifted to the details of the attack. "Was it a torpedo hit or was there also strafing?" a reporter pressed.

"I think there was both."

When asked if the *Liberty* fired on the attacking forces, defense officials again had no answer. "Was the attack without warning, sir?"

"As far as we know, yes."

Across the river at the White House, Christian addressed reporters for his afternoon briefing at 4:35 P.M. in the West Lobby. It had remained a hectic day at 1600 Pennsylvania Avenue as the president juggled the *Liberty* crisis and the visit of the Malawian president Hastings Kamuzu Banda. At one point, he made his guest quietly sip coffee in the Oval Office so he could review the transcript of Christian's morning briefing.

Soviet premier Kosygin had responded to Johnson's earlier message over the hotline, letting him know that he had passed word about the *Liberty* to Egyptian president Gamal Nasser. About an hour before Christian's afternoon news conference, the president hotlined another message to Kosygin. "I deeply appreciate your transmitting the message to President Nasser," he wrote. "We lost 10 men, 16 critically wounded, and 65 wounded, as a result of Israeli attack, for which they have apologized."

When Christian opened up the afternoon briefing for questions, journalists soon returned to the morning's unanswered question of President Johnson's secret meeting with Secretary of State Dean Rusk. Reporters demanded to know who else attended the meeting, how long it lasted, and the topic of discussion.

Christian conceded that the meeting focused on the attack on the *Liberty.* Yes, McNamara attended, he told them, so did National Security Adviser Walt Rostow and special consultant McGeorge Bundy. Despite the fact that the latest reports listed as many as ten killed and up to seventy-five wounded, Christian downplayed the violence of the assault, referring to it merely as a "ship incident," a phrase he repeated in varying forms a half-dozen times throughout the twenty-eight-minute briefing.

The reporters even noted his blasé description. "Can you tell us what the president's feeling was about what you refer to as the 'ship incident'?" one asked.

Christian didn't seem to notice the inference. Instead, he informed the press corps that Rusk had summoned the Israeli ambassador to the State Department hours earlier to protest the attack. "The Ambassador expressed apologies on behalf of his government," Christian said. "A formal United States protest is also being delivered to the Government of Israel."

The story that had sparked a barrage of questions earlier in the day seemed to deflate, as reporters soon appeared far more interested in the use of the hotline that morning than in a questionable attack by an ally that had killed at least ten Americans. Is the hotline located in the

White House or Pentagon? Did the Russians send the first message? Had the White House ever used the hotline before?

Christian tried to satisfy the reporters' curiosity as best he could. He explained when the hotline was installed and briefly described how it worked. More importantly, he noted the context of why the United States and Russia depended on it. "One reason it was installed, as you will recall, was to prevent misunderstandings or misinterpretations of government activities."

"Why was it considered necessary to use the hotline?" a reporter asked moments later, referring to the *Liberty*.

"As I said, the purpose is to prevent misinterpretation," Christian replied.

"I wondered what they might misinterpret about our picking up survivors from our own ships," a reporter commented.

"We wanted to inform them that one of our ships had been struck."

Questions soon gravitated back to the specifics of the hotline. The volley of hotline-related questions—more than three dozen over the course of the briefing—irritated the press secretary. Each time he tried to return to the White House's daily talking points, reporters sidetracked him with questions about the hotline, prompting Christian to finally declare: "I have given you all of my knowledge on it."

Toward the end of the briefing the press secretary returned to the *Liberty*, informing the reporters on background that the United States had launched aircraft to go to the spy ship after news arrived of the attack.

"Carrier-based planes?"

"Yes. Carrier-based planes went to that area when we learned that the ship had been hit," he answered. "That is why I mentioned this as one means of avoiding a misunderstanding."

Only in the remaining minutes of the briefing did a reporter finally ask if the United States knew who had attacked the *Liberty* at the time it sent its hotline message to Russia. The journalists appeared to now sense the gravity of the situation as it had unfolded hours earlier. A ship had been torpedoed and fighters launched to defend it—and America had not known at the time which country its pilots might soon engage.

Christian delicately answered these questions. Just as he had done in the morning, he gave only limited responses, refusing to entertain the reporters' speculation. "The notification of the incident was sent on the initial report of the incident, prior to the time the Israelis advised this government that they had accidentally hit the ship," he told the press corps. "We knew that a ship had been damaged."

"We didn't know who had hit it?" a reporter asked.

"At that time the Israelis had not advised us," Christian replied.

"Had our navy advised who had hit the ship?"

"It was prior to the time we had information on what had happened."

"That leaves the impression we might have thought it was the Russians?" a reporter questioned.

"I don't want to leave any impressions," Christian responded. "We advised them of the incident, without knowing."

"Did we inquire of them whether they by any chance were involved, or was it to explain our planes' flight?"

"There was an advisory that something had happened to one of our ships and we were sending our planes in to see what was the trouble," answered the press secretary.

"Did we do this because we had scrambled some of our planes off of our carriers and we wanted them to know that we wanted them to protect an American ship that was under attack?"

"That is the reason."

Ten minutes into Christian's afternoon briefing—and unbeknownst to the press corps—the National Military Command Center in the Pentagon phoned the Situation Room to relay the latest casualty figures: "10 killed, about 100 wounded—(1 doctor aboard, just hasn't been able to complete rounds on all)—15 to 25 wounded seriously (so far)." The grim picture of life on the *Liberty* now began to emerge as the casualties climbed and help still remained hours away. The attack had evolved into far more than a "ship incident."

CHAPTER 8

The mess deck was a bloody mess that night. People were dying. It was a ghastly sight.

—LLOYD PAINTER, TESTIMONY
BEFORE *LIBERTY* COURT OF INQUIRY

After the attack, with the sickbay destroyed by a rocket, the *Liberty*'s medical corpsmen converted the spy ship's mess hall into an emergency room for the wounded. Cavernous and centrally located, the mess hall was designed to feed nearly three hundred hungry sailors three hot meals a day. Like much of the *Liberty,* the mess deck was austere, even prisonlike, offering little more than steel walls, exposed steam pipes, and fluorescent lights. Sailors ate off metal trays with bent utensils. Roughly two dozen tables, each with attached stools, sat end to end in rows, all bolted down to weather rough seas.

A mural ran the length of the forward wall, providing the mess hall with its only dramatic flair. Painted by homesick sailors on an earlier cruise, the mural depicted a towering canopy of trees with several wood-frame homes nestled beneath them. A waterfront stretched across the mural's foreground. This idyllic American landscape, which could have been copied from the pages of the *Saturday Evening Post,* offered a touch of color and a change of scenery for sailors who spent weeks staring at an empty horizon.

Dr. Richard Kiepfer, fueled by adrenaline, fear, and the responsibility of being the ship's lone doctor, had not stopped working since the attack began. Rocket and cannon explosions had turned even the most benign objects into weapons. When the torpedo tore apart the *Liberty*'s forward compartments, it converted coffee mugs, chairs, and wastebaskets into projectiles. An hour of such physical violence translated into scores of shrapnel and gunshot injuries along with compound fractures and penetrating chest wounds. The torpedo blast had even fused one sailor's eyelids shut.

In the hours since the attack, Kiepfer and his medical corpsmen had performed a tracheotomy, cut open a sailor's chest to relieve pressure on a collapsed lung, and stopped the bleeding from dozens of gunshot and shrapnel wounds. All this time Kiepfer's own lacerated stomach was protected by a cinched life jacket that held his bandages in place. Nearly one hundred injured sailors crowded the mess hall, though the doctor suspected the total wounded was much higher since many of the able bodied continued to work. Two dozen sailors remained missing, most likely sealed inside the flooded compartments. Much of what Kiepfer saw as he made his rounds was unsettling, even with his Columbia University medical training. When he pulled back a piece of torn scalp on one sailor's head, he stared down at the man's brain. To combat shock, Kiepfer recruited volunteers to distribute water, salt pills, and bicarbonate of soda to hydrate the wounded. As the afternoon faded to evening—and anxiety levels rose—the crew switched to brandy.

The *Liberty* was not prepared to handle mass casualties. Ships its size lacked comprehensive medical facilities because the vessels normally traveled as part of a larger fleet. In any other situation, injured sailors would have been transferred to an accompanying aircraft carrier complete with an operating room, intensive-care ward, and a generous sick bay staffed by as many as sixty people. The larger ships carried stocked pharmacies, laboratories, and x-ray machines. Dental officers even performed the occasional oral surgery. Before the attack, Kiepfer's most complicated procedure had been to cauterize a leaky blood vessel in McGonagle's nose. Most days he froze off warts, iced fingers jammed from tossing a football on deck, or removed errant fishing hooks.

It was only by chance that Kiepfer had landed on the *Liberty* instead of in Vietnam. The Navy had assigned Kiepfer to the spy ship because his mother had been diagnosed with end-stage cancer. Because of the

Liberty's four-month assignment, Kiepfer would return home in time to see his mother before she passed away. To keep from dwelling on that painful fact, the thirty-year-old New Yorker had busied himself during cruises. He started a program to remove faded tattoos from sailors who now regretted the drunken body art. Even though he was a medical officer and excluded from many of the mundane chores, Kiepfer volunteered to stand deck watch, often taking the dreaded midnight-to-4 A.M. shift.

Now, in the absence of medical staff, surgical gear, and even drugs, the doctor had to be creative. Intravenous fluid bags dangled from overhead lights and transfusions were given arm to arm. Uninjured sailors were given surgical soap and taught to wash wounds while others learned to sew stitches in the wounded. To stretch the ship's limited supply of penicillin, Kiepfer diluted it with sterile water. Record keeping wasn't an option, so to prevent an accidental overdose of morphine, the medical corpsmen threaded used needles, like a lapel pin, through each wounded man's shirt, pants, and even boxer shorts to signify the men had received the drug. When he ran out of surgical tubing, Kiepfer inserted his finger into one man's chest wall and rolled him on his side to drain the blood.

Standing over Seaman Gary Blanchard at 1:30 A.M. on June 9, Kiepfer realized he needed more than creativity to save the Kansas sailor. Blanchard typified many of the *Liberty*'s enlisted men. Barely out of his teens, the burly sailor sported a sandy crew cut and thick arms. The son of a mechanic—his father was "Mechanic of the Year" several years running at Bob Moore Oldsmobile in Wichita—Blanchard grew up building and racing model cars. Shortly after turning seventeen, he told his parents he wanted to enlist. Because of his age, the Navy required his parents to sign a waiver. His father, an Army veteran, agreed. Blanchard's mother refused to sign. She was particularly close with her son and wanted him to wait a year. Blanchard and his father persuaded her that it was the right decision. He was doing something he felt he needed to do. In the end, she relented. He left his junior year of high school, anxious for chance to see the world.

Over the past several years, Blanchard had pinballed around the world, scrubbing decks and chipping paint. On visits home he loved to describe for his family the unexplainable phenomena—the mysterious lights, brilliant stars, and even fire—he saw in the empty oceans. It made him stop and think of God Almighty. He reveled in the countries he had visited and despaired over the poverty he saw. "You wouldn't believe how fortunate we are to live where we live," he often told his family. But after several years, the novelty had faded. During card games in the *Liberty*'s sleeping quarters or over glasses of his favorite Johnnie Walker Black Label in foreign ports, he told his shipmates that he planned to finish his tour in the coming months and return home to Wichita. He had another motive: his girlfriend was pregnant.

Blanchard had been on deck when the fighter jets first strafed the *Liberty*. He had darted for cover when an explosion steps away knocked him facedown. Shrapnel riddled his lower back. He writhed in pain before sailors dragged him to the mess deck below. There men hoisted him onto a table covered by a mattress. The corpsmen gave him morphine to ease his pain. Kiepfer determined during an exam that Blanchard might need surgery, but he and his senior corpsman agreed to hold off until help arrived. The afternoon turned to evening. Blanchard's abdomen swelled like a balloon from internal bleeding. Blood soaked through his mattress.

"I'm on my way out," he groaned when Kiepfer checked on him again at approximately 1:30 A.M.

Kiepfer knew he was right. The doctor's efforts to stabilize Blanchard had failed. His injuries were too severe. Despite repeated radio requests for help, no helicopters, planes, or ships had materialized in the nearly twelve hours since the attack. Blanchard's blood pressure plummeted. His skin, normally tanned from scrubbing decks under the hot sun, drained of color. The sailor stared at the lights above and appeared disoriented and confused. Kiepfer recognized the signs of shock. Stabilization was no longer an option.

To open Blanchard up and stop the bleeding, Kiepfer needed at least two more doctors, several nurses, and a crash team. He had no operating room, no anesthesiologist, and no skilled help. Kiepfer was terrified.

"If I don't do the surgery, you will die," the doctor said, leveling with him. "If I do the surgery, you may still die."

"Take your best shot," Blanchard whispered.

Kiepfer recruited several volunteers to help move Blanchard from the crowded mess deck to the wardroom above, which the Navy doubled as a makeshift operating room in emergencies. With the doctor's guidance, the sailors rolled Blanchard onto his side and slipped a stretcher beneath him. Kiepfer cinched canvas straps around Blanchard's calves, waist, and torso, careful not to exacerbate his injuries. Wounded sailors on the floor cleared a path for the men to pass. At the far end of the mess deck, the men maneuvered through the door frame and hoisted the injured sailor up the narrow ladder, struggling to keep his stretcher level. Despite a heavy dose of morphine, Blanchard groaned.

A rectangular table stood in the center of the wardroom where the ship's officers dined using china, silverware, and cloth napkins. In one corner sat a red vinyl couch and a glass-top table with a couple of aluminum ashtrays, normally filled with Lucky Strikes. Portholes with blue curtains dotted the wood-paneled walls. A carved African mask stared down from one wall and a painting of a man cane-poling in a river at sunset hung on another, both mementos from previous ports of call. On any other night, McGonagle might have entertained a local dignitary, if the *Liberty* was in port, or retired alone to enjoy one of his favorite Doris Day movies on the ship's projector.

Kiepfer drew two pints of blood from volunteers in the mess deck. He then gathered as many sterile gauzes and bandages as he could carry. A battle lantern served as his surgical lamp. Because the *Liberty* was not outfitted for surgery, it carried no ether, meaning Kiepfer could offer only a spinal anesthetic to numb Blanchard's pain. Unless the injured sailor passed out, he would be awake during surgery. The doctor ordered his impromptu surgical team to roll Blanchard onto his side so he could insert a needle into his back between his vertebrae. Kiepfer felt a slight pop as the needle penetrated the protective sack covering Blanchard's spinal column. A touch of fluid emerged, his cue that he had hit the mark. He slowly injected the anesthetic. He removed the needle and the men rolled Blanchard onto his back.

Lieutenant Painter and Ensign Scott held Blanchard down as Kiepfer made his first incision into the patient's abdomen. The doctor discovered what appeared to be several liters of blood in the abdominal cavity. Without equipment to suction the wound, Kiepfer could only use large surgical sponges to soak up the blood. The process was slow and arduous. The doctor wiped the wound and within moments the sponge saturated. Tom Van Cleave, the senior corpsman, handed him another sponge. Then another and another. Blanchard stared at the ceiling and occasionally rolled his head to the side. "Mama," he repeated. "Mama."

It took nearly an hour to soak up most of the blood. When Kiepfer finally was able to see inside Blanchard's abdomen, he noted with despair that shrapnel had punctured his liver and right kidney. The injuries appeared massive. Even more concerning, the doctor discovered fresh bleeding. Some of the blood appeared bright red, meaning it was oxygen-rich and likely coming from Blanchard's aorta. He also observed oxygen-depleted dark blood, returning to the heart from Blanchard's vena cava. Both the aorta and the vena cava, two of the body's most important blood vessels, had been either injured or torn. With each heartbeat, more blood flowed into the cavity.

Kiepfer sank in defeat. There was nothing he could do to save Blanchard from bleeding to death. The doctor pressed packs over the open ends of Blanchard's major blood vessels to slow the bleeding, then he and his assistant stitched up the incision. The men gave him a final dose of anesthetic to ease his suffering. Blanchard's blood pressure dropped. The men gathered around to watch as the twenty-year-old sailor stared at the lights above. His breathing grew labored. At approximately 3 A.M., he died.

Kiepfer pulled off his surgical gloves and ordered the corpsman to retrieve a body bag and haul Blanchard's remains to the ship's refrigerator. The doctor collapsed on the red vinyl couch in the corner of the wardroom. Thirteen hours had passed since the attack. He wondered where the helicopters and the extra doctors were. Why had no one arrived to help? How had he, an inexperienced doctor who had never completed a surgical residency, been left alone to tackle such an operation?

The doctor felt the throb of his own injury return, a pain he had forgotten during the surgery. He unfastened his life jacket to find his bandage and shirt soaked with blood. Kiepfer peeled off the soiled bandage and replaced it with a fresh one. He pulled on a new shirt and cinched up his life jacket. He paused long enough to devour a ham sandwich for energy as he returned to the mess deck.

It was time to go back to work.

An uneasy calm settled over the *Liberty*'s bridge that night as the injured ship steamed northwest at ten knots to rendezvous with the Sixth Fleet. The bridge had been one of the most dangerous spots during the attack as jet fighters and torpedo boats repeatedly targeted the command hub to kill senior officers and spark chaos among the crew. The barrage of rockets, cannons, and machine gun rounds had shattered portholes and left bowling-ball-sized gashes in the metal walls. The fire from napalm and burning fuel barrels charred the exterior walls and ladders and the acrid smell of burnt paint still hung in the air. Machine gun rounds, .50 caliber, fired from the Israeli torpedo boats littered the deck, mixed with shards of broken glass that crunched as the officers paced. The decks, once slippery with blood, were now sticky.

The ship's engineers had restored limited power. Lights flickered and the two boilers generated enough steam to power the turbines, but teams of sailors had to crank the rudder manually to steer the ship, leaving a sinuous wake that trailed for miles. Complicating the challenge, the attack had destroyed most of the *Liberty*'s navigational systems. Both the radar and gyrocompass were fried and the officers distrusted the magnetic compass. The fathometer was the only operable piece of equipment—despite having stopped working briefly right after the attack—but the depth finder could do little to guide the injured *Liberty*. The sophisticated spy ship, designed to sniff out radio communications of foreign countries, now operated at the same navigational capacity as an eighteenth-century ship.

Ensign Lucas had remained on the bridge since moments after the attack began. He had become a crutch for the injured captain, even loaning him his belt to use as a tourniquet. "He was so weak and had lost so much blood that several times he almost passed out. He gave me orders as to what course to steer in case he did pass out. He never blacked out, but for a while he was lying on the deck being given medical aid and yet was still giving orders and was in full command," Lucas would later write to his wife. "How he managed to keep going is beyond me. He kept his head and his cool the entire time and if it hadn't been for his outstanding leadership we all might not have been able to live. He is the greatest in my book."

Despite the severity of his injuries, McGonagle refused to relinquish his command. Kiepfer gave the skipper a saline solution to help hydrate him during an exam soon after the attack and fixed his poorly cinched tourniquet to slow blood loss. The ship's doctor would later tell the Navy's investigating board that he would have insulted McGonagle had he suggested he go below for medical care. The skipper's presence on the bridge proved therapeutic for the crew. "The Commanding Officer at that time was like a rock upon which the rest of the men supported themselves," the doctor would later testify. "To know that he was on the bridge grievously wounded, yet having the conn and the helm and through the night calling every change of course, was the thing that told the men, 'we're going to live.'"

Lucas watched the skipper's strength return as the hours slipped past. McGonagle chased salt tablets with endless cups of black coffee. His injuries made it difficult to get comfortable. The skipper alternated between stretching out on the deck and reclining in a mounted chair on the port-side wing. When the temperature dropped that evening, he traded his life jacket for a Windbreaker. He left the bridge only to go below to the restroom. Even then, he often chose instead to urinate in a coffee can on the bridge that someone retrieved for him. The two officers spent much of the night in silence. McGonagle appeared deep in concentration. His few comments to Lucas focused on the *Liberty*'s course. That afternoon, the skipper had guided the ship by studying the wake and ordering turns of the rudder. Now in the dark, he periodically stretched out and gazed at the heavens, navigating by the North Star.

Another officer relieved Lucas in the middle of the night, allowing him to retreat below to his stateroom for a few minutes of rest. He found the quarters he shared there with Ensign Scott uninhabitable. A shell had ripped through the ceiling. Blast holes riddled the metal walls. Six inches of salty firefighting water now sloshed on the deck. Lucas spied his roommate's new Polaroid camera, now submerged.

The young officer had quit smoking a few weeks earlier, but he opened the drawer beneath his bunk and salvaged a half carton of Marlboros. Miraculously the cigarettes were dry. Lucas collapsed in an empty stateroom on the deck above and lit a cigarette. He closed his eyes but found sleep impossible. The attack played out in his mind as he stubbed out a cigarette and lit another.

Lucas had seen some of the worst carnage that afternoon. He had felt the warm air of a round zip past his head as he fished his battle helmet out of a locker and crawled into the bridge. The wounded were sprawled all over the deck. Smoke had made breathing difficult. Deafening blasts of rockets and cannons had reverberated. During the torpedo boat attack, Lucas had seen the ship's quartermaster killed just steps away from him. One moment, the sailor stood at the helm. The next, a round zinged through the bridge and hit him from behind. Lucas heard the man gasp and watched him drop to the floor dead. Lucas wasn't spared. Shrapnel scraped his forearm and hand and another piece dug into the back of his head. A sliver of metal lodged beneath his right eye, so hot it sliced the skin as it entered so that he didn't feel it. Only after McGonagle pointed out blood on his cheek did Lucas realize he had been hit. Every time he moved his jaw, he could feel it.

The trauma had not stopped when the attack ended. Lucas helped put out fires and haul the injured to the mess decks. There he had seen the two dozen tables covered with bloodied men and scores of others stretched out on mattresses below. The makeshift hospital smelled of fuel oil, smoke, and blood. Injured sailors occasionally moaned. Lucas had comforted his friend Lieutenant Jim O'Connor, who bled through his mattress on the floor and would later lose a kidney. Lieutenant Commander Dave Lewis, who had been about ten feet from where the torpedo exploded, lay silently, his face charred. On another table, Lucas spotted a man from the deck force stripped completely naked, his body covered with bloody shrapnel wounds.

Alone in the stateroom, Lucas worried that the battered ship might sink. Many uninjured sailors napped in lifejackets topside, just in case. How would he get off the ship? he wondered. His thoughts turned to his daughter, born the day after the *Liberty* sailed for Africa. Her birth announcement had consisted of a telegram from his mother-in-law that rattled off the ship's teletype at 6 P.M. on May 3. He knew his five-week-old daughter only through photographs his wife mailed, which he had proudly shown the other officers and crew as he handed out fifty cigars. More recently, Lucas had missed her baptism, held in a Maryland church four days before the attack. He lit another cigarette. The edginess of the adrenaline and nicotine pumped through him. Like many on the ship, he felt alone and scared, but also fortunate. He had lived. "The night was one of the longest I ever spent," he would write to his wife two days later. "I consider all of us who made it through this to be extremely lucky."

Ensign Scott had worked nonstop since the attack to make sure the crippled ship did not sink. Sailors had sealed off the torpedoed spaces minutes after the strike, but damage control teams still had to plug hundreds of other shell holes. Scott ordered crews to begin a compartment-by-compartment search for leaks, which revealed as much as a foot and a half of seawater in some of the lower compartments. Many of the shell holes had been above the waterline prior to the torpedo strike, but with the Liberty now listing nine degrees, those holes had dropped beneath the waterline, causing the compartments to flood. The Liberty carried various sized wooden cones that sailors now hammered into the holes. The fire on the port-side deck had burned up the fuel for gas-powered pumps. The ship's remaining electrical pumps, weaker than the gas-driven ones, now struggled to bail water.

Scott had examined the top of the torpedo hole earlier in the afternoon from a perch on the main deck. Only a few feet poked above the waterline. Some debris floated out. Engineers could shift the remaining fuel in the lower tanks to stabilize the ship and reduce the list. But Scott realized that such a move risked the possibility that classified documents and bodies might wash out into the sea that night. With no other ships around to retrieve them, those men and records would be lost. He decided to wait until help arrived. His initial assessment of the ship hours after the attack revealed a significant amount of damage. He also appreciated how close the Liberty had come to sinking. He later captured those early impressions in a letter to his parents. "One more torpedo hit and we would have gone down," he wrote. "The entire ship looks like hell—burned and full of rocket and shell holes."

Scott felt the awesome burden of being the *Liberty*'s damage control officer. Though Lieutenant George Golden technically held that title, Golden's battle station was in the engine room. Golden had remained there throughout the attack and now worked with crews to restore power to the ship's systems. Damage control duties fell to Scott.

The young officer had attended a ten-week damage control school in Philadelphia before his assignment to the *Liberty*. There he had climbed inside a mock compartment armed only with a bag of wooden plugs and a mallet. Water began to flood the space. Scott hammered wooden plugs into holes as the cold water rose from his ankles to his knees. He grabbed more cones and pounded. The lights went out as he hammered, feeling for holes with his hands. When the water reached his neck, supervisors ended the simulation. Scott crawled out and toweled off. The simulation chambers were the closest many sailors would ever come to actual combat conditions. Scott learned. When the torpedo tore open the side of the *Liberty* and the power died and the ship began its roll, he was thankful that he had.

The *Liberty* was his first sea assignment fresh out of Officer Candidate School in the spring of 1966. Scott spent his first cruise along the west coast of Africa in the fall of that year, learning the ship's intricate systems. He studied the ship's blueprints and explored the passageways, compartments, and engine room. There was not a compartment on the *Liberty* he had not visited. Though he lacked top-secret clearances required for the research spaces, Scott even had ventured beyond the cipher-locked doors, though the spooks had covered the equipment with black tarps. Scott applied the lessons he learned in damage control school to his crews. He often used smoke grenades during damage control drills to better simulate battle. His men would later thank him for that.

McGonagle summoned Scott to the bridge in the middle of the night. He arrived to find the skipper in his chair, his leg bloodied. The rigid McGonagle, never one to buck regulations, still wore his officer's hat. The skipper demanded a report on the damage control efforts.

Scott told him the flooded spaces were sealed and the bulkheads that supported the water appeared stable at the moment. Crews used plywood and beams to shore up some of the bulkheads for added protection. Other sailors plugged shell holes and pumped seawater out of some of the compartments. McGonagle listened in silence as Scott ticked off the efforts of his crews. When the young officer finished, McGonagle didn't ask any questions, but offered only a comment: "The drill we had earlier today was not very realistic, was it?"

"No, sir," Scott answered.

The stress of the attack and the exhaustion increased as the hours slipped past and help failed to materialize. The officers opened up the ship's storage and rounded up several bottles of liquor from the guarded supply locker. They hauled the liquor below and distributed the bottles to the senior petty officers. Crews had worked nonstop. Nerves were frazzled and tensions soared. The men needed a break, something that might calm them. "We don't want any drunks," Scott told his men. "But if anybody wants to have a little shot of whiskey after what we've been through, they're welcome to it."

Scott climbed to the main deck later that evening for some fresh air. The faint light of stars shone down from above. A warm breeze blew across the deck as the ship now steamed in the dark. Scott tried to keep his crews and others busy, believing it best for the men to focus on a job rather than dwell on the horror of the afternoon. It also kept sailors out of the mess deck, where the ship's doctor and corpsmen remained busy. Extra men were added to watch. Scott ordered teams to walk the ship to reinspect each compartment for leaks and report back to him every hour. He also demanded that crews open the sealed hatch to the flooded research spaces each hour in the off chance others below might have survived. One of the ship's cooks approached Scott on deck and wanted to know the *Liberty*'s prognosis: "Are we going to sink?" the cook asked.

"I don't know," Scott replied. "Ask me in the morning."

Shortly before 6 A.M. on June 9, the gray light of dawn appeared on the horizon, offering many the first view of the *Liberty*'s damage since the attack had ended. The spy ship still listed nine degrees and the bow rode low in the water from the weight of the flooded forward compartments where two dozen of the dead remained sealed inside. Investigators would later count 821 rocket and cannon holes—some as much as a foot in diameter—in the ship's bridge, decks, and smokestack. Nearly all of the forty-five antennae had been wiped out, including four softball-sized shell holes blasted in the towering forward dish. The attack had shattered portholes, ripped open metal doors, and destroyed the forward machine gun tubs, where sailors had died desperately trying to defend the ship. Charred and blistered paint covered much of the port side from the combination of napalm and the 110 gallons of gasoline that had furiously burned on deck. A scorching fire on the ship's starboard side had vaporized the *Liberty*'s motor whaleboat and reduced many of the ship's life rafts to ashes.

Few of the ship's officers and crew had slept much that night. Those who did mostly dozed on the *Liberty*'s outside decks, afraid of venturing to the berthing compartments below in case the injured ship sank. Even at daybreak—roughly sixteen hours after the attack—crewmembers wandered around in life jackets, some still clutching battle helmets. Many of the sailors used the morning light to explore the damage, take photographs, and scavenge bits of twisted shrapnel and spent bullets that littered the decks. More than a few paused to look at the dried blood on the machine gun tubs and the walls of the forecastle. Others peered over the rail to see the top of the torpedo hole that poked above the waterline and fingered the nubs of machine gun rounds lodged in the ship's exterior walls. Many of the crewmembers brought bullets and shrapnel of varying sizes to the bridge so that investigators could later identify the ordnance. One officer even scooped up a vial of unburned napalm jelly.

Daybreak brought a sense of relief for many after an exhausting night alone at sea. The skipper, still on the bridge, remained in the pilothouse chair, where he had spent much of the night, silently sipping coffee from a paper cup, the tourniquet still cinched around his right leg. The ship's doctor and his two corpsmen continued to make rounds, administering morphine, checking vital signs, and comforting the wounded. Down in the engine room, teams worked to restore electrical systems and monitor the ship's boilers and generators. Damage control crews combed the *Liberty*'s compartments for leaks, checked for water intrusion in the fuel tanks, and hammered wooden plugs into the remaining shell holes. Topside deck crews began the grisly task of cleaning up the carnage. The bodies had been removed soon after the attack the day before—stored in the ship's freezer and air-conditioned transmitter room—but sailors now trained high-powered hoses on the dried blood, washing bits of flesh, bone fragments, and even a shoe with a foot still inside over the edge.

Soon after sunrise, the first silhouette of a ship emerged on the empty horizon, dark smoke streaming behind. Many of the *Liberty*'s uninjured sailors and walking wounded lined the rails and watched as the distant specks grew larger, evolving into the destroyers U.S.S. *Davis* and the U.S.S. *Massey*. The sleek ships had plowed through the Mediterranean at thirty knots to rendezvous with the *Liberty* at 6:27 A.M. The aircraft carrier *America* trailed farther behind. For nearly seventeen hours, many on the *Liberty* had desperately waited for help to arrive. Signalmen had spent the night on the ship's bow, aiming lights skyward to alert rescue planes that never materialized. The men in the *Liberty*'s radio room had transmitted updates and the names of the dead over a weak signal. The deck log records that the first ship the *Liberty* spotted on the desolate seas at 4:40 A.M. was the Russian merchant ship *Proletrsk*. For many of the sailors, the arrival of the destroyers served as the first tangible sign of hope. Danger now seemed to pass.

The *Massey*'s motor whaleboat departed the destroyer at 6:52 A.M., carrying Dr. Peter Flynn and a small medical team to the *Liberty*. The *Davis*'s whaleboat sailed about the same time, ferrying medical and damage control teams. A thirty-five-year-old lieutenant commander, Flynn served as a general surgeon on board the aircraft carrier *America*. When news of the attack on the *Liberty* arrived, the Navy flew Flynn, a hospital corpsman, and operating room technician to the *Massey* on a helicopter, lowering the trio in harnesses to the deck below at 7:30 P.M. as the destroyer cut through the waves. The Navy flew other *America* personnel to the *Davis*. Flynn had met with the *Massey*'s commanding officer upon arrival and received the latest casualty figures and the estimated dawn rendezvous. Thirty minutes after he arrived on the destroyer, he had met with the medical corpsmen to formulate a plan. Flynn knew little about the nature of the injuries, but speculated that with a strafing and torpedo attack, he would encounter shrapnel, gunshot, and burn wounds. The team decided to take only limited supplies to the spy ship. Anything necessary could be ferried over later.

The whaleboat motored alongside the *Liberty* in the calm sea. The American flag—the same one hoisted during the attack the afternoon before—fluttered from the mast. The medical team climbed a Jacob's ladder to the deck above. There Flynn scanned the topside, noting the bloody guntub and the hundreds of shell holes. In one spot, the doctor could see through the entire superstructure where a shell had passed through every bulkhead, revealing daylight on the far side. Many of the *Liberty*'s sailors crowded around to watch as the whaleboats from the *Massey* and the *Davis* ferried personnel and equipment. Lieutenant Hubert Strachwitz, who boarded the *Liberty* from the *Davis,* captured the first moments in a letter to his wife. "The reality of the situation struck home as we climbed aboard and looked into the faces of the men. No Hollywood makeup man nor actor could ever produce those faces," the officer wrote. "There were sunken eyes, bristly, dirty faces, dark bloodstains, ripped clothes covered with oil and charcoal. There were no hysterics, no crying, no cursing—just tired bodies trying to do necessary jobs."

Flynn's medical team headed below. When he arrived in the mess deck, the doctor paused. Silence permeated the cavernous room as the injured all stared at Flynn and the corpsmen. Kiepfer, exhausted after being up for twenty-four hours, welcomed the men. The team evaluated the most seriously injured for evacuation to the *America.* Fifteen of the sailors appeared critically injured. Four would require immediate exploratory surgery upon arrival on the carrier. Two sailors who had been in the compartment where the torpedo exploded suffered burned faces. Many others had compound fractures, shrapnel wounds, and lacerations. Shrapnel had lodged in one man's brain and the doctors found another already had developed gangrene. Two of the *Liberty*'s injured suffered amputations. "A rapid survey revealed that almost all had suffered missile and shrapnel wounds with or without

underlying injuries depending on the area, angle, and force of penetration," Flynn later wrote in a seventeen-page report he coauthored
on the rescue effort. "Considering all they had experienced, the long
anxious night many had spent, and that all were nearly exhausted, their
calmness and excellent morale was remarkable."

The medical team discovered that the long night had exhausted
the *Liberty*'s supply of sterile bandages, dressings, and medicine. The
ship's doctor and two corpsmen likewise needed rest. All the seriously
injured would have to be evacuated. The team expected the first helicopters from the *America* to arrive midmorning. In the meantime,
corpsmen began cleaning and dressing wounds. Others inserted intravenous drips to hydrate the wounded sailors and Foley catheters to
allow teams to monitor urine output for complications like blood or
reduced urine that might indicate kidney problems. The corpsmen
swapped Ringer's lactate solution—nicknamed "white blood"—for
the 5 percent dextrose and water mixture that Kiepfer had used to fight
shock. Every injured man received a tetanus booster. Corpsmen soon
prepared an evacuation route to the *Liberty*'s forward deck to make
it easier for volunteers to carry the injured in Stokes litters, a special
basket-style stretcher with raised sides that can be easily hoisted into a
hovering helicopter. The corpsmen conducted a second survey of the
critically injured to determine which sailors had to be airlifted first.

Flynn visited the bridge to check on McGonagle at 8:45 A.M. The
skipper, who had regained some of his strength, greeted the men,
though he remained largely quiet. The few comments he directed at
the doctor centered on the condition of his crew below. McGonagle's
right pant leg had been cut off the day before and the doctor found the
tourniquet tied around his upper thigh. The skipper's leg finally had
stopped bleeding, but it remained stained with dried blood. The combination of the tourniquet and the skipper's refusal to lie down had left
McGonagle's leg grossly swollen and forced him to limp. It appeared to
the doctor that shrapnel had lacerated the skipper's greater saphenous
vein, a large vein located just beneath the skin that runs the length of
the leg and thigh. "His leg was extremely edematous since he had been
on his feet continuously with a tight pressure dressing over the wound
for eighteen hours. This was the only treatment that he had permit-

ted," Flynn later wrote in the report. "This is typical of his outstanding performance during the entire incident."

McGonagle may have performed heroically, but the doctor recognized that the injured skipper needed rest. He had remained on the bridge throughout the attack and the long night afterward, piloting the *Liberty* despite his injuries. Black coffee no longer could combat his exhaustion. Flynn's report shows that the doctor wanted to evacuate McGonagle to the carrier *America* along with the other injured. Flynn met with Kiepfer, Golden, and Captain Harold Leahy, the destroyer division commodore. McGonagle had begged Kiepfer the night before not to let the Navy evacuate him. The *Liberty*'s doctor spoke up on behalf of his commanding officer. The men decided that McGonagle could remain aboard the *Liberty* and in command despite the potential danger his injuries posed. With its staggering number of injured and killed, the *Liberty* needed every available man. McGonagle eagerly accepted the increased personal risk, bolstered by the Navy's decision to provide an additional senior officer to help manage the ship and crew. The skipper soon climbed down to his wrecked cabin below. The deck log shows that at 10:04 A.M., Lieutenant Commander William Pettyjohn, a member of Leahy's staff, boarded the *Liberty* and assumed the duties of the spy ship's executive officer, replacing Philip Armstrong, Jr., who had been killed in the attack.

Volunteers carried the injured to the *Liberty*'s forward deck at 10:10 A.M. Twenty-seven minutes later, the first helicopter from the *America* thundered over the horizon. The *Liberty*'s elaborate antenna configuration prevented the helicopters from landing. Hovering barely twenty feet above the ship, crews lowered cables. The wind from the rotors blew across the deck as volunteers attached the litters and watched as crews hauled up the injured. The *America*'s deck log recorded the arrival of the first injured sailor on the flight deck at 11:15 A.M., where a swarm of reporters and photographers greeted the crew. Throughout the morning and early afternoon, helicopters transported fifty *Liberty* sailors, followed by the bodies of nine dead, completing the transfer at 1:43 P.M. Soon after the flights began, the *America* rendezvoused with the *Liberty*. Captain Donald Engen, skipper of the carrier, sailed his ship down the side of the *Liberty*, passing as close as 150 yards away.

Crewmen from the carrier lined the deck, marveling at the hundreds of blast holes, burned decks, and the spy ship's nine-degree list. The American flag fluttered from the mast. Engen called the air boss—the officer in charge of flight operations—with a unique request. "Let's give them three cheers!"

With nearly two thousand officers and sailors crowding the *America*'s deck, the air boss came over the public address system. "Let's hear it for *Liberty!*"

The roaring cheer that followed thundered over the open sea and echoed back to the men on the carrier's deck, making the hair on the skipper's neck rise in a moment he would never forget. "Hip, hip, hooray! Hip, hip, hooray! Hip, hip, hooray!"

CHAPTER 9

I grieve with you over the lives that were lost, and share in the sorrow of the parents, wives and children of the men who died in this cruel twist of fate.

—EPHRAIM EVRON, MINISTER OF THE ISRAELI EMBASSY
IN A LETTER TO PRESIDENT JOHNSON

Dean Rusk hustled over to Capitol Hill on the morning of June 9 to privately brief the Senate Foreign Relations Committee—the secretary of state's third visit this week—on the latest developments in the Middle East war. The affable Georgia native had just sat down with the committee at about 10:35 A.M. the day before when the White House abruptly summoned him to the Situation Room for the emergency meeting on the *Liberty*. By the time Rusk had returned to Capitol Hill later in the day, committee members already had adjourned.

The frustration Rusk felt over the attack—and his disbelief in Israel's assertion that it was an accident—had not been reflected in the newspaper reports now on doorsteps nationwide. Many of the critical questions concerning the *Liberty* focused on America's role in the attack. Newspapers already doubted the Pentagon's cover story and hinted that the ship likely was eavesdropping on the war at the time of the assault. Other stories questioned whether America had informed Israel of the ship's presence. Few if any articles challenged Israel's assertion that its forces had attacked in error.

Some lawmakers quoted in the morning newspapers appeared to

131

endorse Israel's claim. "With Israel we know it was a mistake," Senator Jacob Javits told reporters. "A miscalculation that could take place any place in the world," added Senator Robert Kennedy. Senate Majority Leader Mike Mansfield told reporters he doubted the attack would spark any lasting complications between the allies. "It certainly wasn't deliberate," declared the Montana Democrat. "It could have happened on either side."

The printed comments of some elected leaders stood in sharp contrast with the hostile mood Rusk encountered when he sat down at 10:05 A.M. in Room S-116, the committee's cavernous hearing room. The contents of this closed-door discussion would remain classified for the next forty years. Soon after Chairman J. W. Fulbright gaveled the meeting to order, the thirteen senators demanded answers.

The secretary of state could offer little more than the basic facts of the attack. Outside the admission that its pilots and torpedo boat skippers had targeted the *Liberty,* Israel had yet to explain the assault in any detail. Absent more information, Rusk shared his opinion: "The incident was extremely distressing, not only because of the dead and the wounded which were involved, but because it was a very reckless act."

Senator Bourke Hickenlooper interrupted. The Iowa Republican had developed a reputation among his colleagues as the "consummate skeptic." The conservative lawmaker previously had demonstrated that he was not afraid of confronting Israel, once accusing its leaders of lying like "horse thieves" over the country's secret nuclear program. The attack on the *Liberty* outraged him. "It seems to me it was completely inexcusable."

"I called in the Israeli ambassador and protested in the strongest possible terms," Rusk told the committee. "He had no explanation. We have had nothing but an apology from the Israeli Government. But there it is."

Senator Frank Carlson of Kansas told fellow committee members that he had a constituent on the *Liberty.* Others probably did as well. The families demanded more than Israeli remorse. "They are not happy with just an apology. They are really complaining. Is there anything more that can be done on this?" asked the Republican. "I cannot understand it."

Hickenlooper interrupted again, blasting Israel for what he perceived as its "cavalier attitude." The United States needed to hold the Jewish state accountable. "We should file for reparations. We should press for them, for the families, the people that were killed," he urged. "Has the Israeli Government indicated any real sorrow about this thing, or is it a perfunctory apology?"

"Oh, yes," Rusk replied. "They have been profuse."

"Have they said whether any disciplinary action will be taken against the stupidity of this crew or—"

"I asked for that yesterday," Rusk said.

"Or the commanding officers of the area or anything?" Hickenlooper pressed.

"We have not heard any more except what I have told you."

The committee turned to the renewed fighting in the Middle East. Despite the Egyptian cease-fire, which had brought cheers from thousands of American Jews in Lafayette Park the day before, the latest reports revealed the war still raged. Israel had opened a new front in the north against Syria in an effort to seize the Golan Heights. Other questions also arose, including the settlement of thousands of refugees and the future of Israel's seized territories. The frustrated lawmakers complained that America appeared to have little influence over Israel, prompting Hickenlooper to suggest the United States consider revoking tax-exempt donations for Israel.

Later in the two-hour briefing, Senator Karl Mundt, a South Dakota Republican, returned to the *Liberty*. "What is the position of the United States when somebody shoots one of these ships down on the high seas?" Mundt asked. "Do we just say, 'Well, you are sorry, it's all right with us,' or is there some indemnification?"

Rusk assured the committee that the United States would make Israel pay for the losses. "We do not have a report of the condition of the ship itself or the damage, but we have laid the basis for a very strong protest for going back to them on that kind of thing," he said. "They, too, I am sure, are investigating, but the only thing we have had from them is a flash report that it occurred."

Carlson interjected moments later, noting the challenging questions lawmakers would soon face about the attack. "Most every member of the Senate and many of Congress are going to have families involved as a result of the deaths and the casualties in this unfortunate situation about this ship. We are going to have to answer some questions," he said. "Was it there on the orders of the Defense Department?"

Rusk confirmed that it was. When pressed to explain the *Liberty*'s location, the secretary of state fell back on the Defense Department's lie that it was there to help relay messages. "This was a communication ship," he said. "During the period in which our embassies and consulates were being closed down and we were having to resort to all sorts of improvised communications, it was there to help in the relay process of messages that our people wanted to go back and forth."

The senators didn't appear to believe him. "Were we intercepting or receiving messages for Israel on this ship?" Carlson asked. "These are questions that have come to me from families—"

"I would think pretty soon somebody had better talk about what type and character of ship this was," interrupted Senator Stuart Symington of Missouri. "I think this is a rather important situation as far as—"

"It has the capacity to listen," replied Rusk, cutting him off. "But we were not involved in transmitting messages from one side to the other, if that is what you have in mind."

Carlson urged the United States to come up with some answers soon. "The people out in the country are asking questions, and we are going to have to answer whether—this can all be off the record as far as I am concerned now—but we are going to have to have answers to those questions from the parents of those boys."

Rusk emphasized that the *Liberty*'s mission had no bearing on whether the ship had a legal right to be in international waters. "You should understand on the question of what it was doing there, it was there under proper orders, on behalf of the United States Government, in the high seas," Rusk said. "And therefore, from our point of view, was not subject to attack by anybody."

At the Pentagon, chief spokesman Phil Goulding reviewed the latest reports on the attack and prepared to brief the defense reporters camped out in the second-floor pressroom at 10:30 A.M. Much of

Goulding's information remained circumstantial. He relayed the *Liberty*'s coordinates and the speed of the ship, and informed reporters of the arrival of the destroyers *Davis* and *Massey*. Helicopters from the aircraft carrier *America* so far had evacuated fifteen of the *Liberty*'s most seriously wounded. The Pentagon expected to airlift another thirty-five injured plus the remains of the deceased.

"The latest recent casualty report from the *Liberty* is as follows: nine dead and twenty-two missing, and seventy-five wounded. At least fifteen of the seventy-five are seriously wounded," Goulding told the reporters. "I do not have any firm information of the twenty-two who are missing. The commanding officer of the *Liberty* has reported that he believes that some of the missing are in flooded compartments in the forward part of the ship. Next of kin are being notified as rapidly as possible. Names will be released once next-of-kin notification has been completed."

Reporters returned to the question of whether the United States had informed Israel and Egypt about the *Liberty*'s presence prior to the attack, given that the ship's mission allegedly was to serve as a benign communications relay. The question had stumped Secretary of Defense Robert McNamara and his deputy, Cyrus Vance, during the afternoon press briefing the day before and exposed a major weakness in the hastily concocted cover story. Early news reports emphasized the Pentagon's failure to answer what many perceived as a simple question.

The United States had not notified either country because the *Liberty* was a spy ship tasked to eavesdrop on foreign nations, a mission that would be compromised if target countries knew about the ship's mission. Government lawyers determined that the *Liberty* had done nothing wrong. The spy ship sailed in international waters at the time of the attack, where it had a legal right to be. The United States had no obligation under international law to inform Israel or Egypt of the *Liberty*'s presence. International law also did not require neutral ships to exit war zones or even adjacent areas. In fact, international law mandated that neutral nations retained neutral status even in war zones.

Furthermore, if the government conceded that it should have informed Israel of the *Liberty*'s presence, then America risked other nations' demanding it alert them when U.S. ships sailed nearby. That would undermine the entire seaborne intelligence program. Hostile countries might seize on any failure to give notice as an excuse to attack an American ship in international waters, then hide behind the *Liberty* precedent.

The Pentagon had its answer. "No countries were informed of the presence of the U.S.S. *Liberty* in the eastern Mediterranean," Goulding told reporters. "The ship was in international waters at all times. It is a noncombatant converted merchant ship armed only with four .50-caliber machine guns. There was no requirement whatever to notify any other nations of the presence of an American noncombatant ship in international waters."

Defense leaders, who sensed the media shifting blame for the attack from Israel to the United States, grew frustrated. "The main issue was not whether we had notified Israel of our intent to be there," Goulding later wrote in a memoir. "The real issue could not have been simpler: A United States ship was operating in international waters; it was identified, as are United States ships anywhere in the world, with the American flag, distinguishing letters and number, and name; it was attacked without provocation."

George Christian greeted reporters at 11:25 A.M. for his morning White House news briefing in the West Lobby. He began with the announcement of the president's 1 P.M. swearing-in ceremony in the East Room of a new member of the Equal Employment Opportunity Commission.

When Christian opened up the briefing for questions moments later, reporters seized on the Vietnam War. Did the president plan to continue pressure on the North Vietnamese until the bombing stopped? Would Moscow help negotiate a peace deal? Did the administration see a decrease in fighting in recent days as a possible sign of deescalation? What other reason could the administration cite for the sudden combat lull?

Questions shifted to the war in the Middle East. Reporters asked about resumption of fighting. What was the president's reaction? Where did the administration stand on the question of seized territories? Who was Johnson talking to about the war? Did the United

States know who fired the first shot and did the administration plan to condemn the aggressor?

The morning before, the attack on the *Liberty* had dominated the press briefing as reporters doggedly tried to ferret out information about the emergency meeting under way between the president and his advisers in the Situation Room. Just twenty-four hours later, interest in the *Liberty* had almost vanished, even as the casualty figures soared.

After more than two dozen questions of the twenty-eight-minute briefing, a reporter asked the press secretary if he had any reaction from the president to the attack. The casualty numbers had jumped as it became increasingly apparent that those sailors initially listed as missing were in fact deceased. "The President is deeply grieved at the fact that, at last report, a possible thirty-one deaths were caused by the attack," replied Christian. "As you know, the United States Government has delivered a strong protest on the matter."

The press secretary read a three-sentence letter received at 5:35 A.M. that morning from Israeli prime minister Levi Eshkol, apologizing for the attack. "I was deeply grieved by the tragic loss of life on the U.S. naval ship *Liberty*. Please accept my deep condolences and convey my sympathy to all the bereaved families," he read. "May all bloodshed come to an end, and may our God grant us peace evermore."

"Did the Israeli Government explain to the American Government why they attacked an American ship?" asked a reporter a moment later. "The reason?"

"The explanation, as given publicly yesterday by the Israeli Government—was that it was a mistake," Christian replied.

"Does the U.S. accept this explanation?"

"As I said, the United States has made a formal protest to the Israeli government and that is the way it stands."

"Then we expect a further explanation of why this mistake was made?"

"We will just have to see what comes about later."

President Johnson's advisers on the Special Committee of the National Security Council gathered at 6:30 P.M. in the Cabinet Room on the first floor of the White House. Built-in bookcases lined the room's western wall. A portrait of Thomas Jefferson hung above the fireplace on the room's northern end and a bronze bust of John F. Kennedy, assassinated three and a half years earlier in Dallas, stood in a nearby corner. A series of French doors with arched transoms on the room's eastern side led out to a colonnade overlooking the Rose Garden on this warm June evening.

In the leather chairs surrounding the elongated conference table sat thirteen of the president's senior advisers. Those present included Dean Rusk, Robert McNamara, CIA director Richard Helms, Joint Chiefs of Staff chairman General Earle Wheeler, Undersecretary of State Nicholas Katzenbach, Assistant Secretary of State for Near Eastern and South Asian Affairs Lucius Battle, President's Foreign Intelligence Advisory Board Chairman Clark Clifford, National Security Adviser Walt Rostow, and his older brother Eugene, a senior official at the State Department. National Security Council staff member Harold Saunders recorded the meeting minutes on a legal pad.

The president's diary shows that Johnson popped in and out of the meeting several times, accompanied by Vice President Hubert Humphrey and Democratic senator Joseph Clark of Pennsylvania. The last time the president left—for just four minutes at 7:34 P.M.—he asked McNamara to join him in the nearby office of his personal secretary. There the president presented his defense secretary with a letter, an inscribed portrait of himself by popular illustrator and artist James Bama, and an Accutron wristwatch in honor of McNamara's fifty-first birthday. "My goodness, Mr. President," the startled McNamara replied. "Thank you, thank you!"

After brief comments on the latest developments in the war in the Middle East—Egypt's President Nasser had announced his resignation earlier in the day—Johnson's advisers turned to the attack on the *Liberty*. Casualty numbers had continued to climb. Only hours earlier, American Naval Attaché Commander Ernest Castle had cabled Israel's first explanation for the attack to the White House, State Department, and Pentagon, among others. The government of Israel reiterated its explanation that its forces had attacked in error, and now blamed the *Liberty* for contributing to that mistake.

Israel claimed that its military had received reports of a shore bombardment near the Egyptian town of El Arish. Soon afterward its forces detected an unidentified naval vessel thirteen miles offshore. The mysterious ship sailed outside normal shipping lanes and in an area Egypt had declared closed to neutrals. When spotted, Israel claimed the ship appeared to escape at a high speed toward Egypt, flew no flag, and resembled the Egyptian ship *El Quseir*, a thirty-seven-year-old cargo ship designed to haul 400 men and forty horses.

In his telegram, Castle criticized Israel's explanation. How could trained naval officers be so inept as to make such a blunder? The *Liberty* bore only a "highly superficial resemblance" to the *El Quseir*. "Certainly IDF Navy must be well drilled in identification of Egyptian ships," the attaché wrote. "*El Quseir* is less than half the size; is many years older, and lacks the elaborate antenna array and hull markings of *Liberty*." Castle attributed the attack to "trigger happy eagerness to glean some portion of the great victory being shared by IDF Army and Air Force and in which Navy was not sharing."

Israel's explanation did little to defuse the anger of the advisers or assuage the growing belief that the attack was more than a trigger-happy error. Rusk began the discussion by recounting the hostility he encountered in his closed-door meeting earlier in the day with the Senate Foreign Relations Committee. The secretary of state relayed the committee members' insistence that Israel pay reparations. "Senators outraged," the minutes record the secretary of state telling his colleagues. "Put in a bill for damages."

McGeorge Bundy took a more tempered view. The former national security adviser, he had returned as a special consultant to the president after the war started days earlier to solve the administration's perception problem. Johnson had too heavy a roster of Jewish and pro-Israel advisers. Bundy offered a different face for the administration. A pragmatist, Bundy urged the United States to wait for Israel to make an offer, then respond.

Lucius Battle took Bundy's suggestion further. The soft-spoken southerner had recently served as America's ambassador to Egypt before returning to Foggy Bottom in his current position. Battle described the *Liberty* attack as "incomprehensible" and urged the United States to take "action." Rather than wait for an offer, he advocated that the administration push the Jewish state to publicly show remorse. "Israel make offer of damages public," Battle urged, according to the minutes. "Then we'll take posture of responding and figure out bill."

Clifford then spoke up. One of the president's most pro-Israel advisers, the former lawyer had been instrumental in President Harry Truman's decision to recognize Israel when it declared independence nineteen years earlier. Clifford demanded America hold Israel accountable. "My concern is that we're not tough enough. Handle as if Arabs or USSR had done it," the minutes show he argued. "Manner egregious. Inconceivable that it was accident. 3 strafing passes, 3 torpedo boats. Set forth facts. Punish Israelis responsible."

Clifford's strong views offended Eugene Rostow. The third-ranking official at the State Department and a Jew, Rostow was shocked that Clifford dare compare Israel, an ally, to its neighboring Arab countries. Clifford's views may have angered Rostow, but the meeting minutes reveal that his impassioned argument swayed Johnson. Saunders penned a note next to Clifford's comments in the margins of his legal pad that read: "President subscribed 100%."

Rusk outlined a plan. The United States would treat this as it did any other assault: demand reparations, punish the attackers, and guarantee it never happened again. The committee agreed that the State Department would take a "strong and firm line." The secretary of state dashed off a 9:32 P.M. telegram to the American Embassy in Tel Aviv, relaying the outrage and ordering the ambassador to press Israel's foreign minister. "There is very strong feeling here about the incomprehensible attack on the USS *Liberty*," he cabled. "We shall be in touch with his government by means of a note on this subject later."

Minutes show that Johnson sat mostly silent through the portions of the meeting he attended, doodling various geometric shapes on White House stationery. The president's few comments revealed his frustration with Israel and America's lack of influence on the Jewish state, the same gripe the senators made earlier in the day to Rusk on Capitol Hill. At one point, the president complained of his failed efforts to restrain Prime Minister Eshkol. "I had a firm commitment from Eshkol & he blew it," reads a note scribbled at the top of one page. "That old coot isn't going to pay any attention to any imperialist pressures."

The president left the cabinet room at 7:53 P.M. and headed to the Oval Office. Even though it was Friday night, Johnson had two more appointments. Two minutes later, the president met in his private lounge with *Newsweek*'s Charles Roberts. The small lounge, just steps from the Oval Office, provided the men an informal place to chat for the seventy-one-minute interview. Christian joined the men.

The president handed a great scoop to the magazine reporter, but with conditions. Attribution had to be indirect with references only to senior or high-ranking administration officials. The president told Roberts that the United States had accepted Israel's apology, but had rejected its explanation for how the attack occurred. Israel's assault on the *Liberty*, he told the reporter, was deliberate. The Jewish state's motive was to prevent the American ship from eavesdropping on Israeli transmissions during the war.

Six minutes after his meeting with *Newsweek* ended, the president sat down with Hugh Sidey of *Time* magazine for an off-the-record interview. During this meeting, the president read a memo from his national security adviser, outlining Eshkol's offer to pay retribution to the families of the men killed on the *Liberty*. The president handed the memo to Sidey. "Imagine what would happen," Johnson quipped, "if we had bombed an Israeli ship by mistake?"

"Well imagine what would've happened if the Soviets had bombed it?" replied Sidey. The men laughed.

CHAPTER 10

I think you know about as much about it as we do.

—PRESIDENT JOHNSON, COMMENTING ON
U.S.S. *LIBERTY* AT A NEWS CONFERENCE

Medical teams on the aircraft carrier *America* hustled nonstop since the first helicopters ferried over the wounded Friday morning. The one-day lead time between the attack and the arrival of the injured gave medical staff a chance to prepare. Corpsmen retrieved sterile dressings normally stored in battle stations around the 1,048-foot carrier. Technicians inspected all the sterilized gear in the operating room and the anesthesiologist prepared for up to thirty surgeries. Other techs readied portable and regular x-ray units, gathered extra film and cassettes, and mixed fresh developing solution. The ship's laboratory converted a physical therapy room into a blood donation center. That night, as the carrier steamed toward the *Liberty*, corpsmen drew ten units of O-negative blood from donors, a relatively rare and special blood type found in only 7 percent of the population that can be given safely to anyone. The medical staff put thirty more sailors with O-negative blood on standby.

The medical department needed more than supplies to handle the expected high volume of casualties. Senior officers suspended all routine medical care, reassigned administrative personnel, and requested volunteers from the ship's crew of approximately five thousand to help. The crew converted the second ward into an intensive care unit, and dental technicians now served as hospital corpsmen. The supply department took over feeding the wounded from the ward's galley, a move that allowed corpsmen there to work full-time caring for the injured. The ship's weapons department assumed trash detail and the carrier's Marines and masters-at-arms sealed off the sick bay, blocking reporters and curious sailors from straying too close. Crewmembers from other departments served as stretcher bearers. Hours before the first wounded arrived, medical personnel screened the remaining patients in sick bay and discharged as many patients as possible to free up the necessary seventy-five beds.

By the time the first helicopters lifted off that morning, the carrier was ready. Inbound helicopters radioed the numbers and types of casualties to the flight deck, where controllers relayed the details over a special independently powered phone line that ran directly to the medical department. When the helicopters landed on the four-and-a-half-acre flight deck, stretcher bearers raced the litters to a forward bomb elevator and through a prearranged and sealed-off route that allowed fast access to the carrier's medical complex five decks below. The walking wounded followed the same path. Medical teams examined each incoming patient in the sick bay, diagnosed major ailments, and determined the necessary x-rays and lab work, jotting details in the medical charts. Dental officers escorted the wounded into the wards, grouping similar injuries together, such as fractures and abdominal wounds, to maximize efficiency. Technicians transfused blood and inserted chest tubes to help drain fluids and air. Others inserted nasogastric tubes to feed and medicate the injured. The ship's surgeon and senior medical officers roamed the wards, examining the patients.

Surgery began immediately on the first of *Liberty*'s four gravely wounded sailors. Doctors paused long enough to cross-match the patient's blood type before rolling him into the carrier's operating room at 1:20 P.M. Doctors performed an exploratory surgery of the sailor's abdomen and removed part of his small intestine. A second surgery followed at 6:30 P.M. and the third at 9:10 P.M., which involved a loop colostomy. Doctors rolled the fourth patient into the operating room at 3:20 A.M. Saturday. The only rest came during the one-hour turnover between surgeries, time used to clean the operating room, resterilize the equipment, and swap out the patients. The gravity of the sailors' injuries—and the fact the men had lived through the exhausting night on the *Liberty*—stunned the doctors. "As is expected from shrapnel injuries, there were often multiple serious injuries," the medical report later stated. "To have survived so long before definitive care could be initiated was miraculous indeed."

The flow of injured slowed after twenty-four hours and the most serious patients—including the four gravely injured—soon stabilized. The doctors focused on setting compound fractures, digging out shrapnel, and removing dead and damaged tissue from wounds. The shrapnel injuries proved challenging because many of the shards were aluminum, a light metal difficult to spot on the ship's x-ray equipment. The medical department's final report shows the tremendous work of the carrier's staff. Teams took 311 x-rays, including sixty-three skull and jaw x-rays and ninety-six chest and abdomen x-rays. Technicians performed another 313 lab tests, ranging from urinalyses and liver batteries to one hundred complete blood counts. Doctors transfused twenty-two pints of blood with no reactions. Many of the wounded had arrived depressed. Doctors noted that morale improved when it became clear all of the injured would survive. To bolster spirits, the supply department plied the wounded with hot food. The staff also provided sailors with toiletries, uniforms, and stationery to write letters home. For those too injured to write, volunteers sat bedside and took dictation.

Two days after the attack, the *America* hosted a 1 P.M. memorial service on the carrier's flight deck to honor the thirty-four officers and crew of the *Liberty* who were killed in the attack. About forty of the injured limped out onto the flight deck that sunny afternoon, many depending on crutches. Photographs of the ceremony show the bandaged sailors, seated in metal chairs alongside a small stage, still dressed in hospital gowns, blue robes, and slippers. Crew from the *America* lined the rails of the decks above. Captain Engen officiated at the memorial service along with the carrier's chaplain. During the ceremony, the chaplain read aloud the names of the men known killed as the *Liberty* survivors seated nearby bowed their heads. Sailors from the *America* fired ceremonial guns and the men saluted the flag as taps played. The sailors sang the Navy Hymn, the familiar chorus rolling across the flight deck. "Oh, hear us when we cry to Thee, for those in peril on the sea."

Vice Admiral William Martin hosted a news conference on the *America* Saturday to brief as many as thirty embedded reporters on the latest details about the *Liberty*. Martin served as the commander of the Sixth Fleet and the highest-ranking officer on scene. The Missouri native and Naval Academy graduate had earned a reputation as a daring pilot during World War II, flying a record of 440 night landings on aircraft carriers in the Pacific. Even after Martin ascended the Navy's bureaucracy, the admiral and former test pilot refused to give up flying. In one nighttime training flight over Alexandria, Virginia, he ditched his fighter in the Potomac after it developed engine trouble, forcing him to swim to shore despite injuries to his arms and legs.

The day after the attack Martin had flown out to the *Liberty* in a helicopter, where crews lowered him to the deck in a sling. Ensign Lucas had greeted the three-star admiral upon arrival and escorted him to Commander McGonagle's cabin. Martin and his aides observed that McGonagle, confined to bed, still had dried blood on his leg. The violence of the attack bothered the veteran officer, who years later summed up his visit in a personal letter to a friend with two words: "Unbelievable carnage!!" Later that day, the admiral met with eight of the *Liberty*'s injured in the sick bay of the cruiser U.S.S. *Little Rock*, his flagship, which sailed with the Sixth Fleet.

Though moved by the violence of the attack, Martin remained a Pentagon loyalist. At fifty-seven, his career continued to rise. He had landed the prestigious job as the commander of the Sixth Fleet only two months earlier. In his press conference this morning—recorded and sent back to Washington—the admiral refused to stray from the Pentagon's previous talking points. Though he briefed reporters on the ship's damage, details of the attack, and McGonagle's condition, it soon became clear that the admiral intended his press conference to counter growing media speculation that the *Liberty* was a spy ship. Martin had even prepared a speech addressing that issue.

"That ship was under my operational command. She was told to remain in international waters in a position which she could carry out her primary mission, which was communications," the admiral told reporters. "Her communications mission was to be available for an evacuation operation if it should be ordered. Her position makes complete logic to me. In a position where she could be contacted by any embassy or consulate involved. This contact might be a very low powered transmitter and some communications as you know that is limited to line of sight. For she's the only ship of her kind engaged in that type of communications in that area."

Unconvinced by the admiral's response, a reporter pressed him again, this time more bluntly. "You emphatically deny that she was functioning as a spy?"

The admiral didn't hesitate to deceive. "I emphatically deny it," he declared. "I emphatically tell you that she was there to be a communications guard in case we had to mass evacuate."

Another reporter asked the same question that had dogged the Pentagon's senior leaders two days earlier during the background briefing in Robert McNamara's private dining room. If the *Liberty* served as a communications relay, did the United States inform Israel and Egypt of its presence? Martin handled this question better than his superiors, stating that he saw no reason for the government to alert either country since the *Liberty* sailed in international waters.

"When you spoke of low-powered transmitters," a reporter asked, "do you mean the emergency transmitters that these ships have?"

Martin answered that he didn't know what communications the *Liberty* had and instead emphasized the dangers facing American foreign-service workers stranded in the Middle East. "We do all know that these embassies and consulates have been ransacked and have been under attack and that they would communicate with whatever they have," he replied. "They might even try to communicate with an amateur set."

Later in the briefing, a reporter asked the admiral where the *Liberty* had sailed from prior to the attack. Rather than just note that the ship had visited Africa and Spain, Martin used the question as another opportunity to reinforce the *Liberty*'s cover story. "She was sent into that area as a communications guard. Pure and simple," he declared.

"It is so essential to get a communications guard close enough that our embassies can get in touch with some help."

When a reporter asked moments later if the United States knew Israel had attacked at the time it launched fighters, Martin spotted a chance to derail speculation that the *Liberty* was a spy ship. "I would like to dispel any ideas that you have that this ship was in there for any other purpose except for an evacuation operation," he told reporters. "It was fortunate to have ships that are good communicators."

The admiral's efforts to kill speculation about the *Liberty*'s mission appeared to grow more desperate as the news conference unfolded and he grasped at any opportunity to reiterate the Pentagon's cover story. As a result, his answers often had little connection to the questions the reporters asked. At times, the admiral confused the spy ship's cover stories, mixing the Pentagon's hastily concocted explanation as to why the ship sailed so close to the war zone with the *Liberty*'s official cover story as a research ship tasked to conduct scientific studies. That became clear when a reporter asked what job the *Liberty*'s civilians performed.

Martin flubbed. Rather than simply decline to answer, he offered a rambling and even comical response. "I would imagine them to be the people that know something about our efforts to improve the satellite communications and bouncing these things off the moon and the electro-magnetic areas. There are many areas right here in the Mediterranean where communications are not good and we don't know exactly why, and this is why this ship was going—to try to find out where these areas are," he babbled. "I frequently move the flagship from an area where I am not getting communications into another and I improve communications. There may be a pattern to this and I hope that ships like the *Liberty* can find out where these patterns are, and I hope that one of them with poor communications is not my homeport."

The admiral appeared to sense that he had strayed and soon wrapped up the news conference. He told reporters that the United States operation had been as "clean as a hound's tooth." "I have tried to be just as open and frank with you as I know how to be," the admiral concluded. "I would hope and expect that any interpretations that you try to make out of it would be in the line of the facts that you have been given and to avoid speculations that might be misinterpreted. I see no occasion for speculation other than the facts that you have been given."

A sense of routine returned to the *Liberty* by the weekend as the ship steamed west at about ten knots toward Malta. The destroyer *Davis* escorted the crippled spy ship and the fleet tug *Papago* trailed behind, scanning the water for bodies and classified records that might have drifted from the torpedo hole. Officers periodically mustered the crew for head counts while others once again assumed deck watch. Crews continued the cleanup of the ship, including a saltwater wash-down of the forecastle and forward deck. Deck hands tossed ruined fire hoses, bloodied mattresses, desks, and four boxes of .50-caliber machine gun rounds damaged by shrapnel overboard. Others carefully sanitized the personal belongings of the men killed, including destroying one officer's letters that showed he was having an affair. The *Liberty*'s deck log shows that navigational glitches still plagued the ship. The gyrocompass broke at 6 P.M. Friday. Two and a half hours later, just as teams restored the compass, the navigation lights failed. The mast lights went out at 12:49 A.M. Saturday and engineers discovered a steam leak at 2:33 P.M. that afternoon. At 10:26 P.M. Sunday night, the gyrocompass broke again.

The ship's damage control teams worked nonstop. The day after the attack, crews from the destroyer *Davis* joined the effort. To the men on the *Davis,* the *Liberty*'s competent sailors appeared fatigued, some shell-shocked. Adding to the strain, many of the *Liberty*'s electricians, engineers, and senior officers had been killed or injured. The well-rested sailors from the *Davis* infused energy and brought needed tools. Major concern centered on the flooded forward compartment. The bulkhead that held back the swirling seawater sprouted cracks and leaks. Ensign Scott immediately assembled sailors to use plywood, four-by-fours, and jacks to stabilize the bulkhead with shoring. With the bulkhead secure—and a sailor posted at all times to monitor it— damage control crews focused on other priorities. Teams repaired the ship's ventilation system to pump out oily fumes that might spark a fire, rewired damaged circuits, and pumped water from the ship's fuel tanks. The *Liberty*'s crew had resisted leveling the ship for fear that classified materials and bodies would wash out to sea. Now with the tug in its wake, crews transferred fuel from the starboard to port tanks to balance out the weight of the flooded compartment and right the ship.

McGonagle's strength began to return by the weekend. Other than meeting with Martin, the skipper had passed much of Friday recovering alone in his stateroom. After spending the entire night after the attack on the bridge, he welcomed the chance to sleep, shower, and dress in a fresh uniform. The ship's doctor removed shrapnel from his right leg Saturday and his officers watched his voracious appetite return over meals in the wardroom. By Sunday night, the skipper felt strong enough to host the guests from the *Davis* for a wardroom screening of Elizabeth Taylor's 1963 film *Cleopatra*. Privately, McGonagle's thoughts centered on his crew and the families of the men killed. The traditionally reserved skipper revealed his anguish in a telegram to his wife. "My Dearest Jean. Am well but brokenhearted," he wrote. "They gave their lives and blood to save their ship. Their valiant efforts were not in vain. Please convey my heartfelt condolences to dependents and help in any way possible." He signed it: "Love Bill, USS *Liberty*."

The Navy planned a special mail pickup to boost morale. Many of the officers and crew dashed off letters home during breaks, capturing initial thoughts and recollections of the attack. Few were as prolific as Lucas. Between standing watch and having x-rays taken of his injuries, the young officer wrote four letters to his wife and his parents in just twenty-four hours. Like many on the *Liberty*, Lucas longed for home. "Honey, I love you so much. I would give anything to be with you right now," he wrote. "I've had a good cry in the presence of the Admiral and several times when the Captain and I have been talking alone. The Captain has cried several times too. I need to have a good cry with you—tears of joy that I'm okay and won't ever have to go through anything like this again. It was pure hell."

Other sailors voiced the disbelief many felt about Israel's explanation that the attack had been a tragic accident. Sitting at the rectangular table in the wardroom where thirty-six hours earlier he had held down Seaman Gary Blanchard during surgery, Scott detailed his views in a five-page letter to his parents. "I don't see how they made a mistake," the officer wrote. "It was too well planned & coordinated. They knew exactly where to hit us and they did." He signed the letter: "Alive & unscathed, Ensign John." Seaman Apprentice Dale Larkins echoed Scott in a letter to his parents in Nebraska. "Close to thirty-five boys died," he wrote. "That's one hell of a mistake isn't it?"

Families of the sailors soon learned who died as chaplains visited homes. The names of the dead and injured appeared that weekend in the Norfolk newspaper and in the papers of towns and cities nationwide. Ruth Scott, the ensign's mother, captured the agony many felt in a letter to her son on the envelope of which she scrawled: *Speed it!* "I just don't know how to start this letter but to say your safety is the greatest gift we have ever had," she wrote. "You have not been out of our minds a minute since we heard the horrible news about your ship, and we are still with you in spirit wherever you are now."

The fleet tug *Papago* soon became a fixture in the *Liberty*'s wake, at times sailing as close as a thousand yards behind the injured ship. The 205-foot-long tug often towed target rafts for fleet bombing practice, coming so close to the explosions that scalding shrapnel rained down on deck. Other times, the tug and its crew of about eighty-five helped tow wrecked or grounded ships. The *Liberty* could sail under its own power, but the gaping torpedo hole concerned the Navy. The majority of the damage was below the waterline and in the ship's most sensitive spot, the NSA's top-secret hub. Seawater flowed freely through flooded compartments as the *Liberty* steamed west, washing classified papers and bodies into the Mediterranean. Soviet trawlers lurked on the horizon, eager to salvage anything. After an unsuccessful attempt by divers to string four cargo nets over the hole, the *Papago*'s crew trolled for papers with an eighteen-foot boat hook and crab nets. On the journey to Malta, the tug ultimately fished out eight pounds of classified materials, which the skipper promptly locked in his safe. The tug backed over any papers that could not be recovered, grinding them up in the ship's propeller. The skipper ordered several sailors to stand watch on the bow at all times, scanning the sea with binoculars. At night, the

Papago's searchlights illuminated the *Liberty*'s wake, making visibility even better than during the day.

At 9:41 Sunday morning, *Papago* sailors spotted the first body floating in the sea. The men alerted the bridge and the tug slowed to idle. Navy diver Ensign John Highfill slipped into his wet suit, climbed overboard, and stroked out to the body on the sea's surface. Far out in the Mediterranean, the water was warm and clear. Highfill noted that the body floated facedown. When he approached within ten feet, he paused, unsure of what the body might look like. The sailor had been in the water for three days, first trapped in the *Liberty*'s flooded compartments and now floating freely in the sea. Highfill held his breath and ducked beneath the surface to look. The scene stunned him. A piece of shrapnel had hit the sailor in the back of the head. The exit wound had caused his face to explode. Peering through his mask, Highfill saw what looked like the man's brains and skin hanging down in the water. It reminded him of jellyfish tentacles. He eyed the rest of the sailor's body and noted the man's left arm was missing, leaving only a piece of jagged bone. Highfill had no other options: he reached out and grabbed the bone. The diver turned and paddled back, towing the sailor by his bone. When he reached the *Papago*, deck crews lowered a metal litter. Highfill floated the body onto it and at 9:55 A.M., the body left the water. That afternoon at 1:36 P.M., the *Papago* pulled alongside the *Liberty* and transferred the remains.

Papago searchers spotted a second body at 6:39 P.M. that evening floating down the starboard side of the tug. Many of the sailors had just settled into the tug's mess deck to watch Jane Fonda and Lee Marvin in the 1965 western comedy *Cat Ballou*. When the bridge again called man overboard, sailors slipped into life jackets and headed topside. Petty Officer 3rd Class Kit Rushing watched from the upper deck as Highfill swam out and retrieved his second body of the day. The crew lowered a litter into the water and then hoisted the body up at 6:53 P.M. The body thudded onto the deck. The dark skin led Rushing to conclude the dead sailor was black. Only when a *Papago* corpsman bent over and unfastened the man's dungarees did the young radioman realize he was wrong. He stared down at the man's bright white stomach. Oil coated the parts of the body not covered by his uniform.

In the water, the challenge magnified. "You couldn't grab anything except the hair or the collar and swim with them," Highfill recalled years later. "Everything was just greasy." The corpsman on deck yelled the dead sailor's name to the bridge, where a signalman flashed the information to the *Liberty*. Sailors retrieved a body bag and zipped the remains inside. Crews hauled the body to the ship's refrigerator, where vegetables had been cleared to make room. Searchers spotted the third and final body at 4:44 P.M. the next day. Eighteen minutes later, divers retrieved the body, this one unidentifiable.

CHAPTER 11

What LBJ didn't know—and I don't think we knew—was who had approved the attack and how far up it went in the Israeli government.

—UNDERSECRETARY OF STATE NICHOLAS KATZENBACH

President Johnson suffered through a long night Friday. After meeting with reporters from *Newsweek* and *Time*, the president dined alone at 10:37 P.M. and retired to the personal residence less than an hour later. Israel's continued battle with Syria mandated that he spend most of the night on the phone. By 3:30 A.M., he had made five calls to the Situation Room, Pentagon, State Department, and America's ambassador to the United Nations. The strain of the week's pressure led him to summon his doctor at 4:05 A.M. over a muscular pain in his left shoulder. After a brief examination, the doctor determined Johnson was fine. Less than an hour later, the president picked up the phone again and dialed his national security adviser.

Not until 6 A.M. did Johnson finally doze. His telephone continued to ring this morning, but the White House operator told callers that on doctor's orders the president was not to be disturbed unless it was an emergency. Two and a half hours later, the president rose, showered, and shaved. In what had become an almost daily routine that week, he descended to the basement Situation Room for another tense meeting with his advisers. More than a half dozen of them had gathered to review Soviet premier Alexei Kosygin's latest hotline message about the war in the Middle East. Johnson digested the latest news while he ate his breakfast and figured out how to immediately pressure Israel to stop fighting.

The *Liberty* in contrast sparked surprisingly little controversy for the president. In just forty-eight hours, the attack had dropped from the front pages of most national newspapers, replaced by headlines about the Middle East war, Vietnam, and debate over a record-breaking $70 billion defense spending bill. Each day as the *Liberty*'s casualty numbers climbed, news stories moved farther back in the pages. The dwindling coverage appeared to reflect reporters' diminishing interest in the story that had once seemed so tantalizing, but had fizzled out following Israel's confession that its forces had attacked in error. The barrage of press speculation that surrounded the spy ship the morning of the attack had waned to the point that no one even asked about the *Liberty* during the afternoon press briefing Friday at the White House.

Many of the first editorials on the attack now appeared. Most newspapers unquestioningly accepted Israel's claim, even though no investigation had been conducted or a more thorough explanation given. Editorial writers, unaware of the doubts that permeated the closed-door meetings in the White House and on Capitol Hill, had no reason to doubt Israel's assertion. In its editorial, the *New York Times* described the attack as one of the "many mistakes that invariably occur in war." "The Israelis, flushed with victory, apparently mistook the *Liberty* for an Egyptian ship—a major error in ship identification, since there are no ships under the Egyptian flag with the silhouette and the peculiar and distinctive radio and radar antennas that distinguish the *Liberty* and her sisters," the paper wrote. "Nevertheless, it is clear that accident rather than design snuffed out the lives of some and caused injuries to others of the *Liberty*'s crew."

The *Washington Post* took a more tempered stance, arguing that the attack "must disturb and depress the whole country." "Israel has made a prompt and complete apology, but this, of course, cannot restore the lives of the dead or make whole the wounded," the paper wrote. "Americans will wish to have, and are entitled to have, a more complete explanation from Israel and from their own government." Even the *Virginian-Pilot*, the daily newspaper serving the *Liberty*'s home port of

Norfolk, failed to challenge the official story. War's chaotic nature rendered such errors "inevitable." "Its confusion, its haste, its inaccuracy have produced numerous examples in Vietnam: Americans shelling Americans and South Vietnamese, bombing raids on military targets killing and maiming helpless civilians," observed the paper. "These same qualities were present in the *Liberty* incident."

Hints of disbelief did emerge, often from small newspapers outside the Beltway. Many puzzled over how Israel's exceptional military could make such a blunder. The facts conflicted with common sense. The *News and Courier* in South Carolina described the attack as "shocking." "It is hard to understand how an Israeli pilot could fail to identify the vessel as American," the Charleston paper wrote. "The Egyptians don't have any similarly configured ships, and all U.S. vessels fly the stars and stripes." The *Shreveport Times* in Louisiana went further, describing Israel's assertion that its forces attacked in error as "far fetched." "It is not easy in clear daylight to mistake the red, white and blue and the stars of the American flag for the flag of some other nation," the paper wrote. "Mere apology is not enough in a case of this kind. Israel should guarantee stiff punishment for those responsible for the attack."

Despite these overtures, the overall lack of criticism of Israel baffled some senior government leaders. The dogged press corps consistently challenged the administration on its Vietnam policy and ambitious social programs. In the case of the *Liberty*, the press aimed most of its critical questions at the American government. Israel in contrast enjoyed a reprieve. Reporters soon adopted the phrase "accidental attack," a description that frustrated Pentagon officials, who felt it minimized the ferocity of the sustained assault that had killed or injured two out of every three men on board. "There was nothing accidental about it," Phil Goulding later griped in his memoir. "It was conducted deliberately—by aircraft and by motor torpedo boat, by rocket and bomb and torpedo and gun fire. Whether it was a tragic mistake in identity is a separate question, but it was no accident."

The administration's political reprieve on the *Liberty* ended Saturday just as the war in the Middle East concluded. The exhausted president prepared to spend a relaxing night with friends on his yacht on the Potomac. Israel had aggressively defended the actions of its air force and navy in the days after the attack on the *Liberty*. Within the first twenty-four hours, an Israeli military spokesman issued a statement declaring that the *Liberty* was unmarked. Israeli forces therefore had assumed the ship must be Egyptian. Now news reports on the wires—attributed to unnamed Pentagon sources—said some American military officials agreed that circumstances surrounding the attack made Israel's claim of mistaken identity "plausible."

The White House dialed Robert McNamara soon after the story rattled off the news ticker. The unprovoked strike on the *Liberty* was an atrocity. The Pentagon still did not even have a concrete tally of how many sailors had been killed, a figure that climbed each day. Grieving families nationwide now struggled with the unexpected news of dead and missing loved ones. Many *Liberty* sailors faced catastrophic injuries and a lifetime of disability, impairment, and pain. The United States did not need to exacerbate that grief and suffering by indicating in any way that the deaths and injuries were acceptable or even faultless.

Beyond the concerns of the families and the injured, the story also promised political problems for the administration. Only the night before, the president's advisers had agreed to take a hard line with Israel to guarantee that the Jewish state paid reparations and punished the attackers. If comments from American officials appeared in news reports stating that Israel's rationale for the attack was "plausible," that would only weaken America's bargaining position. Israel no doubt would use the comments to justify the attack and likely argue that it did not have an obligation to pay the families or the American government for the loss of life, for injuries, and for damage to the ship.

After he hung up with the White House, the defense secretary picked up his hotline to Goulding. McNamara barked that the attack was neither plausible nor excusable. He refused to tolerate anyone in the Pentagon suggesting otherwise. McNamara ordered the Defense Department put out a statement immediately refuting the comments that now appeared on the wires. Goulding dictated a three-sentence statement that the *Chicago Tribune* would later declare came "close to setting foreign policy." Within twenty minutes, Goulding's superiors approved the statement and the Pentagon released it to the press.

"We in the Department of Defense cannot accept an attack upon a clearly marked noncombatant United States naval ship in international waters as 'plausible' under any circumstances whatever," the release read. "The suggestion that the United States flag was not visible and the implication that the identification markings were in any way inadequate are both unrealistic and inaccurate. The identification markings of U.S. naval vessels have proven satisfactory for international recognition for nearly 200 years."

Eugene Rostow summoned Israeli ambassador Avraham Harman for a meeting Saturday at the State Department's headquarters. Two days had passed since the attack on the *Liberty* and many of the president's senior advisers still fumed. The latest news reports buried on page 12 of the *Washington Post* this morning listed thirty-three killed, including nine confirmed dead and twenty-four missing, presumably sealed inside the *Liberty*'s flooded forward compartments. The news showed that the number of injured hovered at seventy-five with fifteen sailors seriously wounded. Those publicly released numbers were far less than the 171 who were actually injured.

The Special Committee of the National Security Council had agreed during its meeting in the Cabinet Room the night before that the State Department would oversee the negotiations with Israel concerning the attack. The administration's hard-line approach included demanding a better explanation for how the attack occurred, pushing for financial reparations for the killed and injured, and guaranteeing that Israel punish the attackers. Rostow's job this morning was to hammer these points with the Israeli ambassador.

The third-ranking officer in the State Department, Rostow possessed a gifted intellect. He had enrolled at Yale University in 1929 after scoring 100 percent on his entrance exam, a feat that led the *New York Times* to dub him the "perfect freshman." Rostow graduated Phi Beta Kappa at age nineteen. He then studied economics at Cambridge and earned a law degree from Yale, where he edited the university's prestigious law journal and later served as dean of the law school until joining the State Department in 1966.

Rostow ranked as one of the president's most pro-Israel advisers. Born in Brooklyn to a socialist father, Rostow was proud of his Jewish heritage and even slipped Yiddish into casual conversations. His support of Israel was so pronounced during the Middle East crisis that one senior intelligence official would later say he acted as though he were a lawyer for Israel. In contrast to his colleagues, whose strong comments on the *Liberty* the night before offended him, Rostow refused to believe Israel knowingly targeted the spy ship. "I could never imagine any Israeli, no matter what his politics were, deliberately firing on the American flag," Rostow later recalled. "I was convinced, and I am convinced, that it was a pure accident."

Regardless of his personal views, Rostow soldiered on this muggy Saturday morning in his meeting with Ambassador Harman. He demanded Israel give the United States a "complete explanation" for the attack. The British-born ambassador produced a letter addressed to Dean Rusk, outlining Israel's commitment to pay damages to the affected families and the American government. Harman's message echoed Prime Minister Eshkol's offer the day before to the American ambassador in Tel Aviv to "make retribution to the families of the victims."

"The Government of Israel deeply regrets this tragic accident. The Ambassador of Israel has been instructed to inform the Honorable Secretary of State that the Government of Israel is prepared to make amends for the tragic loss of life and material damage," Harman wrote in the one-page letter. "The Ambassador of Israel expresses once again in the name of the Government of Israel its deep condolences to the Government of the United States and its sympathy to all the bereaved families."

Elsewhere in the State Department that afternoon, Rusk channeled his hostility over the attack into a stinging three-page letter to the ambassador. Aided by Katzenbach and Walt Rostow, Rusk left no doubt that he didn't believe Israel's assertion that its forces had attacked in error. A rough draft of the letter—complete with scratch-outs and handwritten edits—states that the attack "cannot simply be dismissed as an accident."

The men toned down the final draft of the letter only slightly.

Rather than call the attack deliberate, Rusk instead outlined the facts surrounding the assault and questioned how Israeli forces could have made such an incredible blunder. "At the time of the attack, the U.S.S. *Liberty* was flying the American flag and its identification was clearly indicated in large white letters and numerals on its hull. It was broad daylight and the weather conditions were excellent," Rusk fumed. "Experience demonstrates that both the flag and the identification number of the vessel were readily visible from the air."

The secretary of state pointed out that the United States knew Israeli planes had circled the *Liberty* several times prior to the attack in an apparent effort to identify the spy ship. Unbeknownst to Rusk this afternoon, State Department legal advisers would later determine that at least eight reconnaissance flights buzzed the spy ship, starting at dawn the day of the attack. Rusk wrote that the United States believed that Israel had identified the *Liberty*—or at least its nationality—prior to the attack. Under the circumstances, he described the assault as "quite literally incomprehensible."

"As a minimum, the attack must be condemned as an act of military recklessness reflecting wanton disregard for human life," Rusk wrote. "The silhouette and conduct of the U.S.S. *Liberty* readily distinguished it from any vessel that could have been considered hostile. The U.S.S. *Liberty* was peacefully engaged, posed no threat whatsoever to the torpedo boats, and obviously carried no armament affording it a combat capability. It could and should have been scrutinized visually at close range before torpedoes were fired."

Rusk concluded his letter by informing the ambassador that he expected Israel to compensate America for the damages and guarantee that the Israeli military never again endanger American forces. But reparations and promises were not enough. To convince the American people, Israel needed to punish the attackers. "The Secretary of State wishes to make clear that the United States Government expects the Government of Israel also to take the disciplinary measures which international law requires in the event of wrongful conduct by the military personnel of a State."

Later that afternoon, Eugene Rostow gave the secretary of state's stern letter to Harman. Before reading the note, Harman told Rostow that Israel had decided to appoint a military inquiry to investigate the attack. The ambassador defended Israel's position. He pointed out the Jewish state did not know in advance of the *Liberty*'s presence, noted that the ship sailed in a war zone, and reminded Rostow that Israel promptly apologized for the attack. Harman urged the United States to treat the attack as a "tragic mistake" for which the Israeli government had accepted "full responsibility."

Rostow told the ambassador that he agreed that the attack was a tragic mistake, but in keeping with the State Department's firm line, he "added that circumstances surrounding it very mysterious. Word used in our note was 'incomprehensible.'" Rostow then echoed Rusk's demand that Israel punish the attackers. The United States planned to treat Israel no differently from any other nation under the same circumstances. Harman reiterated his hope that the United States would treat the attack as a "tragic mistake."

The stress of the week had exhausted Johnson, who decided to take the rest of the weekend off. At 5:12 P.M. Saturday he left the White House and headed to the Anacostia Naval Yard. There Johnson boarded the presidential yacht at 5:23 P.M. to spend the night on the Potomac River, leaving behind the Situation Room, ringing phones, and clattering teletypes. Nine minutes after the president's arrival, the captain steered the 104-foot *Sequoia* away from the pier. Built in 1925, the wooden yacht served as the flagship of the secretary of the Navy, though Johnson commandeered it as his own. The president spent so much time on the *Sequoia* that he had ordered upgrades. He had the tiny doorknob in his stateroom replaced with a larger one and the shower floor lowered several inches to accommodate his six-foot-three-inch frame. Johnson ordered the removal of former President Franklin Roosevelt's elevator in the main salon to make room for a bar. After an 8 P.M. dinner, the president and his friends reclined on the top deck to watch the short films *Journey to the Pacific* and *Helicopter Rescue in Vietnam* in the warm June evening, the *Sequoia*'s smokestack serving as the movie screen. The president wished his guests goodnight at 11 P.M. and retreated to his stateroom.

The president woke early Sunday morning. He enjoyed breakfast and then read the newspapers and reviewed classified papers sent out from the Situation Room. Even though he told guests he had a "fair night's rest," the president remained tired. The sudden war in the Middle East, coupled with the associated political pressures, had exacerbated the strains he already felt because of Vietnam. Nearly every day this week, he had either been up late or awoken early because of the swift moving war in the desert. Following breakfast, the president retired to his cabin for a nap. That afternoon following lunch, he again retreated to his cabin to rest. The president rallied in the afternoon and even led the singing of happy birthday for a staff member before the *Sequoia* tied up at the pier at 7:10 P.M. On his own until Lady Bird returned from a four-day trip to New England, the president enjoyed a quiet dinner at aide Jack Valenti's home in northwest Washington, before returning to the White House at 10:39 P.M. and bed soon after. He faced another difficult week ahead that would include sorting out the mess in the Middle East.

The Special Committee of the National Security Council sat down at 6:30 P.M. Monday in the White House cabinet room to discuss the latest developments in the war. The president, busy meeting with the speaker of the Texas legislature, then with a union leader, slipped into the Cabinet Room an hour late, where he doodled cartoon faces on White House stationery. Since the committee's meeting Friday evening, events had changed dramatically in the Middle East. The fighting had ended over the weekend and the full scope of Israel's victory had begun to emerge. In only six days, Israel had trounced its Arab neighbors. For every Israeli killed or injured, the Arabs suffered twenty-five casualties. Captured territories totaled forty-two thousand square miles, more than tripling the size of the Jewish state. Israel had seized the Golan Heights from Syria, reached the Suez Canal in Egypt, and captured the Old City of Jerusalem and the West Bank from Jordan. The thirteen advisers gathered around the elongated table likely felt a sense of relief that the war had ended without drawing the United States and Soviet Union into the conflict. Concerns over the war's messy aftermath soon replaced any feeling of reprieve. The United States now had to help hammer out a lasting peace plan, limit arms proliferation in the region, and determine the future of Israel's captured territories.

The *Liberty* was the first topic of discussion during the two and a half hours the committee met. Many of the president's advisers had voiced outrage at the previous meeting, calling the attack "incomprehensible" and urging the president to treat Israel no different than the Arabs or Soviets. The circumstances surrounding the attack—combined with the fact that the *Liberty* flew a flag and had freshly painted hull markings—ruled out friendly fire in the eyes of many. "People in office assumed that it was not just an accident," recalled NSC staff member Harold Saunders. "Most of us knew that they were guilty of a deliberate attack," added Lucius Battle. "There was nobody I think who did not believe that the Israelis knew it was an American ship that they were attacking," remembered Nicholas Katzenbach.

The evening's discussion centered on a letter Israeli ambassador Harman had given to the State Department earlier that day. Harman's three-page letter served as a rebuttal to Rusk's stinging note delivered Saturday. The ambassador was no longer conciliatory. Rusk's letter had infuriated the Israeli diplomats. Ephraim Evron, the embassy's second in command, had described it as "vicious" in an urgent telegram to Jerusalem. He complained that American officials had already determined—even before an investigation had taken place—that Israeli forces had positively identified the nationality of the *Liberty* prior to the assault. "The clear conclusion is that our forces had attacked deliberately," Evron wrote to the Foreign Ministry. "This is contrary to the initial reactions of the Administration and the Pentagon, that had a lower tone and were directed towards calming down."

Eugene Rostow had stoked the anger when he tipped off the ambassador over the weekend that the administration's hard line on the *Liberty* "made things easier" with the Arabs. McGeorge Bundy in fact had even urged Johnson to capitalize on the attack to weaken accusations of American support for Israel. Bundy drafted talking points on the Middle East crisis for the president and placed the *Liberty* at the top of his list. He noted that his suggestion was "probably for more use in the Middle East than in the United States." "The U.S. continues to take very seriously the careless and destructive attack on the USS

Liberty," Bundy wrote. "There is no excuse for repeated attacks on a plainly marked U.S. naval vessel and while in the President's language the prompt Israeli acknowledgment and apology was 'to their credit,' these acknowledgments do not change the fact that this most unfortunate attack occurred."

In his reply to Rusk, Harman now challenged the assertion that Israeli forces had identified the spy ship prior to the attack and rejected the insinuation that Israel deliberately tried to sink the *Liberty*. "The Government of Israel feels that the statement that 'there is every reason to believe that the U.S.S. *Liberty* was identified, or at least her nationality determined, by Israeli aircraft approximately one hour before the attack' is unfounded," Harman wrote. "Nor can the Government of Israel accept the statement that 'the attack must be condemned as an act of military recklessness reflecting wanton disregard for human life.'" The ambassador went further, blaming the United States for failing to alert Israel of the *Liberty*'s presence. "The area was in fact being used by the United Arab Republic for purposes of hostilities against Israel," he wrote. "It would be appreciated if the Government of Israel could be given timely information of the approach by United States vessels to shores where the Israel Defense Forces are in authority."

Harman's letter only fueled the hostility of the president's advisers. Saunders, who recorded the meeting minutes on a legal pad that evening, captured the frustration. "Consensus: reaction sour. 'Terrible note.'" The United States now faced a larger problem. The "strong and firm line" the committee had agreed to pursue with Israel had backfired. Harman's letter clearly showed that the Jewish state would not be bullied. The challenge facing the men this evening was how to proceed. The advisers debated releasing Rusk's letter to the press. Nearly three dozen sailors had been killed in the attack and many more injured. An American ship almost had been lost. Rusk's letter would reveal to the public the disbelief senior officials felt over Israel's explanation and show that America did not tolerate the killing of its sailors. The move also promised to deflate the swelling pro-Israel fervor that had gripped much of the nation, giving the administration a political reprieve from the stifling pressure. Saunders had suggested a similar strategy days earlier, before America even knew the full extent of the casualties. "With 10 men killed and 100 wounded, should we make public our protest?" he asked in a memo to McGeorge Bundy, the president's special consultant. "If we don't we'll look like real Israeli patsies. Would protest help cool off the Jewish community?"

Releasing Rusk's letter guaranteed other problems. American leaders already complained about the lack of leverage over the Jewish state. The United States had urged Israel not to launch the war, but it was now clear Israel had been the aggressor. The Jewish state also had claimed that it had no territorial ambitions. The United States had publicly affirmed its commitment to the "political independence and territorial integrity" of all Middle Eastern nations. The president had used those exact words in a speech broadcast on radio and television twenty days earlier. American leaders had grown alarmed that Israel now planned to keep at least some of the captured lands. Failure to relinquish the seized territories promised to further complicate American relations in the Arab world, given the close ties between the United States and Israel. The committee's meeting minutes reflect the president's concern. "How do we get out of this predicament?" he asked. McNamara agreed. "We're in a heck of a jam on territorial integrity." A public airing of Rusk's letter about the *Liberty* promised only to anger the Israelis and further erode American leverage.

The Middle East war served as only one variable in a larger foreign policy equation. Despite the recent attention on the conflict, the president and his advisers remained focused on Vietnam. That war would prove the deciding factor in Johnson's decision not to run for reelection in 1968. The news that clattered off the teletype remained grim. Two more American fighters had been shot down Sunday, bringing the total number of planes lost to 581. The unpopular war claimed an average of twenty-six American lives each day. Though thousands of miles separated Vietnam and the Middle East, the two were intrinsically linked in the arena of domestic politics. That connection had only strengthened in the past week. Many American Jews who played a prominent role in the antiwar movement had emerged as hawks on the Middle East conflict, urging the United States to protect Israel and even protesting outside the White House and State Department. The president needed only to check with the mail department for confirmation.

The Middle East war produced the largest surge of letters, telegrams, and postcards of any single issue during Johnson's presidency. The burden of the overwhelming mail was reflected in a memo to Rusk. "During the past ten days, we have analyzed upwards of 50,000 letters and other messages," the memo stated. "The White House has an additional 120,000 letters, which will all be answered. I'm relieved to report that several other agencies are being asked to help with this job."

Set against the backdrop of these foreign policy concerns and the president's weakened domestic political standing, the *Liberty*'s importance faded. The unprovoked attack angered the president and many of his advisers, but the leaders took a pragmatic view. The *Liberty*'s death toll amounted only to roughly one day's casualty count in Vietnam. The week of the attack saw 176 Americans killed in Vietnam and 928 injured, down from 214 killed the week before and 1,161 wounded. The United States wanted to make sure Israel compensated the families and punished the attackers, but the attack did not warrant a break with the Jewish state. The United States had to focus on peace in the Middle East and Vietnam. "There are lots of terrible things that happen in wars," recalled Saunders. "Given the other stakes—as horrible as this was—this was not something that belonged on the geopolitical stage." Even Rusk, who appeared particularly troubled by the attack, agreed. "However outrageous the attack on the *Liberty* was, there remains the policy question as to whether that episode should have been blown into a major confrontation between Israel and the United States," he later wrote in a letter to one of the *Liberty*'s officers. "Those who carry the ultimate responsibility, however, know that there are times when one has to pick up the pieces and not let everything fall apart because of an occurrence of this sort."

The "strong and firm line" softened. Saunders recorded the decision in the meeting minutes. "Consensus: Publishing exchange wouldn't do any good." The State Department would seek a better explanation for the attack, but otherwise the administration reversed course. Rather than openly confront Israel, the United States moved to protect it from possible public relations fallout, the same rationale that had prompted some senior officials to previously suggest sinking the *Liberty* at sea to prevent reporters from photographing it. The advisers agreed that

Harman's letter blaming the United States for the attack represented a domestic political liability for the president. If the United States were forced to release it to the press—or if it leaked—the callous letter would outrage the American public. Many American Jews, already angry over the neutrality blunder, would blame the administration for stirring up anti-Israel sentiment. The beleaguered president, anxious to retain Jewish support and refocus on Vietnam, couldn't afford the domestic political controversy. "It was no help if you had a lot of people getting angry at the Israelis," recalled Katzenbach. "If the Israelis screw up the relations, then the Jewish groups are going to bail out the Israelis. It ends up with you having a more difficult situation than you would have otherwise."

There was only one answer: urge the Israelis to quietly take back the letter, tone it down, and resubmit it. The meeting minutes show the advisers all agreed: "Get Israelis to recall it." Bundy drafted a secret memo for the record following the meeting, outlining the committee's actions. The *Liberty* was the first item on Bundy's memo and would be the last declassified more than three decades later. "After reviewing the Israeli Government's reply to our note protesting its attack on the U.S.S. *Liberty,* the Committee decided (a) to clear up our own pre-liminary understanding of the facts surrounding the attack and (b) to suggest unofficially to the Israelis that they take back their note and rewrite it in a more moderate vein." The job of negotiating with the Israelis fell to Katzenbach. The undersecretary of state days later summoned the Israeli ambassador to Foggy Bottom. The secret memo recording the meeting—declassified thirty-three years later—shows Katzenbach "suggested Harman think about the possibility of making some amendments in the Israeli note, which we think contains some statements they might find it hard to live with if the text some day became public. There was a tentative agreement that the best procedure might be to make a few revisions in both notes and back-date them to replace the originals."

CHAPTER 12

That evening and thru the night we got the boys out that had been trapped down below where the torpedo hit. Found 25 in all. It was a pretty sorry day.

—SEAMAN APPRENTICE DALE LARKINS,
LETTER TO HIS PARENTS

The *Liberty* sailed past the Ricasoli lighthouse at daybreak Wednesday, June 14, and entered the Grand Harbor in Valletta, Malta. Nearly a week had passed since the attack. A maritime crossroads dating back seven thousand years, Valletta offered the nearest drydock in the Mediterranean that could patch the *Liberty*'s steel skin. The destroyer *Davis* escorted the injured ship; the tugboat *Papago* continued to trail behind. Bandaged crewmembers, including one with an eye patch, lined the rails. McGonagle appeared on deck, binoculars around his neck, relieved his ship had completed the thousand-mile journey.

Reporters watched the *Liberty*'s arrival from a nearby hillside, jotting notes about its riddled hull and superstructure, torched life rafts, and the torpedo hole that poked above the waterline. Television journalists shot grainy video of the spy ship as it eased into the crowded harbor. The *Chicago Tribune* observed that the shell marks, which exposed the *Liberty*'s orange primer, matched "the colors of the dawn." A reporter with the Associated Press wrote that the ship's "funnel had more holes than a pepperpot." *Life* magazine described the *Liberty* as "shot up as a tin can on a firing range."

Harbor pilots moored the spy ship to a pier in the British Royal Navy base. By 7:45 A.M., the *Liberty* had secured its mooring lines, set the in-port watch, and mustered the crew. Senior Navy officers waited to board. Divers slipped into wet suits and scuba tanks to make a final inspection. Unlike the Mediterranean's clear waters, the Valletta harbor was murky, forcing the Navy's divers to feel along the *Liberty*'s hull for rips or gashes that might trigger the ship to collapse once workers drained the water from drydock.

A Maltese harbor pilot climbed aboard at 1:52 P.M. Twenty-seven minutes later, the ship's log shows that the pilot assumed control of the *Liberty* and guided the injured ship into drydock No. 2. There the *Liberty* settled onto a row of more than one hundred keel blocks positioned in a line along the drydock floor. Workers anchored the ship to the walls with wooden timbers. The Navy rigged a canvas tarp over the torpedo hole to block reporters from photographing the secret research spaces and concocted a cover story: the tarp protected the privacy of the dead trapped inside.

Dockworkers pumped out the seawater. To prevent the loss of classified papers, the Navy covered the drains with screens. Divers and men in rafts paddled around, searching for classified tapes, memos, or messages that might have floated out of the hole as the water level fell. At sea, only the tip of the torpedo hole jutted above the waterline. In drydock, the crew leaned over the rails to watch its full jagged profile emerge. The torpedo had ripped a teardrop-shaped gash twenty-four feet tall and thirty-nine feet wide, nearly large enough for the tugboat *Papago* to sail through.

The aftermath of the torpedo blast awaited the body recovery team, who now crowded around the sealed hatch that led to the destroyed compartments below. Some sailors dressed this afternoon in rubber boots and coveralls. Others wore only T-shirts and dungarees. Officers handed out battle lanterns, flashlights, and a few pair of gloves. Some of the men would have to work barehanded.

The watertight hatch divided the living and the dead. Soon after the attack, Dr. Kiepfer had recruited several sailors to check for the remote possibility of survivors trapped inside the torpedoed compartments. Heavy fumes of fuel oil spilled out when the men unsealed the hatch.

The mix of oil and seawater had receded since engineers stabilized the *Liberty* and corrected its nine-degree list. The men spotted a body stretched out at the bottom of the ladder.

"What do we do?" one sailor had asked.

"Get a body bag," Kiepfer replied.

Kiepfer's men roped the oil-coated corpse from the compartment and zipped it into a body bag. Sailors lugged the remains to the ship's walk-in freezer and once again sealed the compartment. Each day as the *Liberty* crawled west toward Malta, the smell of the rotting bodies trapped below intensified, prompting one officer to describe the *Liberty* as a "death ship." Sailors slept with the stench, showered with it, and choked down coffee with it. Seaman Jack Beattie, a fireman in the engineering department, captured the conditions in a letter to his parents: "The smell was so bad that you couldn't even eat."

With drydock now dewatered, Lloyd Painter readied a team for the gruesome job of recovering the dead. Painter had worked in the *Liberty*'s research spaces before the attack, reviewing intelligence reports and determining the NSA's spy targets. The Navy allowed only crewmen with top-secret clearance, like Painter, to clean up the torpedoed compartment. The few engineers and medical corpsmen needed to help with the grisly task were ordered to recite oaths promising never to reveal what they saw inside. A guard stood watch at the entrance and forced sailors to sign in and out.

Painter undogged the hatch and crawled first into the dark compartment, navigating the oil-coated ladder that had somehow survived the blast. When he reached the deck below, Painter switched on his flashlight. He panned the room. The compartment had been divided into several rooms and offices equipped with receivers, transmitters, desks, chairs, and filing cabinets. The torpedo had blown out all of the interior walls, leaving only a single expansive space. Piles of tangled debris, mangled metal, and broken furniture were rammed in piles up against the remaining interior bulkhead.

Fuel oil from busted tanks in the bowels of the ship coated the corrugated metal deck, walls, and even the ceiling. Painter aimed his flashlight upward. Electrical wires and cables that once powered this secret intelligence hub now sagged from the ceiling. He froze. Wrapped in the wires, one of the dead officers, eyes open, stared down at him. Painter recognized his former colleague even though the remains were bloated from days in the salty seawater. Painter moved his flashlight down the length of the body. Only the head and torso remained. Good Lord, he thought.

Other sailors crawled down the ladder, handing shovels and body bags through the narrow hatch. The men picked through the piles of warped filing cabinets, broken chairs, desks, and typewriters in search of friends and colleagues as well as classified manuals, records, and equipment that the government wanted cataloged. The work proved difficult. Oil coated everything and the men often slipped. Battle lanterns and flashlights provided only minimal light. The hot summer day—and the lack of ventilation—made the air thick and the stench of death unbearable.

The searchers easily located some of the dead. Other remains proved more difficult to find as the bodies often lay buried beneath piles of heavy debris or stuffed between steam pipes, the only clue a protruding hand or foot or the intense smell. Six days in the salty seawater had left the dead grotesquely swollen and distended. The skin had bleached white—the color of nursing stockings, one sailor later recalled—and the hair largely had fallen out. "You'd puke, then go back at it," recalled Petty Officer 2nd Class Robert Schnell, a twenty-four-year-old from Montana. "It had to be done."

Petty Officer 2nd Class Dennis Eikleberry spotted feet protruding from a pile of twisted metal. Eikleberry, who had been in a room across the hall when the torpedo exploded, let his eyes wander up the body, past the legs, torso, and arms. Instead of a head, Eikleberry found only a long piece of skin that looked like string. Another body he found resembled hamburger meat. The smell was horrendous. "When they picked him up by the belt and the breastbone," Eikleberry recalled, "his arms fell off."

Though many of the bodies were largely intact, some of the recovered remains consisted of only decaying tissue and intestine littered amid teletype papers, tapes, and work manuals, much of it unrecognizable. "Not just arms and legs," recalled Seaman Don Pageler, "inside pieces of bodies and all sorts of stuff." Pageler, a twenty-one-year-old from Kansas, picked up a piece of equipment and found a severed arm. Pageler stared at it in shock. "I looked at the muscle structure," he remembered, "and I knew whose arm it was."

The men tied ropes on the end of the body bags and hoisted them through the same hatch where many had escaped six days earlier. Sam Schulman, the *Liberty*'s junior corpsman, unzipped each bag and removed the shoes and socks. He wiped ink on the bottom of the feet and hands and took prints to help identify the men. "You knew who they were, but they didn't look anything like they did when they were alive," Schulman recalled years later. "The texture of the tissue was such that you were afraid that if you pulled too hard, you would pull the skin off the bone."

Petty Officer 1st Class Ron Kukal helped Schulman. The twenty-seven-year-old Nebraska native said the partial bodies presented the greatest challenge. The men depended on names stenciled on the dead sailors' shirts and pants to help reassemble the remains. "Some of the bodies had arms and legs. Other times you had to take arms and legs and figure out who they belonged to," recalled Kukal, who had supervised communications technicians before the attack. "It was just like a jigsaw puzzle."

Many of the men took breaks from the grisly chore. Kiepfer poured brandy into four-ounce bottles and passed it out. Later he washed out the oil that had clogged Painter's ears and rendered him nearly deaf. The crew worked through the night, picking through piles of debris, shoveling up papers, and identifying and packing the remains of friends. An early status report filed from the *Liberty* revealed that the team identified twelve bodies found in the flooded compartments. Four others were unidentifiable. The team also found a head and an arm.

Recovery of the bodies concluded by the following day. The men continued to sift through piles of classified records, much of it little more than soggy mush, before zipping it inside 168 canvas bags for future sorting. "Twenty remains have been shipped to Naples. It may not be possible to identify all twenty," a final report read. "Bodies of five of the twenty-five originally reported missing have not been found. It is reasonable to assume that the five not found were lost at sea."

*   *   *

The attack had slipped from the front pages of most American news-papers, but media speculation over the *Liberty*'s mission intensified. Press queries swamped the Pentagon as reporters demanded to know if it had been spying. The Pentagon responded by shutting down. The day the *Liberty* reached Malta, McNamara ordered a news blackout. No one could speak to reporters. If pressed, officials could say only that the Navy had convened a court of inquiry to investigate and planned to release a statement when the court concluded.

To explain the Pentagon's sudden news blackout, spokesman Phil Goulding released a five-sentence statement. "Many rumors and reports about the attack have been circulating," Goulding wrote. "The Department of Defense has no evidence to support some of these rumors and reports. Others appear to be based on partial evidence. Some appear to be accurate on the basis of present information here, which is incomplete. Until the Court has had an opportunity to obtain the full facts, the Department of Defense will have no further comment."

The Pentagon's news release—described by the *Chicago Tribune* as "one of the most intriguing pieces of prose that ever came out of the department's press office"—followed rigid precautions the Navy adopted soon after the attack. Reporters had no access to the *Liberty* or the majority of its crew as the injured ship steamed to Malta, which made it easy to control the news during that time. The few interviews with the evacuated sailors on board the aircraft carrier *America* were rigorously monitored by Navy public affairs officials.

The day after the attack, four sailors sat for a filmed interview. A second interview followed two days later with Seaman Kenneth Ecker, who showed reporters his dinged battle helmet, with several holes in it and a piece of shrapnel still lodged near the temple. The Navy prepped the sailors in advance and made them sign agreements to conceal the *Liberty*'s mission and acknowledge that Israel had claimed the attack "was made in error." Public affairs staff monitored—and occasionally interrupted—the interviews. Afterward staff cabled summaries of the interviews, and in Ecker's case, a complete transcript, to Navy commanders.

In a sign of how politically sensitive the attack remained, a public affairs officer highlighted one of Ecker's comments later in a report. "At one point, when asked of the general feeling among *Liberty* crewmen as they spent the night in distress, Ecker answered rather passionately: 'We wanted to get them sons of bitches whoever attacked us.' When pressed for the feeling after it became known that the attackers were Israelis, Ecker replied: 'We still wanted to get them. We didn't care whether they were friends or enemies. They hit our ship and we wanted to make them pay.'"

Another example of the Navy's unease centered on a story filed the day after the attack by Associated Press reporter Bob Horton. The reporter quoted an unnamed officer on the *America* who stated that the *Liberty* was loaded with eavesdropping equipment and tasked to spy on the Middle East war. "To put it bluntly, she was there to spy for us. Russia does the same thing," Horton quoted the officer. "We moved in close to monitor the communications of both Egypt and Israel. We have to. We must be informed of what's going on in a matter of minutes."

That quote sparked a secret investigation to uncover whom Horton talked to and how he fooled the Navy's minders. The results did not please the brass. Reporters typically filed stories using the carrier's teletypes. But Horton smuggled his scoop off the carrier on a routine delivery flight to Greece. "Mr. Horton's copy was not submitted for review for security or accuracy and it was not transmitted by Navy communications," stated a telegram. "It is believed to have been sent ashore in a sealed envelope placed together with other media material."

Malta presented a far greater challenge in attempting to conceal the truth. Unlike the tight confines of an aircraft carrier, which made keeping tabs on journalists easy—except in Horton's case—the Mediterranean island was wide open. Reporters roamed bars, restaurants, and beaches, the spots sailors sought out to unwind. The battered ship also would be on display, undergoing weeks of repairs in the drydock. Days before the *Liberty*'s arrival, the Navy and the American Embassy developed a plan. Additional public affairs officers soon began arriving in Malta to help.

The embassy arranged for the *Liberty* to dock that morning at the British Royal Navy base to "minimize immediate scrutiny." The Navy also barred reporters from the drydock. Most reporters watched the *Liberty*'s arrival from a nearby hillside, a vantage point that prevented them from viewing the side of the ship with the torpedo hole. To satisfy the press, a Navy photographer shot six photographs of Commander McGonagle pointing out blast holes on the bridge and staterooms. The Navy gave the undeveloped roll to the Associated Press to disseminate over the news wires.

After completing the body recovery, the Navy planned a "rigidly controlled" tour of the *Liberty*'s topside and one or two lower compartments "to prevent lending credence" to the spy ship story. "McGonagle would meet with newsmen and be photographed, but aside from paying tribute to his crew he would make no comments about the attack nor would he answer questions about it. "Believe that if newsmen know captain will continue to be unavailable for some time," a Navy message states, "this tour will close out story here and out of town newsmen will depart."

The Navy also banned interviews with the crew by pointing out that members of the crew were potential witnesses before a naval court of inquiry into the incident. But despite the Navy's efforts, uncensored information still leaked. The parents of eighteen-year-old Seaman Apprentice Robert Reilly, whose older brother Thomas also served on the *Liberty* and was critically injured in the attack, released a letter he wrote to the press. Wire services picked up Reilly's letter, and his graphic account of the attack immediately ran in papers nationwide. "We were just sitting ducks," Reilly wrote. "Guys were just torn in half. Some of my best buddies lay dead in three pieces."

Reilly's letter triggered stern warnings to the crew, some of whom wrote to family members and begged them not to release personal letters. "That sort of thing is really bad because we aren't to say a damn word about the attack until the Board of Inquiry comes out with a formal statement," Dave Lucas wrote to his parents. "All of my comments have been off the record, as I'm sure you are well aware." Lucas also warned his wife. "Everything I've said to you is for your info only, as you know," he wrote. "I won't be able to talk to any reporters or anyone outside the family for a long, long time."

*   *   *

A court of inquiry began in the *Liberty*'s wardroom at 7:55 A.M. on June 14, less than two hours after the spy ship tied up in port. The Navy convened these fact-finding panels to investigate catastrophes, from collisions at sea and fires to the loss of ships in battle or storms. Previous inquiries focused on the sinking of the U.S.S. *Maine* in 1898, the attack on Pearl Harbor in 1941, and the torpedoing of the U.S.S. *Indianapolis* by a Japanese submarine in 1945. The court functions much like a grand jury. Witnesses give sworn testimony. Exhibits are marked and entered into the record. A president oversees the inquiry, similar to a judge in a civilian court. At the end, court members compile a report of findings and offer recommendations that can include disciplinary action, from a letter of reprimand to court martial.

Admiral John McCain, Jr., the commander of the Navy's European and Middle East forces, convened the inquiry soon after the attack on the *Liberty*. McCain symbolized the Navy's aristocracy. His father had served as a vice admiral during World War II, commanding one of the most powerful aircraft carrier task forces. The elder McCain's bombers and fighters sank forty-one Japanese ships and damaged twenty-eight others in a single day in an incredible battle near the end of the war. When the senior McCain died suddenly of a heart attack days after the Japanese surrender ceremony on the deck of the battleship U.S.S. *Missouri* in Tokyo Bay, the *New York Times* lauded him in an editorial. "He combined the hot fighting tradition of John Paul Jones with the cold, scientific precision that wins modern battles," the paper observed. "Small, wiry and tense, he looked like a hawk and struck like a hawk."

The younger McCain possessed the drive and ambition of his father. A Naval Academy graduate, McCain was stubby—only five feet six inches tall—and smoked big cigars that he often threw when angry. He routinely barked at his underlings and used foul language, though never around women. His favorite expression was "God bless you, goddammit." Many of McCain's peers viewed the feisty admiral as politically motivated, or as one former aide remarked, "always on his way up." McCain turned his deft political radar not just to the Navy, but also to Congress. During a previous assignment at the United Nations, he had befriended American ambassador Arthur Goldberg, a personal adviser to President Johnson and the Israeli Embassy. The admiral depended on this network of advisers. One of his aides later recalled that McCain "never did anything without checking with ten people all over the world."

Some of McCain's staff blamed his incessant politicking in part for the attack on the *Liberty*, a fact that would neither be included in the Navy's court of inquiry nor ever made public. When the conflict in the Middle East started, McCain's staff had ordered a covert submarine operating in the eastern Mediterranean to pull farther back from shore. McCain's aides requested that the admiral also move the spy ship. Unlike the submarine, which fell solely under Navy jurisdiction, the *Liberty* operated at the request of the National Security Agency, its orders routed through the Joint Chiefs of Staff. If he moved the *Liberty*, McCain risked a clash with the Joint Chiefs or the NSA. He hesitated. "Our staff begged McCain to pull *Liberty*," recalled Rear Admiral Joseph Wylie, Jr., McCain's deputy in London. "He claimed he didn't have the authority. Enough said? He should have. And she was plugged."

McCain understood the geopolitical challenge of the *Liberty* mess. This was no typical collision at sea or ship fire the Navy could handle internally. The attack involved an American ally, one that commanded significant support from American Jews. A court of inquiry report critical of Israel would trigger diplomatic ramifications for the State Department and create domestic political trouble for the beleaguered White House, which now wanted to deemphasize the attack. "It was a little bigger than just a Navy problem," recalled one senior officer. "It was a national problem." Faced with political pressure to conclude the episode as soon as possible, McCain had set strict parameters on his investigators, including barring travel to Israel to interview the attackers. The admiral also allowed his team only one week to investigate, though the court's lawyer would later admit that a proper investigation would have required six months.

McCain appointed Rear Admiral Isaac Kidd, Jr., president. Like McCain, Kidd came from a storied Navy family. His father died on the U.S.S. *Arizona* when the Japanese sank the battleship during the surprise attack on Pearl Harbor. The blast vaporized Kidd's body. Salvage divers later found his Naval Academy class ring fused to the ship's conning tower. The rear admiral was the highest-ranking officer killed that infamous December day and the Navy posthumously awarded him the Medal of Honor, the nation's highest award for heroism.

The younger Kidd strode across stage at the Naval Academy's graduation ceremony less than two weeks after his father's death. The sudden war had prompted the academy to graduate its class six months early. Kidd greeted Secretary of the Navy Frank Knox with a salute as he received his commission as an ensign. "The U.S. Naval Academy and its guests broke into a thunderous cheer," reported *Time* magazine, "an unprecedented demonstration in honor of Ensign Kidd and his father." During the Allied landings in Italy and Sicily, Kidd served as a gunnery officer on a destroyer. He later commanded a destroyer and served as commodore of a guided-missile destroyer division. The forty-seven-year-old Kidd, now heavyset, spoke with a slow drawl and often called younger sailors "son."

Kidd picked Captain Ward Boston, Jr., as the court's attorney. Nearly four years his junior, Boston had flown fighters off aircraft carriers in World War II and later served as an agent with the FBI. Boston and Kidd had met about a year earlier at a dinner party. The feisty son of a locomotive engineer, Boston once challenged Kidd after the admiral had reprimanded a young ensign over a trivial matter. Boston thought the punishment too severe. Boston's sense of fairness stuck with Kidd. At the time Kidd summoned him to help with the *Liberty* inquiry, Boston worked in Naples as a Navy lawyer. Captain Bert Atkinson, Jr., Captain Bernard Lauff, Lieutenant Commander Allen Feingersch, and a court reporter rounded out the court.

Two days after the attack, the court had briefly convened in London. Kidd and Boston flew to Crete and traveled out to the *Liberty* on the destroyer U.S.S. *Fred T. Berry,* arriving on board the injured ship at 6:15 A.M., four days after the attack. The other court members awaited the *Liberty*'s arrival Wednesday morning in Malta. The court's presence, along with other senior military commanders, impressed the *Liberty*'s crew. "Talk about brass!" Dave Lucas wrote to his wife. "Two admirals, seven captains, and yesterday a general from the Joint Chiefs of Staff. The wardroom hat rack has more scrambled eggs than a short order kitchen at breakfast time."

The wardroom still bore the scars from the attack, including jagged shell holes in the wood-paneled walls. The examining officers sat around the same table where Seaman Gary Blanchard had died. The foot-powered suction pump that helped clear the postal clerk's lungs as he took his final breaths now supported a microphone. Lucas testified first so he could go ashore and have shrapnel in his head examined. To help the twenty-five-year-old officer relax, Kidd poured him a cup of coffee and a glass of water. Feel free to smoke, the admiral told him. Lucas had remained on the bridge with McGonagle during much of the attack and served as a key witness.

Lucas testified for most of the morning, describing shells flying through the bridge, the torpedo blast rolling the ship, and spotting the hull number on one of the Israeli torpedo boats. He recounted using his belt as a tourniquet on McGonagle's wounded leg and seeing the American flag flying from the *Liberty*'s mast during the attack. The court showed Lucas the quartermaster's notebook—a primary source for the ship's deck log—and asked him if the splatters on page 102 were blood. Lucas, who had maintained the log during the latter portion of the attack, confirmed. Court members also asked Lucas to read an entry in the log that described one of the gunboats, then showed him a photo of an Israeli torpedo boat. Did the picture match the torpedo boats he saw? Lucas again confirmed.

The court pressed Lucas for details of his skipper's performance. Was McGonagle on the bridge throughout the attack? Did you see him get injured? How did he react to his injuries? Did he stop for medical care? Did the doctor at any point order him to leave the bridge to seek care? Lucas defended his captain. "It would have taken ten people the doctor's size to even begin to get him off the bridge," he told the court. "He was giving orders to us in the pilothouse, he was taking photographs of the aircraft, the patrol craft, attempting to identify them with his binoculars, giving orders to the gun mounts when they were still manned, was directing the fire-fighting parties, seemed like he was everywhere at one time."

The court recessed from 10:45 A.M. until early afternoon, when it summoned the skipper. McGonagle had started the cruise worrying—and blasting junior officers—over mundane matters, such as reviewing routine messages and drill performance. Those early concerns must have seemed trivial now, considering that two-thirds of his men were dead or injured. The spy ship no one was supposed to know existed had appeared in front-page articles in the nation's top newspapers, on the evening news broadcasts, and was discussed and debated among senior leaders of the Pentagon, State Department, and even the White House.

In the hours after the attack, McGonagle's officers had reported him aloof and pensive, likely replaying the assault in his mind. He said little that first night as he sipped black coffee, sighted the North Star, and ordered turns of the rudder. Days later, alone in his stateroom, he nursed Spanish brandy the ship's doctor gave him and prepared for the court of inquiry. Lieutenant Commander William Pettyjohn, who came aboard for the voyage to Malta, had checked on McGonagle periodically, finding the skipper stretched out in his bunk, writing and editing his notes. Unlike Kidd, McGonagle had no family legacy or contacts to protect him. He knew his career was at risk, that commanding officers rarely emerged from inquiries unscathed, much less lauded.

The court began by acknowledging McGonagle's injuries. "Let the record show that although the witness is experiencing considerable pain from shrapnel wounds in his leg, that he willingly appeared at this hearing." McGonagle then recounted details as he remembered them. He discussed the precautions he took entering the war zone, including stationing sailors at the *Liberty*'s machine guns. The skipper described reconnaissance planes he saw buzz the *Liberty* that morning and how he watched through binoculars as the first wave of fighter jets rolled in for the attack. "It seemed to me that the attacks were made in a crisscross fashion over the ship, with each attack coming at approximately forty-five seconds to one minute intervals," he testified. "It is estimated that the total air attack was completed in approximately five to six minutes."

The skipper also downplayed his shrapnel injuries. "I was not knocked off my feet, I was only shaken up and it made me dance around

a little bit, but my injuries did not appear to me to be of any consequence," he said. "Since I could walk and there was no apparent pain, I
gave no further consideration to these minor injuries." When the torpedo boats were about fifteen miles away, he noticed the American flag
had been shot down so he ordered a new one hoisted. McGonagle told
the court that he spotted the Israeli flag on the torpedo boats about
the time one appeared to signal the *Liberty*. He ordered the *Liberty*'s
machine gunners to hold fire, but the gunners failed to hear him and
fired anyway. To McGonagle, the machine gun fire appeared "extremely
effective." "As far as the torpedo boats are concerned," he said, "I am sure
that they felt that they were under fire."

Moments later a torpedo passed the stern of the ship, missing the
Liberty by only twenty-five yards. McGonagle told the court that a
minute later a second torpedo ripped open the ship's starboard side.
The *Liberty* immediately rolled nine degrees and the skipper watched
oil and debris wash out of the hole. The *Liberty* lost power and steering. The torpedo, he testified, had left the spy ship "dead in the water."
"Immediately, I determined that the ship was in no danger of sinking
and did not order the destruction of classified material and did not
order any preparations to be made to abandon ship," the skipper testified. "It was my intention to ground the ship on shoal areas to the left
of the ship's track to prevent its sinking, if necessary."

Though he downplayed his injuries earlier in his testimony, McGonagle later described how he felt he might black out from blood loss,
but still remained on the bridge through the night, only breaking long
enough to use the restroom. Despite the confusion and chaos of the
attack, the skipper could find no fault in the performance of his officers
and crew. He congratulated his men for saving the ship and told the
court that he intended to commend Lucas, Scott, and Golden, among
others. "I have no complaint to lodge against any officer or man on
board U.S.S. *Liberty* for any acts of commission or omission during
the attack and post attack phase," McGonagle told the court. "I have
nothing but the greatest admiration for their courage, their devotion
to duty, and their efforts to save the ship."

Throughout Wednesday and Thursday, a dozen more officers and
crewmembers testified. These witnesses represented a fraction of the

ship's crew of nearly three hundred. Many of the best witnesses—those topside during the attack—had been injured and evacuated to the aircraft carrier *America*. The Navy had since relocated many to hospitals around the Mediterranean. Lieutenant Jim Ennes, Jr., perched on the flying bridge at the start of the attack, would have testified that the fighters made no effort to identify the *Liberty* but immediately opened fire. Seaman Larry Weaver, who had his colon blown out on deck, would have told the court that the fighters executed far more than the half dozen strafing runs claimed. Lieutenant Jim O'Connor, also on the flying bridge, had a clear view of the flag at the start of the attack. None of these men or dozens of others would ever testify.

The few sailors who did testify painted a gruesome picture. Lucas recounted the death of Francis Brown, who had stepped back from the helm as the Israelis shelled the bridge. "He still had his hand, one hand on the wheel. I was two paces to his left, and two paces behind him," Lucas said. "A fragment hit him, I think from behind. It must have come through the bulkhead in the chart-room. He let out a gasp, fell backwards into the chart-room, and within, say a minute, was dead." Chief Petty Officer Carl Lamkin told the court that the rocketed remains of the ship's navigator sickened him. On another occasion, Lamkin recounted slapping a crying sailor, who was paralyzed by fear. "I remember seeing one boy throwing up," Lamkin added. "He had evidently seen one of the bodies that they had brought down."

Lieutenant Lloyd Painter recalled the deaths of the machine gunners stationed on the bow at the start of the attack as he frantically tried to warn them of the approaching fighters over the sound-powered phone. "I still had the phone in my hand," Painter told the court. "I was looking through the porthole when I was trying to contact these two kids, and I saw them both; well, I didn't exactly see them as such. They were blown apart, but I saw the whole area go up in smoke and scattered metal." McGonagle described blood streams on the deck and spotting the body of one of the gunners with "his head nearly completely shot away." Ensign Scott reported that the attack injured so many that the ship ran out of stretchers, forcing men to use blankets and mattresses to haul the injured below.

Dr. Kiepfer described the twenty-eight hours he cared for the wounded while humbly excluding the fact that shrapnel had lacerated his stomach when a rocket hit the sick bay. He recalled his insertion of a chest tube in one sailor with a collapsed lung and explained how he slipped his finger inside another sailor's chest wall to drain the blood. He also told of diluting penicillin with sterile water to make sure the ship's meager supply lasted. The doctor described in detail his surgery on Gary Blanchard, aided by Tom Van Cleave and others.

Testimony revealed the crippling damage to the *Liberty*. Rockets and cannons shredded interior staterooms. Firefighting water flooded others. Rounds sliced through every uniform hanging in George Golden's closet and even blasted his shoes stored in a drawer while saltwater ruined his $219 tape recorder. The torpedo not only split open the side of the *Liberty*, but also destroyed the ship's steering system, blew open the safe in Damage Control Central, and even froze clocks. A tally of the shell holes, included as exhibit 33, revealed 821 blast holes, including 164 in the bridge and smokestack. Damage control crews didn't bother to count machine gun and shrapnel holes, which were "innumerable." So extensive was the damage that repairs to the ship and order and replacement of equipment could take a year and cost up to $12 million, enough money to operate, feed, and staff the spy ship for nearly five years.

The court members questioned whether any of the men in the torpedoed spaces might have drowned. Those who helped recover the bodies testified to finding such horrific injuries that it was doubtful. Kidd, fearing that families might question whether loved ones drowned, inserted the grisly detail into the record. "Wholesale dismemberment resulting in many remains virtually being blown to bits made the recovery particularly difficult and identification even more complicated," Kidd stated. "The degree of dismemberment was so extreme as to be typified by the fact that the last few cases we packed in the small hours this morning contained, for example, a head and an arm in one and similar partial bodies."

The graphic testimony bothered the court members, who also explored the damaged ship. Captain Boston watched men haul bodies out of the torpedoed spaces during a recess. He spotted a sailor emerge from the hole, crying and vomiting after finding a headless body.

These sights, coupled with the testimony of the crew, led Boston to conclude the attack must have been deliberate. The excessive damage, the pre-attack reconnaissance, and the sustained and violent assault ruled out friendly fire, he believed. Alone in a stateroom at night, Kidd confided in his lawyer that he agreed, describing the attackers as "murderous bastards." Boston, who would not voice his opinions publicly for thirty-five years, hinted at his true beliefs in his summation. "After living intimately with the facts of this case for the past week, I have become more and more appalled that such a tragedy should have ever occurred," he told the court. "No matter what conclusions are reached as to the cause of the incident, the horrendous impact of the effect should disturb even the most impassioned."

Despite two days of often-gruesome testimony that would fill 158 pages of transcripts, the court failed to answer the central question: How and why did the attack happen? The Navy had tasked court members to examine all relevant facts. The final transcript, however, revealed a shallow investigation, plagued by myriad disagreements between the captain and his crew. Reconstructing the assault had proved challenging. No one wrote in the quartermaster's notebook for fifty-one minutes during the most intense part of the attack. The bloodstained log jumped from the arrival of Ensign Patrick O'Malley on the bridge at 1:55 P.M. to Lucas's identification of one of the torpedo boat's hull numbers at 2:46 P.M. Thirty-four men had either been killed or mortally wounded in the interim. The court recognized this weakness. After the first day of testimony, it asked McGonagle to gather with his officers and crew and assemble a concrete timeline to present to the court the next day. Even then the men's testimony clashed.

McGonagle testified that he observed the first reconnaissance flight at 10:30 A.M. followed by others at roughly half-hour intervals. Other witnesses told the court that reconnaissance flights began as early as 5:15 A.M. and that planes reconned the ship at least eight times, a figure the State Department later adopted in its report. The skipper also said that the fighter jet attack lasted only five to six minutes, much less time than his men recalled. Painter, who testified immediately after McGonagle, told the court that the jets pounded the ship for at least twenty minutes. Chief Petty Officer Harold Thompson also testified that the air attack lasted between twenty minutes and a half hour. Other witnesses including Lucas, Lamkin, and Kiepfer described fighting fires, rescuing the injured, and even performing surgery as the fighters strafed the *Liberty*, impossible actions to accomplish in the brief time the skipper recalled.

The skipper also stated that he never issued an order to prepare to abandon ship. His men again refuted him. Painter recalled the order and said he ran out on deck to prepare liferafts for the wounded. Scott testified that he torched confidential messages and publications in a wastebasket. Kiepfer mobilized an evacuation of the wounded from the mess deck and Chief Petty Officer Wayne Smith burned radio authentication codes. Petty Officer 2nd Class Charles Cocnavitch, whose testimony was not included in the transcript, told Kidd that he heard the order passed over the sound-powered phones. Someone eventually produced a handwritten copy of the *Liberty*'s Combat Information Center log—entered as exhibit 14—showing that at 2:33 P.M. the demolition bill was set, an order that often means to destroy classified materials, set explosive charges, and open valves to scuttle a ship.

McGonagle and Lucas, who stood just feet apart during much of the attack, offered contradictory views on vital events. McGonagle testified that Francis Brown, who was on the helm during the attack, died before the torpedo strike. Lucas took Brown's place at the helm upon his death. He told the court that Brown died after the torpedo hit as the patrol boats strafed the ship with cannons and machine guns. Cocnavitch pulled Brown's body off the bridge seconds after he was killed. Though not asked by the court, Cocnavitch later confirmed Lucas's account. Lucas and the skipper also clashed on the issue of when the Israelis signaled the *Liberty*. McGonagle testified that he believed the signaling occurred before the torpedo attack. Lucas again disagreed. "This was definitely after the torpedo attack," he told the court.

"The flashing lights from the boats were after the torpedo attack?" court members pressed.

"Yes," Lucas answered. "That is correct."

The officers also differed on the *Liberty*'s machine gunning of the torpedo boats. McGonagle testified that a *Liberty* sailor accurately fired on the Israeli boats and that the Israelis likely believed the spy ship had fired on them. Lucas told the court that he investigated the gunfire and found only ammunition cooking off in a blaze. Thompson also testified that ammunition exploded in the fire. Had the court called Dale Larkins, its members would have heard another witness with a clear view of the bridge's guntub fire. Larkins, who likely fired the *Liberty*'s only effective defensive round during the entire assault, watched the machine gun ammunition cook off. The mounted gun barrel never rose. "The barrel basically was laying on the edge of the tub," Larkins recalled. "I'm sure there wasn't anybody there."

The crewmembers even painted opposing pictures of McGonagle during the attack and immediate aftermath. Lucas testified that while the skipper bled profusely, he continued to bark orders and "insisted on being everywhere that he could." Painter said one of the quarter-masters summoned him to the bridge immediately after the attack to take over for the injured skipper. He arrived to find McGonagle unconscious on a stretcher, his leg soaked with blood. Painter photographed the captain on his back, life jacket cinched tightly around him, bathed in sunlight with his eyes closed, a photo the court never saw. Kiepfer's testimony corroborated Painter. The doctor told the court that shortly after the attack he found the captain sweating, having difficulty standing, and showing excessive anxiety, all signs of shock.

Though it is common for witnesses to remember events differently, none of these significant discrepancies prompted the court to recall any of the officers or crewmembers other than McGonagle. Even with the skipper the court members failed to address any of the contradictions. Rather the court asked McGonagle to submit various records, including a timeline of the attack, a breakdown of the projectile hits, and the chart that showed the *Liberty*'s projected track. Kidd appeared more interested in McGonagle's account of guiding the ship that night by the North Star. He asked the skipper to recount the story as the court members listened in silence. The court's final report relied almost exclusively on the testimony of McGonagle, who according to some of his men had passed out from blood loss and shock.

Many of the officers said the court appeared afraid of uncovering information that might prove the Israelis deliberately targeted the *Liberty*. Scott photographed the first reconnaissance flight at dawn the morning of the attack. He believed he gave the court a "critical piece of information" that showed Israel had detected the *Liberty* almost nine hours before the attack. The court appeared uninterested, asking instead whether Scott had attended damage control school and whether he found it useful. The court's final report dismissed his testimony, stating that reconnaissance flights began hours later than he said. Declassified Israeli records show the plane Scott observed was in fact the reconnaissance flight that first identified the *Liberty*. "It was all perfunctory," Scott later said of the court's interview. "The questioning was not probing or in-depth. It was all superficial."

Other officers who testified described the court as "shallow," "cursory," and focused on "process rather than product." The transcript shows that some of the witnesses testified for only a few minutes, if even that long. The court asked Golden, the *Liberty*'s chief engineer, only thirteen questions, including such basic information as his name, how many years he had served in the Navy, and the cost of his waterlogged tape recorder. Court members asked Lamkin, who fought fires on deck as the planes strafed the ship, just eleven questions and Thompson only eight, ranging from whether he had attended damage control school to whether he was aware that a court had been convened to examine the attack. Mac Watson, another of the *Liberty*'s officers, was asked only five questions.

The court ignored other important details. No one followed up on Painter's testimony that the *Liberty* sailed seventeen and a half miles from shore moments before the attack, a fact that clearly established that the *Liberty* was in international waters and well beyond the territorial limits of either Israel or Egypt. Another fact absent from the discussion was that the *Liberty*, attacked off the coast of Egypt, never approached within thirty-eight miles of the Israeli coast. The court also failed to explore the testimonies of Wayne Smith or Lamkin that the attackers jammed the *Liberty*'s communications, indicating possible foreknowledge of the ship's identity. James Halman, the radioman who made the calls for help, was available to testify, but the court never summoned him. The jamming convinced Halman that the Israelis knew the *Liberty* was an American ship.

Other crewmembers said the court deleted testimony unfavorable to Israel and the Navy from its published report. Lucas submitted a container of unburned napalm jelly that he scraped off the front of the *Liberty*'s superstructure after the attack. Nowhere in the court's printed transcript or in any of its findings is that mentioned, though court members did ask the ship's doctor if he treated any napalm burns. Painter's testimony that the torpedo boats machine gunned the life rafts—witnessed by other crewmembers and recalled years later by Captain Boston—also is absent from the court's final transcript. Cocnavitch said he was ordered to report to the wardroom, sworn in, and asked about the abandon ship order he heard passed over the sound-powered phones. None of the radarman's testimony appears in the court's final record, nor is Cocnavitch even listed as a witness.

More importantly, the court failed to challenge Israel's story despite a directive "to inquire into all the pertinent facts and circumstances leading to and connected with the armed attack." The American government never forced Israel to produce its pilots, torpedo boat skippers, or commanders to testify. Likewise, the government never demanded that Israel submit its ship logs, flight books, or recordings of its pilot communications, all reasonable requests between allied nations. The only evidence submitted on Israel's behalf were telegrams from Ernest Castle, the American naval attaché in Tel Aviv. These telegrams repeated Israel's claim that the *Liberty* was unmarked, acted suspiciously, and resembled an Egyptian cargo ship a fraction of the *Liberty*'s size. When shown one of these messages, McGonagle refuted it.

Kidd confessed years later that his superiors had handicapped the investigation. Israel had been off-limits. "Our Navy's Inquiry was tasked to paint but one part of the picture," the admiral wrote in a letter to one of the *Liberty*'s officers. "Any dealings with any other Nation or any like sources beyond our own people were precluded." Inside the *Liberty*'s wardroom that picture became clear to the testifying officers. Many believed that the court was more interested in whether the *Liberty* and its crew had erred than what actually prompted the attack. "The court didn't seem interested at all in who attacked us and why," recalled Painter, who described the court as a "sham." "It was all about whether we had done something wrong."

Despite contradictions in testimony, the witnesses agreed on one fact: the *Liberty* flew the American flag. Scott testified that he looked up at dawn to check the wind direction and saw the flag flying. Painter told the court he observed the flag later that morning and again right after the torpedo attack as he prepared life rafts in response to the abandon-ship order. Golden recalled that after lunch, while sunbathing with McGonagle, he observed two recon flights circle the ship. When the latter plane buzzed the *Liberty*'s smokestack, Golden couldn't help but notice the flag.

"Was it extended?" the court's lawyer asked.

"Yes, sir," he replied. "There was a slight breeze blowing."

"And it was standing out where it could be seen?" the court pressed.

"Yes, sir," he answered. "Not completely the full length, but it was standing out."

Watson also told the court he saw the flag flying during lunch that afternoon. Like Golden, the young officer noted the wind was blowing while he tracked a recon flight as it zoomed over the ship's radar mast.

"Extended?" the court asked.

"Yes, sir," Watson replied.

Wayne Smith testified that during the attack he sprinted from the main radio room to the transmitter room in part so that he personally could check to make sure the flag was hoisted. Lucas recounted spotting it on the mast during the attack. Even McGonagle, whose testimony differed from his men on other points, agreed with his crew that the *Liberty* flew the American flag. The skipper testified that when he first observed the torpedo boats approaching from about fifteen miles away—long before the torpedo hit the ship—he ordered the signalman to hoist the *Liberty*'s largest flag.

Jim O'Connor, who was en route to a military hospital in Germany to have his blasted kidney removed when the inquiry took place, later provided one of the clearest accounts of the flag at the start of the attack. He told officials at the NSA that an explosion knocked him to the deck of the flying bridge during the first strafing run. When he fell, he looked up to check the flag. "That question was in my mind," O'Connor recalled. "The American flag was up there and it was flying."

"It was not obscured by any smoke or any of that stuff?" NSA officials asked.

"No," O'Connor replied. "The flag was ahead of where the smoke stack was. We hadn't taken that many hits at that point."

"And there was enough wind to have it—"

"It was standing straight up."

CHAPTER 13

Thursday and Friday were the longest days we have experienced.

—GEORGE SCOTT, LETTER TO HIS SON,
ENSIGN JOHN SCOTT

Less than a week after the attack *Newsweek* broke the story that many senior Washington officials believed Israel had deliberately targeted the *Liberty*. President Johnson was the magazine's source. The 178-word article headlined "Sinking the *Liberty*: Accident or Design?" observed that the assault left a "wake of bitterness and political charges of the most serious sort." Previous speculation about the mission vanished. The article defined the *Liberty* as a spy ship tasked to intercept battle-field messages. "One top-level theory holds," *Newsweek* reported, "that someone in the Israeli armed forces ordered the *Liberty* sunk because he suspected it had taken down messages showing that Israel started the fighting. (A Pentagon official has already tried to shoot down the Israeli claim of 'pilot error.') Not everyone in Washington is buying this theory, but some top Administration officials will not be satisfied until fuller and more convincing explanations of the attack on a clearly marked ship in international waters are forthcoming."

Similar articles followed in other newspapers and magazines. *U.S. News & World Report* declared that "questions outnumbered answers" and "the full story may never be made public." "Pending investigations, the U.S. Government's position is that it has accepted the Israeli apology but rejected the explanation that the attack was entirely acci-

190

dental," the magazine wrote. "Well-informed officials feel the attack was too deliberate to have been made without a key decision by some Israeli officer." *Life* magazine echoed the skepticism, calling the *Liberty* an "unexplained casualty" in a two-page article that included a photograph of sailors offloading the injured from a helicopter on the deck of the carrier *America*. "A storm of controversy about the incident immediately swelled," the magazine reported. "As the listing vessel headed for repairs, the only indisputable facts about the episode were the grim casualty figures."

Newspaper editorials berated Israel and accused the American government of lying. "When the essentials of an espionage operation have been exposed, continued secrecy or obfuscation only serves to plant more seeds of doubt," wrote the *Washington Post*. "The insinuations, carefully circulated by Pentagon officials, that the attack was deliberate and conscious only compound the impression of a shabby cover-up." Syndicated columnists Drew Pearson and Jack Anderson urged Congress to investigate the "puzzling circumstances." "The facts are that the *Liberty* was seen by the Israelis off the Egyptian coast at dawn. They did not attack until 2:30 P.M. This gave them ample time to ascertain the identity of the ship," the journalists wrote in a joint column. "Furthermore, a coordinated attack by both torpedo boats and airplanes means that the action was planned in advance."

The families of *Liberty* sailors raised some of the same questions in telephone calls and letters to the men in Malta. Many of the wives and parents had received detailed accounts from loved ones that discussed Israel's reconnaissance of the ship, the efficiency of the attack, and the crew's doubts that it was an accident. Some family members even speculated about possible motives. In a two-page letter to her son, Ruth Scott questioned whether America's failure to support Israel in the 1956 Suez Canal crisis might have been a factor in the attack. "No one can figure out why the Israelis did it," she wrote. "Could they have thought you were giving information to the Arabs? Everything they struck they did swiftly and that is why they won so easily. I don't know. They struck you, apologized to Johnson before our planes got to you. I would like to know what was behind all this."

Many of the *Liberty*'s officers, frustrated by the court's shallow probe, feared the government planned to downplay the attack. George Golden disobeyed orders and talked to the Associated Press. The *Liberty*'s chief engineer told a reporter in a Malta bar that the assault's duration and intensity convinced senior crewmen the attack was intentional. The reporter wrote a story attributed to an unnamed sailor and it appeared in newspapers nationwide. "We were flying the Stars and Stripes and it's absolutely impossible that they shouldn't know who we were," the reporter quoted his source. "This was a deliberate and planned attack and the remarkable thing about it was the accuracy of their air fire." The Navy in response ordered McGonagle to silence his men: "Because other reporters may attempt to follow up, you may feel it appropriate to repeat previous admonition to your fine crew to refrain from speaking about matters under investigation."

These powerful allegations failed to gain the expected traction throughout the mainstream press. More in-depth news reports analyzing the Jewish state's victory over its Arab neighbors overshadowed the mounting press speculation about the *Liberty*. In the same issue of *Life* magazine that raised concerns about the *Liberty*, a grinning Israeli sailor cooling off in the Suez Canal appeared on the cover under the headline "Wrap-up of the Astounding War." Israeli defense minister Moshe Dayan graced *Newsweek*'s cover while the magazine's one-paragraph article questioning the *Liberty* attack ran on page 21. *Time* magazine, which ignored the questions raised by its competitors, also featured on its cover the famed Israeli general with his signature black eye patch, set against the backdrop of the burning desert.

Other media outlets discounted the charges or published articles based on Defense Department spin. Such stories often exonerated Israel. "Former Navy skippers in the Pentagon were frank to forgive the Israelis for not seeing or not believing the identity of the *Liberty*, and then attacking it," wrote George Wilson in the *Washington Post*. Pentagon officials told the Associated Press that the attackers likely were unfamiliar with the *Liberty*'s design, though hundreds of identical vessels had sailed for decades. "The Israelis may have thought the *Liberty* was an Egyptian ship masquerading as a U.S. ship," reported Seymour Hersh. "Officers noted that such deceits are as old as sea warfare."

A few editorials and columns blamed the United States. Questions included whether the *Liberty* might have accomplished its mission from a safer distance and was the intelligence gathered worth the risk to the ship and crew. One unnamed Pentagon official sniped at McGonagle for steaming too close to a war zone: "Couldn't that skipper have at least gotten over the horizon?" Syndicated columnist David Lawrence challenged whether the Navy could have done more to make the *Liberty*'s identity recognizable. "Greater precautions should have been taken by spreading out the American flag on the deck or painting it on the side, so that there could be no chance of mistaking the identity of the ship either from the air or the surface," Lawrence wrote. "There is always the possibility that, even if the American flag had been flown conspicuously, the resemblance to the Egyptian ship could have misled the Israeli airmen into believing the whole thing was merely a ruse to protect an enemy vessel."

The news coverage of the attack ranged widely in point of view. Some magazines and newspapers appeared on a crusade while others took a more tempered stand and a few chose to ignore it. Some of the same media outlets that questioned the assault on the editorial pages published news articles that contradicted the paper's position. One of the best examples that illustrated this inconsistency appeared in the *New York Times*. The newspaper printed the Associated Press story that quoted the unnamed Golden. The same day it published a Reuters dispatch that contradicted the story and claimed the *Liberty*'s officers "rejected the idea that the attack was deliberate." *Liberty*'s officers concluded that the Navy was behind the Reuters three-paragraph story. The *Times* neither investigated nor explained the inconsistency, but rather chose to run the opposing stories alongside each other.

The waffling news coverage likely confounded some readers and made it easy for Congress to ignore the *Liberty*. Some lawmakers questioned the attack in closed-door sessions, including members of the Senate Foreign Relations Committee. But the *Congressional Record* shows that most elected leaders said little or nothing in public. Many chose to congratulate Israel on its victory—congratulations that at times bordered on fawning—rather than press for answers about the *Liberty*. Democratic representative Wayne Hays of Ohio quipped that the United States should trade four hundred fighter jets for Moshe

Dayan. One of his colleagues proposed the United States unload defense secretary Robert McNamara in the trade. Other lawmakers urged the United States to back Israel in peace negotiations, halt foreign aid to Egypt, and provide emergency economic help for the Jewish state.

The same day *Liberty* sailors sifted through the tangled debris of what was once the National Security Agency's hub, Representative Jonathan Bingham of New York proposed America lift the travel ban to Israel so tourists might pump money into the economy. "Israel is suffering economic stresses and strains brought about by the original Arab aggression, and sorely needs the foreign exchange which visitors from the United States can bring," the Democrat urged. "I hope that the State Department will move quickly and take the action now." Hours after *Liberty* sailors packed the last of the dead into body bags, Republican representative Seymour Halpern of New York suggested that the United States relocate its embassy from Tel Aviv to Jerusalem and called for an emergency economic aid plan for Israel. "We can yet redeem our pledges to Israel," he argued. "What we did, or failed to do, is behind us. We now have the opportunity to fulfill our commitment to Israel by standing up for Israel's rights in the peace settlement to come."

Ambassador Avraham Harman pored over the latest news reports in his office at the Israeli Embassy just off Massachusetts Avenue, set amid the tree-lined streets and townhouses in one of northwest Washington's most affluent neighborhoods. Harman was concerned. Newspapers quoted injured sailors and published excerpts from the letters of others detailing the horror of the attack. Some of the nation's most prestigious media outlets reported that American leaders believed Israeli pilots and torpedo boat skippers had deliberately targeted the *Liberty*. These stories represented a stark change from days earlier when the press and administration had appeared satisfied that the attack was a tragic error. Some newspaper editorials now accused Washington of a cover-up, criticized elected leaders for settling for Israel's apology, and called for a congressional investigation. Letters to newspaper editorial pages, which the ambassador read, captured the hostility of the American public. Grieving families soon would file into cemeteries to bury the dead. The attack, as Harman's deputy observed, contained "very dangerous elements for us."

The ambassador's concern turned to anger after Israeli diplomats discovered that President Johnson was *Newsweek*'s anonymous source. Twenty-four hours after the president met with reporter Charles Roberts in his private lounge, a "very reliable journalistic source" tipped off Israeli officials to the details of the briefing. The embassy dashed off an urgent message that Johnson claimed Israel had "carried out a deliberate attack because the *Liberty* had intentionally engaged in electronic espionage." Diplomats learned that information at a State Department background briefing the next day was "presented pretty much the same way."

Ephraim Evron, the Israeli Embassy's second in command, accused the administration of politicizing the *Liberty*. He wrote in a confidential memo that the news leaks were designed to dampen enthusiasm for Israel that only days earlier had sparked thousands to rally in American streets and raised millions in donations. If the administration could marginalize Israel's political influence it would have greater freedom to take positions contrary to Israeli interests, dangerous ground for the Jewish state as it prepared to negotiate a peace deal that would involve controversial issues, such as territorial gains and refugees. "We can assume that the US Department of State and the White House are both party to this decision, each for its own reasons. The US Department of State, and especially Rusk, who had tried throughout the crisis to create the impression of not identifying with us, are attempting to use the incident to create a bridge to the Arab countries," Evron wrote. "The President has been showing in the past few days special sensitivity and dissatisfaction with respect to Jewish pressures on him. He thinks that an information-based treatment of the matter of the ship in the aforesaid manner will lead to weakening of the pro-Israeli pressure that envelopes many circles, even outside the Jewish public."

The Israeli Embassy now countered with its own spin campaign. "We are facing a clear and deliberate attempt to turn public opinion against us," Evron cabled Jerusalem. "Our informative process must avoid confrontation with the United States Government, since it is clear that the American public, if faced with a direct argument, will accept its government's version." Silencing President Johnson was the top priority. Evron suggested the embassy remind the president "of the dangers facing him personally if the public learns that he was party to the distribution of the story that is on the verge of being blood libel." The embassy turned to Supreme Court justice Abe Fortas, a close friend of Johnson's, and Washington lawyer David Ginsburg—referred to in Israeli documents as "Ilan" and "Harari," respectively—for advice and to help pressure the president. Fortas and Ginsburg urged the embassy to publicly propose a joint U.S.-Israeli commission to investigate the attack. America would reject the proposal, because that would expose the *Liberty*'s officers to interrogation by Israel. But diplomats recognized that even the rejection would "improve our position in public opinion" as Israel would appear more cooperative and open than America.

Embassy staffers hammered the media to kill critical stories and slant others in favor of Israel. Before *Newsweek*'s story appeared, embassy spokesman Dan Patir had reviewed an advance copy of the article. He successfully pressured editors to run a "toned down" version. Editors added a question mark to the headline and deleted the words "deliberate attack." The magazine also killed an accompanying commentary that said the leak was designed to free American leaders from pro-Israel pressure. When *Newsweek*'s story broke, embassy officials pounced, labeling the allegations "malicious" in competing newspapers. "Such stories are untrue and without foundation whatever," an unnamed embassy spokesman told reporters. "It was an unfortunate and tragic accident which occurred in an area where fierce land and air fighting took place in recent days." Patir derailed another story about a House Armed Services Committee member under pressure from constituents to launch a congressional investigation: "We have made sure that the journalistic source will refrain from writing about this for now." Israel's spin frustrated American officials, who increasingly bore the media's hostility. Phil Goulding later accused Israel of "floating one self-serving rumor after another" with the mission "to make this tragedy the fault of the United States instead of the fault of the Israeli government."

Rumors evolved into deception. Israeli officials told the press that the day the war began, the Jewish state contacted the American Embassy in Tel Aviv and asked if the United States planned to operate any ships off the Sinai Peninsula in the eastern Mediterranean. Israel claimed that the American Embassy failed to answer, so it was left to assume that no American ships steamed nearby. The implication was clear: America was to blame. When the story appeared in the *Washington Post*, Rusk fumed. The only request Israel had made about American ships came *after* its forces torpedoed the *Liberty*. The secretary of state telegrammed the American Embassy in Tel Aviv, demanding "urgent confirmation" that no prior inquiry was made. Ambassador Walworth Barbour confirmed Israel's story was bogus. "No request for info on U.S. ships operating off Sinai was made until after *Liberty* incident," Barbour cabled back. "Had Israelis made such an inquiry it would have been forwarded immediately to the chief of naval operations and other high naval commands and repeated to dept."

Israel's problems magnified. "A personal friend in the US Department of State just told me that they have proof that we attacked the ship intentionally, and that the purpose was to remove an independent American intelligence source, and force them to depend only on information we are feeding them," Evron cabled Jerusalem. "This man warned me, as a friend, against trouble that we might have in this case." The tip wasn't isolated. Arthur Goldberg, the American ambassador to the United Nations, confided in Harman that the United States had intercepted the communications of Israeli pilots identifying the ship as American. Democratic fund-raiser Abe Feinberg—code-named "Hamlet" in Israeli telegrams—told Evron that the United States had "clear proof that at a certain stage the pilot had discovered the identity of the ship and had still continued the attack." Fortas told the ambassador that many administration officials believed a local commander ordered the attack, fearing the spy ship eavesdropped on "Israeli combat orders, and that they might reach the enemy." Fortas added "the entire city already knows" Israeli "planes circled above the ship a long time before the attack."

But Israeli diplomats continued their defense. Harman told Fortas that he was certain no local commander ordered the attack. Even if Israeli planes had circled the *Liberty*, he insisted, the pilots must have misidentified it. Evron cautioned Feinberg that there was "a significant difference between blaming a single pilot and making a public claim that the Israeli Government I repeat that the Israeli Government had initiated the attack intentionally." The charges only intensified. Ginsburg advised Israel to hurry up and finish its investigation into the attack and turn over the results to the American government. Feinberg urged the embassy to halt what he called its "guerrilla war." Goldberg warned Ambassador Harman that the president was furious and that the embassy needed to be "very careful." He told the embassy that the "only chance of getting out of this crisis is to punish someone for negligence." The frantic ambassador cabled his concerns back to Jerusalem. "In light of the serious developments in this matter, it is essential that our inquiry will end within a day or two at the latest," Harman wrote to the Foreign Ministry. "The faster this thing is behind us, the healthier for all of us!"

CHAPTER 14

His loss to the present day Navy and the Navy of the future is incalculable but irrevocable and regrettable.

—COMMANDER WILLIAM MCGONAGLE, CONDOLENCE
LETTER TO THE FAMILY OF LIEUTENANT STEPHEN TOTH

Soon after the *Liberty* docked in Malta, Commander William McGon-agle checked into the Hotel Phoenicia, a World War II–era hotel set amid acres of manicured gardens overlooking the harbor. His wounded leg still healing, the skipper settled into a spacious room on an upper floor of the grand hotel that once housed the British Royal Air Force and barely survived the German and Italian bombings during the Siege of Malta. McGonagle closed the shutters, blocking the Mediterranean sun as he stretched out in bed to write letters to the families of his thirty-four dead men.

Repair work on the *Liberty* had prevented concentration. Teams of Maltese shipfitters now hammered from 6 A.M. until 10 P.M. to patch the 821 shell holes. The workers replaced shattered portholes, pried machine gun rounds from the walls, and scraped charred paint. Others cut away bent steel and reengineered the warped and destroyed interior decks. Dave Lucas captured the chaos in a letter to his wife. "Damn, the noise in the office is unbelievable!" he griped. "It sounds like the workmen are right next door hitting the metal beams with a sledge hammer."

A short cab ride from the drydock and an easy stroll to the city's waterfront, the Hotel Phoenicia provided McGonagle a refuge to work and reflect. The skipper asked Patrick O'Malley to help. O'Malley served as the ship's secretary and assistant operations officer. Early in the mission—O'Malley's first after he graduated from Officer Candidate School—McGonagle often berated the junior officer for mundane foul-ups that reflected his inexperience. Now the men worked side by side, skipper and young ensign, sharing one of the military's most difficult tasks.

McGonagle sat up in bed, drafting each letter by hand to the wives, parents, and siblings of the men killed. O'Malley, perched in a chair beside him or on the foot of the bed, reviewed the drafts that he later typed for the skipper to sign. To prepare the letters, McGonagle demanded to know the gruesome details of how each of his men died. He reviewed pages of typed medical records and scribbled notes that charted with clinical precision each sailor's fatal wounds: "Blast injury to brain," "Multiple bullet and shrapnel wounds," "Exsanguination from complete transection of body."

The notes in some cases provided a snapshot of a man's final seconds. Some described the smoke-filled compartment moments before the torpedo hit while others detailed the attacks on the forward machine guns, deck, and the bridge. "When the torpedo exploded, a fragment struck him in the back of the head, fracturing his skull and injuring vital parts of his brain," the medical records noted for one sailor. "He had another similar injury lower on his back, indicating that he was turned away from the explosion, and that he probably never knew, until the moment of his death, what was about to occur."

McGonagle omitted the horrific details in his letters, but recounted what each man was doing at the moment he died. He wrote how one sailor had fought a gasoline fire on deck when rocket shrapnel hit him in the chest and face. He praised another man who climbed over the bodies of the dead to try to operate one of the *Liberty*'s machine guns before he too was killed. McGonagle told the parents of Francis Brown that their son had refused to abandon his post at the helm, though it was "engulfed in flames." Whenever possible, McGonagle noted death was "instantaneous."

The torpedo had vaporized some of the men and the remains of a few drifted out of the hole as the ship steamed to Malta. McGonagle had to explain this difficult fact to families who expected to bury loved ones. "It is with profound regret that your husband's body was lost at sea and is unrecoverable or has not yet been positively identified. Everything possible was done to recover those who drifted away from the ship through the enormous torpedo hole and no effort is being spared to identify your husband as one of the three as yet unidentified remains," he wrote to the wife of one man. "It is a painstaking and time consuming task, but will be completed as soon as possible."

In the case of Gary Blanchard, McGonagle told his family that shrapnel had pierced his back and ruptured his liver and right kidney. He described Dr. Kiepfer's middle-of-the-night surgery. "He was given copious fluids and two units of whole blood as a transfusion to arrest the shock. There was no lack of volunteers to provide the blood he so desperately needed. Unfortunately his condition continued to deteriorate and no effort was spared to save his life," the skipper wrote. "You will be grateful to know he was spared pain and suffering during this entire period."

McGonagle and O'Malley worked alone for days in the darkened room at the hotel, immune from the sounds of vacationing guests who strolled the gardens and the hallways. The letters proved emotionally taxing. At times, McGonagle wept. During breaks, the skipper shared his experiences in the Korean War with O'Malley. He described for the young ensign the excitement he had felt as a gunnery officer, firing on enemy shore batteries from the deck of a minesweeper. The rush of combat had thrilled him. O'Malley soaked it up. The earlier friction between the men vanished.

"I was wrong about you," McGonagle confessed. "I apologize for how I treated you."

"Forget it," O'Malley told his skipper. "It's no big deal."

McGonagle tried to add a personal touch to each letter whenever possible, though with a crew of nearly three hundred, coupled with his reserved personality, he knew few of them well. The skipper referred to his men by nicknames—Ike, Dick, and Smitty, for example—and warmly recalled attributes that might comfort the families. He described one sailor's "agile mind and sparkling manner." Another, he wrote, had "contagious enthusiasm." McGonagle complimented the "outstanding pride" one sailor took in the appearance of the mess deck and commended another for being a "competent caterer." He wrote that one of his young officers "unselfishly let the praise shower down" on his men.

The skipper was careful to use only information approved by the Pentagon to describe the attack. But he refused to minimize the violence perpetrated upon his men or their valor in combating it. One of the earliest letters he wrote was to Weetie Armstrong, wife of the *Liberty*'s executive officer, Philip Armstrong, Jr. Despite differences in leadership, education, and personality, McGonagle had respected his second in command. "Words alone cannot express my personal anguish at the untimeliness of his death and the great burden it places on you," McGonagle began. "My thoughts and prayers are with you at this time of need and sorrow."

McGonagle described Armstrong's effort to knock burning gasoline drums overboard, which resulted in his death. "He had several bones broken, including three in his right leg and two in his left. He lived for several hours after the attack and was given morphine so he would be in no pain. Despite herculean efforts by Dr. Kiepfer and others to tend his wounds and restore his strength, he passed away," McGonagle wrote. "Apparently the strain and shock induced a fatal heart attack." The skipper wrote that the men loved Armstrong, who left behind five small children. "You and the children have every right to be proud of the way Philip performed his duties," McGonagle concluded. "Philip was truly a leader in every sense of the word in our hour of awesome peril."

True to his nature, McGonagle did not ignore the Pentagon's insistence that Israel had proclaimed the attack an accident. But neither did he hold back his defense of his ship or his belief that the *Liberty* had done nothing to provoke the attack. "The ship was in international waters steaming on its peaceful purpose when the unidentified jet fighter aircraft and torpedo boats attacked the ship without warning. Their fire was overwhelmingly accurate and effective. The ship was virtually defenseless against the hail of bombs, rockets, and machine gun fire," McGonagle wrote in each letter. "The Israeli Government has apologized to the United States Government for the tragic mistaken attack on USS *Liberty*. That the ship is still afloat today and has not been required to publish a larger casualty list is a result of the outstanding courage, devotion to duty, and uncommon valor on the part of each officer and man in the crew."

The skipper concluded each letter with an apology for missing the funeral and a promise that the deceased's personal belongings would be collected and returned home soon. He asked family members to take pride in the actions of loved ones and told them to please call on him or his wife if needed. He wrote that he considered himself fortunate and privileged to have known and served with each man. McGonagle, who rarely if ever showed any religious leanings, ended each letter with a sentence of prayer, as illustrated by the one he wrote to the executive officer's wife: "May God in His infinite mercy grant you peace as He shelters and gives Philip rest."

The personalized anguish of McGonagle's letters contrasted with the diplomatic considerations the White House applied to its correspondence. Presidential aides wrote thousands of condolence letters to the families of men killed in Vietnam. The White House would mail approximately ten thousand in 1967 alone, prompting aides to create additional templates. The politically delicate nature of the *Liberty* and the administration's desire to deemphasize the attack presented a challenge for Johnson's staff. The three-paragraph form letter used for Vietnam wouldn't work.

James Cross, the president's senior military aide, whose office prepared the condolence letters, consulted Harry McPherson, Jr., the administration's liaison with the Jewish community. "The attached condolence letters, which have been prepared using basic formats approved for Vietnam war casualties, strike me as inappropriate in this case," Cross wrote in a memo. "Due to the very sensitive nature of the whole Arab-Israeli situation and the circumstances under which these people died, I would ask that you review these drafts and provide me with nine to ten different responses which will adequately deal with this special situation."

McPherson wrote several possible paragraphs that neither mentioned Israel nor touched on the violence of the attack. He instead refocused the spotlight on the president's push for peace in the Middle East and how the *Liberty*'s sailors had died for that cause. "It is my fervent hope that from the ashes of war in the Middle East may rise a new opportunity for peace," McPherson suggested. "We sought to avert that war. Now that we must help deal with its consequences, we will do whatever is in our power to assure that those who died will have contributed to building a lasting peace."

Malta proved a welcome respite for the officers and crew after the chaos of the attack and the unease of six days at sea in a crippled ship. While Maltese shipfitters tackled repairs, the *Liberty*'s crew handled administrative duties. The deck force unpacked twenty-four new life rafts. Sailors stored the *Liberty*'s machine guns and ammunition below in the ship's magazine. Others swabbed decks, cleaned filters, and inventoried gear. Officers took turns on watch.

Scores of letters arrived daily from as far away as California and Germany as schoolchildren and adults alike requested details of the spy ship whose existence just weeks earlier had been a government secret. Collectors even mailed self-addressed, stamped envelopes, requesting the *Liberty*'s canceling stamp. In response to the massive interest, a Malta print shop created one thousand postcards with a photo of the *Liberty* on the front and the ship's official history on the back.

News trickled in about the injured, many of whom had left the aircraft carrier *America* for military hospitals in Italy, Germany, and the United States to begin what for some would be months and even years of physical therapy. Sailors with minor injuries returned to the *Liberty* and received warm greetings from shipmates. "All our wounded lived and are doing well," John Scott wrote to his parents. "Ship will be in Malta for another month for refitting. It will be seaworthy—I'll see to that."

With the recovery of the bodies and the cleanup of the research spaces complete, the *Liberty*'s intelligence operators had no more work. The attack had destroyed all the equipment and ended the mission. Less than a week after arriving in Malta, fifty-nine of the spooks returned to the United States and new assignments. Those left behind felt their absence. "Almost all of the Research people are gone now," one of the officers observed in a letter. "The ship is emptier than I've ever seen it."

The remaining sailors mustered each morning for head count and announcements. Afternoons were free. Many explored the cobblestone streets, shops, and historic forts of Malta. Others visited catacombs, caverns, and Roman ruins. Sahara Desert winds kept the days warm and dry, prompting men to rent boats and motor out to desolate coves. Using fins, masks, and snorkels, sailors explored shipwrecks in the clear Mediterranean waters. Beer and wine flowed. Crewmembers challenged North Atlantic Treaty Organization soldiers to a softball game one afternoon. The *Liberty* team throttled them 27–7.

Scott and Painter befriended a cab driver named Shortly, who also owned a bar. Shortly waited each afternoon at the port's entrance to drive the officers to his bar, where he fired up the jukebox free of charge. The officers listened to Elvis and the Beatles and downed cold Budweiser that Shortly ordered specially for them. Dr. Kiepfer rented a beachfront apartment, where he hosted parties until the early morning hours for the *Liberty*'s officers and the nurses he befriended at the British Royal Navy base.

The ship's projector showed grainy movies on the walls of the mess decks other nights, occasionally interrupted by the banging of repairmen. Sailors watched James Stewart's western *Night Passage*, Henry Fonda's nuclear thriller *Fail-Safe,* and Frank Sinatra's classic heist film *Assault on a Queen.* The *Liberty* operated on shore power in drydock that was weaker than the power the ship's engineering plant produced. As a result, the actors' voices were unusually deep, prompting snickers from the men.

The initial euphoria of having survived soon waned. "I just finished counseling one of my seamen. He's down in the dumps and wants to get married to a British girl that he's known for two nights. His gal in the States hasn't written to him in quite a while. He's all of 19 years old," Lucas wrote to his wife back home in Virginia Beach. "He's just depressed and rightly so. What we went through last week was enough to depress anybody. The need for companionship right now is strong."

Many of the men wrestled with grief and loneliness. Don Pageler wrote a postcard to his parents in Kansas that captured the shock many felt. "I'm O.K. Just a few bruises and cuts. I still can't believe it happened. Seems like a dream," he wrote. "Right now all I want to do is come home and see everyone." Dale Larkins echoed Pageler. "Please don't worry any as I am all right," he assured his parents in Nebraska. "The only hurt I have is inside and only time will let me forget."

Family members noted the sadness. "I guess the delayed grief has set in now for the ones who didn't make it. Our first reaction was of joy that you were unhurt and now we are thinking of the others and their families," Ruth Scott wrote to her son. "This sounds silly, but just seeing your handwriting again was proof that you were really all right!" She speculated in another letter that the *Liberty* "must be a sad place for you all." "It seems that a week ago's events couldn't have really happened and yet I think I have some scars. I guess you appreciate everything now," she wrote. "It is a strange world. But isn't it nice to be still in it? I feel that you are indestructible now."

Some of the men experienced appreciation of what it meant to survive, as one sailor noted in a letter: "it's still a great joy to get up in the morning." A British naval officer and his wife invited Patrick O'Malley to the beach one afternoon. O'Malley swam, relaxed, and flirted with a young woman the couple had invited as a blind date for him. The young officer plopped down in the sand and felt the sun on his shoulders. The sounds of other beachgoers swirled around him and for a moment he felt the world pause. O'Malley realized then the awful tragedy he had somehow escaped. "I remember just sitting on the beach and feeling the warmth of the sun on my back and being alive," he later recalled. "I was just so grateful."

Sadness and loneliness erupted in other ways, including fights. Scott, Lucas, and Painter stumbled across an altercation in Valletta one night after dinner. A Maltese man shouted at a *Liberty* sailor in the street. The man charged the sailor, who punched him. Shore patrol and the police soon arrived. Scott drafted a handwritten memo about it for McGonagle. Sailors wrecked a bar later that same night. Lucas described the frustration many felt in a letter. "It's just not right for me to be lounging around like this, but if I didn't I'd go buggy," he wrote.

"It's hard to work, it's hard to relax, it's hard to do anything but think about coming home."

The attack affected everyone, including McGonagle. The rigid skipper, who rarely fraternized with his men, softened. He bought his officers drinks and ignored their long hair and late nights. "The Capt. has changed quite a bit. He is much more relaxed than I've ever seen him," Lucas observed. "He's calling almost all of the officers by their first names." McGonagle too longed for home. In a letter the skipper praised his eight-year-old son for helping his mother. He assured him he would be home soon and planned to take the family on vacation to Florida. "Sure hope we will be able to wrent [sic] a boat sometime after I get home," McGonagle wrote. "Hope you have been winning lots of ball games. The season will probably be over before I get home, but maybe next year I'll be able to see you play more. Bet you are looking forward to camp arn't [sic] you? Have lots of fun." He signed it: "Will see you then, son. Love, Dad."

CHAPTER 15

Did 34 Americans die and were 75 wounded because of another Pearl Harbor–type communications fumble?

— *THE PLAIN DEALER*, CLEVELAND

Israeli chief of staff Yitzhak Rabin picked Colonel Ram Ron to investigate the attack. Ron's family had immigrated to Israel from Poland in the mid-1920s when he was still a child. He was not certified as a lawyer or judge; he had served as an army paratrooper and later a military attaché in Washington. Unlike the American court of inquiry, made up of a panel of senior officers aided by a legal staff, Israel's investigation into the *Liberty* attack consisted only of Ron. Some of the witnesses who testified before him—including the head of the Israeli Navy—outranked him, meaning he would have to pass judgment on his superiors. All told, Ron's investigation lasted only four days.

Soon after Ron submitted his report to Rabin, the Israeli Foreign Liaison Office summoned American naval attaché Commander Ernest Castle to review the findings on the evening of June 17. A South Dakota native and graduate of the Naval Academy, Castle had served in the Korean War and later on defense secretary Robert McNamara's staff during the Cuban Missile Crisis. The Navy assigned Castle to the American Embassy in Tel Aviv in 1965. There he worked as a member of a small team of American officers to hunt down intelligence about Israel's military, a job that often involved such basic tasks as counting ships in the harbor or cruising around in a black Ford station wagon with diplomatic plates.

Castle, who had flown out to the battered *Liberty* hours after the assault, had learned little more about the attack in the subsequent days. He relayed apologies and official messages from the Israeli government, but any efforts to investigate the assault proved futile. The only promising lead—a distraught Israeli sailor who initially discussed the torpedo attack with his embassy staffer neighbor—failed to develop when the sailor suddenly declined to answer any more questions. Israel refused to allow Castle to interview any of the pilots or torpedo boat commanders nor was he offered any government records. Castle confessed his frustration in a telegram to Rear Admiral Isaac Kidd, Jr. "From information available," he wrote, "it can be presumed that only the IDF knows with certainty the exact sequence of events that led to the tragic incident."

Rabin aide Lieutenant Colonel Raphael Efrat dictated the report's findings, translating them from Hebrew to English as Castle jotted down the points. Ron's probe concluded that a series of several mistakes led to the attack, beginning with an erroneous report at 11:24 A.M. that an unidentified ship had shelled the Egyptian town of El Arish. The Navy dispatched three torpedo boats from Ashdod at 12:05 P.M. to investigate. One of the torpedo boats radioed at 1:47 P.M. that the unidentified ship steamed toward Egypt's Port Said at thirty knots. Under standing Israeli orders, commanders could consider any ship traveling more than twenty knots in a conflict zone as hostile, since only warships normally sailed at such high speeds. The Navy ordered the torpedo boats to check the speed again. A second report moments later determined that the *Liberty* sailed at twenty-eight knots—nearly twice the *Liberty*'s maximum speed and almost six times its actual speed at the time.

Israeli reconnaissance planes had identified the *Liberty* early that morning, according to Ron, but when the torpedo boats zoomed in hours later, commanders failed to consider that the target might be the *Liberty*. "Even if the unidentified ship were thought to be *Liberty*," Ron concluded, "the fact that she was reported to be making 30 knots would have denied the identification." The torpedo boats called in an air strike. When the boats arrived after the air assault, two officers on separate vessels mistakenly concluded that the *Liberty* was the Egyptian horse and troop transport *El Quseir,* a thirty-seven-year-old ship a fraction the size of the *Liberty* and lacking the spy ship's unusual antennae configuration. The Israeli skippers, believing that the *Liberty* fired at them, launched the torpedo attack.

Ron concluded that each error was either reasonable or outside the scope of his investigation. He refused to examine the source of the erroneous report that an unidentified ship had shelled El Arish, the catalyst for the attack. Ron also ruled that the gross miscalculation of the *Liberty*'s speed was understandable after the head of the Israeli Navy testified "that such estimations require expertise." Ron conceded that torpedo boat officers might have been reckless in identifying the *Liberty* as a warship because "serious doubts" had surfaced about whether the ship was Egyptian. Despite those doubts, Ron determined that the officers' conduct was acceptable because the *Liberty* failed to identify itself, was engulfed in black smoke, and "behaved suspiciously."

The colonel reserved his harshest criticism for the United States, accusing the *Liberty* of inviting the attack. He blasted the American government for failing to alert Israel to the ship's presence and criticized the *Liberty* for steaming near a war zone and outside normal shipping routes. Ron even accused the *Liberty* of hiding its identity by "flying a small flag" and trying to escape once Israeli forces attacked. In the end, Ron exonerated the attackers. "It is concluded clearly and unimpeachably from the evidence and from comparison of war diaries that the attack on USS *Liberty* was not in malice," Ron determined. "There was no criminal negligence and the attack was made by innocent mistake."

Israel's report stunned Castle. Thirty-four Americans had been killed and nearly two hundred others injured. An American ship had been strafed, torpedoed, and almost sunk in an attack that raged for approximately an hour. Israel's investigation had now exonerated all those involved of criminal negligence. The attack, in Ron's words, was merely an "innocent mistake." Castle wrote to his superiors the next day that Efrat must have noted his "appearance of surprise and incredulity" as he read off the report's findings. Efrat asked for Castle's "off the record" opinion when he finished. The attaché pretended not to hear the question and thanked the colonel for his time. Castle wrote that "the burden of diplomacy bore heavily" on him.

Castle challenged Israel's findings in a report to the White House, Pentagon, and State Department, among others. He called Israel's standing order to attack ships sailing more than twenty knots "incomprehensible" and described its justifications for the assault as "mutually contradictory." If the thirty-knot speed of the unidentified ship ruled out the *Liberty*, it also eliminated *El Quseir* since its maximum speed was only fourteen knots, four less than the *Liberty*. Castle also questioned how "a professional Naval officer of the rank of commander could look at *Liberty* and think her a 30 knot ship." Castle also criticized Israel's excuse that thick smoke made it difficult to identify the *Liberty*, since the smoke had resulted from the attack.

Military and civilian leaders in Washington slammed Ron's report soon after Castle's synopsis rattled off the teletype. Walt Rostow complained to a senior diplomat at the Israeli Embassy that the report made "no goddamn sense at all." Captain Mayo Hadden, Jr., in the Navy's Politico-Military Policy Division, prepared a two-page secret analysis. Hadden based his review on his decades of experience in the Navy. The veteran officer, who ultimately would achieve the rank of rear admiral, had served as a fighter pilot during World War II, where he earned three Distinguished Flying Crosses and had eight confirmed shoot-downs of Japanese planes. Hadden later served as a navigator on the aircraft carrier U.S.S. *Yorktown* and shortly before landing at the Pentagon, the two-time Silver Star recipient had commanded the carrier U.S.S. *Hornet*. Ron's report struck Hadden as a cover-up. The senior officer wrote that the "report blandly glosses over" critical areas that he hoped the United States would refute.

The Israeli explanation for the attack conflicted with the fundamentals of Navy logic. Like Castle, Hadden seized on Israel's claim that its forces had determined the *Liberty* sailed at thirty knots. "How could a ship clearly identifiable as a cargo vessel be credited with a speed of 28–30 knots either visually or by Radar?" he questioned. "Why did Israelis, knowing *Liberty* capable of only 18 knots and *El Quseir* capable of only 14 knots, attribute either ship with the 28–30 knot capability?"

Hadden also puzzled over how trained Israeli commanders failed to recognize that the spy ship was unarmed. Likewise, he noted *El Quseir* had only two small cannons largely used for self-defense. Israeli naval officers should have recognized that neither ship could have shelled El Arish. Lastly, Hadden challenged Israel's assertion that the *Liberty* behaved suspiciously. "How?" he asked. Hadden's conclusion: "the Israelis apparently are attempting to whitewash the incident."

Meanwhile, diplomats from the Israeli Embassy pressured the United States for an advance copy of the report of the Navy's court of inquiry, even before American leaders had completed a review of Israel's findings. Ephraim Evron told one senior Pentagon official that Israel wanted to swap reports prior to publication so the two governments could avoid a "public clash" over the facts. Evron noted that the American naval attaché in Tel Aviv already had been given the synopsis of Israel's report. The United States should reciprocate. Evron added that Eugene Rostow had already agreed to such a swap in a recent talk with Harman.

Israel's military attaché simultaneously pressured his contacts. Brigadier General Joseph Geva met with Hadden the same day the captain drafted his secret analysis of Israel's report. Hadden reluctantly agreed to listen to Geva but as a precaution arranged for two officers to witness the meeting. Geva stated that the attackers "had made grievous errors and mistakes." He felt certain Ron's report contained many flaws. To guarantee its accuracy, he asked the United States to share its findings with Israel before making them public. Hadden recorded the fourteen-minute conversation in a confidential memo. "In short, there was no reason for both Courts to go parallel and never meet, when by coordinating they could travel along the same track and using some of the same facts, they could arrive at similar conclusions," the memo shows Geva suggested. "The whole thing could be done covertly."

The Navy balked. Vice Chief of Naval Operations Admiral Horacio Rivero, Jr., ordered the Israeli attaché to direct his request to the State Department. A secret memo to Chief of Naval Operations Admiral David McDonald—labeled "Private for the CNO" and "Original and Only Copy"—outlined Rivero's concerns. Swapping reports before publication offered no advantage to the U.S., but carried considerable risk if news of the exchange leaked. "Such benefit to the United States is not apparent at this moment," the memo stated. "To the contrary, it is clear that exchange prior to publication would have the appearance of US/Israel cooperation to the point of collusion, at least as it might be viewed by, for example, such persons as relatives of *Liberty* crewmen killed and their Congressmen."

Ambassador Harman anxiously awaited the results of Ron's investigation in his office at the Israeli Embassy. Press criticism had intensified and the ambassador feared officials in Jerusalem did not take the attack seriously enough. Hours before Ron's report arrived in Washington, the ambassador outlined his frustrations in a telegram. "The American press has already interviewed injured from the *Liberty*, and these days 34 Americans are being brought for burial in various cities in the United States, and this reaches national and local newspapers, with the public getting the impression that the Israeli attack may have been deliberate since this was an electronic intelligence ship," Harman wrote. "Each of the family and friends has representatives in the Congress, and there's no doubt that the Congress is under great pressure on this subject, including, in the past few days, pressure to initiate a congressional inquiry into the circumstances of this incident."

Harman's concerns spread beyond the press. Reports from some of President Johnson's closest advisers—Arthur Goldberg, Abe Fortas, and Abe Feinberg—suggested America had proof Israel intentionally targeted the *Liberty*. The United States also knew no ships had shelled the coast, Israel's alleged catalyst for the attack. The Pentagon expected to release the report of the Navy's court of inquiry soon. Harman worried the report would prove damning for Israel. "There is no doubt now that these findings will give basis to the assumption that our people had identified or could have identified the ship long before the attack," the ambassador wrote to Jerusalem. "In addition, as far as we know these findings could give basis to the assumption (very possibly, based on recorded conversations) that although our pilots had doubted the identity of the ship in the midst of the operation, they were still ordered to continue the attack that was later followed also by a torpedo attack."

Ron's report failed to satisfy Harman when it arrived. Unlike his American counterparts, who received only the brief synopsis dictated to the American naval attaché, Harman reviewed the full six-page analysis. Even before delving into its findings, the ambassador homed in on what he considered a fatal flaw: How could Israel settle for a one-man inquiry to investigate such a serious attack? He knew Washington would never accept such a report. Harman took the drastic step of cabling his reactions to Jerusalem with the demand that his memo be handed immediately to Prime Minister Levi Eshkol. "I have no doubt that this treatment is inappropriate for a case in which 34 citizens of a friendly country were killed and 75 more were injured. Treatment of the matter at this level itself could anger the US Government and the delegations," he wrote. "Such a grave matter requires an inquiry committee comprising several commanders, as well as a legal expert who is proficient in inquiries."

The ambassador observed that Ron, a former military attaché, lacked the proper credentials to investigate such a severe attack. "We should also take into consideration that Ram Ron is well known in Washington. It is known that he is not an expert on the Air Force and the Navy," he wrote. "There is no chance that the President, the People and the parents will perceive the fact that we have drawn conclusions based on the inquiry of one person, as appropriate response on our behalf to the severity of the matter." Harman singled out other errors. Ron's report failed to include details from the *Liberty*'s logs that the State Department provided Israel. Harman questioned some of the times listed in the report and why Ron neglected to call expert witnesses. More importantly, Ron interviewed only twelve witnesses—none of them the attacking pilots. Harman's conclusion: "Ron's investigation does not withstand the test of analysis and does not envelop all facts."

The ambassador's opinion would prove incredibly astute. Ron's report did not accurately reflect the record in many important respects. For example, Israel told American reporters that the *Liberty* was unmarked and flew no flag. Not until after the jet fighter and torpedo boat attacks ended, Israel maintained, did its forces identify the spy ship. Evidence gathered for Ron's report contradicted these claims. Israel in fact discovered the *Liberty* almost nine hours before the attack when a reconnaissance plane circled the ship at sunrise. An Israeli naval observer on board the flight spotted the *Liberty*'s distinct hull number: GTR-5. The crew radioed the information to ground control. The naval observer reported the same identification in a debriefing soon after landing. Officers looked up the ship's identity. Hours before the attack, Israel knew not only that an American ship sailed nearby, but that it was the spy ship *Liberty*.

The transcript of radio communication between the pilots and air controllers—a copy of which was included as an exhibit in Ron's report—also revealed that moments before the attack began, Israeli forces questioned whether the ship might be American. Approximately two minutes before the pilots first strafed the *Liberty*, a weapons system officer in general headquarters blurted out: "What is it? Americans?"

"Where are Americans?" one of the air controllers asked.

The officer didn't answer. Lieutenant Colonel Shmuel Kislev, the chief air controller at general headquarters in Tel Aviv, queried his counterpart at Air Control Central. "What are you saying?"

"I didn't say," the other replied, his tone implying that he didn't want to know.

Despite the doubts about the ship's identification, Kislev—seated just a few feet away from the commander of the Israeli Air Force—neither halted the impending assault nor ordered his fighters to inspect the ship for identifying markings or a flag as the planes zeroed in on the *Liberty*. His only concern seemed to be whether any antiaircraft fire targeted his fighters.

"Does he have authorization to attack?" one of the controllers asked.

"He does," Kislev snapped.

The pilots blasted the *Liberty*'s bridge, machine guns, and antennae, killing and injuring dozens of stunned sailors, firefighters, and stretcher bearers. Fires erupted on deck and blood soaked the bridge. Kislev ordered a pair of Super Mystère fighters to join the attack with napalm, which he deemed "more efficient."

One of the pilots then instructed another. "We'll come in from the rear. Watch out for the masts," the pilot warned. "I'll come in from her left, you come behind me."

"Authorized to sink her?" asked one of the controllers.

"You can sink her," Kislev ordered, asking a minute later for a report on the pilot's progress in the attack. "Is he screwing her?"

"He's going down on her with napalm all the time," replied another controller.

A pilot joked during the strafing runs that hitting the defenseless ship was easier than shooting down MiGs, a reference to Soviet jet-fighters often used by Arab militaries. Another quipped that to sink the *Liberty* before the torpedo boats arrived would be a "mitzvah." "Oil is spilling out into the water," one pilot exclaimed. "Great! Wonderful! She's burning! She's burning!"

One of the air controllers parroted the pilot. "She's burning!" the controller cried out. "The warship is burning!"

Shortly before planes exhausted all their ammunition, Kislev finally asked the pilots to look for a flag. He then ordered a third pair of fighters to join the attack. One of the pilots buzzed the ship moments later and spotted the *Liberty*'s hull number. He radioed it to ground control, albeit one letter off. The air controller ordered him to disengage.

"What country?" asked one of the air controllers.

"Probably American," replied Kislev.

"What?"

"Probably American."

More than twenty minutes before the fatal torpedo strike that killed twenty-five sailors, Israel's chief air controller conclusively identified the *Liberty* as an American ship. Years later Kislev confessed that when the pilot radioed in the *Liberty*'s hull number, any doubt about the ship's identity vanished. "At that point in time, in my mind, it was an American ship," he admitted in a British television documentary. "I was sure it was an American ship."

Pilots and air controllers were not the only Israelis aware of the *Liberty*'s identity. Ron's report revealed that two naval officers—one in the Navy war room in Haifa, the other a senior liaison in the air force command center in Tel Aviv—testified that before the torpedo attack, both suspected the target was the *Liberty*. Neither officer intervened to halt the attack. Ron's report also revealed that Captain Yitzhak Rahav, the Israeli navy's second in command, dismissed the pilot's report of the *Liberty*'s hull number, even though Egyptian ships are marked with Arabic script, not Roman letters. Rahav's testimony reflected his belief that the *Liberty*'s hull number "was camouflage writing in order to allow an Egyptian ship to enter the area."

The Israeli ambassador in Washington felt the only solution was for someone to go to jail. Despite Ron's exoneration of the attackers, Harman wrote to Jerusalem that the report showed that several parties were guilty of negligence. The ambassador questioned why the identification of the *Liberty* as an American ship that morning was not communicated to the navy's top leadership. He also challenged Ron's attempt to justify the torpedo boat attack by blaming the *Liberty*. What conclusion will the Americans draw from the conversations between the pilots and air controllers? Harman asked. More importantly, he questioned how Ron ruled the attack reasonable "when he determined that two of the officers testified that after the aircraft attack and before the attack of the torpedo ships they feared that the ship being attacked was the *Liberty*. . . . The question is, was what had happened reasonable in accordance with existing IDF procedures," Harman asked. "I doubt this is for us to claim."

The ambassador knew that the *Liberty* attack could have dire implications for U.S.-Israeli relations. Ron's report did not help matters. The ambassador suggested in a telegram to the prime minister and other recipients that the only way Israel might resolve the issue without jeopardizing ties between the countries was to tell the United States that the "military prosecutor insisted on continuing the investigation and deepening it." Harman demanded his government appoint more investigators and legal counsel. The ambassador urged the investigators immediately to begin interviews with the pilots and torpedo boat skippers. "This matter has turned into an open wound that has inherent in it severe dangers to our relations on all levels the friendship of which we'd had until now, friendship that is essential for our status in the US, that is: the President, the Pentagon, public opinion and the intelligence community. Do you understand that the President is also the Supreme Commander of the US forces?" Harman wrote. "Only a thorough handling of the problem and our coming to clear-cut and serious conclusions could make our situation better."

The ambassador reiterated his message the following day in an urgent telegram, again to the prime minister and other senior leaders. "It is difficult to overstate the explosive potential of this issue," Harman wrote. "Even a superficial analysis of Ron's findings provides basis to the assumption that there was negligence and rash action on the part of several parties." Harman repeated his fears that the American naval court of inquiry would show that Israeli forces had identified the *Liberty* hours before the attack. To defuse the situation, Harman again urged Israel to indict the attackers. "In the severe situation created, the only way to soften the results is if we could let the US Government know already today that we intend to prosecute people in connection with this disaster," the ambassador wrote. "This action is the only way to impress both on the US Government and on the public here, that the attack on the ship was not the result of malicious intent of the Israeli Government or authorized IDF parties."

Harman's answer came within hours. Rather than indict the attackers, Chief of Staff Rabin compromised. Israel would hold a judicial inquiry to determine whether the pilots, torpedo boat skippers, or commanders should stand trial on criminal charges. The military planned to announce the inquiry to the press in Tel Aviv at 8 P.M. that evening, June 20. Though not as dramatic a response as Harman might have hoped, the expanded probe at least promised to shield Israel from accusations that it had whitewashed the attack and provided extra time to await the outcome of the U.S. naval court of inquiry, since the United States had refused to share its findings in advance. If pressed about the attack, diplomats could always tell American leaders that the investigation continued and indictments were still possible.

Embassy officials hustled to deliver the news. Ephraim Evron passed Israel's one-paragraph press release to NSC staffer Harold Saunders and asked that he immediately forward it to Rostow and Bundy. The ambassador also sent a copy of the release to Katzenbach and then briefed Eugene Rostow at the State Department, informing him that a military judge would oversee the inquiry. American officials remained convinced that Israel needed to punish the attackers. The announcement of the Israeli inquiry sparked optimism that might still happen. A State Department telegram to the American Embassy in Tel Aviv relayed the news: "Israeli Judge Advocate General now calling judicial inquiry that could bring persons to trial."

NSA deputy director Louis Tordella climbed the steps of the Capitol on the afternoon of June 20 to brief select members of the House Appropriations Committee about the *Liberty*. The NSA's second in command had a reputation as a brilliant mathematician who excelled in classical number theory and algebra, a natural skill set for cryptology. The tall and slender Tordella had earned a doctorate in mathematics from the University of Illinois and once taught at Chicago's Loyola University. Following the attack on Pearl Harbor, Tordella had served as a Navy cryptanalyst, where he applied his math skills to help break the German Enigma machine used to encrypt messages. Colleagues at the agency viewed Tordella as hardworking and conservative, a trait that was reflected in his daily wardrobe of brown suits and white shirts.

Democratic representative George Mahon of Texas sat down with Tordella in a private room across the hall from the committee's defense appropriations office. Republican representative Glenard Lipscomb of California and senior clerk Robert Michaels joined the meeting. Mahon began by asking about the *Liberty*'s mission and why it had sailed in the Mediterranean. Tordella explained that the spy ship had been diverted from its assignment off Africa in response to the increased tensions in the Middle East. The move had allowed the agency to better serve the national intelligence interests, including those of the Sixth Fleet in case the United States had been forced to intervene in the conflict. Tordella used a map to show the lawmakers the *Liberty*'s track across the Mediterranean and told the men the spy ship never strayed from international waters.

Mahon asked for details of the attack and why the *Liberty* steamed so close to the Egyptian coast. Tordella explained that line-of-sight communications dictated the ship's position. Tordella described the effort to move the *Liberty* hours before the attack, though the veteran spy deliberately chose not to go into any more details than required on the communications foul-up and refused to blame any individual or agency for the failure to contact the *Liberty*. Tordella's hostility over

Israel's assault was reflected in the tone of his comments, as he recorded in a secret memo for the record. "I wryly mentioned that the apology from the Israelis was received and the order to the commanding officer of the *America* was sent with such speed as to enable the recall of the planes which had been sent out to sink the attacking torpedo boats on the assumption they were Egyptian."

Mahon pressed Tordella to explain why Israel attacked. The senior spy could offer little. The NSA lacked concrete proof that Israel deliberately targeted the *Liberty*. A Navy spy plane overhead the afternoon of the attack had intercepted the communications of Israeli rescue helicopters sent out afterward, but failed to record the fighters or torpedo boats. The limited conversations between Israeli helicopter pilots and ground control were ambiguous and showed some confusion over the nationality of the ship. "If they are speaking Arabic (Egyptian), you take them to El Arish," the transcript shows ground control ordered the pilots. "If they are speaking English, not Egyptian, you take them to Lod." Transcripts of the intercepts confirmed that the *Liberty* flew the American flag as the pilots reported spotting it on the *Liberty*'s mast along with the ship's hull numbers: "We request that you make another pass and check once more if this is really an American flag."

The absence of concrete proof of a deliberate attack did not persuade Tordella and other NSA leaders that the assault was an accident. Many realized that only the attackers' communications could answer that question and even that might not reveal what Israeli commanders in headquarters actually knew. An NSA task force created to examine the attack prepared a fact sheet for the agency's leaders. Under the question of whether the attack was premeditated, analysts listed a half dozen bullet points that highlighted Israel's exceptional military and pointed to the fact that it was unlikely to make such a blunder. Information the agency received from a source in Israel later made it clear to senior leaders the attack was no accident.

Tordella explained to Mahon what the agency knew from the limited intercepts. "I told him we simply did not know from either open or intelligence sources but that, by now, there probably was a fair amount of denial and cover-up by the Israelis for the sake of protecting their national position." Mahon asked if a mistake of this nature was common. Tordella doubted it. "I told him that I thought a ship the size of the *Liberty* was unlike and much larger than Egyptian ships and that an obviously cargo-type vessel should not reasonably be mistaken by competent naval forces or air pilots for an Egyptian man-of-war. At best I estimated the attacking ships and planes were guilty of gross negligence and carelessness." Mahon asked Tordella's personal opinion. "I said that, for what it was worth, I believed the attack might have been ordered by some senior commander on the Sinai Peninsula who wrongly suspected that the *Liberty* was monitoring his activities."

Tordella's beliefs echoed those of his boss, Lieutenant General Marshall Carter. The NSA director, who had served as a senior aide and confidant to George Marshall during his tenure as general and then secretary of state and of defense, had a background in intelligence and was politically well connected in Washington. President John Kennedy had chosen him in 1962 to serve as the deputy director of the CIA, where he remained until 1965, when Johnson appointed him head of the NSA. Soon after the *Liberty* attack, Carter appeared before a subcommittee of the House Appropriations Committee to discuss the *Liberty.* Cyrus Vance joined him for the closed-door session. Lawmakers asked whether Carter believed Israel deliberately tried to sink an American ship. "It couldn't be anything else but deliberate," he testified. "There's just no way you could have a series of circumstances that would justify it being an accident."

"I think it's premature to make a judgment like that," Vance countered. Carter would later tell an NSA historian that the *Liberty* was "where I first parted company with Vance." Gerard Burke, Carter's chief of staff, remembered when his boss returned to the NSA afterward, appearing in Burke's ninth-floor office with stunning news. "Cy Vance just told me to keep my mouth shut," Burke recalled his boss telling him. "Those were his exact words." The implication was clear. Regardless of the opinions of Carter, Tordella and other senior leaders, Vance demanded the men remain silent. Carter fumed, but Burke described his boss as a loyal soldier who knew to follow orders. "There was absolutely no question in anybody's mind that the Israelis had done it deliberately," Burke said. "I was angrier because of the cover-up—if that's possible—than of the incident itself, because there was no doubt in my mind that they did it right from the outset. That was no mystery. The only mystery to me was why was the thing being covered up."

These views were shared by many of the NSA's senior leaders. Soon after the attack, a team had flown to Malta to inspect the ship. The extensive damage stunned the men. "Just looking at the damage, it would be hard to say that was an accident," said Allan Deprey, a Navy lieutenant assigned to the NSA who traveled to Malta. "One shot would be an accident or even one torpedo, but there was damage from all directions." Oliver Kirby, deputy director for operations, said he believed Israel wanted an impenetrable defense line. The *Liberty* proved a threat. "We knew it was deliberate," Kirby said of the attack. "It was very well planned, premeditated. They knew exactly what they were doing." Brigadier General John Morrison, Jr., assistant deputy director for operations, said an accidental attack defied logic. "We just couldn't believe that. We knew what the *Liberty* stood for. We knew what it looked like. It was not a small ship. It was a large ship," Morrison said. "They being a bright bunch of folks, we had to believe that they knew. They saw the silhouettte of the ship. They knew when they looked at it what it was. Our flag was flying."

Many senior officers in the State Department's Bureau of Intelligence and Research also doubted Israel's explanation. Thomas Hughes, director of the department's intelligence office, sent a detailed memo five days after the assault to Nicholas Katzenbach, outlining the details of the assault, the helicopter intercepts and his conclusions. The intercepts of Israeli helicopters failed to convince Hughes that the attack was an accident. He wrote that transcripts pointed to "an extraordinary lack of concern on the part of the attackers as to whether the target was hostile." Hughes's June 13 memo raised other questions about the extent and duration of the attack that eroded the credibility of Israel's explanation.

"In six strafing runs, it appears remarkable that none of the aircraft pilots identified the vessel as American," Hughes wrote. "The torpedo boat attack was made approximately 20 minutes after the air attack. The surface attack could have been called off in that time had proper air identification been made." Hughes pointed out what was obvious to many. "*Liberty* crew members were able to identify and record the hull number of one of the small, fast moving torpedo boats during the two minutes that elapsed between their attack run and the launching of the first torpedo, but the Israeli boat commanders apparently failed to identify the much larger and more easily identifiable *Liberty* (11,000 tons, 455 feet long, large identification numbers on hull)."

Israel's explanation, Hughes believed, "stretched all credibility." "We were quite convinced the Israelis knew what they were doing," he later said. "It was hard to come to any other conclusion." Other senior staffers agreed, believing that Israel did not want the United States reading its wartime message traffic. "It wasn't an accident," recalled William McAfee, who served as the department's liaison with other intelligence agencies. "Everybody knew it wasn't an accident." Granville Austin, director of the bureau's Near East and South Asia office, reviewed intelligence reports that described Israel's extensive reconnaissance of the *Liberty* hours before the attack. Despite Israel's protestations that the attack was an accident, Austin believed that Israeli forces knew the *Liberty* was an American ship. "They knew damn well what it was," he said. "That it was an accident, of course, was nonsense."

Despite Jerusalem's close ties with Washington, many State Department officials—and others in the intelligence community—believed the Jewish state's survival instinct was so strong that, if necessary, Israel would attack a close ally in the interest of self-preservation. "Our reports were devastating," recalled William Wolle, who worked on Arab-Israeli issues in the State Department's Bureau of Near Eastern and South Asian Affairs. "The feeling of those of us at the working level in NEA was that the Israelis had deliberately done this so that we couldn't read all of their communications, etc. We are their ally but they are not going to trust us when it comes to a wartime situation in terms of what information might get out, what we might pass along to someone. We all felt it was no accident."

In contrast to the strong views of many in the NSA and State Department, CIA officials backed Israel's explanation days after the attack. A top-secret June 13 memo stated that the helicopter intercepts "leave little doubt that the Israelis failed to identify the *Liberty* as a US ship before or during the atack." The memo also determined that even though the weather was clear and the *Liberty*'s hull number and flag were displayed, the attackers might have confused the spy ship for *El Quseir,* a position contrary to the beliefs of many in the Navy. "Although the *Liberty* is some 200 feet longer than the Egyptian transport *El Quseir,* it could easily be mistaken for the latter vessel by an overzealous pilot," the memo stated. "Both ships have similar hulls and arrangements of masts and stack."

A top-secret memo prepared on June 21 that evaluated Ron's report cast greater doubts on Israel's explanation, but reaffirmed the agency's earlier opinion that the attack likely was an accident and "not made in malice." The report, which blamed the assault on "overeager Israeli commanders," challenged how qualified naval commanders could twice miscalculate the *Liberty*'s speed and fail to note that such a cargo ship could not travel thirty knots and was unarmed and incapable of a shore bombardment. "To say the least, it is questionable military policy to authorize an attack upon an unidentified ship based solely upon a radar track of over 20 knots and erroneous reports that Israeli positions were being shelled," the memo stated. "The Israeli statement that the *Liberty* could not be identified because it was covered with smoke also is a piece of self-serving over rationalization. Clearly the smoke was the result of the Israeli attacks."

The CIA based its analysis in part on the telegrams of the American naval attaché in Tel Aviv, who raised serious questions about the attack but still attributed it to trigger-happy commanders. However, other senior officers inside the American Embassy in Tel Aviv believed the attack was no accident. William Dale, the embassy's second in command, suspected that the Israelis feared that the intelligence collected by the *Liberty* might fall into Arab hands. The department often sent telegrams with intelligence information to multiple embassies. A pro-Arab American diplomat stationed in Damascus, Beirut, or Cairo might pass along information to his contacts, a dangerous wartime proposition for Israel. Heywood Stackhouse, the embassy's principal political officer, also said he didn't believe Israel's explanation. "The Israelis are very, very smart people," Stackhouse said. "I just find it very hard to believe it was an error."

But the CIA's position on the attack soon changed. A secret internal history report declassified in 2006 shows that the agency's faith in its two initial intelligence memos vanished. The emerging details of the sustained assault, coupled with the mounting evidence against Israel, swayed many senior leaders at the agency that the assault likely was no accident. "Although Israeli authorities in Tel Aviv immediately apologized for the grievous 'accident,' many informed Americans soon came to believe that the assault had been anything but accidental. CIA initially resisted this judgment," stated the agency's history report. "But the cumulative weight of the evidence rapidly undermined this position."

Vice Admiral Rufus Taylor, the agency's deputy director at the time of the attack, voiced his disbelief of Israel's explanation in a June 22 memo to Director Richard Helms. Taylor had served as the head of naval intelligence and as the deputy director of the Defense Intelligence Agency. The three-star admiral concluded that Israel deliberately attacked the *Liberty*. "To me, the picture thus far presents the distinct possibility that the Israelis *knew* that *Liberty* might be their target and attacked anyway," Taylor wrote to his boss, "either through confusion in Command and Control or through deliberate disregard of instructions on the part of subordinates."

Several agency field memos produced in the summer and fall of 1967 highlighted the fact that Israel rarely made mistakes. One report even suggested Moshe Dayan had ordered the attack. The CIA considered these field reports—based on unnamed agency contacts—as unevaluated intelligence. Many senior agency leaders by then had already concluded the attack was deliberate. "I don't think there can be any doubt that the Israelis knew exactly what they were doing," Helms told a CIA historian in an oral history interview declassified in 2008. "Why they wanted to attack the *Liberty*, whose bright idea this was, I can't possibly know. But any statement to the effect that they didn't know that it was an American ship and so forth is nonsense."

CHAPTER 16

There was a suspicious feeling around town that we were attempting to back up the Israelis.

—LUCIUS BATTLE, ASSISTANT SECRETARY OF STATE FOR NEAR EASTERN AND SOUTH ASIAN AFFAIRS

Captain Merlin Staring began his legal review of the American court of inquiry in his fifth-floor office of the Navy's headquarters on North Audley Street in central London on June 17. Staring had served throughout World War II and later earned his law degree at Georgetown University. Over the years, the New York native rose from a staff lawyer to a senior member of the Judge Advocate General's Corps. Now the top lawyer for Admiral John McCain, Jr., the commander of American naval forces in Europe and the Middle East, Staring had the duty to review the investigative report on the *Liberty* and make recommendations to McCain before the admiral forwarded it to his superiors at the Pentagon.

The top-secret volume on Staring's desk for review totaled more than seven hundred pages, including a 158-page transcript of witness testimony and forty-nine exhibits that consisted of logs, telegrams, and photographs. The report even included the business card naval attaché Castle had dropped to the deck after the attack and the detailed breakdown of the 821 shell holes that riddled the spy ship's hull and superstructure, handwritten on a piece of lined notebook paper. Staring saw evidence of the inquiry's haste in its sloppy final report, replete with misspellings, typos, and scratch-outs. Some of the exhibits appeared incorrectly labeled and out of order and the names of some of the *Liberty*'s crewmembers were misspelled. The name of Dr. Richard Kiepfer, one of the central witnesses, was spelled two different ways throughout the report, both incorrect. The court even repeatedly misspelled *Israeli*.

The lawyer's concerns grew as he delved into the report's seemingly contradictory findings, which appeared to Staring designed to exonerate the *Liberty* of wrongdoing and provide political cover for Israel. The court determined that the *Liberty* sailed in international waters, flew the American flag, and sported clean and freshly painted hull markings. The Israelis reconned the ship throughout the morning and jammed the *Liberty*'s communications. The court congratulated the heroism of the officers and crew who fought to keep the ship afloat. The report at times even seemed in awe of the assault's efficiency. "Attackers were well coordinated, accurate and determined. Criss-crossing rocket and machine gun runs from both bows, both beams, and quarters effectively chewed up entire topside," the report stated. "Well directed initial air attacks had wiped out the ability of the four 50 cal. machine guns to be effective."

The court criticized Israel's explanation that its forces confused the *Liberty* with the *El Quseir*, noting any resemblance was "highly superficial." "*El Quseir* is less than half the size and lacks the elaborate antenna array and distinctive hull markings of *Liberty*," the report stated. "The location of the superstructure island, a primary recognition feature of merchant type ships, is widely different. By this criteria as a justification for attack, any ship resembling *El Quseir* was in jeopardy." The report also refuted Israel's accusation that the *Liberty* steamed too close to a war zone and outside normal shipping routes, flew no flag, and that its forces mistakenly determined the *Liberty* had shelled Israeli troops onshore. "It is inconceivable that either the IDF Navy or Air Force would associate *Liberty*, with her 4 .50 caliber machine guns, or *El Quseir*, armed with two 3 pounders, with a shore bombardment."

Despite the court's apparent effort to discredit Israel's explanations for the attack, the report ultimately concluded that the assault was a case of mistaken identity. The report asserted that the *Liberty*'s slow speed and the calm weather likely made it difficult for the attackers to spot the American flag during the hour-long assault. The westerly direction of the ship, the report ruled, possibly reinforced the attackers' conclusion that the ship was Egyptian. The contradictory findings baffled Staring as he pored over the report until nearly 3 A.M., breaking only for the occasional cup of coffee or cigarette. How could the court blast Israel's claim that its forces confused the *Liberty* for *El Quseir*, but still rule the attack a case of mistaken identity? Nowhere in the pages of testimony or exhibits could Staring find evidence to support that principal ruling.

Larger questions loomed. If Admiral McCain had barred investigators from traveling to Israel, and court members never received the war logs, diaries, or radio communications from the attackers, how could the court prove what had happened? Court members had no idea what had occurred inside the Israeli chain of command and could offer little more than guesswork. Didn't the families of the men killed, the Navy, and the American public deserve real answers? "The number one paragraph on the preface to that record was that this was a case of misidentification, but I encountered nothing even touching upon that," recalled Staring, who was later promoted to the rank of rear admiral. "No self-respecting lawyer or naval officer could look at the limited nature of the evidence taken by or available to that court of inquiry and find it adequate to support the conclusions the court professed to have reached."

Other senior officers in the London headquarters also doubted Israel's explanation, though most would remain silent for decades. One of the more stinging repudiations of the report came decades later from Captain Ward Boston, Jr., the court's attorney. "The evidence was clear," Boston later said in a sworn affidavit. "I am certain that the Israeli pilots that undertook the attack, as well as their superiors who had ordered the attack, were well aware that the ship was American. I saw the flag, which had visibly identified the ship as American, riddled with bullet holes, and heard testimony that made it clear that the Israelis intended there be no survivors." Even Rear Admiral Wylie, McCain's deputy, confessed years later in an oral history interview with the Naval War College that he did not believe the attack was an accident. "That was deliberate," Wylie told an interviewer. "I don't know why in God's name those idiotic people did it, but—I think I'll not talk about it."

Boston arrived in Staring's office the morning of June 18. Staring had been up most of the night, taking a break only long enough to catch a few hours of sleep before returning to the office at sunrise. Boston asked Staring when he would finish his review. "I have some real problems with it," Staring said. "I have yet to find any evidence in the record, so far as I have read it, that bears out some of the important findings of fact that the board has submitted." Boston left and returned twenty minutes later. McCain now demanded the report back. Staring's legal review was no longer necessary. McCain then signed his five-page endorsement of the court of inquiry. Court President Rear Admiral Isaac Kidd, Jr., handcuffed a briefcase containing the top-secret report to his wrist, packed a pistol, and boarded a flight to Washington.

Kidd delivered the voluminous report to the Pentagon soon after he landed. The Defense Department's senior leaders planned to shrink the report into an unclassified summary for the press. Deputy defense secretary Cyrus Vance organized the effort. The former secretary of the Army under President Kennedy, Vance was promoted in 1964 to the Pentagon's second-in-command where he spent so much time with McNamara that he sometimes spoke in the same staccato manner as his boss. In the intelligence community, Vance had developed a reputation for handling the Pentagon and White House's dirty jobs. He now tapped Pentagon spokesmen Phil Goulding and Richard Fryklund to help Kidd draft the abbreviated *Liberty* narrative.

The Navy's full report concluded that the attack was a case of mistaken identity. But as Staring discovered in his review in London, witness testimony about the pre-attack reconnaissance, clear weather conditions, and the duration of the assault undermined the conclusions that appeared tacked on top. Neither the press nor the American public, however, would see the complete report or have access to its top-secret findings until it was declassified nearly a decade later. The Pentagon's fourteen-page condensed version, in contrast, omitted all the evidence that contradicted Israel's explanations, from the jamming of the spy ship's communications to the court's stinging denunciation of Israel's claim that its forces had confused the *Liberty* for an aged Egyptian cargo ship.

The summary instead amplified details that supported Israel's account. It noted that the attackers must have had difficulty spotting the American flag because of the ship's slow speed, a lack of wind, and smoke from the fires on deck. It also singled out McGonagle's testimony that the *Liberty* effectively fired its machine guns at the torpedo boats, even though other witnesses had refuted the skipper's account. The abbreviated report also included the failure to move the spy ship hours earlier, subtly implying that the United States shared the blame for leaving a defenseless ship in harm's way, though the *Liberty* sailed in international waters. Page after page, the summary reiterated statements and conclusions supporting Israel's weak defense:

"The court found no evidence which indicated that the Israeli units which fired on *Liberty* knew they were attacking an American ship."

"The court found 'no available indications that the attack was intended against a U.S. ship.'"

"'As far as the torpedo boats are concerned,' the commanding officer testified, 'I am sure that they felt they were under fire from USS *Liberty*.'"

"Her flag, while flying, was hanging fairly limply due to a lack of wind and the ship's slow speed."

"The court found that 'The calm conditions and slow ship speed may well have made the American flag difficult to identify.'"

"Smoke from the burning whaleboat and other topside fires, and from the ship's own stack—she was now building up speed—may have obscured her flag."

The summary arrived in the fourth-floor office of Chief of Naval Operations Admiral David McDonald for review on June 22, exactly two weeks after the attack. The accompanying memo warned that "strong Navy non-concurrence in the draft is anticipated" and that the Pentagon's press officers had "their marching orders from Secretary Vance." Like many of the military's senior officers, the sixty-year-old McDonald despised Robert McNamara's leadership of the Pentagon. McNamara and his civilian analysts—dubbed the Whiz Kids—had centralized power, ignored the chain of command, and discounted the views of senior military leaders, whose experience was deemed parochial. Many in the military believed McNamara made decisions based on studies, spreadsheets, and cost-benefit analysis equations, often at the expense of human lives.

Despite his dislike of McNamara, McDonald knew to keep his criticisms of the controversial defense secretary private. He had landed his job as the Navy's senior officer after his predecessor, Admiral George Anderson, who had graced the cover of *Time* magazine in the wake of the Cuban Missile Crisis, publicly challenged McNamara and was fired. The soft-spoken son of a Georgia country preacher, McDonald told the press that McNamara was "probably the best Defense Secretary ever," though in private he often ridiculed McNamara and his deputies with a harshness that made his aides uncomfortable. A pragmatist, McDonald realized that quitting would only hurt the Navy. "I have more influence and more chance of changing it by staying where I am than quitting in a huff," he confided in an aide after a fight with McNamara. "I wouldn't want to do that."

The *Liberty* inquiry presented McDonald with another chance to challenge the Pentagon's civilian leaders. McDonald attacked the draft summary of the *Liberty*'s court of inquiry with a red pencil. The veteran sailor immediately seized on the summary's bold declarations that exonerated the attackers. In a note on the page, McDonald challenged the statement that the court found no evidence that Israel's forces knew the *Liberty* was an American ship. "Was there any which indicated that they didn't know?" McDonald wrote. Likewise, he questioned the statement that there was no available indication that the attack was intended against an American ship. "Any that the attack wasn't intended?" he scribbled.

Other passages in the draft intended to prop up Israel's weak explanations also bothered McDonald. He highlighted references to the poor visibility of the flag, the firing of the *Liberty*'s machine guns, and the failure to order the spy ship farther to sea hours before the attack. The Pentagon's goal, McDonald soon realized, was to protect Israel. He articulated his frustration in a handwritten memo. "I think that much of this is extraneous and it leaves me with the feeling that we're trying our best to excuse the attackers," the admiral wrote. "Why not let them make the case of (a) unidentified, (b) non deliberate, etc.? Were I a parent of one of the deceased this release would burn me up. I myself do not subscribe to it."

The office of the secretary of defense refused to relent. A follow-up draft of the summary prepared hours later addressed some of McDonald's concerns, though the release largely contained many of the original passages that troubled the admiral. The draft still mentioned that calm weather and fires might have obscured the flag and that the *Liberty* fired on the attackers. An accompanying memo made it clear that despite having asked for the Navy's participation, the Pentagon's senior leaders had little interest in making any substantial changes to the draft. "Unfortunately, although Mr. Fryklund states that he agrees with the CNO's position, he is bound by Mr. Vance's guidance," the memo stated. "Therefore while some of the wording has been shaded more toward the Navy stand, I am unable to get further changes or deletions."

Vice Chief of Naval Operations Admiral Horacio Rivero, Jr., marked his "suggested deletions" on the revised draft with a green pen. McDonald's senior deputy crossed out sentences that stated the court found no evidence that Israel had deliberately targeted the *Liberty*. The admiral also marked through passages about the poor visibility of the flag, the firing of the *Liberty*'s machine guns, and communications failures, many of the same sentences that troubled his boss. McDonald then reviewed a third draft of the press release and noted the same sections with his red pencil. The admiral dashed off another handwritten memo, again questioning why the United States appeared so interested in protecting Israel. "I see no reason whatsoever to mention *Liberty*'s firing of her .50 cal. machine guns," McDonald wrote. "I still say let Israel say whether or not she could see the U.S. flag. Why volunteer the 'perhaps *they* couldn't see it, etc.'"

Senior officers also challenged the Pentagon's insistence that the draft include the failure to contact the *Liberty* before the attack. "We have no business whatsoever accepting any burden of blame by indicating that we were trying to change her position at the last minute for reasons which are nobody's business but ours," Kidd wrote in a secret memo to McDonald. "I am convinced that the minute we open up

Pandora's communication box on the *Liberty* situation, the burden of responsibility will immediately shift in the American press, and probably the world press, from Israel's irresponsible action to U.S. Naval Communications deficiencies." McDonald echoed Kidd's concerns in a handwritten memo. "I still do not agree to including possible Communication problems," he wrote. "This is an *internal* matter and not germane."

The admiral's refusal to protect Israel reflected the general disbelief of many on his staff that the attack was an accident. To these senior officers, the idea that trained naval forces could fail to recognize the *Liberty* on a clear afternoon was incomprehensible. Captain Jerome King, Jr., McDonald's executive assistant and senior aide, said many years later that at the time no one believed the Israeli claim that its forces confused the *Liberty* for a thirty-seven-year-old Egyptian horse and troop transport. "It certainly was not mistaken identity," King, later a vice admiral, recalled. "I don't buy it. I never did. Nobody that I knew ever did either. It wasn't as though it was at night or a rainy day or anything like that. There wasn't any excuse for not knowing what the ship was. You could divine from just the apparatus on deck—all the antennae and so on—what its mission was."

The struggle between senior Navy officers and the Pentagon's civilian leaders to draft the narrative soon leaked to the press. The *Evening Star* ran a story headlined "Report on Israel Ship Attack A Touchy Task for Pentagon," outlining the political challenge of exonerating the *Liberty*'s officers and crew while not blaming Israel. "One of their big problems has been to find a way to tell the truth and nothing but the truth without telling the whole truth," the article stated. "Pentagon officials would like somehow to emphasize that the ship was attacked without warning while she was in international waters, where she had every right to be, and yet to avoid damaging relations with the Israelis, who immediately apologized for the attack."

McDonald and his staff achieved some success in shaping the public summary of the court of inquiry's report. The final draft noted that the court determined that resemblance to *El Quseir* was "highly superficial" and that the attackers had "ample opportunity" to identify the *Liberty* prior to the assault. It also stated that the court had "insufficient information" to determine why the Israelis attacked and noted that the court heard no evidence from Israel, language absent in early drafts. But McDonald's power had limits. The final draft stated that "witnesses suggested that the flag may have been difficult for the attackers to see," even though that contradicted the testimony of every witness. References to the *Liberty*'s firing of its machine guns and botched orders to move the ship also remained. "You had fine comments on the previous draft," stated a handwritten briefing memo that accompanied the Vance-approved release. "The other three objectionable passages, machine gun firing, difficulty in seeing the flag, and the communication delays, are still in this draft."

The Pentagon released its censored summary of the Navy's court of inquiry on June 28, twenty days after attack. The release included a nine-page summary of the court's findings accompanied by nineteen edited pages of McGonagle's testimony that captured the drama of the assault. The final narrative reflected the dueling interests of the Navy, anxious to keep the focus on Israel's culpability, and the Pentagon's civilian leaders, concerned with providing political cover for Israel and preserving diplomatic relations. As a result, the report appeared both to exonerate the crew of the *Liberty* and provide a plausible rationale that might explain how and why Israel attacked.

Major news outlets from the *New York Times* to the *Chicago Tribune* and *Dallas Morning News* seized on the bungled effort to move the *Liberty*. The *Washington Post* called it an "ironic twist" that the Navy's most sophisticated spy ship "failed to get a message to move farther out to sea the day she was attacked." In follow-up articles, many papers including the *Baltimore Sun, Philadelphia Inquirer,* and *Virginian-Pilot* of Norfolk questioned whether the firing of the spy ship's machine guns had triggered the torpedo attack.

Only deep into the stories did most newspapers address the question of Israeli responsibility. Many articles noted that the court ruled that Israel "had ample opportunity to identify *Liberty* correctly." Other stories quoted the report's finding that the court had "insufficient information before it to make a judgment on the reasons" for the attack. In the twenty-second paragraph of its story, the *New York Times* wrote that the court did not interview any Israeli witnesses, a fact most newspapers omitted.

The insinuation that *Liberty* gunfire and the failed effort to move the ship triggered the assault shifted the responsibility for the attack from Israel to the United States, just as Kidd warned would happen in his secret memo. Press accounts implied that if the Pentagon's communications system had not failed, the attack would not have happened. Likewise, had the sailors not fired the *Liberty*'s machine guns, the Israeli torpedo boats might have spared the spy ship the torpedo strike that resulted in twenty-five of its thirty-four fatalities. The subtle suggestion of American culpability overshadowed the court's determination that the *Liberty* had a legal right to sail where it did.

The press coverage angered the *Liberty*'s officers in Malta. Many were particularly upset by the implication that the ship's futile self-defense effort served as the attack's catalyst. The men had only done what was expected of them and try to save the ship and themselves. Ensign Lucas described the allegations in a letter to his wife as "far fetched." "If they had been pounding the hell out of us for half an hour, a little machine gun fire from our .50 cal. pea shooters wouldn't have made much difference," Lucas wrote. "Many of the articles are barking up the wrong tree."

Editorials and opinion columns also spread blame widely. Some charged Israel with deliberately attacking the spy ship. Others zeroed in on the *Liberty*'s bungled orders. The *Washington Daily News* blamed McGonagle for not pulling his ship from the war's sideline. Despite the varying accusations, editorials largely agreed on one point: the Pentagon's summary failed to explain what had happened. The *Washington Post* slammed it as "not good enough." *Time* griped that it offered only "fragmentary answers" while the *Chicago Tribune* complained that the report produced "more fog and unanswered questions than clarification." The *Evening Star* called it an "affront" filled with "irrelevant tidbits of fact" that revealed "little of consequence that has not been public knowledge since the day of the attack."

Many editorials doubted Israel's explanations and criticized the Pentagon for its silence on that point. The conservative *National Review* urged Congress to investigate. "One thing at least is proved by analysis on the facts already at hand. The incident was *not* 'an accident,'" the magazine opined. "It was an act either of stupidity gross enough to be negligence, or of aggression." The *National Observer* blasted Israel's supporters for blaming the United States. "The apologists are still maintaining that the Israelis made an understandable mistake because they thought the ship was Egyptian. This has to be sheer hokum," it wrote. "Only the blind—or the trigger-happy—could have made such a mistake." The *Evening Star* accused the Pentagon of failing to address the critical question of what Israel knew and when. "Did the attackers, in fact, know that the *Liberty* was an American ship? It seems to us they must have known. If so, why was the attack made and who ordered it?" the paper asked. "Surely the Defense Department knows the answers to these and other pertinent questions by this time. If it does not, there is something radically wrong in the Pentagon."

Other editorials challenged the Pentagon's failure to contact the *Liberty* hours before the attack, often evoking apocalyptic scenarios should the communications system fail again. "The prompt transmittal of orders, in this nuclear age, is the first essential of effective military command," argued the *Washington Post*. "A similar lapse could result in the destruction of the Nation itself." The *Chicago Tribune* exclaimed that the failure to pull the spy ship from harm's way evoked "shades of Pearl Harbor!" "A warning to the *Liberty* was imperative enough, but what if a great world holocaust demanded an instant warning to the field?" the paper questioned. "Would we find again that defense communications failed at zero hour?"

Some columnists and editorial writers doubted the military had released all the facts. Syndicated columnist James Kilpatrick urged reporters to "keep digging." "It surely will be some years, and it may be next to never, before the whole story is told," Kilpatrick wrote. "Mum officially is the word." The *Baltimore Sun* cautioned that Americans "have become wary of official announcements" and that readers must remember that public reports "are not necessarily the full story." "The lay citizen, without access to the Navy's classified information, cannot arrive at an informed judgment on the unfortunate event—beyond the point that it obviously should not have happened," argued the paper.

"So long as part of the episode remains shrouded in security secrecy, the rest of it cannot be expected to come into clear focus."

Editorial pages in small towns and cities far removed from the Beltway's insider gossip reflected frustration and disbelief with the efforts to explain the attack. The *Edwardsville Intelligencer* in Illinois said that the Navy's report only confirmed what many already suspected: the *Liberty* did not provoke the attack. "Still unknown—and this is a question which can only be answered by the Israeli government—is whether the attack was accidental or deliberate. This question never may be answered to the satisfaction of everyone unless someone confesses," the paper observed. "Portions of the testimony before the court of inquiry by the *Liberty*'s commanding officer, Cmdr. William L. McGonagle, would seem to indicate that the attack was deliberate."

CHAPTER 17

I have mixed emotions about leaving the ship. I would like to come home right now, that's for sure. But I also want to ride the ship back to Norfolk—after getting this far I want to go all the way.

—ENSIGN DAVE LUCAS, LETTER TO HIS WIFE

Representative Craig Hosmer took the floor of the House of the Representatives on the morning of June 29 to voice his outrage over the assault on the *Liberty*. The Pentagon's censored report dominated headlines in most of the nation's top newspapers that morning. The California Republican viewed the attack through his own military experience. Hosmer had enlisted in the Navy in July 1940 and served throughout World War II. He remained in the Naval Reserves when the war ended, eventually earning the rank of rear admiral. Hosmer understood seamanship, ship identification, and naval warfare.

After the House convened at 11:00 on this Thursday morning—exactly three weeks after the attack—Hosmer told his colleagues that he had concluded that the coordinated strike by fighters and torpedo boats meant Israel must have deliberately targeted the *Liberty*. "I do not believe the attack was ordered at the highest command level of the Israeli military, but that it was ordered at a sufficiently high level to permit coordination of the Israel air and naval forces involved," he declared. "This means that some officer or officers of relatively high rank must have acted on their own initiative."

Hosmer said he doubted Israel's claim that its forces had confused

238

the *Liberty* for an Egyptian cargo ship. "The fact that the U.S.S. *Liberty* was a Victory hull vessel, hundreds of which were produced and used by the U.S. Navy during World War II and since, rules out the possibility of mistaken identity. Every ship recognition book in the world has, for years, identified the characteristic Victory hull and superstructure of the U.S.S. *Liberty* as U.S. Navy property," he argued. "What those responsible for this outrage sought to gain can, at this point, be only a matter of speculation."

The conservative lawmaker suggested that Israel might have hoped that the attack would trigger intervention by the United States and the Soviets or might have served as a signal to keep the superpowers out. He also speculated that Israel, euphoric with victory on land, thought the sea attack might "further demonstrate Israeli military might." Regardless of motive, Hosmer concluded that the Jewish state now had an obligation to pay retribution to the families of the men killed and punish those involved. "Whatever is the reason for the attack, it was an act of high piracy," he declared. "Those responsible should be court-martialed on charges of murder, amongst other counts."

Mississippi representative Thomas Abernethy rose moments later. Like his colleague, the southern Democrat doubted Israel's explanations, but he also believed the American government was covering up the truth. He watched in disbelief the day after the attack as State Department officials fanned out across Capitol Hill, assuring lawmakers that it was an accident. Abernethy's efforts to ferret out information drew elusive answers. He could tolerate it no longer. "This useless, unnecessary and inexcusable attack took the lives of 34 American boys, wounded 75 others, and left many others in a state of horrified shock, to say nothing of what it did to a flag-flying vessel of the U.S. Navy," he roared. "How could this be treated so lightly in this the greatest Capitol in all the world?"

The lawmaker noted that the spy ship sailed more than fifteen miles from shore, far beyond the territorial waters recognized by Israel and Egypt. He pointed out that reconnaissance flights had buzzed the *Liberty* that morning and that the "attack was incessant, heavy and hard." "The ship was well marked, so said the Pentagon. Its name was painted on its stern. U.S. letters and numbers were on its bow. The day was clear. And it was distinctly flying the flag that you and I stood here and so praised and respected just a few days ago on Flag Day," Abernethy said. "But what respect have we shown for it since it was so recklessly shot down by the Israel attackers? What complaint have we registered? What has Washington said? To tell you the truth, this great Capital as well as this great Government—if it can still be called great—was and is as quiet as the tomb regarding this horrible event."

Abernethy criticized the government for settling for an apology. If any other nation had attacked the *Liberty,* the government would have roared back and possibly even retaliated. "It is not enough to let it drop with a simple statement that the attackers just happened to make a mistake," he argued. "This is too serious a matter to accept a simple 'Excuse us, please' sort of statement. There must be more than this to assure our men, our people, and our Nation that another nation must not make such unprovoked and vicious attacks upon us." Abernethy reminded his colleagues in closing that the families of the *Liberty*'s sailors and the rest of the nation awaited Congress's response. "The world has been standing by looking at us now for days since the *Liberty* was pounced upon," he concluded. "What do we do? What do we say?"

Few other elected leaders said or did anything. Of the 435 House members, only Hosmer and Abernethy spoke out during the three and a half hours that legislative body met. No one in the Senate, which met for less than two hours, mentioned the attack. Some lawmakers quietly appealed for information through committees. More than sixty wrote letters to the State Department and Navy—roughly five per day—asking the status of reparations for the dead and injured. Many of the letters were pro forma, written in response to constituent requests, including family members of men killed. A memo to Secretary of State Dean Rusk two weeks after the attack, analyzing the State Department's voluminous mail, summarized the outrage felt by many Americans: "The attack on the *Liberty* was almost unanimously condemned."

Diplomats at the Israeli Embassy in Washington learned the outcome of the court of inquiry days in advance of the Pentagon's planned publication. A journalist who managed to read a draft of the release tipped off embassy spokesman Dan Patir. Five days before the Defense Department released its summary to the press, Patir cabled a detailed description of the report's contents to Jerusalem. He noted the hefty size of the full report and that it contained the testimonies of roughly twenty officers, crewmembers, and other Navy officials. Patir reported that a special team at the Pentagon had spent three days editing the voluminous report into a declassified summary. Senior leaders with the Navy, Defense, and State departments reviewed the draft prior to publication.

Patir wrote that the Pentagon summary chronicled the attack in detail and exonerated McGonagle of wrongdoing. The Navy also had nominated the skipper for the Medal of Honor. More importantly, Patir wrote that the report might prove politically damaging for Israel. "This announcement includes denunciation of the Israeli attack, that is defined as a 'rash act.' It insists that the incident took place in international waters, and that the *Liberty* had the right to be in them," Patir wrote. "It notes that Israeli airplanes were seen circling above the ship about 6 hours before the attack itself. It assumes with certainty that these aircraft had identified the *Liberty* immediately and had communicated this observation to the headquarters in Tel Aviv."

The embassy's problems soon compounded. Ambassador Avraham Harman learned that the Senate Foreign Relations Committee, particularly Bourke Hickenlooper of Iowa, had shown increased interest in the attack. Another member of the committee even had suggested the United States launch a congressional investigation. Such a probe would only jeopardize U.S.-Israeli relations. Harman wrote a desperate message to Yitzhak Rabin, Israel's chief of staff. He reiterated the need to indict the attackers. "Our main goal is to emphasize the truth, that the attack was not conducted maliciously by the Israeli government and IDF," he wrote. "I am convinced that the only way is for the legal inquiry to end in negligence and recklessness charges."

Harman's suggestion drew a heated response from Rabin. Israel had followed the ambassador's earlier advice and expanded its probe of the attack after Harman noted myriad flaws in Colonel Ram Ron's report. But Rabin now denounced Harman for what he believed was the ambassador's effort to sway the outcome of that investigation. Harman needed to back down. "Do you or your American colleagues even consider that the US Administration would try to influence the work of a Supreme Court judge?" Rabin wrote in a highly confidential and restricted telegram. "Please understand once and for all that no interference or pressure are possible in the direction you're suggesting."

Israeli officials failed to recognize how far the U.S. government had gone to help the Jewish state's public position, including slanting the court of inquiry's public summary. When the Pentagon released that summary, Israel again resorted to a spin campaign. News reports appeared in American papers, often with vague attributions, that challenged many of the Navy's findings. Israel disputed the fact that the *Liberty* flew a flag. Other press reports claimed that the Israeli boats had approached the *Liberty* prior to the torpedo attack and demanded the ship identify itself. The *Liberty* instead had signaled back "A-A," a maritime code that means "identify yourself first." Israel said an Egyptian destroyer used the same signal in the 1956 war. The alleged use of the identical message led Israeli sailors to conclude the *Liberty* must be Egyptian.

The press reports frustrated senior Navy officers. Kidd re-interviewed McGonagle and his signalmen. Kidd reported that Israel's claim that the *Liberty* had signaled the torpedo boats was bogus. McGonagle was unable to read Israel's signals. Even if the skipper had wanted to reply, he couldn't because the attackers had shot out the signal lights. "Nothing intelligible was received by light from any of the Israeli torpedo boats prior to the offer of help which was received from the torpedo boats after the torpedo hit," stated a Navy memorandum for the record. "The only available installed signaling apparatus on *Liberty* was destroyed early in the attack and the hand-held Aldis lamp was not 'unlimbered' until after the torpedo hit." Kidd elaborated in a telegram: "I am convinced these men know what they are talking about."

The Associated Press soon published an article written by an Israeli Naval Reserve officer who served on one of the torpedo boats. The first-person account by Micha Limor appeared in newspapers nationwide, including the *New York Times, Washington Post,* and *Chicago Tribune.*

Limor wrote that crews tried to identify the *Liberty* with binoculars as two fighters circled the spy ship. The jets fired two rockets then retreated to base. "About 2,000 yards from the ship, a strange spectacle met our eyes. The high masts and the many weird antenna showed that this was a warship. The side of the vessel was blotted out by smoke, and apart from three numbers along her side, which meant nothing to us, we could not discern a thing. We could see no flag on the mast, nor was anyone to be seen on the decks and bridge," he wrote. "We spent several minutes trying to contact the ship and demanding identification. We tried by radio and by heliograph, in accordance with internationally accepted means. But she gave no answer."

Torpedo boats zoomed past the *Liberty* in battle formation and fired across the bridge and bow to demand identification. "Suddenly, a sailor appeared in view and started firing at us with a heavy machine gun from the bridge. We took the challenge and directed cannon fire against him," he wrote. "A moment later he fell, together with the machine gun. Thus there was no doubt that we were faced by the enemy. The prolonged refusal to identify herself, the absence of any flag, the shooting at us, and above all, the weird contraptions on the ship left us without doubt." Limor wrote that Israel hoped to capture the *Liberty* rather than sink it. The torpedo boats circled the ship and repeatedly fired to try to stop it. "This had no effect. No one appeared. No one reacted. The shells caused little damage to the hull and the ship proceeded on her way," he wrote. "You could almost hear the men's teeth grinding aboard our boat. Nothing can annoy a torpedo boat crew more than being completely ignored."

Unable to stop the ship, commanders ordered it torpedoed. "We drew up along the left side of the ship and advanced at full battle speed. Just as in dozens of training exercises we reached the right angle and range—and let go. We thought only a miracle would save the ship," he wrote. "One of the torpedoes hit amidships. There followed an enormous explosion and a huge water spout. And then fires broke out and the ship leaned sideways as if about to sink." Only when Israeli crewmembers plucked a rubber life raft from the water—marked "U.S. Navy"—did the sailors realize their mistake. Limor wrote that after the attack ended, Israeli sailors watched the American flag rise up the mast. "Dozens of shells, rockets and torpedoes were needed to drag a sign of identity from them, said one of my seamen who, like the rest of his mates, was bitterly upset at this surprising turn of events," Limor wrote. "He was right. The showing of the Stars and Stripes at the first stage would have prevented all that happened subsequently."

Limor's story, described by a *Liberty* officer in a letter as the product of a "wild imagination," infuriated the *Liberty*'s men. Fighters did not circle the ship prior to the attack and the torpedo boats were too far away to have witnessed the air assault. The American flag was shot down, but replaced by a larger flag long before the Israeli Navy arrived. None of the torpedo boats fired across the bow, circled the ship, or radioed the *Liberty*. The only markings Limor reportedly saw were the *Liberty*'s hull numbers, which he claimed meant nothing to him. That alone was a shocking statement. How could a naval officer not understand the significance of a ship's hull number? Even Israeli torpedo boats carried similar markings. The Israeli officers should have at a minimum noted the *Liberty*'s markings were not in Arabic, as Egyptian ships are identified. But these gripes were trivial compared to Limor's largest blunder: he attributed the torpedo strike to the wrong side of the ship.

Liberty sailors anxious to challenge Limor's story were barred from talking to reporters. That left many Americans to assume his story was accurate. The Pentagon ended the news blackout after the release of the summary of the court of inquiry, but limited the *Liberty*'s crew—still in Malta awaiting the completion of repairs—from discussing anything outside the summary's contents. Restrictions on crewmember interviews, published in the *Liberty*'s Plan of the Day, soon evolved into a ban on all press contacts. The one-page memo was read aloud at morning quarters and posted throughout the ship for the crew to read. "Interviews and statements to news media concerning the attack on *Liberty* 08 June are not to be given by individuals. If you are approached by someone wanting an interview or statement inform them that they must contact the Public Affairs Officer," the memo read. "The only information that ships company is allowed to discuss is that already made available to the press. Therefore, there is nothing new that we would be able to tell them in an interview."

*   *   *

Maltese workers flooded the *Liberty*'s drydock on the afternoon of July 14 in preparation for the return home. The *Liberty* had arrived in Valletta at dawn exactly one month earlier, greeted by reporters on a hillside who marveled at the scorched spy ship. Shipfitters had worked daily to patch the hundreds of shell blasts and the torpedo hole that warped interior decks. Fresh paint masked the smell of the dead. The repairs served as a temporary remedy so the *Liberty* could cross the Atlantic. The Navy would decide later whether to overhaul the ship's mechanical and electrical systems and fix its battered hull. "After getting to Norfolk, what happens to the ship and the crew is still anybody's guess," one officer wrote in a letter. "We'll just have to wait and see."

Sailors fanned out across the ship's lower compartments to monitor the outward bulkheads as the water rose. McGonagle ordered crews to report problems immediately to Damage Control Central. The skipper refused to allow the ship to leave drydock until each team confirmed the absence of leaks. Four hours after workers began to flood the drydock—and with the ship now afloat—the *Liberty* eased out of its dock and tied up alongside a Valletta pier. After a month of depending on shore power, the ship's engineering plant now hummed. The crew could finally use the *Liberty*'s toilets rather than the foul outhouse perched on the end of the pier.

The *Liberty* completed its dock trials at 9:45 A.M. the next morning. Engineers ran the propeller up to five knots forward and five knots in reverse to test the ship's main propulsion plant. Men also checked the ship's generators, evaporators, and the main feed water pump to guarantee the *Liberty*'s steam-powered system still functioned after a month of no use. Crews swabbed the decks with fresh water and removed the extra mooring lines. Many of the sailors dashed off letters, alerting loved ones of the *Liberty*'s expected homecoming in two weeks. "Everybody on board is eagerly awaiting our arrival in Norfolk," Ensign Scott wrote to his parents in North Carolina. "Malta has been very good to us but it will be good to be back in the States."

The *Liberty* sailed for home at 7 A.M. on July 16, once again passing the Ricasoli lighthouse at the entrance of Valletta's Grand Harbor. The tugboat *Papago*, which had trailed the *Liberty* on its voyage to Malta, again fell in line. Sailors lined the decks and watched as the ancient maritime crossroad that had served as the *Liberty*'s home port for the past month faded on the horizon. Vice Admiral Martin congratulated the crew on the eve of the ship's departure. "USS *Liberty* has become a legend in her own time," he wrote. "We have shared your grief for those who lost their lives, we remind ourselves that you were classic examples of unswerving devotion to duty."

Malta had provided the officers and crew a relaxing place to decompress, reflect, and grieve. An early morning fire in a storeroom that produced a lot of smoke but few flames had served as the month's most exciting event. The ship's new executive officer, Lieutenant Commander Donald Burson, who reported aboard shortly before departure, brought with him a familiar rigidity that had once been routine on the *Liberty*. He ordered one officer to get a haircut and barked at the enlisted men over minor infractions. "The new XO is beginning to get rather picky on some things," an officer griped in a letter. "I realize that we have been rather lax in some areas, but then again, everything has been so jumbled up since the 8th of June, I don't know what he expects."

The task of sorting the jumbled recollections fell to the officers, who gathered in the wardroom after the court of inquiry to discuss medals. Reports of heroic actions surfaced. Men on the forward machine guns had died protecting the ship. Damage control teams had fought fires and kept the *Liberty* afloat. The doctor and his corpsmen had performed surgeries while others rescued men from flooded spaces and the main decks as the fighters attacked. Officers investigated each case. The men learned that not everyone had acted heroically. Stories arose of sailors found hiding. Fear paralyzed others and some cried. One officer claimed to have rescued a blinded colleague in the torpedoed compartments when the investigation revealed an enlisted man made the rescue.

Purple Hearts presented a dilemma for the Pentagon. The medal's criteria required that recipients be killed or injured fighting opposing armed forces. Israel was an ally, so the *Liberty*'s crewmen weren't eligible. Admiral McCain's office intervened. *Liberty* men no doubt believed the attackers represented a hostile force. "Suggest that failure to award Purple Hearts could later become known to press and could generate unwelcome public discussion of procedures which could be interpreted as discriminating not only against the dead and wounded but against cases of unquestioned heroism in action which are only now beginning to become known."

The Pentagon acquiesced, but soon discovered that combat pay posed a similar challenge. Troops in war zones received roughly an extra fifty dollars a month. The Pentagon didn't recognize the eastern Mediterranean as a war zone. McCain's office again advocated for the crew: "A favorable determination would be of financial benefit, a boost to their morale and tangible recognition of the heroic deeds and sacrifices of the officers and men of the USS *Liberty.*" This time the Pentagon compromised. Rather than pay the entire crew—a minimal expense given the Navy's $21 billion budget that year—Pentagon penny-pinchers decided that only the injured men and the families of those killed were entitled to combat pay. The uninjured got only regular pay.

Lost in the Pentagon's arithmetic was the incalculable toll the attack took on the sailors and their families. Many of the families still grieved and sought answers to explain how loved ones had been killed. Others wanted guarantees that Israel would be held accountable. William Allenbaugh, whose son died in the torpedoed research spaces, expressed that in a letter to President Johnson. He asked what action, if any, the government planned to take against the Israeli government. "This was a dastardly deed," Allenbaugh wrote. "We feel that something should be done to correct the loss we have all felt so keenly. Please advise, if possible, what course we can take in regards to this matter."

Soon after her husband's burial in Arlington, Weetie Armstrong wrote a letter to the crew. "You lost your XO and I lost my husband but we were fortunate to have been a part of his life. I know all of you prayed and did what you could for him in his last hours and for this I thank you. I don't understand why God chose to take Philip but I accept God's will. This was His plan for Philip. My children and I are fine. Of course our future looks a bit dim but God will give us the strength to take life a day at a time," she wrote. "I'm not going to make any definite plans until I have some time to think. In any case please feel free to call on me and my children when you are home again. May God bless and keep all of you safe. My prayers are with you."

CHAPTER 18

Almost as shocking as the attack itself has been the manner in which Washington—especially the Defense Department—has seemed to try to absolve Israel from any guilt right from the start. Some of these efforts would be laughable but for the terrible tragedy involved.

—*SHREVEPORT TIMES*

Clark Clifford ranked near the top of President Johnson's roster of pro-Israel advisers. Chairman of the President's Foreign Intelligence Advisory Board, the sixty-year-old Clifford recognized the significant role Jews played in American politics, particularly for Democrats. But Clifford's views were based on more than votes. Though he was Episcopalian, Clifford had regarded the creation of a Jewish state as a moral necessity following the Holocaust. His support for Israel had become a defining moment early in his political career when he served as an aide to President Harry Truman.

On the eve of Israel's independence in 1948, Clifford had urged Truman to recognize the Jewish state. Truman sympathized with the Zionists, but faced pressure from Secretary of State George Marshall not to grant recognition. Most of Truman's senior advisers sided with Marshall. To settle the issue, Truman asked Clifford and Marshall to debate during an afternoon meeting in the Oval Office. The president perched behind his desk, adorned with his famous plaque: THE BUCK STOPS HERE! Marshall sat to his left, Clifford his right. Aides crowded around.

Marshall and his deputies took a pragmatic view. Arabs vastly outnumbered Jews, by some estimates as much as 30 million to just 600,000. Arab nations sat on the Middle East's massive oil reserves. Marshall also warned the president that if Zionists declared independence, neighboring Arab nations would invade. The five-star general, whose economic recovery plan for Europe after World War II would earn him the Nobel Peace Prize in 1953, did not want the United States to be forced to intervene. The best solution was to let the United Nations take over.

Clifford countered that the United Nations' proposed plan for the region called for a single state, an unrealistic solution given that Arabs and Jews already lived separately. A former St. Louis trial lawyer with sixteen years of experience, Clifford argued that the United States had a moral responsibility to support the fledgling state and create a secure homeland for Jews. "Here is an opportunity to try to bring these ancient injustices to an end," he argued. "Perhaps these steps would help atone, in some small way, for the atrocities, so vast as to stupefy the human mind, that occurred during the Holocaust."

The afternoon debate intensified. Clifford watched as the general's face reddened. When Clifford finished, Marshall exploded. The general accused Clifford of cashing in America's foreign policy for a few votes. He then threatened the president: "If you follow Clifford's advice and if I were to vote in the election, I would vote against you." Everyone in the Oval Office froze. If Marshall's threat became public, it would prove politically disastrous for Truman. The president, up for reelection that fall and facing abysmal approval ratings, knew Americans adored Marshall.

Eleven minutes after Israel declared its independence at midnight on May 14, 1948, Truman officially recognized the Jewish state. Clifford had won.

In the two decades since that afternoon, Clifford had remained an advocate for Israel. Still, the attack on the *Liberty* troubled him. Among the president's senior advisers, he had emerged as one of the strongest proponents of forceful action. He described the attack as "egregious" and told colleagues it was "inconceivable" that it could have been an accident. "My concern is that we're not tough enough. Handle as if

Arabs or USSR had done it," Clifford had argued in a meeting of the Special Committee of the National Security Council. "Punish Israelis responsible."

Johnson asked Clifford to prepare a report on the attack but barred him from conducting an independent probe, a handicap he complained about in his memoir: "Because of this limitation, I was never fully satisfied with the results of my report." Clifford gathered records from the Pentagon, including the Navy's court of inquiry and the synopsis of Colonel Ram Ron's report, though Israel had yet to conclude its expanded probe. The veteran statesman also reviewed transcripts of the NSA's radio intercepts of Israeli helicopters. Keeping with the president's wishes, Clifford neither interviewed *Liberty* survivors nor took testimony from Navy, White House, or Pentagon officials. He also did not visit Israel, interview the attackers, or review the Jewish state's war logs, diaries, or radio communications.

Clifford submitted his five-page report to National Security Adviser Walt Rostow two days after the *Liberty* departed Malta for its voyage home. Rostow delivered the top-secret report to the president, describing it in a memo as a "brief but definitive analysis." Clifford's report served as a stinging rebuttal of many of Israel's explanations. He denounced the assertion that Israel had queried the American Embassy in Tel Aviv about the presence of any American ships days before the attack. He also refuted the accusation that the *Liberty* tried to hide itself by flying a small flag. Israel's claim that the *Liberty* refused to identity itself when confronted by torpedo boats, Clifford labeled "demonstrably false."

Clifford's sharpest rebuke centered on Israel's assertion that its forces confused the *Liberty* for an aging Egyptian horse and troop transport. A former Navy captain, Clifford understood ship recognition. He wrote that the *Liberty*'s name was painted in English clearly across the stern with its hull numbers on the bow, a big difference from Egyptian ships marked in Arabic. The American flag flew from the mast. Visibility was excellent. With a gentleman's touch that endeared him to so many presidents, Clifford deemed Israel's excuse a fiction. He supported his position with the trial lawyer's vigor that had made him the first Washington attorney to earn a million dollars a year.

"That the *Liberty* could have been mistaken for the Egyptian supply ship *El Quseir* is unbelievable. *El Quseir* has one-fourth the displacement of the *Liberty,* roughly half the beam, is 180 feet shorter, and is very differently configured. The *Liberty*'s unusual antenna array and hull markings should have been visible to low-flying aircraft and torpedo boats," Clifford wrote. "In the heat of battle the *Liberty* was able to identify one of the attacking torpedo boats as Israeli and to ascertain its hull number. In the same circumstances, trained Israeli naval personnel should have been able easily to see and identify the larger hull markings on the *Liberty.*"

Despite his effort to discredit Israel's explanations, Clifford hedged on the central question of whether its forces deliberately strafed and torpedoed an American ship. He padded his final assessment with qualifiers, though he concluded that Israel's high command and senior government leaders likely did not order the attack. "The evidence at hand does not support the theory that the highest echelons of the Israeli Government were aware of the *Liberty*'s true identity or of the fact that an attack on her was taking place," he wrote. "To disprove such a theory would necessitate a degree of access to Israeli personnel and information which in all likelihood can never be achieved."

Clifford attributed the assault to negligence. He concluded that there was no justification for Israel's otherwise outstanding military to have failed to alert its forces that an American ship sailed nearby. Clifford advocated that the United States demand punishment. "The best interpretation from available facts is that there were gross and inexcusable failures in the command and control of subordinate Israeli naval and air elements," he concluded. "The unprovoked attack on the *Liberty* constitutes a flagrant act of gross negligence for which the Israeli Government should be held completely responsible, and the Israeli military personnel involved should be punished."

President Johnson had confided in a *Newsweek* reporter the day after the attack that he believed Israel had intentionally tried to sink the *Liberty* because it was a spy ship. Press Secretary George Christian, though personally convinced "an accident of this magnitude was too much to swallow," later wrote that Clifford's report swayed the president otherwise. Johnson, who said little publicly about the attack in

1967, dedicated barely a paragraph to it years later in his memoir. He described the *Liberty* simply as a "heartbreaking episode" and a "tragic accident." The president also erred in his memoir in stating that the attack had killed only ten men.

Clifford's report suffered a critical weakness: How could he rule the attack an accident if he didn't believe Israel's explanation? That conundrum plagued the Navy's investigation and embodied American officials' larger struggle to determine precisely how and why the attack occurred. Many recognized that Israel had much to lose by torpedoing the *Liberty,* but simultaneously found its explanations lacked credibility. To resolve that central question required that the United States put the pilots, torpedo boat skippers, and commanding officers under oath—as the Navy did with McGonagle and his crew—and demand answers. It also required investigators to review Israel's radio communications and war logs. Absent Washington's political resolve to pressure Israel, investigators could offer little more than circumstantial guesswork.

Clifford appeared to recognize these failings years later when he described the *Liberty* attack in his memoir. Compared to his original analysis, his views seemed to have sharpened. The *Liberty* did not warrant a break in diplomatic relations, but he believed the attack had been left unresolved. Clifford wrote that he could not bring himself to believe that the highest levels of the civilian government had ordered the strike, but he also felt that Israel failed to make "adequate restitution or explanation." "I do not know to this day at what level the attack on the *Liberty* was authorized, and I think it is unlikely the full truth will ever come out. Having been for so long a staunch supporter of Israel, I was particularly troubled by this incident," he wrote. "Somewhere inside the Israeli government, somewhere along the chain of command, something had gone terribly wrong—and then had been covered up."

Robert McNamara appeared in room S-116 before a closed-door session of the Senate Foreign Relations Committee at 10 A.M. on Wednesday, July 26, ostensibly to talk about America's military aid and sales program. The defense secretary was in for a surprise. In the seven weeks since the attack, the administration had refocused on the Vietnam War, largely viewed as the primary obstacle to the president's 1968 reelection.

McNamara had flown to Southeast Asia earlier in the month to meet with General William Westmoreland, the commander of American military operations in Vietnam. In spite of his increased personal doubts McNamara assured the president and his fellow advisers that victory was possible. "There is a limit to what the enemy can send into the South," he confided in Clark Clifford. "For the first time, I feel that if we follow the same program we will win the war and end the fighting."

McNamara's upbeat report contrasted with the bleak picture the press painted. *Newsweek* noted in a special Independence Day issue titled "The Vietnam War and American Life" that 11,373 Americans had been killed and another 68,341 wounded. The magazine reported that the war's cost had now soared to $38,052 a minute. "There are no statistics to tot up Vietnam's hidden price," *Newsweek* wrote. "But its calculus is clear: a wartime divisiveness all but unknown in America since the Blue bloodied the Gray."

Lawmakers also doubted the assessment. The Preparedness Investigating Subcommittee of the Senate Armed Services Committee planned hearings that would stretch over seven days in August. Senior military officers, angry over McNamara's micromanagement of the war, hoped to use the hearings to pressure the administration to rescind its bombing restrictions. McNamara later described the hearings as "one of the most stressful episodes of my life." The president considered them a "political disaster."

McNamara could not afford to be sidetracked.

Few elected leaders had publicly questioned the *Liberty*, which had dropped from the headlines. Behind closed doors, where legislators could speak openly without fear of offending Israel's powerful lobby, some lawmakers still clamored for more information. The *Liberty* attack had particularly troubled the Senate Foreign Relations Committee, whose members grilled Dean Rusk the morning after the attack.

Hickenlooper, a Republican and senior member of the committee, emerged as one of the more forceful leaders, though his colleagues also voiced concerns. Two days after the *Liberty* arrived in Malta, Hickenlooper had written to Rusk, demanding a detailed report on the attack that he believed "took place under circumstances making it hard to believe that it was accidental."

With McNamara already on Capitol Hill to discuss America's military aid program, committee members seized an opportunity and shifted discussion to the attack. Republican senator George Aiken of Vermont was the first to raise the issue of the *Liberty:* "We have never gotten a very good story on a certain episode."

McNamara understood what he meant. "The attack on the *Liberty,* I think, represented a serious error of judgment and procedure," he replied. "But I have examined the record of the investigation, and I find no intent by the Israeli Government, and no intent by any representatives of the Israeli Government to attack a U.S. vessel."

"Was it an individual rather than a governmental error?" Aiken pressed.

"Yes, sir," McNamara answered. "To the best of my knowledge."

"From what I have read I can't tolerate for one minute that this was an accident," Hickenlooper declared moments later. "I think it was a deliberate assault on this ship. I think they had ample opportunity to identify it as an American ship."

Hickenlooper, known by colleagues as the "consummate skeptic," compared the *Liberty* to the torpedo boat assaults in the Gulf of Tonkin, which the president had used to drum up congressional support for military action against North Vietnam in 1964. "What have we done about the *Liberty*?" he asked. "Have we become so placid, so far as Israel is concerned or so far as that area is concerned, that we will take the killing of 37 American boys and the wounding of a lot more and the attack of an American ship in the open sea in good weather? We have seemed to say: 'Oh, well, boys will be boys.' What are you going to do about it? It is most offensive to me."

McNamara dismissed Hickenlooper's comparison to the Tonkin Gulf Resolution, arguing that the United States had reason to believe North Vietnam intentionally targeted American ships. The defense secretary said the Navy's court of inquiry concluded the *Liberty* attack was an error. He added that the United States had made a strong protest to the Israeli government. "In the case of the attack on the *Liberty*, it was the conclusion of the investigatory body headed by an admiral of the Navy in whom we have great confidence that the attack was not intentional," McNamara told committee members. "I read the record of the investigation, and I support that conclusion."

Hickenlooper questioned whether the intelligence was really any better in the case of the Tonkin Gulf attacks than it was with the *Liberty*. "There is no evidence, then, no evidence that we have at all, that there was any communication between Tel Aviv and the attacking vessels or the airplanes that apparently flew over this ship several times at rather low altitude?" he asked.

"No, there is no evidence that the individuals attacking the *Liberty* knew they were attacking a U.S. ship," McNamara answered. "There is some evidence, circumstantial, that they didn't know it."

"It just doesn't sound very good to me," Hickenlooper complained. "I can't accept these explanations that so glibly come out of Tel Aviv and perhaps some rather confusedly come out of our own investigation, I don't know."

McNamara assured him nothing was left out of the court of inquiry, but Hickenlooper persisted. "It is inconceivable to me that the ship could not have been identified. According to everything I saw, the American flag was flying on this ship. It had a particular configuration. Even a landlubber could look at it and see that it has no characteristic configuration comparable to the so-called Egyptian ship they now try to say they mistook it for," he said. "It just doesn't add up to me. It is not at all satisfactory."

"I don't want to carry the torch for the Israelis," McNamara countered.

"That is what it looks like we are doing in this country," Hickenlooper replied.

"Not only the committee but the public wants better information than they have had so far," Aiken interjected.

"The public is thoroughly dissatisfied with the situation," Hickenlooper added. "It is the seemingly cavalier attitude expressed by Israel in some ways apparently accepted by us on a very tragic situation. I think there is utterly no excuse for it."

"I completely agree with you," replied McNamara. "But it is thoroughly clear, based on the investigation report, that it was not a conscious attack on a U.S. vessel."

"You mean by the pilots?" asked Senator Karl Mundt, a South Dakota Republican.

"By the pilots. They did not identify the vessel as a U.S. vessel prior to the time of attack," McNamara said. "You may consider this inconceivable."

"On the part of the attackers, yes," Mundt replied. "It seemed to be broad daylight."

"They definitely did not," McNamara countered. "All of the evidence points to the contrary."

"You take their word for it?" Mundt asked.

"My conclusion is based on the investigation report which did not discuss the identification with the Israeli pilots or naval personnel involved, but did examine all of the circumstances of the attack and did discuss it with the commander and even the men on the *Liberty.*"

Hickenlooper read the Pentagon's summary of the court of inquiry that dealt with the Israeli reconnaissance prior to the attack, stating that witnesses had testified to "significant surveillance." "If they didn't identify that ship," he quipped, "then they are not as smart as I think they are."

McNamara argued that the earlier recon flights weren't the attackers. "I think it is an inexcusably weak military performance. That, I fully agree with," he said. "But I simply want to emphasize that the investigative report does not show any evidence of a conscious intent to attack a U.S. vessel."

Each time the senators challenged the defense secretary, he pointed to the court of inquiry's conclusions. McNamara's defense grew more forceful as the questions continued. His bluster disguised the fact that others inside the Pentagon disagreed with him, including his own general counsel. "I found it hard to believe that it was, in fact, an honest mistake on the part of the Israeli air force units," that assistant, Paul

Warnke, later would admit. "I still find it impossible to believe that it was. I suspect that in the heat of battle they figured that the presence of this American ship was inimical to their interests, and that somebody without authorization attacked it."

McNamara succeeded in stifling the debate. Despite the heated volley, McNamara insisted there was no evidence of an intentional attack. The defense secretary did concede the critical point that Navy investigators had failed to interview the attackers, though that admission drew no follow-up from the lawmakers. The frustrated senators soon tired and moved on to other topics. Hickenlooper griped that he doubted the committee would ever learn the truth. "That is all we have to go on at the present time. I suppose that is all we will ever get," he conceded. "It creates a sense of utter frustration."

McNamara's rigorous defense of Israel contrasted with Dean Rusk's position. The pragmatic secretary of state appeared several times before the same committee in the weeks after the attack, often meeting behind closed doors. Rusk, who described the attack as a "genuine outrage," doubted Israel's explanation that it was simply a tragic accident. Though Rusk did not seek out opportunities to publicize his disbelief, he likewise showed no hesitation about sharing his doubts when asked. His candor even had sparked a minor diplomatic crisis.

At a meeting of the North Atlantic Treaty Organization in Luxembourg, Rusk shared his thoughts on the *Liberty* with NATO secretary-general Manlio Brosio and other attendees. His blunt comments prompted a frantic telegram to the State Department from Harlan Cleveland, America's ambassador to NATO. "Secretary's comments to Brosio and several foreign ministers at Luxembourg about Israeli foreknowledge that *Liberty* was a US ship piqued a great deal of curiosity," Cleveland wrote. "Would appreciate guidance as to how much of this curiosity I can satisfy, and when."

The same day the Pentagon released its summary of the court of inquiry, Rusk met with the Senate Foreign Relations Committee. Hickenlooper asked if he had any information about the attack, but Rusk could offer few answers. He read the opening paragraphs of the Pentagon's summary and noted that Israel had conducted extensive surveillance of the ship prior to the attack. He told members he had sent a stern letter to Israel's ambassador. The United States still awaited the outcome of Israel's investigation.

Rusk told the committee two weeks later, on July 11, that the United States still had no clear answers. He raised the possibility that America might never know with certainty what had happened. "I might just say at the moment that all the facts we are going to get, I think, are pretty well in, and we still have no satisfactory explanation of how it occurred," Rusk said. "We will be putting a bill in to the Israeli government for reparations and damages for both personnel and for damage to the ship, and that will be coming along as soon as we get all the data together. That will be a very substantial bill."

The secretary of state sat down again with the committee later that same week in the Old Senate Office Building. He reiterated the government's plan to submit reparations claims but could offer no more information on the attack. The United States still had no real understanding of it despite its investigations. Israel had all the answers. "We have now had our Naval Board of Inquiry, and the summary of that report has been made public," Rusk said. "We do not believe that we have had anything that could be called an adequate justification from the Israeli Government."

Chairman J. W. Fulbright voiced his frustration. Senators had hoped to have a thorough report on the *Liberty* before deciding on the foreign aid bill before the committee for approval. Fulbright told Rusk the senators wanted a transcript of the Navy's court of inquiry, a request Rusk said he could arrange. "These matters are very difficult for us to come to conclusion on if we do not have what the members consider to be a full account of it," complained the Arkansas Democrat. "I do not think I am revealing any secret to say that several members were extremely upset about that incident."

"Senator," Rusk replied, "so were we."

Commander McGonagle guided the *Liberty* into the Little Creek Naval Amphibious Base near Norfolk on Saturday afternoon, July 29. Anxious sailors in crisp white uniforms lined the rails as the *Liberty*—still accompanied by the tugboat *Papago*—tied up alongside pier 17 at 5 P.M. A helicopter buzzed high overhead. McGonagle likely felt a mix of relief and sadness as he observed the families gathered on the concrete pier below, many waving signs welcoming the crew home. When the *Liberty* had sailed from Virginia eighty-eight days earlier for its top-secret mission to Africa, the skipper believed his career had stagnated, and he obsessed over inconsequential matters. He now returned with thirty-four of his men dead and nearly two hundred more injured. His spy ship, which no one was supposed to know existed, had briefly dominated the news that summer.

McGonagle had weathered a court of inquiry in the meantime and emerged a hero. Rather than force him to retire, the Navy nominated him for the Medal of Honor and recommended him for promotion to captain. Senior officers in the Pentagon greeted the skipper's success with surprise and admiration, best reflected by a doctored copy of McGonagle's Navy bio that circulated. Someone had underlined McGonagle's unspectacular assignments in blue ink, ranging from salvage ship operator to naval science instructor at the University of Idaho. "A diverse background, the product of our 'system' which some people don't like," read a handwritten note appended to it. "But he had the right skills & experience to do a big job at the right time."

The roughly three hundred wives, children, parents, and reporters gathered could see no outward scars of the attack that had left 821 shell holes and a huge gash in *Liberty*'s side. The only remnants of that violent afternoon sat zipped inside 168 canvas bags under guard in a locked compartment belowdecks, a waterlogged mix of classified records, flesh, and bone fragments. The absence of scars did little to ease the pain for families of the dead, many of whom traveled to Norfolk and climbed the gangway. One woman approached Ensign O'Malley and insisted that her son had survived the torpedo blast. The junior officer, who had helped McGonagle write letters to the families, recognized the woman's name. Her son was one of the sailors lost at sea.

"He swam through the hole," the woman insisted. "Maybe he made it to shore."

O'Malley glanced at the woman's husband. The man remained silent, offering O'Malley only a pleading look.

"Nobody got out. Nobody," O'Malley replied. "He's dead. I'm sorry."

The widow of one of the petty officers killed by the torpedo blast asked Lieutenant Painter if she could visit the place where her husband had died. Painter obliged. He escorted her through the ship's passageways and down a couple of ladders into the torpedoed compartment. The space that for six days was filled with warm seawater, oil, and blood, was now clean and largely rebuilt. The smell of fresh paint filled the air. The woman surveyed the empty room. "Not much was said. There was just an overwhelming sense of sorrow and loss," Painter recalled later. "She was one brave, courageous woman."

The *Virginian-Pilot* captured the sadness many felt in an editorial that appeared that morning. "The arrival here today of the USS *Liberty* is a sobering reminder to this Navy community that no ship that clears this port is assured of returning with her hull intact and all her crewmen alive and uninjured," the newspaper wrote. "Among the casualties were our neighbors—men who walked down our streets, shopped in our stores, chatted with us at lunch counters. The survivors and their families are joyful. But the rejoicing is tempered by the loss of shipmates and friends."

Miss Norfolk, dressed in a white knee-length dress and a flower hat, and Miss Hospitality in a blue dress, white hat, and gloves, greeted sailors. Reporters photographed the tearful reunions of husbands and wives, parents and children. Though the *Liberty* had dropped from the headlines, the Pentagon remained guarded with the press. The day before the *Liberty*'s arrival, the ship's Plan of the Day again ordered crewmembers to defer interviews to senior officers. To satisfy the media, McGonagle led reporters on a brief tour. He described the attack only as "unprovoked and unexpected." The skipper shifted the attention to his men, complimenting the "magnificent job" of his damage control teams and noting that he had recommended forty-two sailors for medals: "The reaction of the crew was everything I could have expected or hoped for."

A team of National Security Agency analysts visited the *Liberty* two days after it arrived in port to inspect the canvas bags stowed below deck. The agency demanded an inventory if possible of all surviving classified materials. The bags, stacked several high, held the remnants of key cards, manuals, and magnetic tapes that crews had shoveled up in Malta. *Liberty* sailors with classified clearances slipped on coveralls, masks, and gloves inside the darkened compartment that morning. The men opened the duffle bags and emptied them one after the other onto the deck. A rancid smell filled the air. Some manuals contained legible material, but many others had been reduced to an oil-soaked pulp. One of the men spotted a finger. "It was a nightmare," recalled John McTighe, a young Navy lieutenant who worked at the NSA. "It was just mush."

The agency's concern centered on whether the *Liberty* might pose an intelligence breach. Soviet ships sailed in the Mediterranean at the time of the attack. Officials had feared the Russians might recover classified records. The *Papago*, stationed a thousand yards behind the *Liberty*, had netted some documents and shredded others in its propeller. A few likely were lost at sea. Benjamin Cwalina, a security officer tasked with determining whether the *Liberty* posed an intelligence breach, looked at the piles of soggy papers and realized that the torpedo had vaporized much of the spy ship's records. After opening only a half dozen bags, Cwalina and others told the sailors to stop. The rest of the materials should be burned. "We declared no compromise," Cwalina recalled. "We didn't have to worry about the Russians getting hold of any of our documents."

The final destruction of the classified records fell to the men on the *Liberty*. A work party from the local base arrived one humid August morning a couple of weeks later with a truck and a crane to help Painter and other sailors dispose of the stacks of canvas bags. The first sailor to venture down inside the torpedoed spaces in Malta, Painter would be the last to deal with the remnants of the attack. The men loaded the bags onto the back of a truck and drove to the base incinerator. There a crane lifted each bag—many containing bone fragments and tissue of the *Liberty*'s dead—and dropped them one by one into the incinerator. The young officer watched as the bags vanished in seconds. "I remember thinking that I had just cremated the remains of many unnamed sailors," Painter later recalled. "I never forgot that day."

Sixteen days after the *Liberty* tied up in Virginia, Ephraim Evron delivered a copy of Israel's final report on the attack to Eugene Rostow at the State Department. Brigadier General Joseph Geva, Israel's military attaché, also submitted a copy to his counterparts in the U.S. Navy. Israeli diplomats urged American officials to downplay the nineteen-page report now that the attack had faded from the headlines. American leaders agreed and limited distribution largely to members of Congress and senior officers at the Pentagon. "I made clear that the document is secret and added that in our opinion, it is best not to re-evoke the matter now that it is being forgotten," Evron cabled to Jerusalem. "Rostow responded that confidentiality will be guaranteed."

American leaders had awaited a satisfactory explanation of the attack for more than two months. The Israeli prosecutor, without naming any defendants, recommended seven charges of negligence. Those ranged from failure to alert senior officers of the spy ship's presence after reconnaissance flights spotted it that morning to the dereliction of the torpedo boat division commander to positively identify the *Liberty* before attacking it. Lieutenant Colonel Yeshayahu Yerushalmi was the judge who presided over the case. Like Ron, Yerushalmi was a native of Poland. He had emigrated to Israel as a teenager in 1935 and later graduated from Tel Aviv's Balfour College. After he studied law at the University of Jerusalem, Yerushalmi joined the military court of appeals as a judge in 1957, where he served at the time of the attack on the *Liberty*. Yerushalmi's report stated that over the course of a month, he heard thirty-four witnesses and considered fourteen exhibits before rendering his verdict. The English-language version of his report provided to the United States identified witnesses by title only and did not include a breakdown of those exhibits.

Yerushalmi's explanation for the attack largely mirrored Ron's, but a close comparison of the reports revealed stark differences. Ron had exonerated the attackers, but his full report contained damaging evidence against Israeli forces. Transcripts of radio communications showed that a pilot reported the *Liberty*'s hull markings more than twenty minutes before the torpedo strike, markings that convinced the chief air controller at general headquarters in Tel Aviv the ship was "probably American." The Navy's second in command had received the pilot's report of the *Liberty*'s hull markings, but dismissed the markings as an Egyptian ruse. Ron's report also revealed that before the torpedo attack, two other Israeli Navy officers believed the target was the *Liberty*. These facts had convinced Ambassador Harman that people needed to go to jail.

Yerushalmi's report in contrast downplayed, omitted, or used ridiculous logic to explain away the most damaging evidence that showed Israeli forces had conclusively identified the *Liberty* in time to halt the fatal torpedo strike that killed twenty-five of the thirty-four sailors. In his poorly written and cumbersome report, Yerushalmi conceded that pilots spotted the *Liberty*'s hull markings but said only that it raised doubts about the ship's identity. Likewise, he omitted the fact that the Navy's second in command had earlier testified that he discounted the pilot's report as evidence of an Egyptian ploy. Also absent was the critical fact that two Israeli Navy officers believed before the torpedo attack that the ship was the *Liberty* but failed to intervene. In referring to one of the officers, Yerushalmi stated only that the officer's suspicion was "aroused" that the target might be wrong.

Yerushalmi's report instead appeared intended to counter many of the criticisms against Israeli forces. He explained away the morning's reconnaissance by stating that shortly before the attack, an officer assumed the *Liberty* had sailed away and ordered the ship's marker removed from the Navy's war room plotting table. He wrote that he examined photographs of the *Liberty* and *El Quseir* and was satisfied that the two ships appeared similar. The smoke, a result of the air strikes, made it harder for Israeli forces to identify it. As for the criticism that torpedo boat skippers should have recognized the unarmed ship was incapable of a shore bombardment, Yerushalmi argued that it could have been an escaping Egyptian supply ship that lagged behind the true culprits or, as one witness testified, was a transport ship that had "come to assist in the evacuation of Egyptian soldiers."

Yerushalmi justified Israel's actions in part by blaming the United States. He conceded the *Liberty* was in international waters, but determined that that didn't matter because the ship steamed in an area Egypt had declared "dangerous for shipping." He wrote that he could only assume Egypt's declaration was known to the *Liberty*. He further noted that the area was not a recognized shipping route and criticized the United States for failing to announce the *Liberty*'s presence. McGonagle also shared the blame for allegedly signaling "identify yourself first" when confronted by the torpedo boats, a claim the United States had disproved. Yerushalmi insisted—despite evidence to the contrary—that Israeli forces did not identify the *Liberty* until after the torpedo strike. "It was only a helicopter, sent after the attack in order to render assistance—if necessary—which noticed a small American Flag flying over the target," he wrote. "At that stage the vessel was finally identified as an audio-surveillance ship of the U.S. Navy."

In his conclusion, Yerushalmi ruled that Israel's pilots, skippers, and commanders all acted reasonably under wartime circumstances. He then dismissed all charges. No Israeli would ever be punished for the attack that killed thirty-four Americans, injured almost two hundred others, and nearly destroyed an American ship. The assault on the *Liberty,* which raged for approximately an hour on a clear afternoon in international waters, was the most violent assault on an American naval ship since World War II. Yet Yerushalmi could find no evidence of wrongdoing, no negligence, no violation of military procedure. "For all my regret that our forces were involved in an incident with a vessel of a friendly state, and its sad outcome," Yerushalmi concluded, "I have not discovered any deviation from the standard of reasonable conduct which would justify the committal of anyone for trial."

American officials slammed Yerushalmi's report. Lucius Battle, assistant secretary of state for Near Eastern and South Asian affairs, questioned why Israeli officers removed the *Liberty* from the war room's plotting table. Reconnaissance planes had flown regular missions since before sunrise. Surely someone could have assured Israel's high command that no ships capable of a shore bombardment had sailed into the area. If it was clear the *Liberty* was not a threat, why did Israeli forces attack? How were fighter pilots able to spot the spy ship's hull markings after the assault—when fires raged on deck—but failed to observe the towering letters and numbers before repeatedly strafing the defenseless ship with cannons and napalm?

Battle's memo to Nicholas Katzenbach, the State Department's second in command, concluded that Yerushalmi's report promised political problems for the administration. Congressional interest remained strong and it would be only a matter of time before word of the report's arrival leaked. To mitigate the backlash, America needed to make sure Israel punished someone. "It seems likely that the decision will be considered a 'whitewash' by the press, public, and Congressional officials," Battle wrote. "The United States cannot accept the report as exonerating the Israeli Government from taking the disciplinary measures which international law requires in the event of wrongful conduct by the military personnel of a state."

Others shared Battle's view. Captain Mayo Hadden, Jr., in the Navy's Politico-Military Policy Division prepared a summary of Yerushalmi's report for senior officers at the Pentagon. Two months earlier, Hadden had written a secret analysis of Ron's report, describing it as a "whitewash." The World War II fighter pilot reiterated his previous analysis in a confidential memo. "A one-word summation," he concluded, "well could be white-wash." NSA deputy director Louis Tordella went further. Tordella, who previously told members of the House Appropriations Committee in a closed-door meeting that he believed Israel intentionally targeted the *Liberty*, was outraged by Yerushalmi's findings. He made his feelings clear in a handwritten note. "A nice whitewash for a group of ignorant, stupid and inept xxx," he wrote, substituting the letter *x* for his true beliefs. "If the attackers had not been Hebrew there would have been *quite* a commotion. Such crass stupidity—30 knots, warship, 2 guns, etc., does not even do credit to the Nigerian Navy."

When Ambassador Harman had urged Israel to expand its investigation, he believed that only a thorough vetting of the assault followed by the prosecution of the attackers would assure Washington that the strike had not been malicious. Yerushalmi's exoneration instead confirmed the belief among many senior American officials that Israel had deliberately targeted the *Liberty*. The question remained: How could trained Israeli naval officers confuse a spy ship with forty-five towering antennae for an aged horse and troop transport a fraction its size? Israel's skilled intelligence services had pinpointed the precise location of Egyptian forces on the eve of the war but days later seemed at a loss to identify the lumbering *Liberty* on a clear day.

Even Israel's convoluted justification as outlined in Yerushalmi's report overlooked the obvious question: Why did senior commanders, when presented with the possibility that the target might be American, not do everything possible to stop the assault? The senior air controller later admitted he was certain the ship was American. Why had neither he nor his supervisors called the Navy, the defense minister, or even the leaders of Israel's civilian government to demand an end to the assault? Surely more could have been done to halt the attack before the torpedo strike more than twenty minutes later that resulted in the majority of the *Liberty*'s casualties. Israeli forces already had determined the ship was unarmed, alone, and incapable of escape. There was no need to hurry.

The possibility of such a catastrophic intelligence breakdown seemed preposterous to American officials, particularly in the wake of Israel's stunning performance in what would later be known as the Six-Day War. To many, Yerushalmi's report appeared orchestrated to provide political cover for Israel's leaders and shield the attackers. The failure to punish those involved, Katzenbach later said, only "confirms that there was some knowledge of it." It also left lingering resentment among many, particularly in the Navy. When asked about his "most prominent memory of the *Liberty*," Admiral Rivero answered: "My anger and frustration at our not punishing the attackers."

Katzenbach shared his disbelief in a private meeting at the State Department in August with Evron, the Israeli Embassy's second in command. Evron said he could add little to the report's findings. He had pressed the issue with Chief of Staff Yitzhak Rabin, but said Israel was now bound by Yerushalmi's conclusion. "Examining judge laid out point after point confirming negligence on part of various Israeli officials in affair, yet ended up finding no deviation from normal conduct. Surely, Under Secretary said, one cannot believe such conduct was consistent with normal Israeli practice and did not involve culpable negligence on part of officials involved," a memo of the conversation stated. "Under Secretary reiterated his surprise at judge's findings though he assured Evron he did not intend publicly to express these personal conclusions."

The State Department continued to seek answers. In a September analysis, Deputy Legal Adviser Carl Salans contrasted Yerushalmi's findings with the Navy court of inquiry and Clark Clifford's report. The Harvard-trained lawyer outlined nearly a dozen significant inconsistencies between the American and Israeli accounts, from the *Liberty*'s speed and direction to the number of reconnaissance flights, visibility of the ship's markings, and the alleged resemblance to *El Quseir*. His five-page report, prepared for Katzenbach and stamped top-secret, convinced Salans that the attack must have been deliberate. "There were a lot of discrepancies. That was the whole point of the memo," recalled Salans, the department's second-ranking lawyer at the time. "My opinion was that very likely the Israelis were not telling the truth."

State Department legal adviser Leonard Meeker agreed. He later wrote that the apparent coordination between the fighters and torpedo boats—followed by hours of close surveillance—ruled out an accidental attack by local commanders. The department's top lawyer concluded that the order to strike must have originated high up the chain of command. "The Israeli and U.S. Navy accounts of what happened on 8 June 1967 plainly do not jibe," Meeker wrote. "The attacks on the *Liberty* cannot be written off as accidental. Nor can they really be seen as the result of mis-identification of the ship. In view of the repeated reconnaissance runs by Israeli aircraft over several hours between 0515 and 1245, the air and torpedo boat attacks must be judged as deliberate."

The discrepancies noted in the State Department's analysis were familiar to many senior American officials, but absent the political motivation to press Israel, the report accomplished little. Phil Goulding later summarized the frustration over Washington's inability to determine precisely what happened. "How in the name of heaven was the Pentagon to learn whether the attackers knew that the *Liberty* was an American ship? How was it to know why the attack had been made and who ordered it? The Israeli government had not offered us its logs or copies of its messages; it had volunteered no witnesses nor affidavits," the Pentagon's chief spokesman wrote in his memoir. "When I left the government, nineteen months after the attack, we still did not have from Israel the answers to why it happened or how it happened or who ordered it or who was to blame. Having acknowledged—rather begrudgingly—its responsibility for the attack, the sovereign government of Israel had not seen fit to disclose details to us."

CHAPTER 19

The average American taxpayer would likely find it hard to reconcile a settlement of less than two cents on the dollar in the case of the Liberty *with our recent large-scale support for Israel.*

—CONFIDENTIAL STATE DEPARTMENT LETTER

Family, friends, and shipmates gathered on the banks of the Potomac River at Arlington National Cemetery on a warm August morning to bury the last of the *Liberty*'s dead. Two tents set up along either side of the grave sheltered rows of folding chairs that protected grieving families from the summer sun. Women in dark knee-length dresses sobbed in the shade, comforted by men in business suits. A single casket suspended over the fresh grave held little more than bone fragments and tissue—shoveled into body bags two months earlier in Malta—of five sailors and one Marine vaporized by the torpedo. The casket and funeral served largely as a symbolic gesture.

Taps soon sounded over the rolling hills of the cemetery as the morning service, performed according to Catholic and Protestant traditions, concluded. Officers in formal Navy whites saluted the flag-draped coffin. Some of the men in suits placed their right hands over their hearts. Others bowed their heads. Seventy-four days after a torpedo ripped open the side of the *Liberty*—and nearly six thousand miles from where it happened—the remains of the men were lowered into the ground. The rectangular headstone that marked the new grave read: "DIED IN THE EASTERN MEDITERRANEAN."

Few newspapers covered the funeral. The press, like much of the country, focused elsewhere. Race riots recently had rocked more than one hundred cities, including Detroit, Newark, and Milwaukee, triggering a presidential commission and congressional probes. News stories depicted armored personnel carriers and even tanks rolling past looted stores. Others showed smoldering city blocks and bloodied bodies strewn on sidewalks. A photo published in *U.S. News & World Report* in early August showed National Guardsmen crouched behind a jeep in Detroit, battling rooftop snipers in what the magazine described as a "guerrilla war." *Newsweek*'s cover that same week displayed an urban inferno beneath the headline "Battlefield, U.S.A."

Beyond the riots, the war in Vietnam slogged on and President Johnson's approval ratings plummeted. An August 13 poll showed that only 39 percent of Americans approved of the president, down nine points from May and marking Johnson's lowest approval rating during his forty-five months in office. A poll released a week later revealed that potential Republican presidential candidate George Romney boasted an eight-point lead over the president in the race for the White House. Johnson's political future appeared dim. At his Texas ranch a few weeks later, the president confided in his friend Texas governor John Connally that he would not run again.

The president, a virtual prisoner in the White House and at his ranch because of the Vietnam War protesters, watched as his team of advisers continued to unravel. Defense Secretary Robert McNamara, who popped sleeping pills some nights and faced mounting doubts over the winnability of Vietnam, stepped down in November after nearly seven years at the head of the Pentagon. McNamara, who became president of the World Bank, would later write that he was not sure whether he resigned or was fired. One thing was clear: the two men had grown apart. Johnson felt isolated. "I have seldom felt as sorry for him," Lady Bird confessed in her diary. "The sense of loneliness and separation is deep."

Against this backdrop of dour news, the *Liberty* faded.

Newsweek, which broke the story that many senior American leaders believed Israel had deliberately targeted the ship, reported in August on McNamara's closed-door session with the Senate Foreign Relations Committee. The magazine noted in a one-paragraph column that the defense secretary was "satisfied that the strafing of the U.S. ship *Liberty* by Israeli pilots during the Mideast war was unintentional." The article failed to mention McNamara's efforts to stifle debate in the contentious session, the frustrated questions of the senators, or Hickenlooper's declaration that he believed the attack was a "deliberate assault."

The magazine reported the next week that Israel's investigation had exonerated the attackers. The Israeli report merited only a four-sentence brief. The magazine printed the Israeli claims that the *Liberty* had refused to identify itself and that the attackers mistakenly confused it with an Egyptian cargo ship, claims that had been discredited by the American government. "An Israeli court of inquiry has just concluded that the *Liberty* was attacked because she greatly resembled an Egyptian supply ship known to be in the area," *Newsweek* wrote. "Moreover, the Israelis say that when the *Liberty* was asked to identify herself, she replied: 'Identify yourself first.'"

Newsweek printed a follow-up story in May 1968, explaining in more detail Israel's account of the attack, but the magazine again failed to question what many in Washington viewed as serious discrepancies. *U.S. News & World Report,* in a story that also appeared that month based on diplomatic accounts, took a more tempered approach, spotlighting the differences between the Israeli and American investigations. Neither article questioned why no one was ever punished. "Why didn't the Israelis take more time to confirm the ship's identity?" the article asked. "Military experts make this point to explain: One of the reasons Israel is alive is that it strikes quickly, asks questions later."

Several congressmen rallied for answers as 1967 waned.

The day after the mass burial at Arlington, Republican representative H. R. Gross demanded to know if American taxpayers were bankrolling Israeli reparations or had provided the weapons used against the *Liberty*. Unbeknownst to the Iowa congressman, a preliminary Navy analysis two months earlier found that torpedo boat gunners had targeted the spy ship with 40-mm tracer rounds made in the United States. "Is this Government now, directly or indirectly, subsidizing Israel in the payment of full compensation for the lives that were destroyed, the suffering of the wounded, and the damage from this wanton attack?" Gross asked. "It can well be asked whether these

Americans were the victims of bombs, machine gun bullets and torpedoes manufactured in the United States and dished out as military assistance under foreign aid."

On September 19, Louisiana Democratic representative John Rarick protested the failure of the government and national press to investigate the *Liberty*. He inserted into the record a couple of articles that raised questions about the attack and a resolution approved at the American Legion's recent national convention in Boston that demanded the government "conduct a complete and thorough investigation." "The more the case is studied the more questions occur. Who planned the attack on the *Liberty*, and why was it made? Why has the report of the naval court of inquiry not been made public?" Rarick asked. "I submit that the attack on the *Liberty* warrants a full and complete investigation by the Congress."

Republican representative Craig Hosmer of California—one of only two lawmakers to challenge the Navy's censored report when it was first published—in October inserted into the *Congressional Record* a letter he wrote to the State Department and Defense Department, demanding answers about the attack and the status of Israel's reparations. "Inasmuch as American lives were lost, American sailors were injured, and an American naval vessel was severely damaged by the attack on the U.S.S. *Liberty*, it seems to me that the U.S. Government by this time should be in a position to say something definitive about the whole affair," Hosmer said. "The U.S.S. *Liberty* incident is, at this point, by no means satisfactorily closed."

When lawmakers considered spending nearly $6 million to build schools in Israel in November, Representative Gross interrupted the debate and returned to his previous concerns over *Liberty* reparations. "Does the gentleman mean to tell me that we are going to embark upon this multimillion-dollar program in Israel before there is a settlement for this loss of life, pain and anguish to the wounded, and damage to the vessel," Gross demanded of his colleague, Representative Otto Passman, a Louisiana Democrat. "I will say to the gentleman that as far as I am concerned not one dollar of U.S. credit or aid of any kind would go to Israel until there is a firm settlement with regard to that attack and full reparations have been made."

Gross introduced an amendment the next day to block aid to Israel until it "provides full and complete reparations for the killing and wounding of more than 100 United States citizens in the wanton, unprovoked attack." Passman objected and demanded Gross explain his amendment.

Gross countered that his amendment was "self-explanatory." "It simply means that none of the funds provided in this bill shall go to the State of Israel until that Government provides full and fair reparations for the more than 100 U.S. servicemen who were killed and wounded—I believe some 34 or 35 were killed and another 75 or 80 were wounded—in the unprovoked attack by Israel's military forces upon the U.S.S. *Liberty.*"

Democratic representative Clarence Long of Maryland defended Israel, arguing that the Jewish state had promised to pay the families and should be given time to do so. "Is it not the purpose of the gentleman's amendment simply to give a slap in the face to a friendly country that has already admitted it made a mistake and has offered to make full reparations?" Long demanded. "I ask the gentleman if he is willing to give them time and not to insult somebody gratuitously."

"This is not an insult," Gross replied. "Let them first compensate those to whom they caused so much pain and anguish."

Long refused to relent. "If this is not an insult, I would like to hear from the gentleman what he regards as an insult."

"I wonder how you would feel if you were the father of one of the boys who was killed or maimed on that U.S. naval vessel," Gross replied. "I do not know what kind of descriptive word you would use to express your feeling in that connection—or perhaps you do not have any feeling with respect to these young men who were killed, wounded and maimed, or their families."

Moments later, Gross's amendment failed.

Long's confidence in Israel's willingness to pay its debts for the *Liberty* proved premature. At 10:30 A.M. on March 25, 1968—more than nine months after the attack—Israeli Ambassador to the United States Yitzhak Rabin arrived in the seventh-floor office of Nicholas Katzenbach, the State Department's second in command. After serving as the chief of staff of the Israel Defense Forces during the Six-Day War, Rabin had replaced Avraham Harman as ambassador to the U.S. in February 1968. Many Israelis believed that Rabin "incarnated the narrative of Israel's courageous fight for independence."

State Department lawyers sensed trouble with Rabin's visit. Washington lawyer David Ginsburg accompanied him. Throughout the summer and fall of 1967, U.S.-government lawyers had calculated claims on behalf of the wives, children, and parents of the thirty-four men killed on the *Liberty*. The American Embassy in Tel Aviv had presented the Israeli government with a bill for $3.3 million on December 29. In its accompanying note, the State Department urged Israel to promptly pay in "view of the substantial economic hardship suffered by these claimants." Israel responded by hiring Ginsburg.

Deputy State Department legal adviser Carl Salans, who drafted the earlier analysis highlighting the myriad discrepancies between the reports of the Israeli and American investigations, dashed off a memo to Katzenbach days before the meeting with Rabin. Salans was blunt. "We clearly do not want to encourage a protracted nit-picking and haggling exercise. An extended 'negotiation' over the death claims would result in considerable delay and added hardship for the claimants and would, we think, be severely criticized in Congress," he advised Katzenbach. "We should again urge the Israelis to proceed expeditiously with payment of the death claims."

Rabin began by stating that Israel "accepted in principle the obligation to pay the claims, but that more than half the compensation claimed related to shock and emotional anguish." Rabin said the Israeli government wanted to know how the United States quantified emotional anguish. Ginsburg then elaborated. The veteran lawyer said Israel was willing to pay $1.54 million for loss of support, but described shock and mental anguish as an "arbitrary figure." He also pointed out that Israel still faced claims for the injured and the *Liberty* repairs, figures the American government had not yet calculated.

Katzenbach responded "that the death claims had been presented first out of humanitarian considerations." Some of the families, the undersecretary said, had a "genuine financial need." The remaining claims for the injured demanded more time to compile. The government still did not know the full extent of the injuries in some cases or did not have long-term medical care estimates. Katzenbach again "urged that the Government of Israel not hold up the death claims." Congress was concerned most, he warned, with compensation for the families of the dead.

If Israel agreed to pay an "arbitrary figure" for emotional anguish, Rabin said he feared it might set a precedent forcing it to "accept other arbitrary figures, such as that for pain and suffering in the personal injury cases." Ginsburg said he wanted details of how the United States determined the figures for emotional anguish in the death cases and asked for the formula the government planned to use for the personal injury cases and an estimate of the *Liberty* repair bill. The embassy's lawyer added that federal statutes don't recognize payments for emotional anguish in claims against the United States. Why should Israel have to pay?

Katzenbach again emphasized that Israel should pay the death claims immediately rather than wait for the other claims. State Department officials warned Rabin after the meeting that any delays would spark victims to "redouble efforts through congressional and other channels to insure their claims not being sidetracked. This could seriously agitate issue of *Liberty* attack at time when it has generally subsided." The threat didn't sway Rabin, who "seemed unimpressed by political risks involved."

State Department lawyers outlined on several occasions in the following weeks how the United States calculated the $3.3 million claim. Israel still waffled. As the one-year anniversary of the attack approached, the Jewish state proposed a compromise. Israel wanted to use the same formula the American government used to pay death claims for service members. State Department lawyers calculated that Israel's proposal slashed its total compensation to $1.25 million. The proposal would hit the parents of unmarried sailors the hardest, cutting payments from $20,000 each to $5,000 each.

State Department officials fumed. The *Liberty* men didn't die in a combat zone or a war in which the United States was involved. The *Liberty* sailed in international waters with an American flag on a clear day.

Liberty sailors had a reasonable expectation of safety. "We think this proposal entirely misconceives the legal situation," the State Department's top lawyer wrote in a memo to Katzenbach. "The payments provided for in United States legislation are in no way related to liability of another government under international law to pay compensation for wrongful death."

Some in the State Department advocated that if necessary, the United States could have a "public airing" of Israel's refusal to pay. Pressure mounted as the days passed and the first anniversary of the attack approached. The public and members of Congress continued to harass the State Department, demanding to know if Israel had paid its reparations. On May 27—354 days after its pilots and skippers strafed and torpedoed the *Liberty*—Israel relented and wrote a check to the United States treasurer for $3,323,500. The two-paragraph press release issued at noon the next day stated that as soon as the check was deposited in the treasury, families would be paid.

On July 3 the United States billed Israel $7,644,146 for the *Liberty*'s repairs. Lawyers still calculated injury claims. The Israeli newspaper *Haaretz* ran an article stating that Israel expected America to reconsider whether it owed further reparations since the Pentagon had failed to order the *Liberty* farther from shore. "It has become clear that the U.S. Naval Command realized that a ship that is virtually in the midst of a battle zone endangers herself and therefore the order was given to the ship to get away," the article read. "It is believed in Jerusalem that the U.S. is likely to take that fact into account when she submits further claims to Israel."

The article, immediately translated and forwarded to the State Department, foreshadowed Israel's new legal theory to avoid claims, a theory it formally presented two weeks later in a note to the American Embassy in Tel Aviv. Israel now stated that various investigations of the attack exonerated the Jewish state of any liability. The previous $3.3 million payment to the families of the dead, Israel now claimed, "was motivated by humanitarian considerations relating to the economic hardship suffered by the families of the deceased."

Israel's posture outraged Rusk, who called it "totally unacceptable." The United States refused to accept Israel's claim that it was "not legally liable for death and material damage resulting from attack." Furthermore, Rusk wrote that no evidence had arisen in any inquiry exonerating Israel from paying. The secretary of state threatened that the United States would release Israel's note to the press. "We have not made either fact of receipt or contents known to public or to Congress," he warned. "If necessary, we will respond formally."

Israel backtracked. Its Foreign Ministry asked that the note be returned and forgotten. In March 1969 the United States presented claims on behalf of injured sailors. Israel paid the full $3,566,457 a month later, a figure that included $92,437 to reimburse the government for medical care and $21,745 to pay for ruined personal property. Awards ranged from a few hundred dollars for sailors with minor wounds to some in excess of $100,000 for more severe injuries, which included brain damage in one case and the loss of a kidney in another. Then the United States returned to the $7,644,146 bill for the *Liberty*'s repairs.

Israel ignored it.

Various memos and telegrams reveal the frustration the State Department faced, describing Israel as "evasive" and "petulant." A telegram to the American Embassy in Tel Aviv urged the diplomats to remind Israel that its "unresponsive attitude towards this claim will not lead to its being forgotten." In August 1971, Israel secretly offered the United States the token sum of $100,000, about 1.5 cents on the dollar. Walworth Barbour, the American ambassador to Israel, urged that the United States accept the deal. Others disagreed. Israel's lowball offer was an insult. "The suggested sum is so small as to call clearly for a courteous rejection out of hand," wrote Heywood Stackhouse, then the State Department's country director for Israel and Arab-Israel affairs. "We think it better to keep the claim outstanding than to make a settlement unsatisfactory in so many ways. It would not be a serious irritant in our relations, and it would be a continuing reminder we are not *that* easy a mark."

The issue dragged on for years. Lawmakers and the press finally began asking questions in 1977 when the *Liberty* repair bill showed up as outstanding debt on the annual claims report of money owed by foreign governments submitted to Congress. The State Department hustled to come up with a deal, but negotiations stalled again as the United

States soon focused on the Camp David peace process. By 1980, Israel's bill had climbed to $17,132,709, a figure that included $9,488,563 in interest. Democratic senator Adlai Stevenson of Illinois, chairman of the Senate select subcommittee on the collection and production of intelligence, threatened a congressional investigation. "Since this ship was on an intelligence mission, I intend to use the subcommittee as a means of looking into this matter further, to try to determine belatedly what the truth is," he told a reporter. "Those sailors who were wounded, who were eyewitnesses, have not been heard from by the American public."

Israel offered to settle for $6 million, payable in three annual installments of $2 million. The final offer was less than the original bill for damages. The United States, weary of the negotiations, accepted the deal in December 1980. Thirteen years had passed since the attack and nearly eight years since President Johnson had died of a heart attack at his Texas ranch. The *New York Times* wrote in a front-page story that the United States and Israel "had finally closed the book on one of the most divisive issues between the two countries." Stevenson dropped his proposed investigation.

Former secretary of state Rusk challenged the idea that the issue was dead in a 1981 letter to one of the *Liberty*'s officers. Rusk wrote that he believed the attack "was and remains a genuine outrage." Despite the years of negotiations, he added that he felt Israel did not pay enough to the families of the men killed or the survivors. Rusk was pragmatic. The bill for the ship was the least important: "It was not a major point because, in light of our aid programs for Israel, we would, in effect, be paying ourselves."

Captain William McGonagle sipped coffee with Secretary of the Navy Paul Ignatius and Chief of Naval Operations Admiral Thomas Moorer at the Washington Navy Yard on the morning of June 11, 1968. The Navy had chosen to honor McGonagle with the Medal of Honor, the nation's highest award for heroism, on this day. The skipper dressed for the occasion in his formal whites. The government offered to pay the transportation and hotel costs for McGonagle's siblings to attend the

11:30 A.M. ceremony in the sail loft. McGonagle's wife, three children, and mother-in-law also came, as did some of the *Liberty*'s remaining officers and crewmembers who lived in the Washington area.

The forty-two-year-old skipper, recently promoted to the rank of captain, had relinquished responsibility for the *Liberty* eight months earlier. McGonagle now commanded the U.S.S. *Kilauea*, a new twenty-knot ammunition ship built by General Dynamics in a Massachusetts shipyard. A little more than a year earlier, as the *Liberty* trolled the west coast of Africa, McGonagle had feared his career was over. Now it had soared. The *Los Angeles Times* noted his heightened status in a story on his promotion: "Command of a new ship is considered a career plum in the Navy." But the Navy readied its greatest plum for McGonagle this morning.

The Medal of Honor often is awarded posthumously because of the extraordinary criteria required to earn it. Those service members fortunate enough to survive combat traditionally are invited to the White House, where the president presents the medal. President Johnson often performed the ceremony, personally placing the medal around the neck of each recipient. Johnson presented at least nine Medals of Honor during the first half of 1968. He had dined with the parents of a deceased recipient in March. Less than a month before McGonagle's ceremony, the president presented medals to four servicemen simultaneously—one from each branch of the military—at the dedication of the Pentagon's new Hall of Heroes.

McGonagle would not be so fortunate. The *Liberty* remained too politically sensitive for the administration even a year later and after Johnson's announcement that he would not run for reelection. James Cross, the president's senior military aide, delivered McGonagle's citation and a Presidential Unit Citation for the rest of the crew to the president for his signature on May 15. Cross urged Johnson not to present either award in person. The president signed both citations that afternoon, then followed Cross's advice. "Due to the nature and sensitivity of these awards, Defense and State officials recommend that both be returned to Defense for presentation, and that no press release regarding them be made by the White House."

The president instead visited former president Dwight Eisenhower,

Supreme Court Justice William Douglas, and Senator Richard Russell at the Walter Reed Army Hospital the morning of McGonagle's ceremony. During his ten-minute visit with Russell, Johnson presented the Georgia Democrat with a signed copy of his speeches, *To Heal and to Build,* scribbling inside: "To my friend Dick Russell with appreciation." The president returned to the White House afterward, less than four miles from the Washington Navy Yard, where he presided over the graduation ceremony of the Capitol Page School in the East Room. Too concerned about domestic politics to present the nation's highest award for heroism, the commander in chief instead handed out diplomas to high school students.

Admiral Moorer, who would go on to serve as chairman of the Joint Chiefs of Staff, years later wrote that he had attended numerous Medal of Honor ceremonies at the White House. The four-star admiral, who was often outspoken in his belief that the Israelis deliberately targeted the *Liberty,* described the president's refusal to present McGonagle his award as a "back-handed slap." "They had been trying to hush it up all the way through," Moorer said of McGonagle's award. "The way they did things I'm surprised they didn't just hand it to him under the 14th Street Bridge."

McGonagle never publicly questioned why the president did not present him his medal. He remained a loyal officer, reluctant to challenge his superiors. He refused efforts years later by some of his crew to have his medal re-presented at the White House. "I do not feel that I 'earned' or 'won' the Medal that was *bestowed* on me," he wrote to one of his crewmembers. "As far as I am concerned, I did no more than fulfill my duties and responsibilities as Commanding Officer, as set forth in U.S. Navy Regulations."

The skipper's reserved demeanor masked his private feelings. Handwritten notes in his personal files show that McGonagle later researched how other service members were awarded their medals. He appeared to locate only two others during that era who, like him, failed to receive medals in person from the president. On a single sheet of unlined paper, McGonagle listed their names: Captain Harvey Barnum, Jr., followed by 1st Lieutenant Walter Marm, Jr. Beneath them, he simply wrote: "ME."

McGonagle kept any concerns he had to himself on this June morning in the Washington Navy Yard. As the men sipped coffee the secretary of the Navy commended McGonagle for saving the *Liberty*. The skipper, as he always did, demurred. The honor belonged to his men. Secretary of the Navy Ignatius disagreed. "When you and Admiral Moorer have finished your coffee," Ignatius ordered, "we're going to go right out there and we're going to have this ceremony."

"Aye, aye, sir," McGonagle replied.

McGonagle, surrounded by friends, family, and *Liberty* crewmembers, listened as the National Anthem played. Moorer then read the medal citation, recounting how the skipper, despite his injuries, had remained at the helm of his battered ship until help arrived nearly seventeen hours later. Like the vaguely worded tombstone in Arlington that marked the mass grave of *Liberty* sailors, McGonagle's citation never mentioned Israel, nor was the Jewish state identified as the attacker in the ceremony, a fact the *Chicago Tribune* noted in an article the next day.

"Despite continuous exposure to fire, he maneuvered his ship, directed its defense, supervised the control of flooding and fire, and saw to the care of the casualties," Moorer read. "Captain McGonagle's extraordinary valor under these conditions inspired the surviving members of the *Liberty*'s crew, many of them seriously wounded, to heroic efforts to overcome the battle damage and keep the ship afloat."

Ignatius turned to McGonagle afterward. The secretary of the Navy, against a backdrop of whirring cameras, placed the Medal of Honor around the skipper's neck. The five-pointed gold star, suspended from a blue ribbon, rested just beneath McGonagle's chin. The son of a sharecropper-turned-janitor, the man who had guided his ship to safety by the North Star, lowered his head and wept.

The *Liberty*'s voyage home from Malta proved its last. The spy ship languished alongside a Virginia pier throughout 1967 and the first half of 1968. The $162,608 the Navy spent to patch the torpedo and shell holes in Malta—the minimum required to allow the *Liberty* to steam home—was a fraction of the estimated $7.6 million needed to fix its battered hull and restore its electrical and mechanical systems. Those extra millions the United States sought from Israel seemed less likely to materialize each day as Israel haggled with the United States over the bill.

Ensign Dave Lucas's journal reveals the routine life of the men still on board the *Liberty* as the summer gave way to fall, then winter. Some sailors left to attend Navy training programs while others studied for promotions and high school equivalency exams. The remaining sailors swabbed decks, chipped paint, and cleaned filters. Others inventoried the narcotics locker, audited the ship's post office, and stood watch. Days off were plentiful.

The Navy continued to reassign officers and crewmembers as it became increasingly clear the *Liberty* would not sail again. Dr. Kiepfer departed for a hospital residency in Boston. The Navy dispatched Painter to Germany. Golden and Watson soon departed. Scott shipped off to Vietnam along with many other *Liberty* crewmembers. The wardroom, where men had traded stories over coffee and cigarettes, soon hosted many of the farewell dinners.

McGonagle returned to the *Liberty* one morning in June 1968 to award medals to some of his remaining men. The Medal of Honor presented to him only days earlier dangled from his neck as McGonagle once again climbed the spy ship's gangway. The morning breeze blew the smell of creosote across the *Liberty*'s port quarter as the former skipper walked down the line, pinning medals on the uniforms of his men. Family members trailed behind, snapping photos.

The Navy awarded more than two hundred Purple Hearts to the *Liberty*'s injured and to the families of the deceased, a staggering figure considering that the ship's crew totaled less than three hundred. The Navy also awarded more than forty medals for heroism and exemplary service, including the Navy Cross, Silver Star, Bronze Star, and the Navy Commendation Medal. Some of the medals were posthumous, including Navy Crosses, an award second only to the Medal of Honor, for Francis Brown and Philip Armstrong, Jr.

McGonagle presented the Silver Star—the nation's third-highest award for heroism—to Lucas, Golden, and Richard Brooks. Ten other *Liberty* officers and crewmembers also were awarded medals. In small ceremonies elsewhere reassigned crewmembers Kiepfer, Scott, Larkins, and Lockwood, among others, received Silver Stars.

For the collective effort to save the ship the Navy honored the entire crew with the Presidential Unit Citation, the nation's highest award for a military unit. The *Virginian-Pilot* noted in a story about the June ceremony that the scars from the assault a year earlier largely were gone. "The ship looked good, dressed for the occasion, with the only hint of the attack in the many patches of new paint," the paper wrote. "But it was really a day for the men."

The sailors sipped punch, ate cookies, and posed for pictures with McGonagle after the awards ceremony. Shortly before the skipper left, someone asked him to share his thoughts on the attack. He declined: "What I have to say, I've already said." McGonagle refused to speak of the attack again, other than to congratulate the efforts of his crew, until he returned to Arlington twenty-nine years later to meet with his men one last time shortly before his death.

Many *Liberty* crewmembers correctly speculated that the Navy would mothball the spy ship. The men prepared final reports, collected charts, publications, and clocks and audited the cash in the ship's post office. The *Liberty*'s engineers opened the valves and removed the nuts, bolts, and gaskets, sealing each inside bags and wiring them in place in case the Navy reactivated the ship. Crews opened the inside hatches to dehumidify the ship and coated the gears with Cosmoline to prevent rust.

The echo of voices down the narrow passageways soon fell silent. The smell of eggs, fried one hundred at a time, no longer flooded the mess deck each morning. Gone was the hum of the engines that had lulled many men to sleep as the ship steamed the oceans. The *Liberty* would never sail again. The Pentagon dismantled the spy ship program the following year. In December 1970, the Navy removed the *Liberty* from its registry. It was then sold to the Boston Metals Company in Baltimore for $101,667. Metal cutters later broke it down for scrap.

Sailors scavenged for souvenirs long before the *Liberty* reached the scrap yard. Men cut up the African mahogany rails, handcrafted by the *Liberty*'s first skipper and still burned and peppered with shrapnel, into two-inch blocks. Other sailors collected tattered flags that once flew from the ship's mast along with Zippo lighters adorned with the ship's insignia of an eagle clutching the *Liberty* bell in its talons. Many sailors clung to bits of twisted shrapnel and machine gun bullets from the attack. Mac Watson took the bloodstained log.

The few remaining officers and crewmembers gathered a final time on board the deck of the *Liberty* to decommission it at 11 A.M. on June 28, 1968. The spy ship was tied up alongside Pier Bravo in the Norfolk Naval Shipyard. During a quiet ceremony on a hot summer morning, the *Liberty*'s executive officer read the ship's history, from its naming in honor of ten American cities and towns to the final attack that killed thirty-four men and injured nearly two hundred others. Some of the families of the deceased listened in the audience. Another officer read the decommissioning order. The skipper lowered the *Liberty*'s flag and a chaplain offered a final prayer.

The sailors shook hands afterward and said good-byes before filing down the gangway. Brooks departed last, pausing at the top. He stared up at the bridge where McGonagle had fought to steer the ship that awful day. He observed the guntubs where the men had died desperately trying to protect the *Liberty*. He looked down at the patch that covered the torpedo hole. This aged cargo ship that had plowed the seas through the final days of World War II and Korea miraculously had survived a torpedo blast and 821 rocket and cannon hits. Brooks felt sad. He knew that a part of him would forever remain on board. He raised his right hand and saluted the *Liberty*.

EPILOGUE

More than four decades have passed since the attack on the *Liberty*, but it remains a vivid part of the daily lives of many of the men who served. Some of the sailors still wrestle with disabilities, while others battle post-traumatic stress disorder that led some to alcoholism and others to divorce court. Many families seemed to unravel in the wake of the tragic and unexpected deaths. Bitterness is common. Sailors and family members I interviewed dealt with the repercussions of the attack differently. One of the officers critically injured in the attack used his settlement money to buy a sports car. Years later the son of one crewmember who was killed named his own daughter Liberty. When I called to interview one sailor, his wife had to prep me. Brain damage caused him to stutter, she warned me, and I would have to repeat questions and be patient.

My father, I realized, was one of the lucky ones. Though he rarely spoke of the *Liberty* when I was growing up, the attack left its mark on him, as evident by the scores of letters he wrote during that era, now brittle and yellowed after spending years in a trunk in my grandmother's attic. The tone of his letters prior to the attack reflected the excitement of a young man eager to see the world. He described the wildlife he saw in Africa, the mechanics of his job on the ship, and the distant ports he visited. That youthful tone vanished in the letters he wrote after the attack. Soon after the *Liberty* returned to Virginia, he left for Vietnam, where he was later injured and medically retired from the Navy.

The *Liberty* attack had other effects, in part because the government's effort to deemphasize the attack meant vital lessons went unheeded. Seven months later, communist North Korea seized the spy ship U.S.S. *Pueblo* in international waters, killing one crewmember and holding eighty-two others hostage for almost a year. The men were beaten and starved. The congressional committee that investigated the *Pueblo* described the loss to American prestige and intelligence as "incalculable." In the more than 500 pages of published testimony on the *Pueblo*, the *Liberty* is barely mentioned. But a passing exchange between Admiral Thomas Moorer, who was then chief of naval operations, and Democratic Representative Otis Pike of New York proved revealing. Pike asked the question that should have been on the minds of everyone: What did the *Liberty* teach us?

Moorer seemed to fumble. He replied that the Navy had provided some extra guns to repel boarders, changed some communication procedures, and told people to remain sharp, all alleged improvements that failed to protect the crew of the *Pueblo*. Under questioning, Moorer admitted that the intelligence missions were riskier than the Navy initially believed. "If the lessons of the *Liberty* had been known to planners and commanders involved with the USS *Pueblo*, the sorry tragedy of that ship would never have happened as it did," Commander Lloyd Bucher, the skipper of the *Pueblo*, later wrote. "The similarities are a terrible confusion in command and control, a lack of response to desperate calls for assistance during attack, and a cover-up for incompetency at the top."

Whether the *Liberty* belonged on the geopolitical stage—as some of President Johnson's advisers questioned—is debatable. Soon after the attack, the president ordered Nicholas Katzenbach to press Israel to pay reparations to the injured and the families of the men killed and make sure payments were generous. With those conditions met, the president was willing to drop the matter. When I interviewed Katzenbach for this book, I asked if he had ever demanded to know why Israel attacked. "No," he said. "What good would it do? What would it tell you?" From a policy perspective, Katzenbach said, Israel's motivation didn't matter. "I don't think it would do any good to know," he said. "I don't like to work at things that don't do any good."

Faced with incredible pressure in Vietnam and with his domestic approval numbers plummeting, Johnson likely felt he had found a compromise that would make sure families were generously compensated and not spark a confrontation with Israel's supporters. But the American government owed the men who served on the *Liberty* an explanation. Johnson downplayed the attack for the wrong reasons: to protect his failed policies in Southeast Asia and his personal political ambitions. Senate Majority Leader Mike Mansfield told a reporter hours after the attack that he doubted the *Liberty* incident would spark any lasting complications in U.S.-Israel relations. If Navy investigators had spent more than eight days probing the attack, if Congress had played a more public and aggressive oversight role, and if Israel had followed Ambassador Harman's advice and prosecuted those responsible, the attack wouldn't have harmed long-term U.S.-Israeli relations.

Some of President Johnson's advisers later regretted the handling of the attack. "We failed to let it all come out publicly at the time," said Lucius Battle, the assistant secretary of state for near eastern and south Asian affairs. "We really ignored it for all practical purposes, and we shouldn't have." George Ball, the former undersecretary of state prior to Katzenbach, wrote that the *Liberty* ultimately had a greater effect on policy in Israel than in the United States. "Israel's leaders concluded that nothing they might do would offend the Americans to the point of reprisal," Ball wrote. "If America's leaders did not have the courage to punish Israel for the blatant murder of American citizens, it seemed clear that their American friends would let them get away with almost anything." Rear Admiral Thomas Brooks, a former director of naval intelligence, described the treatment of the *Liberty*'s crew as a "national disgrace." "The Navy was ordered to hush this up, say nothing, allow the sailors to say nothing," Brooks said. "The Navy rolled over and played dead."

My father found an unlikely sense of closure when he traveled with me to Israel in the fall of 2007. Yiftah Spector, one of the Israeli pilots who had attacked the *Liberty,* declined my request for an interview but invited me to his home in the suburbs of Tel Aviv for coffee. Spector, who also participated in Israel's attack on an Iraqi nuclear reactor in 1981, more recently had drawn criticism for signing a petition, along with other pilots, refusing to conduct airstrikes against militants hiding in densely populated Palestinian areas. I left my father behind and took a cab to Spector's home that afternoon. I arrived to find the sixty-six-year-old brigadier general covered in sweat from building a playground for his grandchildren in his backyard. Over coffee in his kitchen he asked why I was interested in the *Liberty*. Four decades had passed, he said, and it was an old story. I told him my father was one of the officers.

Why had I not brought him along for coffee, Spector asked, remembering my earlier comment that my father had accompanied me to Israel. I told him that I thought that might be awkward. "Nonsense," he said. "I must meet your father. Call him." I phoned my father and relayed Spector's request to see him. Within half an hour a taxi pulled alongside the curb in front of Spector's home, and my father came face-to-face with one of the pilots who attacked his ship that sunny afternoon of June 8, 1967. The two men, both young and confident so many years earlier, were now gray and wrinkled. Spector stuck out his hand for my father to shake. "We came within 300 meters of one another," he told my father. "I'm sorry."

Those were the words my father and many of his shipmates had wanted to hear for decades, the words no one in the Navy, the White House, or Congress had ever been publicly willing to say. The *Liberty* and its crew had become pariahs, shunned for political reasons and the misguided view that it was more important to protect relations with an ally than to support and defend American service members. The unfortunate reality is that America could have done both. Spector had no way of knowing how my father might react when he invited him to his home, but he chose to do so anyway. Even though my father had long ago packed up his memories of the *Liberty* and moved on with his life, I know how much Spector's apology meant to him. A burden had been lifted. My father reached out and took Spector's hand and said: "Thank you."

NOTE ON SOURCES

Many of the records I used to piece together the story of the U.S.S. *Liberty* came from two dozen archives and libraries scattered across the United States and Israel. The Freedom of Information Act pried loose other files from the Navy, State Department, Central Intelligence Agency, and National Security Agency. Litigation proved the only means to obtain some records from the Navy. My diligent research assistant, Gideon Kleiman, scoured Israel's archives for *Liberty* records, which I had professionally translated from Hebrew to English in Israel.

Other journalists, historians, and filmmakers graciously opened their private collections of notes, letters, and interviews. Those include Jim Ennes, Jr., author of *Assault on the* Liberty, who provided me access to more than 5,600 pages of his personal files. Jim Miller, who waged his own legal battle with the U.S. government for *Liberty* records, copied his collection of hundreds of government memos, cables, and reports. Richard Thompson shared hours of interview outtakes from the BBC's documentary *Dead in the Water.* James Bamford, Tim Frank, Joseph Bouchard, and Ahron Bregman also graciously shared interviews, letters, and e-mails.

I relied heavily on hundreds of interviews I conducted with *Liberty* survivors, Navy personnel, Israeli military and intelligence officers, State Department officials, White House advisers, and CIA and NSA operatives, some of whom have never spoken publicly until now. I often interviewed people on multiple occasions and for hours at a time in their homes, in restaurants, in hunting and Masonic lodges, and on long drives. I gained valuable insight from many people by spending personal time with them, including an afternoon drive across the beautiful Texas hill country and a climb up the clock tower of a historic church along the Canadian border.

All quotes in this book come from memos, reports, telegrams, meeting minutes, press conference transcripts, the *Congressional Record,* the court of inquiry, news stories, memoirs, and in a few cases, from the recollections of those involved. I have edited some quotes for length, but without altering the meanings. Memory is never perfect, so when possible I have used multiple sources to confirm dialogue and cross-reference scenes for accuracy. The ship's blueprints along with more than five hundred photographs from the National Archives, Lyndon Baines Johnson Library and Museum, NSA, Navy, and the private collections of many survivors—particularly Dave Lucas, Dennis Eikleberry, and Lloyd Painter—proved an invaluable tool to re-create places described in this book as well as the *Liberty* itself, both before and after the attack.

The best material came from the personal files and records of the sailors who survived that awful day. Many of the officers and crewmembers still have razor-sharp bullets, bits of twisted shrapnel, and edges of blast holes that were excised off the ship's hull and superstructure by welders in Malta more than four decades ago. I wrote this manuscript with a piece of the *Liberty*'s handcrafted African mahogany deck rail—still burned and peppered with shrapnel—sitting atop my computer. Beyond relics, these *Liberty* veterans shared with me scores of never-before-seen personal letters, telegrams, postcards, journals, reel-to-reel tapes, and notes, which opened wide a window on the past. These records make up the soul of this book.

ARCHIVES AND LIBRARIES

Charleston County Public Library, Charleston, S.C.

Congressional Medal of Honor Society, Mount Pleasant, S.C.

Edward L. Doheny Jr. Memorial Library, University of Southern California, Los Angeles, Calif.

Edwin Ginn Library, Fletcher School of Law and Diplomacy, Tufts University, Medford, Mass.

Emil Buehler Naval Aviation Library, Pensacola, Fla.

Frank Melville Jr. Memorial Library, Stony Brook University, Stony Brook, N.Y.

George C. Marshall Research Library, Lexington, Va.

Government Documents/Microforms Collection, Harvard University, Cambridge, Mass.

Lamont, Littauer, John F. Kennedy School of Government, Law School, Widener libraries, Harvard University, Cambridge, Mass.

Herbert Hoover Presidential Library and Museum, West Branch, Iowa.

Hoover Institution Archives, Stanford University, Palo Alto, Calif.

Israel State Archives, Jerusalem.

J. D. Williams Library, University of Mississippi, Oxford, Miss.

Library of Congress, Washington, D.C.

Lyndon Baines Johnson Library and Museum, Austin, Texas.

Marlene and Nathan Addlestone Library, College of Charleston, Charleston, S.C.

National Archives and Records Administration, College Park, Md.

National Cryptologic Museum Library, Fort Meade, Md.

Naval Historical Center, Washington, D.C.

Naval War College Library, Newport, R.I.

Richard B. Russell Library for Political Research and Studies, University of Georgia, Athens, Ga.

Seeley G. Mudd Manuscript Library, Princeton University, Princeton, N.J.

Sterling Memorial Library, Yale University, New Haven, Conn.

U.S. Naval Institute, Annapolis, Md.

Vietnam Archive, Texas Tech University, Lubbock, Texas.

NOTES

PROLOGUE

PAGE

1 *I know what a slaughterhouse:* Gary Brummett interview with author, Sept. 30, 2006.

1 *grave #1817:* Kaitlin Horst e-mail to author, Aug. 19, 2008.

1 *"one of the most bloody":* Michael E. Ruane, "An Ambushed Crew Salutes Its Captain," *Washington Post,* April 10, 1999, p. B1.

1 *He had shied away:* Gene Kramer, "Skipper Breaks Silence on Attack," *Peoria Journal Star,* June 9, 1997, p. A2.

2 *His family had weathered:* William McGonagle interview with Tim Frank, Sept. 27, 1997.

2 *The* Liberty *festered inside him:* Jim Yardley, "A Salute to Bravery, and Modesty, as Medal of Honor Heroes Meet," *New York Times,* June 7, 1998, p. 1; Marguerite Freeman interview with author, Dec. 15, 2007.

2 *Within months:* Marguerite Freeman interviews with author, Dec. 15–16, 2007.

2 *In twenty-two months:* Ruane, "An Ambushed Crew Salutes Its Captain," p. B1.

3 *some analysts argue:* Benjamin Cwalina interview with author, Dec. 3, 2007.

3 *"There wasn't any place":* Patrick O'Malley interview with author, Nov. 26, 2007.

4 *The Navy barred its investigators:* Ward Boston, Jr., interview with author, Oct. 11, 2006.

4 *"with the feeling":* David L. McDonald's Comments/Recommended Changes on Liberty Press Release, Box 112, *Liberty* Press Releases,

Immediate Office Files of the Chief of Naval Operations (CNO), Operational Archives Branch, Naval Historical Center (NHC), Washington, D.C.

4 *"not good enough"*: "Not Good Enough," editorial, *Washington Post,* June 30, 1967, p. A22.

4 *"more fog"*: "Missed Signals Again," editorial, *Chicago Tribune,* June 30, 1967, p. 14.

4 *"Did the attackers"*: "Pentagon Cover-Up," editorial, *Evening Star,* June 30, 1967, p. A14.

5 *"Whatever is the reason"*: *Congressional Record,* 90th Cong., 1st sess., June 29, 1967, p. 17893.

5 *"I can't tolerate"*: Senate Committee on Foreign Relations, *Foreign Assistance Act of 1967: Hearings Before the Committee on Foreign Relations on S. 1872,* 90th Cong., 1st sess., July 26, 1967 (Washington, D.C.: U.S. Government Printing Office, 1967), pp. 266, 268.

5 *"How could"*: *Congressional Record,* 90th Cong., 1st sess., June 29, 1967, pp. 17894–95.

5 *"Blast injury to brain"*: untitled handwritten notes, Box 3, William Loren McGonagle Papers, 1947–99, Hoover Institution Archives (HIA), Palo Alto, Calif.

6 *When asked to attend:* William McGonagle undated draft letter to Stan White, Box 6, William Loren McGonagle Papers, 1947–99, HIA.

6 *One of his officers wrote:* Lloyd Painter e-mail to author, Nov. 27, 2007; Lloyd Painter interview with author, Aug. 22, 2008.

6 *McGonagle had quietly conducted:* Information is drawn from multiple sources, including letters and notes on file with McGonagle's personal papers in the Hoover Institution Archives. Also, the Lyndon Baines Johnson Library and Museum provided copies of McGonagle's charge sheets detailing the records he reviewed on his May 13–16, 1985, and Oct. 19–20, 1998, visits to the archives. McGonagle's questioning and disbelief in the official American and Israeli stories come from his interview with Tim Frank on Sept. 27, 1997, and his interview with Richard Schmucker on Nov. 16, 1998.

7 *"For many years"*: *Dead in the Water,* directed by Christopher Mitchell, Source Films for BBC, 2002.

CHAPTER 1

PAGE

9 *I got my orders today!:* John Scott letter to parents, March 1, 1966.

9 *Commander William McGonagle paced:* Author interviews with Dave Lewis (April 10, 2007); John Scott (March 31, 2007); Dave Lucas (April 25, 2007); Dave Lucas's journal; Dave Lewis e-mails to author, Aug. 5, 2008.

9 *The* Liberty, *squeezed:* Dave Lucas audio letter to Paula Lucas, May 23, 1967; John Scott letters to parents, April 26, 1967, and May 31, 1967; Dale Larkins letter to parents, May 31, 1967.

10 *The* Liberty's *new orders:* COMSERVRON EIGHT msg. 240020Z, May 1967, *Liberty* court of inquiry.

10 *The skipper's haste:* Patrick O'Malley interview with author, Nov. 26, 2007; William McGonagle letter to Clay Brooks with completed Hall of Fame Profile, Nov. 5, 1985, Box 1, William Loren McGonagle Papers, 1947–99, HIA; William McGonagle Navy Bio, July 8, 1971, Box 6, William Loren McGonagle Papers, 1947–99, HIA; William McGonagle letter to Mike Polston with completed questionaire, Dec. 12, 1994, Box 1, William Loren McGonagle Papers, 1947–99, HIA; William McGonagle interview with Tim Frank, Sept. 27, 1997.

12 *"the wrath":* John Scott letter to parents, Feb. 17, 1967.

13 *"My career":* Patrick O'Malley interview with author, Nov. 26, 2007.

13 *Oregon shipbuilders:* James Mooney, et al., eds., *Dictionary of American Naval Fighting Ships,* vol. 4. (Washington DC.: U.S. Government Printing Office, 1969), p. 109; Unclassified Naval Security Group File, U.S.S. *Liberty,* Post 1 Jan. 1946, Command File, Operational Archives Branch, NHC.

14 *Halfway around:* House Committee on Armed Services, *Inquiry into the U.S.S.* Pueblo *and EC-121 Plane Incidents: Hearings Before the Special Subcommittee on the U.S.S.* Pueblo. 91st Cong., 1st sess., March 4, 1969 (Washington, D.C.: U.S. Government Printing Office, 1969), pp. 635–36; Raymond V. B Blackman, ed., *Jane's Fighting Ships, 1966–67* (London: Sampson Low, Marston, 1966) p. 447; Thomas H. Moorer oral history interview with John T. Mason, Jr., Jan. 13, 1976, U.S. Naval Institute, Annapolis, Md.

14 *The Defense Department:* House Committee on Armed Services, *Inquiry into the U.S.S.* Pueblo *and EC-121 Plane Incidents: Report of the Spe-*

cial Subcommittee on the U.S.S. Pueblo. 91st Cong., 1st sess., July 28, 1969 (Washington, D.C.: U.S. Government Printing Office, 1969), pp. 1631–33; Julie Alger, "A Review of the Technical Research Ship Program, 1961–1969," p. 5; "Fact Sheet for DIRNSA," undated, www.nsa.gov; Oliver Kirby interview with author, Dec. 31, 2007; Bobby Ray Inman interview with author, Feb. 26, 2007.

14 *The Navy commissioned:* Alger, "A Review of the Technical Research Ship Program, 1961–1969," pp. 5–12; Howard Lund interview with author, Sept. 25, 2007.

15 *"to discourage":* J. W. Chidsey Memorandum for the Record, Feb. 21, 1967, Box 19, Immediate Office File, of the CNO, Operational Archives Branch, NHC.

15 *Shipfitters:* Mooney et al., eds., *Dictionary of American Naval Fighting Ships,* vol. 4, p. 109; Dave Lewis interview with author, April 10, 2007; William D. Gerhard and Henry W. Millington, *Attack on a Sigint Collector, the U.S.S.* Liberty, National Security Agency/Central Security Service, 1981, p. 16.

15 *"porcupine":* Isaac Kidd, Jr., made the comment during the *Liberty* court of inquiry. His description comes from a magnabelt recording of the session and is not contained in the court's printed transcript.

15 *On the frigid:* U.S.S. *Liberty* Commissioning Program, Dec. 30, 1964, Box 3, William Loren McGonagle Papers, 1947–99, HIA; Donald Peoples interview with author, Dec. 31, 2007.

15 *Like its namesakes:* Author interviews with Warren Heaney (Jan. 28, 2008), John Scott (March 30–31, 2007), Jack Beattie (Dec. 27, 2007), George Wilson (Feb. 1, 2008), Gary Brummett (Oct. 8, 2008), and Mac Watson (Jan. 31, 2008).

16 *A class system:* Author interviews with John Scott (March 30, 2007), Dave Lewis (April 10, 2007), Joe Lentini (April 6, 2007), and Gary Brummett (Oct. 8, 2008); Joe Lentini e-mail to author, Sept. 12, 2008.

17 *Though the government:* Chidsey Memorandum for the Record.

17 *sailed at 7:30:* William McGonagle testimony, *Liberty* court of inquiry.

17 *"I was too hung over":* John Scott letter to parents, May 31, 1967; John Scott interview with author, March 31, 2007.

17 *Lieutenant Commander Philip Armstrong, Jr.:* Author interviews with John Scott (March 30, 2007), Dave Lewis (April 10, 2007), Mac Watson (Jan. 31, 2008, and Sept. 15, 2008), Dave Lucas (April 25, 2007), Tim Armstrong (Sept. 22, 2007), and Richard Taylor (May 30, 2007).

20 *The skipper would deny:* William McGonagle letter to Jim Ennes, Jr., Jan. 1980.

20 *McGonagle rated:* Philip Armstrong, Jr., fitness reports, May 31, 1966, and June 1, 1967, Box 10, William Loren McGonagle Papers, 1947–99, HIA.

CHAPTER 2

PAGE

22 *The circumstances surrounding:* House Committee on Armed Services, *Review of Department of Defense Worldwide Communications Phase I: Report of the Armed Services Investigating Subcommittee,* 92nd Cong., 1st sess., May 10, 1971 (Washington, D.C.: U.S. Government Printing Office, 1971), p. 6.

22 *The cost:* "Vietnam War," editorial, *New York Times.* May 28, 1967, p. E2.

22 *Casualties for May:* Tom Buckley, "Casualties of U.S. Rise in Vietnam," *New York Times,* June 2, 1967. p. 1.

22 *"Vietnam was a fungus":* Stanley Karnow, *Vietnam: A History,* rev. ed. (New York: Penguin, 1991), p. 493.

22 *The 25,000 sorties:* Robert S. McNamara with Brian VanDeMark, *In Retrospect: The Tragedy and Lessons of Vietnam* (New York: Times Books/Random House, 1995), p. 244.

23 *The Pentagon spent:* "Pentagon Triples Spending on Defoliation in Vietnam," *New York Times,* March 15, 1967, p. 2.

23 *"If America's soul":* "Beyond Vietnam," April 4, 1967, www.stanford.edu.

23 *"war without end":* Congressional Record, 90th Cong., 1st sess., April 25, 1967, p. 10611.

23 *"fanatically devoted":* The Vietnam Situation: An Analysis and Estimate, May 23, 1967, Box 14, Central Intelligence Agency Collection, Vietnam Archive, Texas Tech University, Lubbock, Texas.

23 *"resolute stoicism":* Intelligence Memorandum: The Current State of Morale in North Vietnam, May 12, 1967, Box 1, Central Intelligence Agency Collection, Vietnam Archive, Texas Tech University, Lubbock, Texas.

23 *"Short of a major invasion":* Reaction to Various US Courses of Action, May 23, 1967, www.cia.gov.

24 *The first president:* Bruce E. Altschuler, *LBJ and the Polls* (Gainesville: University of Florida Press, 1990), pp. xi–xiii.

24 *Over the past year:* George H. Gallup, ed., *The Gallup Poll: Public Opinion 1935–1971,* vol. 3, 1959–71 (New York: Random House, 1972), pp. 1992, 2062.

24 *Beyond popularity:* Ibid., p. 2058.

24 *Polls taken:* Ibid., pp. 2049, 2055, 2067.

24 *The Georgia-born Rusk:* Joseph A. Fry, *Debating Vietnam: Fulbright, Stennis, and Their Senate Hearings* (Lanthan, Md.: Rowman & Littlefield, 2006), p. 62; Homer Bigart, "War Foes Clash with Police Here as Rusk Speaks," *New York Times,* Nov. 15, 1967, p. 1.

24 *During an April speech:* Thomas W. Zeiler, *Dean Rusk: Defending the American Mission Abroad* (Wilmington, Del.: Scholarly Resources, 2000), pp. 162–63; Richard Rusk e-mails to author, Jan. 10, 2008, and Jan. 15, 2008.

24 *"aspirin, scotch":* Dean Rusk as told to Richard Rusk, *As I Saw It,* edited by Daniel S. Papp (New York: W. W. Norton & Company, 1990), pp. 417–18; Richard Rusk e-mail to author, Oct. 9, 2008.

24 *Twice activists:* McNamara, *In Retrospect,* p. 297.

24 *Once at Harvard:* Ibid., pp. 254–56.

24 *"murderer":* Ibid., p. 258.

25 *"You have blood":* Ibid., pp. 258, 260.

25 *Even the president:* David Halberstam, *The Best and the Brightest* (London: Barrie & Jenkins, 1972), p. 640.

25 *The war's fallout:* Lady Bird Johnson, *A White House Diary* (New York: Holt, Rinehart & Winston, 1970), pp. 362, 347.

25 *"The only difference":* Halberstam, *The Best and the Brightest,* p. 640.

25 *"Now is indeed":* Johnson, *A White House Diary,* p. 469.

25 *The* Liberty *reached:* U.S.S. *Liberty* Deck Log, June 1, 1967, Box 529, RG 24, Logs of U.S. Naval Ships and Stations, National Archives and Records Administration (NARA), College Park, Md.; William McGonagle testimony, *Liberty* court of inquiry; Dave Lucas's journal.

25 *Commander McGonagle had hoped:* USS LIBERTY msg. 241732Z, May 1967, *Liberty* Incident Message File, NHC.

26 *"I can just see":* Dave Lucas letter to Paula Lucas, June 2, 1967.

26 *The celebrity psychic:* Eric Pace, "Jeane Dixon, 79, Astrologer Claiming Psychic Power, Dies," *New York Times,* Jan. 27, 1997, p. B11; Jeane Dixon letter to Jim Ennes, Jr., Oct. 30, 1974.

26 *"Everybody is speculating"*: John Scott letter to parents, May 31, 1967.

26 *Marine Staff Sergeant Bryce Lockwood:* Bryce Lockwood interviews with author, April 4, 2007, and Sept. 7, 2008; Dave Lewis interview with author, April 10, 2007; Dave Lewis e-mails to author, Sept. 9, 2008; Robert L. Wilson oral history interview with Robert D. Farley, Henry F. Schorreck, and Henry Millington, May 6, 1980, www.nsa.gov; Birchard Fossett oral history interview with Robert D. Farley, May 15, 1980, www.nsa.gov; Birchard Fossett interview with author, Feb. 19, 2008.

27 *McGonagle's new orders:* JCS msg. 011545Z, June 1967, Report of the JCS Fact Finding Team, USS *Liberty* Incident, June 8, 1967. The Navy often uses nautical miles, which are slightly longer than regular miles. For the purposes of this book, I have listed everything simply as miles. The differences are negligible and have no bearing on the outcome of events.

27 *McGonagle ordered:* Dave Lucas letter to Paula Lucas, June 2, 1967.

27 *The* Liberty *overtook:* USS LIBERTY msg. 022108Z, June 1967, *Liberty* court of inquiry.

28 *"Shep was like":* Dave Lucas letter to Paula Lucas, June 2, 1967.

28 *President Johnson crawled:* Lyndon Johnson Daily Diary, June 4, 1967, Box 11, The President's Daily Diary, LBJL.

28 *America had set:* Buckley, "Casualties of U.S. Rise In Vietnam," p. 1.

28 *more than 1,400:* Richard Witkin, "Johnson, in City, Vows to Maintain Peace in Mideast," *New York Times,* June 4, 1967, p. 1; Richard Witkin, "Protests to Greet Visit of President," *New York Times,* June 3, 1967, p. 12.

29 *"part Jewish":* Harry McPherson, Jr., oral history interview with T. H. Baker, Jan. 16, 1969, LBJL.

29 *Israel enjoyed:* Glenn Frankel, "A Beautiful Friendship?" *Washington Post Magazine,* July 16, 2006, p. W13; Warren Bass, *Support Any Friend: Kennedy's Middle East and the Making of the U.S.-Israeli Alliance* (New York: Oxford University Press, 2003), pp. 4, 30–33, 44–45; Stephen E. Ambrose, *Eisenhower: The President,* vol. 2. (New York: Simon & Schuster, 1984), pp. 385–87;

29 *"You have lost":* Merle Miller, *Lyndon: An Oral Biography* (New York: Putnam's, 1980), p. 477.

29 *"Take care of the Jews":* Michael Karpin, *The Bomb in the Basement: How Israel Went Nuclear and What That Means for the World* (New York: Simon & Schuster, 2006), p. 243.

29 *"Most, if not":* Remarks of the President to the 125th Anniversary Meeting of B'nai B'rith, Sept. 10, 1968, Box 37, Office Files of White House Aides, Office Files of Harry McPherson, Jr., LBJL.

30 *The nation's six million:* Alan L. Otten, "Politics and People: The Jewish Vote," *Wall Street Journal,* June 7, 1967, p. 16; David S. Broder, "Pressure Mounts for U.S. to Assert Pro-Israel Stand," *Washington Post,* June 7, 1967, p. A10; William V. Shannon, "U.S. Politics and the Middle East Crisis," *New York Times,* June 12, 1967, p. 44.

30 *Johnson surrounded:* Douglas Little, "The Making of a Special Relationship: The United States and Israel, 1957–68," *International Journal of Middle East Studies* 25, no. 4 (Nov. 1993), p. 573; Steven L. Spiegel, *The Other Arab-Israeli Conflict: Making America's Middle East Policy, from Truman to Reagan* (Chicago: University of Chicago Press, 1985), pp. 128–29; Michael B. Oren, *Six Days of War: June 1967 and the Making of the Modern Middle East* (New York: Oxford University Press, 2002), pp. 111–12.

30 *"it might mean":* McGeorge Bundy oral history interview with Paige E. Mulhollan, Jan. 30, 1969, LBJL.

30 *United Artists:* Tom Segev, *1967: Israel, the War, and the Year That Transformed the Middle East,* trans. Jessica Cohen (New York: Metropolitan Books/Henry Holt, 2007), pp. 116–18.

30 *"No one who has":* Peter L. Hahn, "An Ominous Moment: Lyndon Johnson and the Six Day War," in *Looking Back at LBJ: White House Politics in a New Light,* ed. Mitchell B. Lerner (Lawrence: University Press of Kansas, 2005), p. 80.

31 *"Perhaps the best":* "US Help for Israel, 1964–1966," Nov. 2, 1966, Box 140, National Security File, Country File, Israel, LBJL.

31 *"You don't have":* Lucy S. Dawidowicz, "Intergroup Relations and Tensions in the United States," *The American Jewish Yearbook 1967,* vol. 68, ed. Morris Fine and Milton Himmelfarb (New York and Philadelphia: American Jewish Committee and Jewish Publication Society of America, 1967), p. 80.

31 *viewed Vietnam and Israel:* "Jewish War Plea Vexes President," *New York Times,* Sept. 11, 1966, p. 4.

31 *"Viet Nam is a serious":* "1968—American Jewry and Israel," undated, Box 141, National Security File, Country File, Israel, LBJL.

31 *The State Department processed:* Dixon Donnelley memo to Dean Rusk,

June 2, 1967, Box 193, White House Central Files, National Security–Defense, LBJL.

31 *An estimated 125,000:* Maurice Carroll, "Supporters of Israel March Here as the Police Turn Away Arab Group," *New York Times,* May 29, 1967, p. 1.

31 *The president had:* Lyndon Baines Johnson, *The Vantage Point: Perspectives of the Presidency, 1963–1969* (New York: Holt, Rinehart & Winston, 1971), pp. 293–97.

32 *Its military:* Terence Smith, "Reserve Call-Up Costly to Israel," *New York Times,* May 29, 1967, p. 4; Terence Smith, "Israelis in Jerusalem, Often Divided, Unite Calmly to Prepare to Defend City," *New York Times,* June 5, 1967, p. 3; "Trenches Cross City Squares," *New York Times,* June 3, 1967, p. 9; Michael Bar-Zohar, *Embassies in Crisis: Diplomats and Demagogues Behind the Six-Day War,* trans. Monroe Stearns (Englewood Cliffs, N.J.: Prentice-Hall, 1970), pp. 147–48.

32 *The president diverted:* Witkin, "Johnson, in City, Vows to Maintain Peace in Mideast," p. 1.

32 *Abe Feinberg whispered:* Miller, *Lyndon,* p. 480.

32 *He tried to relax:* Lyndon Johnson Daily Diary, June 4, 1967.

32 *The call came at 4:30 A.M.:* Johnson, *A White House Diary,* p. 520; Hugh Sidey, "The Presidency: Over the Hot Line—the Middle East," *Life,* June 16, 1967, p. 24.

32 *At the National Security Agency's:* David Kahn, *The Codebreakers: The Story of Secret Writing* (New York: Macmillan, 1967), pp. 672–88.

33 *The spy ship:* Liberty Deck Log, June 5, 1967.

33 *America had faced:* Michael Dobbs, *One Minute to Midnight: Kennedy, Khrushchev, and Castro on the Brink of Nuclear War* (New York: Knopf, 2008), pp. 184–87.

34 *Richard Harvey and Eugene Scheck:* Richard Harvey oral history interview with W. M. Gerhard, H. Millington, and R. D. Farley, July 16, 1980, www.nsa.gov; Eugene Scheck oral history interview with Robert D. Farley and Henry Millington, Aug. 11, 1980, www.nsa.gov; John A. Connell oral history interview with Henry Millington and Bob Farley, Sept. 15, 1980, www.nsa.gov; USS *Liberty* Chronology of Events, June 8, 1967, www.nsa.gov; Merriwell Vineyard interview with author, Nov. 26, 2007.

34 *Before the* Liberty: CINCUSNAVEUR msg. 271052Z, May 1967, Report of the JCS Fact Finding Team, USS *Liberty* Incident, June 8, 1967.

34 *Concerns increased:* CINCUSNAVEUR msg. 051352Z, June 1967, Report of the JCS Fact Finding Team, USS *Liberty* Incident, June 8, 1967.

34 *"unpredictability":* COMSIXTHFLT msg. 062349Z, June 1967, Report of the JCS Fact Finding Team, USS *Liberty* Incident, June 8, 1967. Military and government telegrams often were written in all caps and lacked proper punctuation. For the readers ease, I have converted such communications into regular sentence use and added some punctuation.

34 *"I don't know why":* J. H. King, Jr., Memorandum for the Record, June 9, 1967, Box 111, *Liberty* Briefing Book, Immediate Office Files of the CNO, Operational Archives Branch, NHC.

35 *"I wouldn't even let":* Ibid.

35 *"several hundred miles":* William D. Gerhard and Henry W. Millington, *Attack on a Sigint Collector, the U.S.S. Liberty,* National Security Agency/Central Security Service, 1981, p. 21.

35 *A senior officer:* CINCUSNAVEUR msg. 081903Z, June 1967, Box 111, *Liberty* Briefing Book, Immediate Office Files of the CNO, Operational Archives Branch, NHC.

35 *"Time is getting":* Report of the JCS Fact Finding Team, USS *Liberty* Incident, June 8, 1967. For additional information, see House Committee on Armed Services, *Review of Department of Defense Worldwide Communications Phase I: Report of the Armed Services Investigating Subcommittee,* 92nd Cong., 1st sess., May 10, 1971 (Washington, D.C.: U.S. Government Printing Office, 1971).

35 *"Looks to me":* Ibid.

CHAPTER 3

PAGE

36 *While we are not:* Walter G. Deeley memo to Louis Tordella, June 14, 1967, www.nsa.gov.

36 *Ensign John Scott assumed:* John Scott interviews with author, March 31, 2007, April 1, 2007, and July 29, 2008.

37 *"All this the armed forces":* "Aqaba Gulf Open," *New York Times,* June 8, 1967, p. 1.

38 *The night before:* James G. O'Connor oral history interview with Bill Gerhard, Henry Millington, Hank Schorreck, and Bob Farley, May 22, 1980, www.nsa.gov.

38 *High above the* Liberty: Israel Defense Forces History Department, "The Attack on the 'Liberty' Incident, 8 June, 1967," June 1982. pp. 6–8, IDF Archives; *Attack on the* Liberty, directed by Rex Bloomstein, Thames Television, 1987.

38 *"It was a gray color":* Attack on the *Liberty.*

39 *"It made 3 runs":* Dale Larkins's journal.

39 *"You're clairvoyant":* John Scott interview with author, March 31, 2007; Scott also described his observations in his testimony before the court of inquiry.

40 *"Maximum effort must":* William McGonagle memo to all OOD/JOOD/CIC Personnel, June 5, 1967, *Liberty* court of inquiry.

40 *"primary function":* Liberty Gunnery Doctrine, *Liberty* court of inquiry.

40 *"Self defense capability":* USS LIBERTY msg. 062036Z, June 1967, Report of the JCS Fact Finding Team, USS *Liberty* Incident, June 8, 1967.

40 *"With all the excitement":* Dave Lucas letter to Paula Lucas, June 6, 1967.

41 *The corpsmen began sick call:* Richard Kiepfer interview with author, Jan. 11, 2007.

41 *Crews prepared:* Dave Lucas's journal.

41 *Down in the engine room: Liberty* Engineering Log, June 8, 1967, *Liberty* court of inquiry.

41 *A faulty steam-line gasket:* William McGonagle and George Golden testimony, *Liberty* court of inquiry.

41 *Research operators:* Robert L. Wilson oral history interview with Robert D. Farley, Henry F. Schorreck, and Henry Millington, May 6, 1980, www.nsa .gov.

42 *A single jet:* Carl F. Salans, "Report of Attack on U.S.S. *Liberty,*" July 28, 1967, Box 1798, RG 59, Central Files 1967–69, POL 27 ARAB-ISR, NARA; *Liberty* court of inquiry.

42 *"Where's our buddy?":* Charles Cocnavitch interview with author, Dec. 10, 2007.

42 *"Would it affect":* Dave Lewis interview with author, April 10, 2007; Dave Lewis e-mails to author, July 31, 2008, and Aug. 1, 2008.

43 *The naval observer:* Israel Defense Forces History Department, "The Attack on the 'Liberty' Incident," pp. 7–8.

43 *The forty-one-year-old skipper:* William McGonagle interview with Tim Frank, Sept. 27, 1997.

43   *The* Liberty *had changed:* Liberty Deck Log, June 8, 1967.

43   *"current situation":* USS LIBERTY msg. 080856Z, June 1967, Report of the JCS Fact Finding Team, USS *Liberty* Incident, June 8, 1967; Dave Lewis e-mail to author, Aug. 5, 2008.

44   *At the start of the drill:* William McGonagle testimony, *Liberty* court of inquiry; *Liberty* Deck Log, June 8, 1967.

44   *Dale Larkins:* Dale Larkins interview with author, Sept. 10, 2007.

45   *Bryce Lockwood:* Bryce Lockwood interview with author, April 4, 2007; Bryce Lockwood e-mail to author, Aug. 5, 2008.

45   *Petty Officer 2nd Class Dennis Eikleberry:* Dennis Eikleberry interview with author, March 22, 2007.

45   *Ensign Scott:* John Scott interview with author, March 31, 2007.

45   *Ensign Dave Lucas:* Dave Lucas interview with author, April 25, 2007.

45   *Dr. Richard Kiepfer:* Richard Kiepfer interview with author, Jan. 11, 2007.

45   *McGonagle remained:* William McGonagle and Lloyd Painter testimonies, *Liberty* court of inquiry.

46   *Ensign Patrick O'Malley:* Patrick O'Malley interview with author, Nov. 26, 2007.

46   *"We've got three":* Lloyd Painter interview with author, March 1, 2007.

46   *"You'd better call":* Lloyd Painter testimony, *Liberty* court of inquiry.

46   *Painter watched:* Ibid.; Lloyd Painter interview with author, March 1, 2007; Lloyd Painter e-mails to author, Aug. 5, 2008; Rick Aimetti interview with author, Dec. 20, 2007.

47   *The fighters zeroed:* Lloyd Painter and Patrick O'Malley testimony, *Liberty* court of inquiry; Patrick O'Malley interview with author, Nov. 26, 2007. Some Israeli sources have disputed the use of rockets during the air attack, stating that the shell holes resulted from 30-mm cannons. Numerous *Liberty* survivors, including William McGonagle, testified before the court of inquiry and in subsequent interviews of Israel's use of rockets. The finding's of the Navy's court of inquiry also described rocket attacks, including the following statement: "Two or more jet aircraft at a time conducted strafing, rocket and incendiary attacks."

47   *Ennes, who had climbed:* Jim Ennes, Jr., e-mails to author, Aug. 22–23, 2008; James M. Ennes, Jr., *Assault on the* Liberty: *The True Story of the Israeli Attack on an American Intelligence Ship* (New York: Random House, 1979), pp. 61–62.

47 *The skipper:* Patrick O'Malley interview with author, Nov. 26, 2007; Patrick O'Malley testimony, *Liberty* court of inquiry.

47 *One sailor:* Larry Weaver e-mails to author, Aug. 7, 2008.

48 *McGonagle grabbed:* William McGonagle testimony, *Liberty* court of inquiry.

48 *Below the bridge:* Ibid.; Patrick O'Malley interview with author, Nov. 26, 2007; William McGonagle letter to Weetie Armstrong, June 13, 1967, Box 3, William Loren McGonagle Papers, 1947–99, HIA.

49 *O'Connor lay:* James G. O'Connor oral history interview with Bill Gerhard, Henry Millington, Hank Schorreck, and Bob Farley, May 22, 1980, www.nsa.gov; Sandy O'Connor Jackson interview with author, Nov. 30, 2007; Sandy O'Connor Jackson e-mails to author, Aug. 11, 2008; Patrick O'Malley interview with author, Nov. 26, 2007.

49 *Lieutenant Stephen Toth:* Patrick O'Malley interview with author, Nov. 26, 2007; Josie Toth Linen interview with author, Aug. 6, 2008.

CHAPTER 4

PAGE

51 *Primary cause of death:* Richard Kiepfer testimony, *Liberty* court of inquiry.

51 *Ensign John Scott strode:* John Scott interviews with author, March 31, 2007, April 1, 2007, and Aug. 7, 2008.

53 *Down in the engine room:* Richard Brooks interviews with author, Nov. 14, 2007, and Aug. 8, 2008; Gary Brummett interviews with author, June 26, 2007, and Aug. 11, 2008.

54 *Petty Officer Eikleberry:* Dennis Eikleberry interview with author, March 22, 2007.

55 *Other instructors:* Joe Lentini e-mail to author, Oct. 10, 2008.

56 *Dave Lewis:* Dave Lewis interview with author, April 10, 2007; Dave Lewis e-mails to author, Aug. 10–11, 2008.

56 *Bryce Lockwood:* Bryce Lockwood interview with author, April 4, 2007.

57 *Petty Officer 1st Class Jeff Carpenter:* Jeff Carpenter interview with author, Feb. 5, 2008; Jeff Carpenter e-mail to author, Aug. 28, 2008.

57 *"No Arab":* Joe Lentini interview with author, April 6, 2007.

57 *Petty Officer 3rd Class Terry McFarland:* Terry L. McFarland oral his-

tory interview with William Gerhard, Henry Schorreck, and R. D. Farley, June 23, 1980, www.nsa.gov.

57 *Petty Officer 1st Class Joe Lentini:* Joe Lentini interview with author, April 6, 2007; Joe Lentini e-mail to author, Aug. 22, 2008.

57 *Shrapnel had broken:* Reginald Addington interview with author, Aug. 20, 2008.

57 *"Somebody's up there":* Ibid.; William D. Gerhard and Henry W. Millington, *Attack on a Sigint Collector, the U.S.S.* Liberty, National Security Agency/Central Security Service, 1981, p. 27.

58 *Dave Lewis found:* Dave Lewis interview with author, April 10, 2007.

58 *Another young sailor:* Bryce Lockwood interview with author, April 4, 2007; Bryce Lockwood e-mail to author, Aug. 17, 2008.

58 *Petty Officer 2nd Class Ronnie Campbell:* Bryce Lockwood interviews with author, April 4, 2007, and Aug. 28, 2008; Mike Allen e-mail to author, Aug. 28, 2008.

58 *Dr. Richard Kiepfer arrived:* Richard Kiepfer testimony, *Liberty* court of inquiry; Richard Kiepfer interviews with author, Jan. 11, 2007, Jan. 27, 2008, Aug. 13, 2008, and Aug. 16, 2008; Thomas Van Cleave interviews with author, May 18, 2007, and Aug. 29, 2008; Sam Schulman interviews with author, May 17, 2007, and Aug. 13, 2008; Frank Spicher interview with author, Jan. 27, 2008; Rick Aimetti interview with author, Dec. 20, 2007; George Wilson interview with author, Feb. 1, 2008; William McGonagle letter to Linda L. Spicher, June 18, 1967, Box 3, William Loren McGonagle Papers, 1947–99, HIA; Larry Weaver e-mail to author, Aug. 7, 2008.

61 *Petty Officer 2nd Class James Halman:* James Halman interviews with author, Jan. 21, 2008, and Aug. 15, 2008; Wayne Smith and Carl Lamkin testimonies, *Liberty* court of inquiry.

62 *"Any station":* Liberty rough and smooth radio logs as contained in the court of inquiry. I consulted both logs to create this scene. James Halman, who helped prepare the logs, told me that he felt the rough log was a more accurate reflection of the communications that day. For the purposes of this scene, I translated the abbreviated radio codes recorded in the logs into actual speech and fixed puncuation accordingly.

63 *The U.S.S.* Saratoga *was steaming:* U.S.S. *Saratoga* Deck Log, June 8, 1967, Box 813, RG 24, Logs of U.S. Naval Ships and Stations, NARA. Details of the *Saratoga* are drawn from Raymond V. B. Blackman, ed.,

Jane's Fighting Ships, 1967–68 (London: Sampson Low, Marston, 1967), p. 347; Roger Hall interview with author, Sept. 2, 2008.

64 *Ensign Dave Lucas:* Dave Lucas testimony, *Liberty* court of inquiry; Dave Lucas interviews with author, April 25, 2007, and Aug. 13–14, 2008.

65 *"firefly-like pieces":* William McGonagle letter to Mike Polston with completed questionaire, Dec. 12, 1994, Box 1, William Loren McGonagle Papers, 1947–1999, HIA.

66 *Fifteen miles:* William McGonagle testimony, *Liberty* court of inquiry.

CHAPTER 5

PAGE

67 *You are authorized:* JCS msg. 081416Z, June 1967, Report of the JCS Fact Finding Team, USS *Liberty* Incident, June 8, 1967.

67 *McGonagle studied:* William McGonagle testimony, *Liberty* court of inquiry.

67 *Dale Larkins climbed:* Dale Larkins interviews with author, Sept. 10, 2007, and Aug. 24, 2008.

68 *Up on the bridge:* William McGonagle and Dave Lucas testimonies, *Liberty* court of inquiry.

68 *McGonagle and his signalmen:* NAVCOMMUNIT NAPLES msg. 061222Z, July 1967, Box 111, *Liberty* Briefing Book, Immediate Office Files of the CNO, Operational Archives Branch, NHC; Dale Larkins interview with author, Sept. 10, 2007.

68 *On the forecastle:* Dale Larkins interviews with author, Sept. 10, 2007, and Aug. 24, 2008.

69 *The starboard machine gun:* William McGonagle and Dave Lucas testimonies, *Liberty* court of inquiry.

69 *The torpedo boats:* Details of the torpedo boat come from Blackman, *Jane's Fighting Ships, 1967–68,* p. 147.

70 *Down in the engine room:* Gary Brummett interview with author, June 26, 2007; Dennis Eikleberry interview with author, March 22, 2007; Jeff Carpenter interview with author, Feb. 5, 2008.

70 *Even if he survived:* John Scott interview with author, April 1, 2007; James Halman interview with author, Jan. 21, 2008; Richard Kiepfer interview with author, Aug. 13, 2008; George Wilson interview with author, Feb. 1, 2008.

70 *Up on the bridge:* William McGonagle testimony, *Liberty* court of inquiry; *Liberty* Deck Log, June 8, 1967.

71 *Eikleberry never heard:* Dennis Eikleberry interview with author, March 22, 2007.

72 *Jeff Carpenter who had been:* Jeff Carpenter interview with author, Feb. 5, 2008.

72 *When the torpedo exploded:* Robert Schnell interview with author, Feb. 1, 2008.

73 *Bryce Lockwood fumbled:* Bryce Lockwood interviews with author, April 4, 2007, Aug. 22, 2008, and Aug. 28, 2008; Phillip Tourney interview with author, Aug. 21, 2008.

74 *The torpedo's explosion:* John Scott interviews with author, April 1, 2007, and Aug. 7, 2008.

76 *Chief Petty Officer Brooks:* Richard Brooks interviews with author, Nov. 14, 2007, and Aug. 8, 2008; Gary Brummett interview with author, Aug. 30, 2008.

76 *Scott bypassed:* John Scott interview with author, April 1, 2007.

76 *Robert Schnell had climbed:* Robert Schnell interviews with author, Feb. 1, 2008, and Aug. 23, 2008; Dave Lewis interview with author, April 10, 2007; Phillip Tourney interview with author, Aug. 21, 2008.

77 *Up on the bridge:* William McGonagle and Dave Lucas testimonies, *Liberty* court of inquiry; *Liberty* Deck Log, June 8, 1967.

77 *Brown stepped back:* Dave Lucas testimony, *Liberty* court of inquiry; Charles Cocnavitch interviews with author, Dec. 10, 2007, and Aug. 28, 2008.

78 *If the* Liberty *were:* William McGonagle, John Scott, and Richard Kiepfer testimonies, *Liberty* court of inquiry; James Halman interview with author, Jan. 21, 2008; Lloyd Painter interview with author, March 1, 2007; Charles Cocnavitch interview with author, Dec. 10, 2007.

78 *The torpedo boats soon:* William McGonagle and Harold Thompson testimonies, *Liberty* court of inquiry; *Liberty* Deck Log, June 8, 1967.

78 *The torpedo boats had not:* William McGonagle testimony, *Liberty* court of inquiry; court of inquiry findings of fact; *Liberty* Deck Log, June 8, 1967.

79 *The only functioning transmitter:* James Halman interview with author, Jan. 21, 2008.

79 *An officer jotted:* handwritten distress message, Box 2, William Loren McGonagle Papers, 1947–99, HIA. This message also is reflected in the

Liberty's radio log that is contained in the court of inquiry. There are slight differences between the handwritten draft of the message and the radio log, so I have used my best judgment to reconstruct the message to what I believe is accurate.

80 *In the mess deck:* John Scott interviews with author, April 1, 2007, and Aug. 31, 2008; Lloyd Painter interview with author, March 1 2007; Lloyd Painter e-mails to author, Aug. 31, 2008.

80 *Another helicopter: Liberty* Deck Log, June 8, 1967; William McGonagle testimony, *Liberty* court of inquiry; Ernest Castle interview with author, March 28, 2007.

81 *Miles above:* Michael Prostinak interviews with author, Sept. 23, 2007, and Aug. 14, 2008; Charles Tiffany interview with author, Feb. 14, 2007; Charles Tiffany e-mails to author, Aug. 1–2, 2008; Marvin Nowicki e-mail to James Bamford, March 3, 2000.

81 *Before the war:* William D. Gerhard and Henry W. Millington, *Attack on a Sigint Collector, the U.S.S.* Liberty, National Security Agency/Central Security Service, 1981, pp. 11–12. Details of the EC-121 are drawn from Martin Streetly, *World Electronic Warfare Aircraft* (London: Jane's, 1983), pp. 75–76.

82 *Strapped in the back:* Marvin Nowicki e-mail to James Bamford, March 3, 2000; Michael Prostinak interview with author, Sept. 23, 2007.

83 *"Hey, Chief":* Marvin Nowicki e-mail to James Bamford, March 3, 2000.

83 *"Following received":* USS SARATOGA msg. 081235Z, June 1967, *Liberty* Incident Message File, NHC.

83 *"3 unidentified gunboats":* USS SARATOGA msg. 081237Z, June 1967, *Liberty* Incident Message File, NHC.

84 *"Under attack":* USS SARATOGA msg. 081245Z, June 1967, *Liberty* court of inquiry.

84 *"Hit by torpedo":* USS SARATOGA msg. 081254Z, June 1967, *Liberty* Incident Message File, NHC.

84 *Soviet warships:* Neil Sheehan, "Russians Continue to Harass 6th Fleet," *New York Times,* June 9, 1967, p. 1.

84 *Martin heard:* William Martin undated letter to James Ramage, Box 18.25, James D. Ramage Papers, Emil Buehler Naval Aviation Library, Pensacola, Fla.

84 *"America launch":* COMSIXTHFLT msg. 081250Z, June 1967, *Liberty* Incident Message File, NHC.

84	*"Your flash traffic":* COMSIXTHFLT msg. 081305Z, June 1967, *Liberty* Incident Message File, NHC.

84	*On the bridge:* Donald D. Engen, *Wings and Warriors: My Life as a Naval Aviator* (Washington, D.C.: Smithsonian Institution Press, 1997), pp. 318–22; Donald D. Engen oral history interview with Paul Stillwell, Nov. 7, 1994, U.S. Naval Institute, Annapolis, Md. Details of the *America* come from Blackman, *Jane's Fighting Ships, 1967–68,* p. 346.

85	*Tully would later write:* Joseph Tully, Jr., letter to Jim Ennes, Jr., May 6, 1981.

85	*Commander Max Morris:* Max K. Morris letter to Joseph Tully, Jr., June 19, 1981.

85	*The* Saratoga *had been ordered:* Details of the aircraft come from John C. Fredriksen, *Warbirds: An Illustrated Guide to U.S. Military Aircraft, 1915–2000* (Santa Barbara, Calif.: ABC-CLIO, 1999), pp. 102, 105.

85	*Intelligence officers:* Brad Knickerbocker, "A Former Navy Pilot Recalls the *Liberty* Incident," *Christian Science Monitor.* June 4, 1982, p. 4; Roger Hall interview with author, Dec. 27, 2007.

85	*The* Saratoga *messaged:* USS SARATOGA msg. 081322Z, June 1967, *Liberty* Incident Message File, NHC.

85	*"We are on the way":* Engen, *Wings and Warriors,* p. 320.

86	*"Not too large":* Ibid. Also, information on American disbelief that the Soviets had attacked comes from J. C. Wylie, Jr., Q&A with Joseph F. Bouchard, March 28, 1988, and Horacio Rivero, Jr., Q&A with Joseph F. Bouchard, March 10, 1988.

86	*"Defense of":* CTF SIX ZERO msg. 081316Z msg., June 1967, *Liberty* Incident Message File, NHC.

86	*"Ensure pilots":* COMSIXTHFLT msg. 081336Z, June 1967, *Liberty* Incident Message File, NHC.

86	*The admiral:* COMSIXTHFLT msg. 081337Z, June 1967, www.liberty-incident.com.

86	*"You are authorized":* COMSIXTHFLT msg. 081339Z, June 1967, *Liberty* Incident Message File, NHC.

86	*The* Saratoga *had estimated:* USS SARATOGA msg. 081322Z, June 1967, *Liberty* Incident Message File, NHC; COMSIXTHFLT msg. 081320Z, June 1967, *Liberty* Incident Message File, NHC.

86	*"Israeli aircraft":* USDAO TEL AVIV ISRAEL msg. 081414Z, June 1967, *Liberty* Incident Message File, NHC.

86 *"Recall all strikes"*: COMSIXTHFLT msg. 081440Z, June 1967, *Liberty* Incident Message File, NHC.

CHAPTER 6

87 *I just don't believe:* Dean Rusk undated oral history interview XXX with Richard Geary Rusk and Thomas J. Schoenbaum, Dean Rusk Oral History Collection, Richard B. Russell Library for Political Research and Studies, University of Georgia, Athens.

87 *President Lyndon Johnson woke:* Lyndon Johnson Daily Diary, June 8, 1967.

87 *Johnson had weathered:* Lyndon Johnson Daily Diary, June 7, 1967.

87 *The morning papers:* "Aqaba Gulf Open," *New York Times,* June 8, 1967, p. 1; Terence Smith, "Israelis Weep and Pray Beside the Wailing Wall," *New York Times,* June 8, 1967, p. 1; Drew Middleton, "Eban Sees Thant," *New York Times,* June 8, 1967, p. 1.

88 *Most mornings:* McNamara's routine and description of his office comes from Henry L. Trewhitt, *McNamara* (New York: Harper & Row, 1971), pp. 14–16; James Carroll, *House of War: The Pentagon and the Disastrous Rise of American Power* (Boston: Houghton Mifflin, 2006), p. 227.

88 *Elsewhere, Secretary of State:* Dean Rusk Appointment Book, June 8, 1967, Box 4, Papers of Dean Rusk, Secretary of State, 1961–69, LBJL.

88 *In the wooded suburbs:* Kahn, *The Codebreakers,* p. 688.

88 *"You are getting":* Ruth Scott letter to John Scott, June 8, 1967.

88 *At 9:11 A.M.:* Charles M. Gettys Memorandum for the Record, June 8, 1967, Box 107 [2 of 2], National Security File, Country File, Middle East, LBJL.

88 *"The* Liberty's *been":* John A. Connell oral history interview with Henry Millington and Bob Farley, Sept. 15, 1980, www.nsa.gov; Eugene Scheck oral history interview with Robert D. Farley and Henry Millington, Aug. 11, 1980, www.nsa.gov.

89 *"USS* Liberty *has been reportedly":* DIRNSA msg. 081328Z, June 1967, www.nsa.gov.

89 *Next the men focused:* Louis W. Tordella Memorandum for the Record, June 8, 1967, www.nsa.gov; USS *Liberty* Chronology of Events, June 8, 1967, www.nsa.gov.

89 *Thirty-eight minutes after:* Lyndon Johnson Daily Diary, June 8, 1967.

90 *"We have a flash report":* Walt Rostow memo to Lyndon Johnson, June 8, 1967, Box 18, National Security File, National Security Council Histories, Middle East Crisis, LBJL.

90 *The president phoned Robert McNamara:* Lyndon Johnson Daily Diary, June 8, 1967; Harriet Dashiell Schwar, ed., *Foreign Relations of the United States, 1964–1968,* vol. 19, *Arab-Israeli Crisis and War, 1967* (Washington, D.C.: U.S. Government Printing Office, 2004), p. 362.

90 *"Get me in twenty minutes":* Lyndon Johnson Daily Diary, June 8, 1967.

90 *By 10:15 A.M.:* unsigned memo, June 8, 1967, Box 18, National Security File, National Security Council Histories, Middle East Crisis, LBJL.

90 *"The* Liberty *is listing":* Walt Rostow memo to Lyndon Johnson, June 8, 1967, Box 18, National Security File, National Security Council Histories, Middle East Crisis, LBJL.

90 *"An American ship":* Memo of telephone conversations, June 8, 1967, in Schwar, ed., *Foreign Relations of the United States, 1964–1968,* pp. 366–67.

91 *Nearly six thousand miles away:* USDAO TEL AVIV ISRAEL msg. 081414Z, June 1967, *Liberty* Incident Message File; USDAO TEL AVIV ISRAEL msg. 151615Z June 1967, *Liberty* court of inquiry; Ernest Castle interview with the author, Feb. 20, 2002.

91 *"Our Defense Attaché":* unsigned memo, June 8, 1967, Box 18, National Security File, National Security Council Histories, Middle East Crisis, LBJL; Charles M. Gettys Memorandum for the Record, June 8, 1967, Box 107 [2 of 2], National Security File, Country File, Middle East, LBJL.

91 *The president ordered:* Lyndon Johnson telegram to Alexei Kosygin, June 8, 1967, Box 19, National Security File, National Security Council Histories, Middle East Crisis, LBJL.

92 *"in connection with":* Memo of telephone conversations, June 8, 1967, in Schwar, *Foreign Relations of the United States, 1964–1968,* p. 367.

92 *At 11:04 A.M.:* Lyndon Johnson Daily Diary, June 8, 1967.

92 *Tensions soared:* Nicholas Katzenbach interviews with author, April 19, 2007, and Feb. 17, 2009. Clark Clifford with Richard Holbrooke, *Counsel to the President: A Memoir* (New York: Random House, 1991), pp. 445–46; Rusk, *As I Saw It,* p. 388; Dean Rusk undated oral history interview XXX with Richard Geary Rusk and Thomas J. Schoenbaum, Dean

Rusk Oral History Collection, Richard B. Russell Library for Political Research and Studies, University of Georgia, Athens; Johnson, *The Vantage Point*, pp. 300–1; Dean Rusk letter to Jim Ennes, Jr., Aug. 12, 1981; Phil G. Goulding, *Confirm or Deny: Informing the People on National Security* (New York: Harper & Row, 1970), pp. 96–98. Rusk and Clifford both write that the president was in the Situation Room when the message arrived that Israel had attacked the *Liberty*. The hotline message Johnson sent to Kosygin, informing the Soviet premier of the attack and Israel's culpability, shows that the president approved it at 11 A.M., six minutes before he arrived in the Situation Room.

92 *At approximately 11:25 A.M.:* Dean Rusk telegram 209218 to the American Embassy in Moscow, June 8, 1967, Box 107 [1 of 2], National Security File, Country File, Middle East, LBJL.

93 *"We were baffled":* Clifford, *Counsel to the President,* p. 446.

93 *"Israelis do not":* AMEMBASSY TEL AVIV msg. 081510Z, June 1967, Box 114, National Security File, Country File, Middle East, LBJL.

93 *"We had better":* AMEMBASSY CAIRO msg. 081545Z, June 1967, Box 107 [1 of 2], National Security File, Country File, Middle East, LBJL.

94 *"Captain Vineyard":* Louis W. Tordella Memorandum for the Record, June 8, 1967. In an interview with the author on Nov. 26, 2007, Merriwell Vineyard said he shared Tordella's outrage over the discussed plan to sink the *Liberty* to protect Israel, a proposal he described as "absolutely preposterous." He summed up the handling of the entire *Liberty* attack and aftermath with the same description. "When I look back and realize the politics of the situation," he said, "I don't know why I would expect anything else."

94 *Reporters for major:* Jack Valenti, *A Very Human President* (New York: Norton, 1975), pp. 260–61; George Christian, *The President Steps Down: A Personal Memoir of the Transfer of Power* (New York: Macmillan, 1970), p. 190.

94 *"prisoner in the dock":* George E. Christian oral history interview with Joe B. Frantz, Dec. 4, 1969, LBJL.

94 *A former reporter:* David Stout, "George Christian, 75, Aide to President, Dies," *New York Times,* Nov. 29, 2002, p. C6.

94 *He started his briefing:* White House news conference transcript 866-A, June 8, 1967, Box 19, National Security File, National Security Council Histories, Middle East Crisis, LBJL. News conference transcripts normally do not include the names of the reporters.

96 *Across the river:* Goulding, *Confirm or Deny,* pp. 96–106.

96 *Since he learned:* Louis W. Tordella Memorandum for the Record, June 8, 1967; USS *Liberty* Chronology of Events, June 8, 1967, www.nsa. gov.

98 *"Vance states":* CINCUSNAVEUR msg. 081517Z, June 1967, *Liberty* Incident Message File, NHC.

98 *Like his:* Phil G. Goulding oral history interview with Dorothy Pierce, Jan. 3, 1969, LBJL.

98 *"A U.S. Navy":* Goulding, *Confirm or Deny,* pp. 102–3.

98 *"What attacked it?":* Ibid., pp. 105–6. Goulding's book does not include the names of the reporters.

CHAPTER 7

PAGE

100 *You can come out:* A. J. Liverman telegram to Lyndon Johnson, June 7, 1967, Box 194, White House Central Files, National Security–Defense, LBJL.

100 *Rusk found it:* Rusk, *As I Saw It,* p. 388; Dean Rusk undated oral history interview XXX with Richard Geary Rusk and Thomas J. Schoenbaum, Dean Rusk Oral History Collection, Richard B. Russell Library for Political Research and Studies, University of Georgia, Athens.

100 *"To Dean Rusk":* "The String Runs Out," *Time,* Feb. 4, 1966, pp. 21–26.

101 *Like Rusk, Harman was:* Marvine Howe, "Avraham Harman Is Dead at 77; Head of University and Diplomat," *New York Times,* Feb. 25, 1992, p. D22.

101 *Rusk told Harman:* Dean Rusk telegram 209253 to the American Embassy in Tel Aviv, June 8, 1967, Box 107 [2 of 2], National Security File, Country File, Middle East, LBJL; Avraham Harman telegram 92 to the Foreign Ministry, June 8, 1967, 4079/HZ-26, Israel State Archives, Jerusalem; William D. Wolle interview with author, Dec. 18, 2007; Dean Rusk Appointment Book, June 8, 1967, Box 4, Papers of Dean Rusk, Secretary of State, 1961–69, LBJL.

101 *"Well, there must":* William D. Wolle oral history interview with Charles Stuart Kennedy, March 6, 1991, Front Diplomacy: The Foreign Affairs Oral History Collection of the Association for Diplomatic Studies and Training, Manuscript Division, Library of Congress, Washington, D.C.

101 *"The implication was clear":* Avraham Harman telegram 92 to the Foreign Ministry, June 8, 1967, 4079/HZ-26, ISA.

102 *Moments after Harman left:* Lyndon Johnson Daily Diary, June 8, 1967.

102 *"Hit him hard":* Schwar, *Foreign Relations of the United States, 1964–1968,* p. 371.

102 *The New York Republican:* Jacob K. Javits, with Rafael Steinberg, *Javits: The Autobiography of a Public Man* (Boston: Houghton Mifflin, 1981), pp. 1–15, 271–90.

102 *"anchor and bastion":* Ibid. p. 271.

102 *"tragic error":* Congressional Record, 90th Cong., 1st sess., June 8, 1967, p. 15261.

103 *"Pooch":* James Janega and Gary Washburn, "Political, Polish and Proud," *Chicago Tribune,* Sept. 26, 2002, p. 1.

103 *"It was with heavy heart":* Congressional Record, 90th Cong., 1st sess., June 8, 1967, p. 15131.

103 *The* Congressional Record *shows:* The three other lawmakers who mentioned the *Liberty* were Senators Robert Kennedy (D-N.Y.), Abraham Ribicoff (D-Conn.), and Frank Lausche (D-Ohio).

103 *Those lawmakers who challenged:* Thomas G. Abernethy letter to Jim Ennes, Jr., Jan. 26, 1980, Box 159, Thomas G. Abernethy Collection, J. D. Williams Library, University of Mississippi, Oxford, Miss.

104 *"neutral in thought":* Schwar, *Foreign Relations of the United States, 1964–1968,* p. 311.

104 *"grotesque":* "The Search for Peace . . . ," editorial, *New York Times,* June 6, 1967, p. 46.

104 *"I was appalled":* John P. Roche memo to Lyndon Johnson, June 6, 1967, Box 107 [2 of 2], National Security File, Country File, Middle East, LBJL.

104 *"There are reports":* Walt Rostow memo to Lyndon Johnson with accompanying statement from Mathilde Krim, June 7, 1967, Box 107 [2 of 2], National Security File, Country File, Middle East, LBJL.

105 *FBI director:* J. Edgar Hoover telegram to the Situation Room, June 6, 1967, Box 107 [1 of 2], National Security File, Country File, Middle East, LBJL.

105 *Closer to the rally:* Thomas L. Johns memo to Marvin Watson, June 8, 1967, Box 193, White House Central Files, National Security-Defense, LBJL.

105 *"There never was"*: McGeorge Bundy oral history interview with Paige E. Mulhollan, March 19, 1969, LBJL.

105 *Americans showed that support:* "A Million a Minute," *Time,* June 16, 1967, pp. 17–18; "'Give as You Never Gave.'" *Newsweek,* June 19, 1967, pp. 35–36; Farnsworth Fowle, "Funds for Israel Pouring in Here," *New York Times,* June 8, 1967, p. 10; David A. Jewell, "$1 Million for Israel Is Raised Here," *Washington Post,* June 10, 1967, p. A13; M. S. Handler, "Donations Pour in for Israeli Fund," *New York Times,* June 9, 1967, p. 1; "Jewish Groups Open Drives to Help Israel," *Washington Post,* June 6, 1967, p. A12.

105 *"Pro-Israeli letters"*: Dixon Donnelley memo to Dean Rusk, June 7, 1967, Box 193, White House Central Files, National Security-Defense, LBJL.

106 *The day of the rally:* Dixon Donnelley memo to Dean Rusk, June 9, 1967, Box 108, National Security File, Country File, Middle East, LBJL; Dixon Donnelley memo to Dean Rusk, June 8, 1967, Box 107 [2 of 2], National Security File, Country File, Middle East, LBJL.

106 *"There should be"*: William L. Taylor telegram to Lyndon Johnson, June 6, 1967, Box 194, White House Central Files, National Security-Defense, LBJL.

106 *"As an elected official"*: West Suburban Temple Har Zion letter to Lyndon Johnson with petition, May 26, 1967, Box 194, White House Central Files, National Security-Defense, LBJL.

106 *"The entire world"*: Harry Miller letter to Lyndon Johnson, June 8, 1967, Box 194, White House Central Files, National Security-Defense, LBJL.

106 *"shaken to the marrow"*: Joseph A. Califano, Jr., *The Triumph & Tragedy of Lyndon Johnson: The White House Years* (New York: Simon & Schuster, 1991), p. 205.

107 *senior White House advisers:* Califano, Jr., *The Triumph & Tragedy of Lyndon Johnson,* p. 205.

107 *"quiet diplomacy"*: Hubert Humphrey memo to Lyndon Johnson, June 8, 1967, Box 18, National Security File, National Security Council Histories, Middle East Crisis, LBJL.

107 *"under control"*: Joe Califano, Jr., memo to Lyndon Johnson, June 7, 1967, Box 193, White House Central Files, National Security-Defense (Gen ND 17 2/20/66), LBJL.

107 *Two hours before:* Joe Califano, Jr., memo to Lyndon Johnson, June 8,

1967, Box 18, National Security File, National Security Council Histories, Middle East Crisis, LBJL.

107 *Busloads of American Jews:* Details of the rally in the park are drawn from Stuart Auerbach, and Jim Hoagland, "Jews and Arabs Rally Here," *Washington Post,* June 9, 1967, p. B1; Phil Casey, "The Yarmulke and the Fez in D.C.," *Washington Post,* June 9, 1967, p. B1; Irving Spiegel, "Jews in Capital Turn Aid Rally Into a Victory Demonstration," *New York Times,* June 9, 1967, p. 10; William Kling, "Jews at Capital Rally Hail News of Truce," *Chicago Tribune,* June 9, 1967, p. 6; Fred Barnes, "Israeli Rally Becomes a Celebration," *Evening Star,* June 9, 1967, p. A11; Mary McGrory, "Instant Israelization of Lafayette Park," *Evening Star,* June 9, 1967, p. A1; "'Give as You Never Gave,'" *Newsweek,* June 19, 1967, pp. 35–36.

108 *McNamara and Vance:* Goulding, *Confirm or Deny,* pp. 114–15.

108 *"Can you tell us":* Background briefing transcript, June 8, 1967, Box 12, Office Files of White House Aides, Office Files of George Christian, LBJL.

109 *Across the river:* White House news conference transcript 867-A, June 8, 1967, Box 19, National Security File, National Security Council Histories, Middle East Crisis, LBJL.

109 *At one point:* Lyndon Johnson Daily Diary, June 8, 1967.

110 *"I deeply appreciate":* Lyndon Johnson telegram to Alexei Kosygin, June 8, 1967, Box 19, National Security File, National Security Council Histories, Middle East Crisis, LBJL.

112 *"10 killed":* Lawrence Baker Situation Room telephone memorandum, June 8, 1967, Box 18, National Security File, National Security Council Histories, Middle East Crisis, LBJL.

CHAPTER 8

PAGE

113 *The mess deck:* Lloyd Painter testimony, *Liberty* court of inquiry.

113 *Dr. Richard Kiepfer:* This scene is based on Richard Kiepfer's testimony before the court of inquiry, and author interviews with Richard Kiepfer (Jan. 11, 2007), John Scott (Jan. 12, 2007, and Sept. 15, 2008), Lloyd Painter (March 1, 2007), Thomas Van Cleave (May 18, 2007), Phillip Tourney (Sept. 5–6, 2007), and Peter Flynn (April 6, 2007); Clyde W. Way oral history interview with Henry Schorreck, William Gerhard, Henry Millington, and Robert Farley, June 8, 1980, www.nsa.gov.

115 *Barely out of his teens:* Background on Gary Blanchard is drawn from author interviews with Glenda Phillips (Dec. 6, 2007), Faith James (Oct. 26, 2008), and Dale Larkins (Jan. 13, 2007, and Sept. 10, 2007).

119 *An uneasy calm:* This scene is drawn from Dave Lucas, William McGonagle, and Richard Kiepfer testimonies before the *Liberty* court of inquiry and author interviews with Dave Lucas (April 25, 2007, and Aug. 13, 2008), Dave Lewis interview (April 10, 2007), and Richard Kiepfer (Jan. 11, 2007); *Liberty* Deck Log, June 8–9, 1967.

119 *"He was so weak":* Dave Lucas letter to Paula Lucas, June 10, 1967.

120 *"The Commanding Officer":* Richard Kiepfer testimony, *Liberty* court of inquiry.

121 *Her birth announcement:* Dave Lucas's journal.

122 *"The night was":* Dave Lucas letter to Paula Lucas, June 10, 1967.

122 *Ensign Scott had worked:* This scene is based on author interviews with John Scott (Jan. 8, 2007, April 1, 2007, July 21, 2008, and Aug. 4, 2008) and Warren Heaney (Jan. 28, 2008).

123 *"One more torpedo":* John Scott letter to parents, June 10, 1967.

124 *Shortly before 6 A.M.:* Description of the *Liberty*'s damage and events the morning of June 9, 1967, are drawn from testimony before the *Liberty* court of inquiry and the author's interviews with John Scott (April 1, 2007), Dave Lucas (April 25, 2007), Richard Kiepfer (Jan. 11, 2007), Dennis Eikleberry (March 22, 2007), Jack Beattie (Dec. 27, 2007), Phillip Tourney (Sept. 5–6, 2007), Rick Aimetti (Dec. 20, 2007), Frank Spicher (Jan. 27, 2008), and William Pettyjohn (Feb. 24, 2008).

126 *at 6:27 A.M.:* *Liberty* Deck Log, June 9, 1967.

126 *The* Massey*'s motor whaleboat:* U.S.S. *Massey* Deck Log, June 9, 1967; U.S.S. *Davis* Deck Log, June 9, 1967.

126 *A thirty-five-year-old:* Peter Flynn interview with author, April 6, 2007.

126 *When news of the attack:* John J. Gordon, Peter A. Flynn, and John A. Peck, "A Report on the Medical Aspects of the USS *Liberty* Incident," August 1967.

127 *"The reality of":* "Damage to Ship Described," *Evening Star,* June 16, 1967, p. A3.

127 *Fifteen of the sailors:* Details of the injuries and chronology of the morning rescue efforts come from John J. Gordon, Peter A. Flynn, and John A. Peck, "A Report on the Medical Aspects of the USS *Liberty* Incident," August 1967.

129 *McGonagle may have:* Ibid.; Peter Flynn interview with author, April 6, 2007; Richard Kiepfer interview with author, Jan. 11, 2007; Lloyd Painter e-mail to author, July 28, 2008.

130 *"Let's give them three cheers":* Engen, *Wings and Warriors,* pp. 321–22; Donald D. Engen oral history interview with Paul Stillwell, Nov. 7, 1994, U.S. Naval Institute, Annapolis, Md.

CHAPTER 9

PAGE

131 *I grieve with you:* Ephraim Evron letter to Lyndon Johnson, June 8, 1967, Box 107 [2 of 2], National Security File, Country File, Middle East, LBJL.

131 *Many of the critical questions:* William Beecher, "Israel, in Error, Attacks U.S. Ship," *New York Times,* June 9, 1967, p. 1; Fred Farrar, "Israelis Rip U.S. Ship; 10 Men Killed," *Chicago Tribune,* June 9, 1967, p. 1; George C. Wilson and Anthony Astrachan, "Envoy Here Apologizes for Attack," *Washington Post,* June 9, 1967, p. A1.

132 *"With Israel":* Beecher, "Israel, in Error, Attacks U.S. Ship," p. 1.

132 *"A miscalculation":* Ibid.

132 *"It certainly wasn't":* Farrar, "Israelis Rip U.S. Ship," p. 1.

132 *the committee's cavernous:* Details of the committee's room are drawn from Joseph C. Goulden, *Truth Is the First Casualty: The Gulf of Tonkin Affair—Illusion and Reality* (Chicago: Rand McNally, 1969), p. 53.

132 *"The incident was":* Senate Committee on Foreign Relations, *Executive Sessions of the Senate Foreign Relations Committee Together with Joint Sessions with the Senate Armed Services Committee,* vol. 19, 90th Cong., 1st sess., 1967 (Washington, D.C.: U.S. Government Printing Office, 2006), pp. 705–17.

132 *"consummate skeptic":* William M. Blair, "'Consummate Skeptic,'" *New York Times,* Sept. 5, 1971, p. 41.

132 *"horse thieves":* Seymour M. Hersh, *The Samson Option: Israel's Nuclear Arsenal and American Foreign Policy* (New York: Random House, 1991), pp. 80–81.

134 *At the Pentagon:* Details for this scene are drawn from SECDEF msg. 091812Z, June 1967, *Liberty* Incident Message File, NHC; Goulding, *Confirm or Deny,* pp. 119–23.

136 *"No countries were informed":* Goulding writes in his memoir that this

statement was put out in a press release before the end of the day. His account conflicts with the transcript of the news briefing telegrammed to senior Navy officials that states that the information was provided to reporters during Goulding's 10:30 A.M. briefing.

136 *"The main issue":* Goulding, *Confirm or Deny,* p. 123.

136 *George Christian greeted reporters:* News conference transcript 868-A, June 9, 1967, Box 19, National Security File, National Security Council Histories, Middle East Crisis, LBJL.

137 *at 5:35 A.M.:* AMEMBASSY TEL AVIV msg. 090810Z, June 1967, Box 114, National Security File, Country File, Middle East, LBJL.

137 *President Johnson's advisers:* Meeting Minutes of the Special Committee of the National Security Council, June 9, 1967, Box 19, National Security File, National Security Council Histories, Middle East Crisis, LBJL.

138 *"My goodness":* Lyndon Johnson Daily Diary, June 9, 1967.

138 *Only hours earlier:* USDAO TEL AVIV ISRAEL msg. 091520Z, June 1967, *Liberty* Incident Message File, NHC; Blackman, *Jane's Fighting Ships,1966–67,* p. 76.

139 *The former:* McGeorge Bundy oral history interview with Paige E. Mulhollan, Feb. 17, 1969, LBJL.

140 *Clifford's strong views:* A. Jay Cristol, *The Liberty Incident: The 1967 Israeli Attack on the U.S. Navy Spy Ship* (Washington, D.C.: Brassey's, 2002), p. 66.

140 *"strong and firm line":* Memorandum from the President's Special Consultant to the Special Committee of the National Security Council, June 9, 1967, in Schwar, *Foreign Relations of the United States, 1964–1968,* pp. 400–1.

140 *"There is very strong":* Dean Rusk telegram 209964 to Walworth Barbour, June 9, 1967, Box 114, National Security File, Middle East, LBJL.

140 *doodling various:* Lyndon Johnson's handwritten notes, June 9, 1967, Box 22, Handwriting File, Lyndon B. Johnson, May 1967–June 1967 [2 of 3], LBJL.

141 *The president told Roberts:* Dan Patir telegram 155 to the Foreign Ministry, June 11, 1967, 4079/HZ-26, ISA.

141 *"Imagine what would":* Lyndon Johnson Daily Diary, June 9, 1967.

CHAPTER 10

PAGE

142 *I think you know:* "Transcript of LBJ's News Conference," *Washington Post,* June 14, 1967, p. A13.

142 *Medical teams on:* Details of this scene are drawn from John J. Gordon, Peter A. Flynn, and John A. Peck, "A Report on the Medical Aspects of the USS *Liberty* Incident," August 1967; Peter Flynn interview with author, April 6, 2007.

142 *the 1,048-foot carrier:* Details of the carrier's size and crew come from Blackman, *Jane's Fighting Ships, 1967–68,* p. 346.

142 *Two days after:* Details of the memorial service are drawn from Engen, *Wings and Warriors,* p. 322; News Release No. 40–67, 66 Responds to Mideast Crisis, Box 709, Press Releases/Briefings, 1967, Post 1 Jan. 1946 Command File, Operational Archives Branch, NHC; J. M. Mahood, ed., *United States Ship America, 1967* (Dallas: Armed Forces Publications/Taylor, 1967), pp. 244–45.

145 *The Missouri native:* "Retired Admiral, Test Pilot William I. Martin Dies at 85," *Washington Post,* April 4, 1996, p. B7; "Vice Adm. W. I. 'Bill' Martin, Ava Native, Dies in Virginia," *Douglas County Herald,* April 11, 1996, p. 1; "Sixth Fleet Gets New Chief," *New York Times,* April 11, 1967, p. 14.

145 *"Unbelievable carnage!!":* William Martin undated letter to James Ramage, Box 18.25, James D. Ramage Papers, Emil Buehler Naval Aviation Library, Pensacola, Fla.

145 *"That ship was under":* This scene is based on press briefing transcript, June 10, 1967, Box 709, Post 1 Jan. 1946 Command File, Operational Archives Branch, NHC; USS AMERICA msg. 152043Z, June 1967, Box 113, Public Affairs Matters, Immediate Office Files of the CNO, Operational Archives Branch, NHC. There are some slight variations between these two transcripts that required me to make certain judgments as to accuracy, spelling, and punctuation.

148 *Crews continued the cleanup:* Dave Lucas's journal; Dave Lucas letter to Paula Lucas, June 11, 1967; John Scott interview with author, July 21, 2008.

148 *To the men on the* Davis: William Pettyjohn interview with author, Feb. 24, 2008; John Scott interview with author, July 21, 2008.

149 *The ship's doctor:* CTG SIX ZERO PT FIVE msg. 101750Z, June 67, www.nsa.gov; Dave Lucas letter to Paula Lucas, June 11, 1967.

149 *"My Dearest Jean":* William McGonagle telegram to Jean McGonagle, June 10, 1967, Box 4, William L. McGonagle Papers, 1947–99, HIA.

149 *"Honey, I love you":* Dave Lucas letter to Paula Lucas, June 11, 1967.

150 *"I don't see how":* John Scott letter to parents, June 10, 1967.

150 *"Close to thirty-five boys died":* Dale Larkins letter to parents, June 10, 1967.

150 *"I just don't":* Ruth Scott letter to John Scott, June 11, 1967.

150 *The fleet tug* Papago: U.S.S. *Papago* Deck Log, June 9–14, 1967.

150 *The 205-foot-long:* Details of the *Papago*'s size come from Blackman, *Jane's Fighting Ships, 1967–68,* p. 439; Kit Rushing interview with author, May 10, 2007.

150 *the* Papago's *crew trolled:* DIRNAVSECGRUEUR msg. 191358Z, June 1967, www.nsa.gov; CTG SIX ZERO PT FIVE msg. 092119Z, June 1967, www.nsa.gov.

150 *The skipper ordered:* Kit Rushing interview with author, May 10, 2007; John Highfill interview with author, Feb. 10, 2008.

151 *At 9:41 A.M.: Papago* Deck Log, June 11, 1967.

151 *Highfill noted:* John Highfill interview with author, Feb. 10, 2008.

151 *Many of the sailors:* Kit Rushing interview with author, May 10, 2007.

152 *"You couldn't grab":* John Highfill interview with author, Feb. 10, 2008.

152 *a signalman flashed:* Dennis Eikleberry interview with author, March 22, 2007.

152 *Searchers spotted: Papago* Deck Log, June 12, 1967.

CHAPTER 11

PAGE

153 *What LBJ didn't know:* Nicholas Katzenbach interview with author, April 19, 2007.

153 *President Johnson suffered:* Lyndon Johnson Daily Diary, June 9–10, 1967; Harold H. Saunders Memorandum for the Record, Oct. 22, 1968, in Schwar, *Foreign Relations of the United States, 1964–1968,* p. 410.

154 *The barrage of press:* News conference transcript 869-A, June 9, 1967, Box 19, National Security File, National Security Council Histories, Middle East Crisis, LBJL.

154 *"many mistakes":* "Death on the *Liberty,*" editorial, *New York Times,* June 10, 1967, p. 32.

154 *"must disturb"*: "American Casualties," editorial, *Washington Post*, June 9, 1967, p. A22.

155 *"inevitable"*: "Tragedy and Triumph," editorial, *Virginian-Pilot*, June 10, 1967, p. 12.

155 *"shocking"*: "Shocking Error," editorial, *News and Courier*, June 9, 1967, p. 10A.

155 *"far fetched"*: "The Big Problems Lie Ahead," editorial, *Shreveport Times*, June 11, 1967, p. 2B.

155 *"There was nothing"*: Goulding, *Confirm or Deny*, p. 128.

156 *Within the first twenty-four hours:* Orr Kelly, "U.S. Ship's Toll May Reach 31," *Evening Star*, June 9, 1967, p. 1.

156 *news reports:* Goulding, *Confirm or Deny*, pp. 123–24; Darrell Garwood, "Israel Vows Amends for Ship Attack," *Washington Post*, June 11, 1967, p. A10; Louis Dombrowski, "Israel Offers to Pay Reparations to U.S.," *Chicago Tribune*, June 11, 1967, p. 10; "Israel Promises Amends for Attack on U.S. Navy Ship," *Evening Star*. June 11, 1967, p. A4.

156 *The White House dialed:* Goulding leaves the impression that Johnson made the call to McNamara, though he does not state that specifically. The president's diary reflects that Johnson made a 12:10 P.M. call to the defense secretary, which McNamara returned at 2:59 P.M.

156 *"close to setting"*: Fred Farrar, "Pentagon Reports of Israeli Ship Attacks Termed Curious," *Chicago Tribune*, June 18, 1967, p. 16.

157 *"We in the Department"*: Goulding, *Confirm or Deny*, p. 124.

157 *The latest news reports:* Seymour M. Hersh, "Toll in Torpedoing of U.S. Ship Put at 33 Killed, 75 Wounded," *Washington Post*, June 10, 1967, p. A12.

157 *Rostow possessed:* Background on Rostow is drawn from "Yale's Perfect Freshman," *New York Times*, Sept. 15, 1929, p. RP33; Todd S. Purdum, "Eugene Rostow, 89, Official at State Dept. and Law Dean," *New York Times*, Nov. 26, 2002, p. C19; Oren, *Six Days of War*, p. 108; Harold Hongju Koh, "In Memoriam: Dean Eugene V. Rostow," *Yale Law Report* 50, no. 2 (Summer 2003), pp. 16–17; Boris I. Bittker, "Eugene V. Rostow," *Yale Law Journal* 94, no. 6.,(May 1985), pp. 1315–22.

158 *His support of Israel:* Thomas Hughes interview with author, May 3, 2007.

158 *"I could never imagine"*: Richard B. Parker, ed., *The Six Day War: A Retrospective* (Gainesville: University Press of Florida, 1996), p. 278.

158 *"complete explanation:* Eugene Rostow memorandum of conversation

with Avraham Harman, June 10, 1967, in Schwar, *Foreign Relations of the United States, 1964–1968*, p. 419.

158 *"make retribution"*: AMEMBASSY TEL AVIV msg. 091115Z, June 1967, Box 108, National Security File, Country File, Middle East, LBJL.

158 *"The Government of Israel"*: Avraham Harman letter to Dean Rusk, June 10, 1967, Box 107 [2 of 2], National Security File, Country File, Middle East, LBJL.

158 *"cannot simply be"*: Dean Rusk draft letter to Avraham Harman, June 10, 1967, Box 108, National Security File, Country File, Middle East, LBJL.

159 *"At the time"*: Dean Rusk letter to Avraham Harman, June 10, 1967, Box 107 [2 of 2], National Security File, Country File, Middle East, LBJL.

160 *"tragic mistake"*: Dean Rusk telegram 210199 to the American Embassy in Tel Aviv, June 11, 1967, Box 1794, RG 59, Central Files 1967–69, POL 27 ARAB-ISR, NARA.

160 *At 5:12 P.M.*: Lyndon Johnson Daily Diary, June 10, 1967.

160 *Built in 1925*: Details on the history of the *Sequoia* are drawn from www.sequoiayacht.com; Blackman, *Jane's Fighting Ships,1967–68*, p. 437.

161 *The president woke*: Lyndon Johnson Daily Diary, June 11, 1967.

161 *On his own*: Johnson, *A White House Diary*, p. 522.

161 *The Special Committee*: Meeting Minutes of the Special Committee of the National Security Council, June 12, 1967, Box 19, National Security File, National Security Council Histories, Middle East Crisis, LBJL.

161 *The president*: Lyndon Johnson Daily Diary, June 12, 1967; Lyndon Johnson's handwritten notes, June 12, 1967, Box 22, Handwriting File, LBJL.

161 *For every Israeli*: Oren, *Six Days of War*, pp. 305–7.

162 *"People in office"*: Harold Saunders interview with author, Oct. 2, 2007.

162 *"Most of us knew"*: Lucius Battle interview with author, Nov. 7, 2006.

162 *"There was nobody"*: Nicholas Katzenbach interview with author, April 19, 2007.

162 *"vicious"*: Ephraim Evron telegram 156 to the Foreign Ministry, June 11, 1967, 4079/HZ-26, ISA.

162 *"made things easier"*: Ibid.

162 *"probably for more use"*: McGeorge Bundy memo to President Johnson,

June 9, 1967, Box 108, National Security File, Country File, Middle East, LBJL.

163 *"The Government of Israel"*: Avraham Harman letter to Dean Rusk, June 12, 1967, Box 107 [2 of 2], National Security File, Country File, Middle East, LBJL.

164 *"With 10 men killed"*: Harold H. Saunders memo to McGeorge Bundy, June 8, 1967, Box 3, National Security File, Files of the Special Committee of the NSC, LBJL.

164 *"political independence"*: Schwar, *Foreign Relations of the United States, 1964–1968,* pp. 80–81.

164 *Two more American fighters:* "Power Plant and MiG Field in North Hit by U.S. Planes," *New York Times,* June 12, 1967, p. 1.

164 *The unpopular war:* Walt W. Rostow memo to Lyndon Johnson, May 25, 1968, Box 35, National Security File, Memos to the President, Walt Rostow, LBJL.

165 *The Middle East war produced:* Whitney Shoemaker oral history interview with Dorothy Pierce, Nov. 25, 1968, LBJL.

165 *"During the past ten days"*: Dixon Donnelley memo to Dean Rusk, June 14, 1967, Box 109, National Security File, Country File, Middle East, LBJL.

165 *The week of the attack:* Bernard Weinraub, "Allied Unit with U.S. Copters Smashes a Vietcong Battalion," *New York Times,* June 16, 1967, p. 16.

165 *"There are lots"*: Harold Saunders interview with author, Oct. 2, 2007.

165 *"However outrageous"*: Dean Rusk letter to Jim Ennes, Jr., Sept. 10, 1981.

166 *"It was no help"*: Nicholas Katzenbach interview with author, April 19, 2007.

166 *"After reviewing"*: McGeorge Bundy memorandum for the Record, June 12, 1967, Box 19, National Security File, National Security Council Histories, Middle East Crisis, LBJL.

166 *"suggested Harman"*: Benjamin H. Read memo, June 16, 1967, Box 19, National Security File, National Security Council Histories, Middle East Crisis, LBJL.

CHAPTER 12

PAGE

167 *That evening:* Dale Larkins letter to parents, June 15, 1967.

167 *The* Liberty *sailed: Liberty* Deck Log, June 14, 1967.

167 *Bandaged crewmembers:* Colin Frost, "Strafed Ship Reaches Malta," *Virginian-Pilot,* June 15, 1967, p. 6; "Ship Attack Puzzles Pentagon," *Chicago Tribune,* June 14, 1967, p. 2.

167 *McGonagle appeared:* "'Liberty' Reaches Malta Port," *Virginian-Pilot,* June 15, 1967, p. 1; William McGonagle interview with Tim Frank, Sept. 27, 1997.

167 *"the colors of the dawn":* "Ship Attack Puzzles Pentagon," p. 2.

167 *"funnel had more holes":* Frost, "Strafed Ship Reaches Malta," p. 6.

167 *"shot up as a tin can":* "Unexplained Casualty: U.S.S. 'Liberty,'" *Life,* June 23, 1967, p. 29.

168 *Divers slipped into wet suits:* John Highfill interview with author, Feb. 10, 2008.

168 *A Maltese harbor pilot: Liberty* Deck Log, June 14, 1967.

168 *concocted a cover story:* CINCUSNAVEUR msg. 120950Z, June 1967, www.nsa.gov.

168 *To prevent the loss:* HQ NSAEUR msg., 161530Z, June 1967, www.nsa.gov; CTF ONE ZERO ZERO msg. 150200Z, June 1967, www.nsa.gov.

168 *Soon after the attack:* John Scott interviews with author, April 1, 2007, and July 21, 2008.

169 *"death ship":* Ibid.

169 *"The smell was so bad":* Jack Beattie letter to parents, June 15, 1967.

169 *With drydock now dewatered:* Lloyd Painter interview with author, March 1, 2007; Lloyd Painter e-mail to author, April, 11, 2008.

169 *The Navy allowed:* HQ NSAEUR msg., 161530Z, June 1967, www.nsa.gov.

170 *The men picked:* Description of the torpedoed compartments are drawn from interviews with Lloyd Painter (March 1, 2007), Ron Kukal (March 14, 2007), Dennis Eikleberry (Oct. 12, 2006, and March 22, 2007), Don Pageler (July 26, 2007), Robert Schnell (Feb. 1, 2008), and Sam Schulman (May 17, 2007).

170 *"You'd puke":* Robert Schnell interview with author, Feb. 1, 2008.

170 *"When they picked":* Dennis Eikleberry interview with author, March 22, 2007.

170 *"Not just arms"*: Don Pageler interview with Joyce E. Terrill, April 25, 1987.

171 *"You knew who"*: Sam Schulman interview with author, May 17, 2007.

171 *"Some of the bodies"*: Ron Kukal interview with author, March 15, 2007.

171 *Kiefer poured brandy*: Richard Kiepfer interview with author, Jan. 11, 2007.

171 *An early status report*: USS LIBERTY msg. 150710Z, June 1967, www. nsa.gov.

171 *"Twenty remains"*: CTF ONE ZERO ZERO msg. 151406Z, June 1967, www.nsa.gov.

172 *Press queries swamped*: Goulding, *Confirm or Deny,* p. 124.

172 *"Many rumors and reports"*: Ibid., p. 130.

172 *"one of the most intriguing"*: Fred Farrar, "Pentagon Reports of Israeli Ship Attacks Termed Curious," *Chicago Tribune,* June 18, 1967, p. 16.

172 *The Navy prepped*: COMSIXTHFLT msg. 090546Z, June 1967, *Liberty* Incident Message File, NHC; USCINCEUR msg. 081650Z, June 1967, *Liberty* Incident Message File, NHC.

172 *Afterward staff cabled*: USS AMERICA msg. 150657Z, June 1967, Box 113, Public Affairs Matters, Immediate Office Files of the CNO, Operational Archives Branch, NHC.

173 *"At one point"*: USS AMERICA msg. 112005Z, June 1967, *Liberty* Incident Message File, NHC.

173 *"To put it bluntly"*: Seymour M. Hersh, "Toll in Torpedoing of U.S. Ship Put at 33 Killed, 75 Wounded," *Washington Post,* June 10, 1967, p. A12; USS AMERICA msg. 092225Z, June 1967, *Liberty* Incident Message File, NHC.

173 *"Mr. Horton's copy"*: CINCUSNAVEUR msg. 111743Z, June 1967, www.nsa.gov.

173 *Days before the* Liberty's *arrival*: CINCUSNAVEUR 110225Z, June 1967, www.nsa.gov.

173 *"minimize immediate scrutiny"*: AMEMBASSY VALLETTA msg. 161815Z, June 1967, Box 1796, RG 59, Central Files 1967–69, POL 27 ARAB-ISR, NARA.

173 *The Navy also barred*: CTF ONE ZERO ZERO msg. 170630Z, June 1967, www.nsa.gov.

174 *To satisfy the press*: CTF ONE ZERO ZERO msg. 150200Z, June 1967, www.nsa.gov.

174   *"rigidly controlled"*: Ibid.

174   *"to prevent lending credence"*: AMEMBASSY VALLETTA msg. 161815Z, June 1967, Box 1796, RG 59, Central Files 1967–69, POL 27 ARAB-ISR, NARA.

174   *"Believe that"*: CTF ONE ZERO ZERO msg. 150200Z, June 1967, www. nsa.gov.

174   *"members of the crew"*: CINCUSNAVEUR msg. 120950Z, June 1967, www.nsa.gov.

174   *"We were just sitting ducks"*: " 'Just Sitting Ducks,' Sailor Says of Attack," *News and Courier,* June 16, 1967, p. 3A.

174   *"That sort of thing"*: Dave Lucas letter to parents, June 24, 1967.

174   *"Everything I've said"*: Dave Lucas letter to Paula Lucas, June 15, 1967.

175   *A court of inquiry:* Material in this section, unless otherwise noted, comes from the transcript of the *Liberty* court of inquiry.

175   *His father had served:* "Admiral J. S. McCain Dies on Coast at 61," *New York Times,* Sept. 7, 1945, p. 1.

175   *"He combined"*: "Admiral McCain," editorial, *New York Times,* Sept. 9, 1945, p. 76.

175   *The younger McCain:* Information on Admiral John McCain, Jr.'s, personality is derived from Herbert E. Hetu oral history interview with Paul Stillwell, June 5, 1996, U.S. Naval Institute; Joseph C. Wylie, Jr., oral history interview with Paul Stillwell, May 22, 1985, U.S. Naval Institute; John McCain with Mark Salter, *Faith of My Fathers* (New York: Random House, 1999), pp. 52–96.

176   *"Our staff begged"*: Joseph C. Wylie, Jr., oral history interview with Paul Stillwell, May 22, 1985, U.S. Naval Institute; J. C. Wylie, Jr., letter to Joseph F. Bouchard, March 28, 1988.

176   *"It was a little bigger"*: Herbert E. Hetu oral history interview with Paul Stillwell, June 5, 1996, U.S. Naval Institute.

176   *Faced with political pressure:* Ward Boston, Jr., interview with author, Oct. 11, 2006.

177   *Salvage divers later found:* Joy Waldron Jasper, James P. Delgado, and Jim Adams, *The U.S.S. Arizona: The Ship, the Men, the Pearl Harbor Attack, and the Symbol That Aroused America* (New York: Truman Tally/St. Martin's, 2001), p. 13.

177   *The rear admiral was the highest-ranking:* "23 High Officers Casualties in War," *New York Times,* May 7, 1944, p. 34.

177 *"The U.S. Naval Academy"*: "June in December," *Time,* Dec. 29, 1941, p. 40.

177 *Kidd served as:* Wolfgang Saxon, "Isaac C. Kidd, Jr., 79, Admiral and Expert on Maritime Law," *New York Times,* July 4, 1999, p. 26; "Navy Hero's Son to Get Ship," *New York Times,* Sept. 7, 1956, p. 5; "New U.S. Destroyer Division," *New York Times,* Jan. 2, 1962, p. 5.

177 *Boston had flown fighters:* Ward Boston, Jr., interview with author, Oct. 11, 2006.

177 *arriving on board the injured ship: Liberty* Deck Log, June 12, 1967.

177 *"Talk about brass":* Dave Lucas letter to Paula Lucas, June 15, 1967.

178 *The wardroom still bore:* "Finis," *Newsweek,* July 3, 1967, p. 24; Dave Lucas letter to Paula Lucas, June 16, 1967.

178 *To help the twenty-five-year-old officer relax:* Dave Lucas letter to Paula Lucas, June 15, 1967.

179 *Days later:* Richard Kiepfer interview with author, Jan. 11, 2007.

179 *Lieutenant Commander William Pettyjohn:* William Pettyjohn interview with author, Feb. 24, 2008.

181 *Lieutenant Jim Ennes, Jr.:* Jim Ennes, Jr., e-mail to author, Oct. 6, 2008.

181 *Seaman Larry Weaver:* Larry Weaver e-mail to author, Sept. 3, 2008.

181 *Lieutenant Jim O'Connor:* James G. O'Connor oral history interview with Bill Gerhard, Henry Millington, Hank Schorreck, and Bob Farley, May 22, 1980, www.nsa.gov.

182 *Captain Boston watched men:* Ward Boston, Jr., interview with author, Oct. 11, 2006.

183 *"murderous bastards":* Ibid.

184 *Petty Officer 2nd Class Charles Cocnavitch:* Charles Cocnavitch interviews with author, Dec. 10, 2007, and Aug. 28, 2008.

185 *"The barrel basically":* Dale Larkins interview with author, Sept. 10, 2007.

186 *"It was all perfunctory":* John Scott interview with author, April 13, 2008.

186 *"shallow":* Lloyd Painter interview with author, April 13, 2008.

186 *"cursory":* Mac Watson interview with author, April 23, 2008.

186 *"process rather than product":* Patrick O'Malley e-mail to author, April 20, 2008.

186 *The transcript shows:* The *Liberty* inquiry's lack of depth is particularly apparent when compared to the court of inquiry that examined North

330 Notes

Korea's 1968 seizure of the spy ship U.S.S. *Pueblo*. The *Pueblo* inquiry took testimony from more than 100 witnesses, generating more than 3,300 pages of testimony.

186 *never approached within thirty-eight miles:* Cristol, *The* Liberty *Incident,* p. 267.

186 *James Halman:* James Halman interviews with author, Jan. 21, 2008, and Aug. 15, 2008.

186 *Other crewmembers said:* This author discovered eleven magnabelt tapes in the Naval Historical Center's archives containing approximately 2.5 hours of testimony from the *Liberty* court of inquiry. These are believed to be the only surviving tapes from that investigation. The Navy, which originally attempted to block the release of the tapes, relented after I filed a Freedom of Information Act lawsuit in federal court. The tapes unfortunately do not cover the portions of testimony that are in dispute. But a comparison of the testimony on the tapes with the court's printed transcript shows multiple omissions and off-the-record exchanges that are not present in the court's official transcript. That transcript, according to Adm. John McCain, Jr.'s, orders, was supposed to be a verbatim record.

186 *Lucas submitted:* Dave Lucas interview with author, April 25, 2007.

187 *Painter's testimony:* Lloyd Painter interview with author, March 1, 2007; Ward Boston interviews with author, Oct. 11, 2006, and April 21, 2007.

187 *Cocnavitch said:* Charles Cocnavitch interviews with author, Dec. 10, 2007, and Aug. 28, 2008.

187 *"Our Navy's Inquiry":* Isaac C. Kidd, Jr., letter to Jim Ennes, Jr., Oct. 10, 1983.

187 *"The court didn't seem":* Lloyd Painter interview with author, April 13, 2008.

188 *"That question":* James G. O'Connor oral history interview with Bill Gerhard, Henry Millington, Hank Schorreck, and Bob Farley, May 22, 1980, www.nsa.gov.

CHAPTER 13

190   *Thursday and Friday:* George Scott letter to John Scott, June 11, 1967.

190   *"wake of bitterness":* "Sinking the *Liberty*: Accident or Design?," *Newsweek,* June 19, 1967, p. 21.

190   *"questions outnumbered answers":* "Mystery of Attack on U.S.S. 'Liberty,'" *U.S. News & World Report,* June 26, 1967, p. 33.

191   *"unexplained casualty":* "Unexplained Casualty: U.S.S. 'Liberty,'" *Life,* June 23, 1967, p. 29.

191   *"When the essentials":* "The Liberty," editorial, *Washington Post,* June 17, 1967, p. A12.

191   *"puzzling circumstances":* Drew Pearson and Jack Anderson, "Explanations Due on Ship Attack," *Washington Post,* June 16, 1967, p. D19.

191   *"No one can figure out":* Ruth Scott letter to John Scott, June 15, 1967.

192   *The* Liberty's *chief engineer:* George Golden interview with Jim Ennes, Jr., Dec. 3, 1972.

192   *"We were flying":* "Crewmen of 'Liberty' Say Attack Deliberate," *Virginian-Pilot,* June 18, 1967, p. A13; "Israelis Knowingly Attacked Ship, Navy Reportedly Told," *Evening Star,* June 17, 1967, p. A2.

192   *"Because other reporters":* CINCUSNAVEUR msg. 181105Z, June 1967, *Liberty* Incident Message File, NHC.

192   *"Former Navy skippers":* George C. Wilson, "*Liberty* Attack Punctured Pentagon Cover," *Washington Post,* June 18, 1967, p. C5.

192   *"The Israelis may have":* Seymour M. Hersh, "Israeli Jets Eyed Ship Before Blow," *Washington Post,* June 14, 1967, p. A11.

193   *"Couldn't that skipper":* Wilson, "*Liberty* Attack Punctured Pentagon Cover," p. C5.

193   *"Greater precautions":* David Lawrence, "Attack on U.S. Ship Stirs Questions," *Evening Star,* June 13, 1967, p. A13.

193   *"rejected the idea":* "Officer Calls It a Mistake," *New York Times,* June 18, 1967, p. 20.

193   *Democratic representative Wayne Hays:* "Washington Whispers: Why Nasser Offered to Bow Out . . . Wrong Guess by Hussein . . . Israel's 'Lesson' to U.S. Generals," *U.S. News & World Report,* June 19, 1967, p. 28.

194   *"Israel is suffering":* *Congressional Record,* 90th Cong., 1st sess. June 14, 1967, p. 15875.

194 *"We can yet redeem"*: Congressional Record, 90th Cong., 1st sess. June 15, 1967, p. 15957.

195 *"very dangerous elements"*: Ephraim Evron telegram 156 to the Foreign Ministry, June 11, 1967, 4079/HZ-26, ISA; Avraham Harman telegram 285 to the Foreign Ministry, June 18, 1967, 4079/HZ-26, ISA.

195 *"very reliable journalistic source"*: Dan Patir telegram 155 to the Foreign Ministry, June 11, 1967, 4079/HZ-26, ISA.

195 *"carried out a deliberate attack"*: Ibid.

195 *"presented pretty much"*: Ephraim Evron telegram 156 to the Foreign Ministry, June 11, 1967, 4079/HZ-26, ISA.

195 *"We can assume"*: Ibid.

195 *"We are facing"*: Ibid.

196 *"of the dangers"*: Ibid.

196 *"improve our position"*: Ibid.

196 *"toned down"*: Dan Patir telegram 163 to the Foreign Ministry, June 11, 1967, 4079/HZ-26, ISA.

196 *"malicious"*: "Raid on Ship Deliberate, Some Claim," *Virginian-Pilot,* June 13, 1967, p. 12.

196 *"We have made sure"*: Dan Patir telegram 115 to the Foreign Ministry, July 11, 1967, 4079/HZ-26, ISA.

196 *"floating one self-serving rumor"*: Goulding, *Confirm or Deny,* p. 128.

196 *"to make this tragedy"*: Ibid., p. 137.

196 *Israeli officials told:* Fred Farrar, "Israel Says U.S. Ignored Query on Ships in Area," *Washington Post,* June 16, 1967, p. A9.

197 *"urgent confirmation"*: Dean Rusk telegram 211695 to the American Embassy in Tel Aviv, June 16, 1967, Box 1796, RG 59, Central Files 1967–69, POL 27 ARAB-ISR, NARA.

197 *"No request for info"*: AMEMBASSY TEL AVIV msg. 162000Z, June 1967, ibid.

197 *"A personal friend"*: Ephraim Evron telegram 160 to the Foreign Ministry, June 11, 1967, 5986/HZ-4, ISA.

197 *Arthur Goldberg:* Avraham Harman telegram 607 to the Foreign Ministry, June 16, 1967, 4079/HZ-26.

197 *"clear proof"*: Ephraim Evron telegram 193 to the Foreign Ministry, June 13, 1967, 4079/HZ-26.

197 *"Israeli combat orders"*: Avraham Harman telegram 245 to the Foreign Ministry, June 15, 1967, 5986/HZ-4, ISA.

197 *Harman told Fortas:* Ibid.

197 *"a significant difference":* Ephraim Evron telegram 193 to the Foreign Ministry, June 13, 1967, 4079/HZ-26, ISA.

198 *Ginsburg advised:* Ibid.

198 *"guerrilla war":* Ibid.

198 *"very careful":* Avraham Harman telegram 607 to the Foreign Ministry, June 16, 1967, 4079/HZ-26, ISA.

198 *"In light of ":* Avraham Harman telegram 200 to the Foreign Ministry, June 13, 1967, 4079/HZ-26, ISA.

CHAPTER 14

PAGE

199 *His loss:* William McGonagle letter to J. C. Toth, June 17, 1967, Box 3, William Loren McGonagle Papers, 1947–99, HIA.

199 *McGonagle closed the shutters:* Patrick O'Malley interview with author, Nov. 26, 2007; Richard Kiepfer interview with author, Aug. 16, 2008.

199 *Teams of Maltese shipfitters:* Dave Lucas letter to Paula Lucas, June 17, 1967.

199 *"Damn, the noise":* Dave Lucas letter to Paula Lucas, June 23, 1967.

200 *"Blast injury to brain":* untitled handwritten notes, Box 3, William Loren McGonagle Papers, 1947–99, HIA.

200 *"When the torpedo exploded":* Chronological Record of Medical Care, Box 3, William Loren McGonagle Papers, 1947–99, HIA.

200 *"engulfed in flames":* William McGonagle letter to W. Brown, June 18, 1967, Box 3, William Loren McGonagle Papers, 1947–99, HIA.

201 *"It is with profound":* William McGonagle letter to Sherry Raper, June 18, 1967, Box 3, William Loren McGonagle Papers, 1947–99, HIA.

201 *"He was given":* William McGonagle letter to F. C. Blanchard, June 18, 1967, Box 3, William Loren McGonagle Papers, 1947–99, HIA.

201 *"I was wrong about you":* Patrick O'Malley interview with author, Nov. 26, 2007.

201 *"agile mind and sparkling manner":* William McGonagle letter to J. H. Hayden, June 18, 1967, Box 3, William Loren McGonagle Papers, 1947–99, HIA.

202 *"contagious enthusiasm":* William McGonagle letter to W. J. Marlborough, June 18, 1967, Box 3, William Loren McGonagle Papers, 1947–99, HIA.

202 *"outstanding pride":* William McGonagle letter to Gail Thompson, June 18, 1967, Box 3, William Loren McGonagle Papers, 1947–99, HIA.

202   *"competent caterer"*: William McGonagle letter to J. C. Toth, June 17, 1967, Box 3, William Loren McGonagle Papers, 1947–99, HIA.

202   *"unselfishly let the praise"*: Ibid.

202   *"Words alone"*: William McGonagle letter to Weetie Armstrong, June 13, 1967, Box 3, William Loren McGonagle Papers, 1947–99, HIA.

202   *"The ship was in international waters"*: Ibid. McGonagle used the same description in all of his letters.

203   *"May God in His"*: Ibid.

203   *The White House would mail:* James U. Cross, *Around the World with LBJ: My Wild Ride as Air Force One Pilot, White House Aide, and Personal Confidant* (Austin: University of Texas Press, 2008), pp. 77–81; James Cross interview with author, April 29, 2008.

203   *"The attached condolence letters"*: James Cross memo to Harry McPherson, Jr., June 20, 1967, Box 42, Office Files of White House Aides, Office Files of Harry McPherson, Jr., LBJL.

204   *"It is my"*: Harry McPherson, Jr., memo to James Cross, June 26, 1967, ibid.

204   *The deck force unpacked:* Dave Lucas's journal.

204   *Scores of letters:* Dave Lucas letter to Paula Lucas, June 20, 1967.

204   *"All our wounded"*: John Scott letter to parents, June 19, 1967.

204   *Less than a week:* "New Duty for 59 of 'Liberty,'" *Virginian-Pilot*, June 24, 1967, p. 4.

205   *"Almost all of the Research people"*: Dave Lucas letter to Paula Lucas, June 20, 1967.

205   *Others visited catacombs:* Details of crew life in Malta are drawn from Dave Lucas letters to Paula Lucas, July 13, 1967, June 18, 1967, June 28, 1967, and June 25, 1967.

205   *Scott and Painter:* John Scott interview with author, July 21, 2008.

205   *Dr. Kiepfer rented:* Richard Kiepfer interview with author, Aug. 16, 2008.

205   *The ship's projector:* Dave Lucas letters to Paula Lucas, June 22, 1967, June 24, 1967, and July 7, 1967.

205   *"I just finished counseling"*: Dave Lucas letter to Paula Lucas, June 17, 1967.

206   *"I'm O.K."*: Don Pageler postcard to parents, June 16, 1967.

206   *"Please don't worry"*: Dale Larkins letter to parents, June 15, 1967.

206   *"I guess the delayed grief"*: Ruth Scott letter to John Scott, July 4, 1967.

206 *"must be a sad place":* Ruth Scott letter to John Scott, June 15, 1967.

206 *"it's still a great joy":* Dave Lucas letter to Paula Lucas, June 23, 1967.

206 *"I remember just sitting":* Patrick O'Malley interview with author, Nov. 26, 2007.

206 *Scott, Lucas, and Painter:* John Scott memo to William McGonagle, June 23, 1967, Box 5, William Loren McGonagle Papers, 1947–99, HIA; Dave Lucas letter to Paula Lucas, June 23, 1967.

206 *"It's just not right":* Dave Lucas letter to Paula Lucas, June 26, 1967.

207 *He bought his officers:* Dave Lucas letter to Paula Lucas, July 7, 1967.

207 *"The Capt. has changed":* Dave Lucas letter to parents, July 2, 1967.

207 *"Sure hope we will":* William McGonagle letter to Mackie McGonagle, June 20, 1967, Box 4, William Loren McGonagle Papers, 1947–99, HIA.

CHAPTER 15

PAGE

208 *Did 34 Americans die:* "Navy Must Explain Order Delay," editorial, *Plain Dealer,* June 30, 1967, p. 16.

208 *Ron's family:* Cristol, *The* Liberty *Incident,* p. 165.

208 *A South Dakota native:* Ernest Castle interview with author, Feb. 20, 2007; Lynn Blasch interview with author, Nov. 13, 2007.

209 *He relayed:* Ernest Castle interview with author, March 28, 2007.

209 *The only promising:* Edward Gibson Lanpher oral history interview with Charles Stuart Kennedy, June 25, 2002, Front Diplomacy: The Foreign Affairs Oral History Collection of the Association for Diplomatic Studies and Training, Manuscript Division, Library of Congress, Washington, D.C.

209 *"From information available":* USDAO TEL AVIV ISRAEL msg. 151615Z, June 1967, *Liberty* court of inquiry.

209 *Rabin aide:* USDAO TEL AVIV ISRAEL msg. 181030Z, June 1967, *Liberty* court of inquiry.

209 *Ron's probe concluded:* Ibid.; Colonel Ram Ron report to Yitzhak Rabin, June 16, 1967, 4079/HZ-26, ISA.

210 *"appearance of surprise and incredulity":* USDAO TEL AVIV ISRAEL msg. 181030Z, June 1967, *Liberty* court of inquiry.

211 *"no goddamn sense at all":* Ephraim Evron telegram 304 to the Foreign Ministry, June 19, 1967, 4079/HZ-26, ISA.

211 *The veteran officer:* Mayo A. Hadden, Jr., biography; Mayo A. Hadden III interview with author, May 6, 2008.

211 *"report blandly glosses over":* Mayo A. Hadden, Jr., Memorandum for the Record, June 19, 1967, Box 111, *Liberty* Briefing Book, Immediate Office Files of the CNO, Operational Archives Branch, NHC.

212 *"public clash":* Ephraim Evron telegram 272 to the Foreign Ministry, June 16, 1967, 4079/HZ-26, ISA; Townsend Hoopes memo to Nicholas Katzenbach and Paul H. Nitze, June 19, 1967, Box 111, *Liberty* Briefing Book, Immediate Office Files of the CNO, Operational Archives Branch, NHC.

212 *"had made grievous errors":* Mayo A. Hadden, Jr., Memorandum for the Record, June 19, 1967, Box 111, *Liberty* Briefing Book, Immediate Office Files of the CNO, Operational Archives Branch, NHC.

212 *"Such benefit":* Jerome H. King, Jr., memo to David L. McDonald, June 19, 1967, Box 111, *Liberty* Briefing Book, Immediate Office Files of the CNO, Operational Archives Branch, NHC.

213 *"The American press":* Avraham Harman telegram 285 to the Foreign Ministry, June 18, 1967, 4079/HZ-26, ISA.

213 *"There is no doubt":* Ibid.

214 *"I have no doubt":* Avraham Harman telegram 705 to the Foreign Ministry, June 19, 1967, 4079/HZ-26, ISA.

214 *"We should also":* Ibid.

214 *Harman questioned:* Avraham Harman telegram 707 to the Foreign Ministry, June 19, 1967, 4079/HZ-26, ISA.

214 *"Ron's investigation":* Avraham Harman telegram 305 to the Foreign Ministry, June 19, 1967, 4079/HZ-26, ISA.

214 *Ron's report:* Colonel Ram Ron report to Yitzhak Rabin, June 16, 1967, 4079/HZ-26, ISA.

214 *Israel in fact discovered:* Information here comes from Colonel Ram Ron report to Yitzhak Rabin, June 16, 1967, 4079/HZ-26, ISA; *Attack on the* Liberty, directed by Rex Bloomstein, Thames Television, 1987; Israel Defense Forces History Department, "The Attack on the 'Liberty' Incident, 8 June, 1967," June 1982, pp. 7–8, IDF Archives.

215 *"What is it?":* Israeli historian Ahron Bregman published excerpts of the attackers' communications in his books *Israel's Wars: A History Since 1947* (New York: Routledge, 2002, pp. 88–90) and *A History of Israel* (New York: Palgrave Macmillan, 2003, pp. 120–22). The *Jerusalem Post* later published a transcript of the communications, but with

slight variations (Arieh O'Sullivan, "Liberty Revisited: The Attack," *Jerusalem Post,* June 4, 2004, p. 20). To assist this author, Bregman graciously listened to the tapes again. He confirmed his translations in e-mails on Oct. 3, 2007. To create this scene, I used both Bregman and the *Jerusalem Post* as sources. When faced with differences between them, I often deferred to Bregman.

215 *seated just a few feet:* Cristol, *The Liberty Incident,* p. 42.

216 *More than twenty minutes:* Exact times are difficult to pinpoint given the chaotic nature of combat. The air controller's statement that he believed the ship was American came at 2:14 P.M., according to the transcript of the recording published in the *Jerusalem Post.* The *Liberty's* deck log recorded the torpedo strike at 2:35 P.M., twenty-one minutes after the identification. Colonel Ram Ron's report determined that the torpedo attack occurred at 2:40 P.M., twenty-six minutes after the identification. Lieutenant Colonel Yeshayahu Yerushalmi's follow-up report concluded that the torpedo attack occurred at 2:36 P.M., twenty-two minutes after pilots identified the *Liberty.*

216 *"At that point in time":* Attack on the Liberty. Shmuel Kislev declined an interview request from this author.

216 *Ron's report also revealed:* The officers were Commander Avraham Lunz in Haifa and Lieutenant Commander Pinchas Pinchasi in Tel Aviv. Lunz declined an interview request from this author. Pinchasi could not be located.

217 *"was camouflage writing":* Colonel Ram Ron report to Yitzhak Rabin, June 16, 1967, 4079/HZ-26, ISA. This author interviewed Yitzhak Rahav in Israel on Oct. 12, 2007. During the interview, Rahav denied testifying in the Israeli court of inquiry or being interviewed by Ron. "I never gave any evidence," Rahav said. "Never." Despite his assertion, Rahav is listed as No. 5 on the witness list.

217 *"when he determined":* Avraham Harman telegram 707 to the Foreign Ministry, June 19, 1967, 4079/HZ-26, ISA.

217 *"military prosecutor insisted":* Avraham Harman telegram 305 to the Foreign Ministry, June 19, 1967, 4079/HZ-26, ISA.

217 *"This matter has turned":* Ibid.

218 *"It is difficult":* Avraham Harman telegram 323 to the Foreign Ministry, June 20, 1967, 4079/HZ-26, ISA.

218 *"In the severe situation":* Ibid.

218 *Rather than indict:* IDF Spokesman Announcement, 4079/HZ-27, ISA;

Harold H. Saunders memo to Walt Rostow and McGeorge Bundy, June 20, 1967, Box 3, National Security File, Files of the Special Committee of the NSC, LBJL.

219 *"Israeli Judge Advocate General":* Nicholas Katzenbach telegram 214682 to the American Embassy in Tel Aviv, June 22, 1967, Box 4, National Security File, Files of the Special Committee of the NSC, LBJL.

219 *The NSA's second in command:* Background on Tordella is drawn from Kahn, *The Codebreakers,* p. 705; Robert McG. Thomas, Jr., "Louis W. Tordella, 84, Who Helped Break German Military Code in World War II," *New York Times,* Jan. 16, 1996, p. B8; Juanita Moody interview with author, Nov. 21, 2007; and Benson Buffham interview with author, Nov. 20, 2007.

220 *"I wryly mentioned":* Louis W. Tordella Memorandum for the Record, June 20, 1967, www.nsa.gov. Tordella remained outraged over the attack on the *Liberty* for years, convinced that it was no accident. In an interview with this author on Feb. 26, 2007, former NSA director Bobby Ray Inman said Tordella visited him soon after Inman took over as head of the agency in 1977. Tordella, who by then had retired from the NSA, shared his views on the *Liberty.* Inman said Tordella believed Israel had learned a lesson from the 1956 Suez Canal Crisis when the United States pressured the Jewish state to withdraw from captured territories. "His view was that they didn't want to run a risk that we would detect exactly what they were going to do and try to bring it to a halt with a lot of pressure before they achieved their objectives," Inman said. "They knew exactly what the ship was and what it was doing and therefore it was, in his view, a deliberate act to try to protect the plans until they finished what they were going to do."

220 *"If they are speaking Arabic":* DIRNSA msg. 221454Z, June 1967, www.nsa.gov.

220 *Under the question:* "Fact Sheet for DIRNSA," www.nsa.gov.

220 *Information the agency:* Edward Koczak interview with author, Jan. 5, 2009.

221 *The NSA director:* Bruce Lambert, "Marshall Carter, 83, Intelligence Official and Marshall Aide," *New York Times,* Feb. 20, 1993, p. 48.

221 *"It couldn't be anything else":* Marshall S. Carter oral history interview with Robert D. Farley, Oct. 3, 1988, www.nsa.gov.

221 *"Cy Vance just told me":* Gerard Burke interview with author, Oct. 4, 2007.

222   *"Just looking at the damage"*: Allan Deprey interview with author, Nov. 25, 2007.

222   *"We knew it was deliberate"*: Oliver Kirby interview with author, Feb. 25, 2007.

222   *"We just couldn't believe that"*: John Morrison interview with author, April 6, 2007.

222   *"an extraordinary lack of concern"*: Thomas Hughes memo to Nicholas Katzenbach, June 13, 1967, in Schwar, *Foreign Relations of the United States, 1964–1968*, pp. 474–76.

223   *"stretched all credibility"*: Thomas Hughes interview with author, May 3, 2007.

223   *"We were quite convinced"*: Thomas Hughes interview with author, April 26, 2007.

223   *"It wasn't an accident"*: William McAfee interview with the author, May 3, 2007.

223   *"They knew damn well"*: Granville Austin interview with author, Oct. 3, 2007.

223   *"Our reports were devastating"*: William D. Wolle oral history interview with Charles Stuart Kennedy, March 6, 1991, Front Diplomacy: The Foreign Affairs Oral History Collection of the Association for Diplomatic Studies and Training, Manuscript Division, Library of Congress, Washington, D.C.; William D. Wolle interview with author, Dec. 18, 2007.

223   *"leave little doubt"*: Intelligence Memorandum: The Israeli Attack on the USS *Liberty,* June 13, 1967, www.cia.gov.

224   *"not made in malice"*: Intelligence Memorandum: The Israeli Statement on the Attack on the USS *Liberty,* June 21, 1967, www.cia.gov.

224   *William Dale:* William Dale interview with author, March 27, 2007.

224   *"The Israelis are very"*: Heywood Stackhouse interview with author, May 15, 2008.

225   *"Although Israeli authorities"*: Robert M. Hathaway and Russell Jack Smith, *Richard Helms: As Director of Central Intelligence, 1996–1973* (Washington, D.C.: Center for Study of Intelligence/Central Intelligence Agency, 1993), pp. 145–46.

225   *Vice Admiral Rufus Taylor:* "Vice Adm. Rufus Taylor, Retired CIA Deputy, Dies," *Washington Post,* Sept. 20, 1978, p. B8.

225   *"To me, the picture"*: Rufus Taylor memo to Richard Helms, June 22, 1967, in Hathaway and Smith, *Richard Helms,* p. 146.

225 *Several agency field memos:* CIA Intelligence Information Cable, Turkish General Staff Opinion Regarding the Israeli Attack on the USS *Liberty,* June 23, 1967; CIA Information Report, [Redacted] Comment on Known Identity of USS *Liberty,* July 27, 1967; CIA Information Report, Prospects for Political Ambitions of Moshe Dayan/Attack on USS *Liberty* Ordered by Dayan, Nov. 9, 1967.

225 *"I don't think there":* Richard Helms oral history interview with Robert M. Hathaway, Nov. 8, 1984, www.cia.gov.

CHAPTER 16

PAGE

226 *There was a suspicious:* Lucius Battle interview with author, Nov. 7, 2006.

226 *Staring had served:* Merlin Staring interviews with author, April 17, 2007, and April 25, 2007; Merlin Staring official Navy biography.

226 *The top-secret volume: Liberty* court of inquiry.

228 *"The number one paragraph":* Merlin Staring interview with author, April 17, 2007.

228 *"The evidence was clear":* Ward Boston, Jr., affidavit, Jan. 8, 2004. Democratic representative John Conyers, Jr., of Michigan inserted a copy of Boston's affidavit in the *Congressional Record* on Oct. 11, 2004.

228 *"That was deliberate":* Joseph C. Wylie, Jr., oral history interview with Evelyn M. Cherpak, Jan. 22, 1986, Naval War College Library, Newport, R.I.

229 *"I have some real":* Merlin Staring interview with author, April 17, 2007.

229 *Court President:* Ward Boston, Jr., interview with author, Oct. 11, 2006.

229 *The former secretary:* "2 Pentagon Aides Sworn to Posts," *New York Times,* July 6, 1962, p. 7; "Vance's Promotion Approved by Senate," *New York Times,* Jan. 28, 1964, p. 19.

229 *spoke in the same:* Russell Jack Smith, *The Unknown CIA: My Three Decades with the Agency* (Washington, D.C.: Pergamon-Brassey's International Defense Publishers, Inc., 1989), p. 184.

229 *dirty jobs:* Thomas Hughes interviews with author, May 3, 2007, and Jan. 4, 2009.

229 *The Pentagon's fourteen-page:* Draft press release, Box 112, *Liberty* Press

Releases, Immediate Office Files of the CNO, Operational Archives Branch, NHC.

230 *"strong Navy non-concurrence":* Mayo A. Hadden, Jr., memorandum to distribution list, June 22, 1967, Box 112, *Liberty* Press Releases, Immediate Office File of the CNO, Operational Archives Branch, NHC.

230 *McNamara and his civilian analysts:* Information on McNamara's leadership comes from David L. McDonald oral history interview with John T. Mason, Jr., Jan. 24, 1976, U.S. Naval Institute; David C. Richardson oral history interview with Paul Stillwell, March 30, 1992, U.S. Naval Institute; Horacio Rivero, Jr., oral history interview with John T. Mason, Jr., Nov. 12, 1975, U.S. Naval Institute; Thomas H. Moorer oral history interviews with John T. Mason, Jr., Feb. 21, 1975, and April 11, 1975, U.S. Naval Institute.

231 *McDonald knew to keep:* Information on David McDonald comes from David L. McDonald oral history interview with John T. Mason, Jr., Nov. 8, 1974, U.S. Naval Institute; Herbert E. Hetu oral history interview with Paul Stillwell, June 5, 1996, U.S. Naval Institute; "Persuasive Admiral," *New York Times,* May 7, 1963, p. 22; "Stormy Days for the Navy," *Time,* Nov. 15, 1963, p. 37; Jerome King, Jr., interview with author, Feb. 6, 2008.

231 *"probably the best Defense Secretary ever":* "Stormy Days for the Navy," *Time,* Nov. 15, 1963, p. 37.

231 *"I have more influence":* Herbert E. Hetu oral history interview with Paul Stillwell, June 5, 1996, U.S. Naval Institute.

231 *"Was there any":* David L. McDonald's Comments/Recommended Changes on *Liberty* Press Release, June 22, 1967, Box 112, *Liberty* Press Releases, Immediate Office Files of the CNO, Operational Archives Branch, NHC.

231 *"I think that much":* Ibid.

232 *"Unfortunately, although Mr. Fryklund":* Mayo A. Hadden, Jr., memo to Jerome H. King, Jr., June 22, 1967, ibid.

232 *"suggested deletions":* Horacio Rivero, Jr.,'s Recommended Changes on *Liberty* Release, ibid.

232 *"I see no reason":* David L. McDonald's Comments/Recommended Changes on *Liberty* Press Release—1300, June 23 version, ibid.

232 *"We have no business":* Isaac C. Kidd, Jr., memo to David L. McDonald, June 21, 1967, Box 111, *Liberty* Briefing Book, Immediate Office Files of the CNO, Operational Archives Branch, NHC.

233 *"I still do not agree":* David L. McDonald's Comments/Recommended Changes on *Liberty* Press Release—1300, June 23 version, Box 112, *Liberty* Press Releases, Immediate Office Files of the CNO, Operational Archives Branch, NHC.

233 *"It certainly was not":* Jerome King, Jr., interview with author, Feb. 6, 2008.

233 *"One of their big":* Orr Kelly, "Report on Israel Ship Attack a Touchy Task for Pentagon," *Evening Star,* June 25, 1967, p. A4.

234 *"You had fine comments":* Jerome H. King, Jr., memo to David L. McDonald, June 26, 1967, Box 112, *Liberty* Press Releases, Immediate Office Files of the CNO, Operational Archives Branch, NHC.

234 *Major news outlets:* Neil Sheehan, "Order Didn't Get to U.S.S. *Liberty,*" *New York Times,* June 29, 1967, p. 1; Fred Farrar, "Delay in Navy Message Bared in Israeli Attack on U.S. Ship," *Chicago Tribune,* June 29, 1967, p. 1; "*Liberty* Move Order Delayed," *Dallas Morning News,* June 29, 1967, p. 1.

234 *"ironic twist":* George C. Wilson, "The *Liberty* Got Order Too Late," *Washington Post,* June 29, 1967, p. 1.

234 *In follow-up articles:* "Firing Accident Thought Cause of 1 Raid on Ship," *Virginian-Pilot,* June 30, 1967, p. 1; Charles W. Corddry, "Ghost Gun Bared in *Liberty* Probe," *Baltimore Sun,* June 30, 1967, p. A1; "U.S. Ship Fired on Israelis Before PT Boats Attacked," *Philadelphia Inquirer,* June 30, 1967, p. 4.

234 *"had ample opportunity":* "Israelis Dispute Finding That *Liberty* Flew Flag," *Evening Star,* June 29, 1967, p. 1.

234 *"insufficient information":* Fred Farrar, "Delay in Navy Message Bared," p. 1.

235 *"far fetched":* Dave Lucas letter to Paula Lucas, July 6, 1967.

235 *The* Washington Daily News: "The USS *Liberty* Report," editorial, *Washington Daily News,* June 30, 1967, p. 30.

235 *"not good enough":* "Not Good Enough," editorial, *Washington Post,* June 30, 1967, p. A22.

235 *"fragmentary answers":* "Inquest for *Liberty,*" *Time,* July 7, 1967, p. 15.

235 *"more fog":* "Missed Signals Again," editorial, *Chicago Tribune,* June 30, 1967, p. 14.

235 *"affront":* "Pentagon Cover-Up," editorial, *Evening Star,* June 30, 1967, p. A14.

236 *"One thing at least"*: "U.S.S. *Liberty*," editorial, *National Review*, June 27, 1967, p. 673.

236 *"The apologists"*: "Observations," editorial, *National Observer*, July 3, 1967, p. 10.

236 *"Did the attackers"*: "Pentagon Cover-Up," *Evening Star*, p. A14.

236 *"The prompt transmittal"*: "Not Good Enough," *Washington Post*, p. A22.

236 *"shades of Pearl Harbor"*: "Missed Signals Again," *Chicago Tribune*, p. 14.

236 *"keep digging"*: James J. Kilpatrick, "Heroism Aboard the USS *Liberty*," *Hartford Courant*, Aug. 1, 1967, p. 16.

236 *"have become wary"*: "The U.S.S. *Liberty*," editorial, *Baltimore Sun*, July 3, 1967, p. A8.

237 *"Still unknown"*: "Attack on USS *Liberty*," editorial, *Edwardsville Intelligencer*, July 7, 1967, p. 10.

CHAPTER 17

PAGE

238 *I have mixed emotions*: Dave Lucas letter to Paula Lucas, June 22, 1967.

238 *Hosmer had enlisted*: "Craig Hosmer Dies; Ex-House Member," *New York Times*, Oct. 14, 1982, p. D23; *Biographical Directory of the United States Congress, 1774–2005* (Washington, D.C.: U.S. Government Printing Office, 2005), pp. 1279–80.

238 *"I do not believe"*: *Congressional Record*, 90th Cong., 1st sess., June 29, 1967, p. 17893.

239 *Like his colleague*: Thomas G. Abernethy letter to Jim Ennes, Jr., Jan. 26, 1980, Box 159, Thomas G. Abernethy Collection, J. D. Williams Library, University of Mississippi, Oxford, Miss.

239 *"This useless"*: *Congressional Record*, 90th Cong., 1st sess., June 29, 1967, pp. 17894–95.

240 *More than sixty*: Mayo A. Hadden, Jr., memo to Charles F. Baird, July 20, 1967, Box 112, *Liberty* Press Releases, Immediate Office Files of the CNO, Operational Archives Branch, NHC.

240 *"The attack on the* Liberty*"*: Dixon Donnelley memo to Dean Rusk, June 23, 1967, Box 17, RG 59, Office of the Executive Secretariat, Middle East Crisis Files, 1967, NARA.

240 *Diplomats at the Israeli embassy:* Dan Patir telegram 369 to the Foreign Ministry, June 23, 1967, 4079/HZ-26, ISA.

241 *"This announcement":* Ibid.

241 *"Our main goal":* Avraham Harman telegram 155 to the Foreign Ministry, June 28, 1967, ibid.

242 *"Do you":* Yitzhak Rabin telegram 158 to Avraham Harman, June 29, 1967, ibid.

242 *News reports:* "Israelis Dispute Finding That *Liberty* Flew Flag," *Evening Star,* June 29, 1967, p. 1; "Israel Says It Tried in Vain to Identify the *Liberty,*" *Washington Post,* June 30, 1967, p. A17; "Israelis Say Signal by *Liberty* Caused Mistake in Identity," *New York Times,* June 30, 1967, p. 2.

242 *"Nothing intelligible":* Jerome H. King, Jr., Memorandum for the Record, July 6, 1967, Box 111, *Liberty* Briefing Book, Immediate Office Files of the CNO, Operational Archives Branch, NHC.

242 *"I am convinced":* NAVCOMMUNIT NAPLES msg. 061222Z, July 1967, ibid.

243 *"About 2,000 yards":* Micha Limor, "Israeli Navy Man Describes Attack on the *Liberty,*" *New York Times,* July 7, 1967, p. 3. In an interview in Israel with this author on Oct. 14, 2007, Micha Limor defended his account of the attack. He said no one ordered him to write the article, but that he volunteered. He said the story was reviewed by Israeli censors prior to publication.

244 *"wild imagination":* Dave Lucas letter to Paula Lucas, July 6, 1967.

244 *The Pentagon ended:* CINCUSNAVEUR msg. 301401Z, June 1967, *Liberty* Incident Message File, NHC.

244 *"Interviews and statements":* *Liberty* Plan of the Day, July 22, 1967; *Liberty* Plan of the Day, June 30, 1967.

245 *Maltese workers flooded:* *Liberty* Plan of the Day, July 14, 1967; Dave Lucas's journal.

245 *"After getting to Norfolk":* Dave Lucas letter to parents, July 5, 1967.

245 *After a month:* Dave Lucas letters to Paula Lucas, July 13–14, 1967; Dave Lucas's journal.

245 *"Everybody on board":* John Scott letter to parents, July 14, 1967.

246 *"USS* Liberty *has become":* *Liberty* Plan of the Day, July 14, 1967.

246 *An early morning fire:* Dave Lucas letter to Paula Lucas, July 9, 1967.

246 *"The new XO":* Dave Lucas letter to Paula Lucas, July 5, 1967.

246 *The task of sorting:* Dave Lucas's journal; John Scott interview with author, June 10, 2008.

247 *"Suggest that failure"*: CINCUSNAVEUR msg. 141737Z, June 1967, *Liberty* Incident Message File, NHC.

247 *"A favorable determination"*: CINCUSNAVEUR msg. 191610Z, June 1967, Box 113, Personal Actions, Casualties, Awards, Immediate Office Files of the CNO, Operational Archives Branch, NHC.

247 *the Pentagon compromised*: CNO msg. 211634Z, July 1967, *Liberty* Incident Message File, NHC.

247 *"This was a dastardly deed"*: William F. Allenbaugh letter to Lyndon Johnson, July 8, 1967, Box 1798, RG 59, Central Files 1967–69, POL 27 ARAB-ISR, NARA.

247 *"You lost your XO"*: *Liberty* Plan of the Day, June 30, 1967.

CHAPTER 18

PAGE

249 *Almost as shocking*: "Let's Have All the Facts," editorial, *Shreveport Times*. June 18, 1967, p. 2B.

249 *His support for Israel*: Clifford, *Counsel to the President*, pp. 3–25; Douglas Frantz and David McKean, *Friends in High Places: The Rise and Fall of Clark Clifford* (Boston: Little, Brown, 1995), p. 16; Marilyn Berger, "Clark Clifford, a Major Adviser to Four Presidents, Is Dead at 91," *New York Times*, Oct. 11, 1998, p. 1.

251 *"Because of this limitation"*: Clifford, *Counsel to the President*, p. 446.

251 *Clifford submitted*: Clark Clifford memo to Walt Rostow, July 18, 1967, Box 115, National Security File, Country File, Middle East, LBJL.

251 *"brief but definitive analysis"*: Walt Rostow memo to Lyndon Johnson, July 18, 1967, ibid.

251 *first Washington attorney*: Berger, "Clark Clifford, a Major Adviser to Four Presidents, Is Dead at 91," p. 1.

252 *"an accident of this magnitude"*: George Christian letter to Jim Ennes, Jr., Jan. 5, 1978.

253 *"heartbreaking episode"*: Johnson, *The Vantage Point*, pp. 300–1, 304.

253 *"adequate restitution"*: Clifford, *Counsel to the President*, p. 447.

254 *McNamara had flown*: McNamara, *In Retrospect*, p. 283.

254 *"There is a limit"*: Clifford, *Counsel to the President*, p. 447.

254 Newsweek *noted*: "A Nation at Odds," *Newsweek*, July 10, 1967, pp. 16–17.

254 *"one of the most stressful"*: McNamara, *In Retrospect*, p. 284.

254 *"political disaster"*: Ibid.

255 *"took place under"*: Bourke Hickenlooper letter to Dean Rusk, June 16, 1967, Box 1799, RG 59, Central Files 1967–69, POL 27 ARAB-ISR, NARA.

255 *"We have never gotten"*: Senate Committee on Foreign Relations, *Foreign Assistance Act of 1967: Hearings Before the Committee on Foreign Relations on S. 1872*, 90th Cong., 1st sess., July 26, 1967 (Washington, D.C.: U.S. Government Printing Office, 1967), pp 266–70. McNamara's insistence before the Senate Foreign Relations Committee that the attack was an accident differed from comments made to this author on April 25, 2007. In that conversation, McNamara said he never understood why the Israelis attacked. "I was uncertain at the time what happened. I haven't seen anything since that adds certainty," he said. "My basic belief is nobody knows what in the hell happened or why."

257 *"I found it hard"*: Paul C. Warnke oral history interview with Dorothy Pierce, Jan. 17, 1969, LBJL.

258 *"genuine outrage"*: Dean Rusk letter to Jim Ennes, Jr., Sept. 10, 1981.

258 *"Secretary's comments to Brosio"*: AMEMBASSY PARIS msg. 171602Z, June 1967, Box 1796, RG 59, Central Files 1967–69, POL 27 ARAB-ISR, NARA.

258 *He read the opening: Executive Sessions of the Senate Foreign Relations Committee Together with Joint Sessions with the Senate Armed Services Committee*, vol. 19, 90th Cong., 1st sess., June 28, 1967 (Washington, D.C.: U.S. Government Printing Office, 2006), pp. 754–56.

259 *"I might just say": Executive Sessions of the Senate Foreign Relations Committee Together with Joint Sessions with the Senate Armed Services Committee*, vol. 19, 90th Cong., 1st sess., July 11, 1967 (Washington, D.C.: U.S. Government Printing Office, 2006), pp. 823–24.

259 *"We have now had"*: Senate Committee on Foreign Relations, *Foreign Assistance Act of 1967: Hearings Before the Committee on Foreign Relations on S. 1872*, 90th Cong., 1st sess., July 14, 1967 (Washington, D.C.: U.S. Government Printing Office, 1967), pp. 233–34.

259 *Commander McGonagle*: Details of the *Liberty*'s arrival are drawn from the following sources: Dave Lucas's journal; " 'Liberty' to Dock Saturday." *Virginian-Pilot*, July 28, 1967, p. 29; Clifford Hubbard, " 'Liberty' Brings in Memories," *Virginian-Pilot*, July 30, 1967, p. 1.

260 *"A diverse background"*: Unsigned memo, June 21, 1967, attached to William McGonagle's April 25, 1966, Officer Biography Sheet, Box 111,

Liberty Briefing Book, Immediate Office Files of the CNO, Operational Archives Branch, NHC.

260 *The only remnants:* DIRNAVSECGRU msg. 191326Z, June 1967, www. nsa.gov.

260 *"He swam through":* Patrick O'Malley interview with author, Nov. 26, 2007.

261 *"Not much was said":* Lloyd Painter e-mail to author, June 8, 2008.

261 *"The arrival here today":* "Welcome, *Liberty,*" editorial, *Virginian-Pilot,* July 29, 1967, p. 8.

261 *The day before the* Liberty's *arrival: Liberty* Plan of the Day, July 28, 1967.

261 *"unprovoked and unexpected":* Hubbard, "'Liberty' Brings in Memories," p. 1.

261 *A team of National Security Agency:* USS *Liberty* msg. 021630Z, August 1967, www.nsa.gov.

261 *The bags:* This scene is drawn from John McTighe interview with author, Nov. 19, 2007; Benjamin Cwalina interview with author, Dec. 3, 2007; Benjamin Cwalina oral history interview with Bob Farley, May 9, 1980, www.nsa.gov.

262 *"I remember thinking":* Lloyd Painter e-mails to author, June 8, 2008.

263 *"I made clear":* Ephraim Evron telegram 106 to the Foreign Ministry, Aug. 14, 1967, 4079/HZ-26, ISA.

263 *The Israeli prosecutor:* Preliminary Inquiry Decision, 4079/HZ-27, ISA.

263 *Like Ron:* Cristol, *The Liberty Incident,* p. 167.

265 *Yerushalmi ruled:* Yitzhak Rahav, the second in command of Israel's navy in 1967, resigned soon after the attack. An American military attaché in Israel reported his resignation in a memo dated Aug. 22, 1967, speculating that it had to do with the *Liberty.* Shlomo Erell, the head of the Israeli Navy in 1967, told this author in an Oct. 9, 2007, interview that he demanded Rahav resign: "I actually fired him, but not in a formal way," Erell said, adding that he told Rehav: "You made a hell of a blunder and you cannot stay." Rahav refuted that account in an interview with this author on Oct. 12, 2007. He said he resigned over Erell's incompetence in managing the Navy, not the *Liberty.*

266 *"It seems likely":* Lucius Battle draft memo to Nicholas Katzenbach, Aug. 18, 1967, in Schwar, *Foreign Relations of the United States, 1964–1968,* pp. 796–800.

266 *"A one-word summation":* Mayo A. Hadden, Jr., memo to Op-06, Aug. 22, 1967, Box 112, *Liberty* Press Releases, Immediate Office Files of the CNO, Operational Archives Branch, NHC.

266 *"A nice whitewash":* Louis Tordella handwritten note, Aug. 26, 1967.

267 *"confirms that there was":* Nicholas Katzenbach interview with author, April 19, 2007.

267 *"My anger and frustration":* Horacio Rivero, Jr., Q&A with Joseph F. Bouchard, March 10, 1988.

267 *"Examining judge laid out":* Dean Rusk telegram to the American Embassy in Tel Aviv, Aug. 31, 1967, Box 1800, RG 59, Central Files 1967–69, POL 27 ARAB-ISR, NARA.

268 *His five-page report:* Carl Salans memo to Nicholas Katzenbach, Sept. 21, 1967.

268 *"There were a lot of discrepancies":* Carl Salans interview with author, March 6, 2007.

268 *"The Israeli and U. S. Navy accounts":* Leonard Meeker e-mail to author, April 4, 2008.

268 *"How in the name":* Goulding, *Confirm or Deny,* pp. 133–34.

CHAPTER 19

PAGE

269 *The average American taxpayer:* H. H. Stackhouse letter to J. Owen Zurhellen, Jr., Sept. 9, 1971.

269 *A single casket:* "Military Honors," *Washington Post.* Aug. 22, 1967, p. A8.

269 *five sailors and one Marine:* Mayo A. Hadden, Jr., Memorandum for the Record, Aug. 21, 1967, Box 111, *Liberty* Briefing Book, Immediate Office Files of the CNO, Operational Archives Branch, NHC; Unclassified Naval Security Group File, U.S.S. *Liberty,* Post 1 Jan 1946, Command File, Operation Archives Branch, NHC.

269 *"DIED IN THE EASTERN MEDITERRANEAN":* In 1982, following requests from *Liberty* veterans, the government changed the headstone to read: "KILLED USS LIBERTY."

270 *Race riots:* "As Rioting Spread . . . The Search for Answers," *U.S. News & World Report,* Aug. 14, 1967, p. 26.

270 *"guerrilla war":* "Looting, Burning—Now Guerilla War," *U.S. News & World Report,* Aug. 7, 1967, p. 23.

270 *"Battlefield, U.S.A.":* Newsweek, Aug. 7, 1967, cover photo and head-line.

270 *August 13 poll:* Gallup, *The Gallup Poll: Public Opinion 1935–1971,* vol. 3, 1959–1971, pp. 2075, 2062.

270 *lowest approval rating:* "War . . . Riots . . . Crime . . . Taxes: Why Demo-crats Worry About '68," *U.S. News & World Report,* Aug. 21, 1967, p. 46.

270 *A poll released a week later:* Gallup, *The Gallup Poll: Public Opinion 1935–1971,* vol. 3, 1959–71, p. 2076.

270 *president confided:* Johnson, *A White House Diary,* pp. 565–67.

270 *McNamara, who became:* McNamara, *In Retrospect,* p. 311.

270 *"I have seldom felt":* Johnson, *A White House Diary,* p. 593.

271 *"satisfied that the strafing":* "The U.S.S. *Liberty*—Tragedy of Errors," *Newsweek,* Aug. 28, 1967, p. 14.

271 *"An Israeli court":* "The *Liberty* Incident—An Israeli View," *Newsweek,* Sept. 4, 1967, p. 11.

271 Newsweek *printed a follow-up:* "Why Israel Attacked the *Liberty,*" *Newsweek,* May 6, 1968, p. 23.

271 *"Why didn't the Israelis":* "When U.S. Ship Was Victim of a 'Shoot First' Policy," *U.S. News & World Report,* May 13, 1968, p. 12.

271 *a preliminary Navy analysis:* NAVSCIENTECHINTELCEN msg. 281548Z, June 1967, www.libertyincident.com.

271 *"Is this Government":* Congressional Record, 90th Cong., 1st sess., Aug. 22, 1967, p. 23606.

272 *"The more the case is studied":* Congressional Record, 90th Cong., 1st sess., Sept. 19, 1967, pp. 26082, 26088.

272 *"Inasmuch as American":* Congressional Record, 90th Cong., 1st sess., Oct. 18, 1967, p. 29370.

272 *"The U.S.S. Liberty incident":* Congressional Record, 90th Cong., 1st sess., Oct. 20, 1967, p. A5167.

272 *"Does the gentleman":* Congressional Record, 90th Cong., 1st sess., Nov. 16, 1967, p. 32885.

273 *"provides full":* Congressional Record, 90th Cong., 1st sess., Nov. 17, 1967, pp. 32968–69.

273 *At 10:30 A.M.:* Memorandum of conversation about U.S.S. *Liberty* claims, March 25, 1968.

274 *"incarnated the narrative":* Segev, *1967,* p. 262.

274 *"view of the substantial":* Dean Rusk airgram to the American Embassy in Tel Aviv with attached draft note for the Israeli Ministry of Foreign

Affairs, Dec. 19, 1967; Carl F. Salans memo to Nicholas Katzenbach, March 22, 1968.

274 *"We clearly do not":* Carl F. Salans memo to Nicholas Katzenbach, March 22, 1968.

274 *"accepted in principle":* Memorandum of conversation about U.S.S. *Liberty* claims, March 25, 1968.

275 *"redouble efforts":* Dean Rusk telegram 136943 to the American Embassy in Tel Aviv, March 27, 1968.

276 *"We think this proposal":* Leonard C. Meeker memo to Nicholas Katzenbach, May 17, 1968; AMEMBASSY TEL AVIV msg. 201115Z, May 1968.

276 *"public airing":* Ibid.

276 *wrote a check:* AMEMBASSY TEL AVIV msg. 271505Z, May 1968; Fabian A. Kwiatek memo to Edward G. Boehm, May 31, 1968; AMEMBASSY TEL AVIV msg. 031100Z, May 1968.

276 *two-paragraph press release:* Press Statement: Payment of U.S.S. *Liberty* Death Claims, May 28, 1968.

276 *the United States billed Israel:* Walworth Barbour airgram to the State Department, July 6, 1968.

276 Haaretz *ran an article:* Walworth Barbour airgram to the State Department, July 23, 1968.

276 *"was motivated":* AMEMBASSY TEL AVIV msg. 061125Z, August 1968.

276 *"totally unacceptable":* Dean Rusk telegram 219537 to the American Embassy in Tel Aviv, Aug. 12, 1968.

277 *Its Foreign Ministry asked:* AMEMBASSY TEL AVIV msg. 031130Z, September 1968.

277 *Israel paid the full $3,566,457:* State Department airgram to the American Embassy in Tel Aviv with list of claimants, March 18, 1969; Ernest L. Kerley memo to George H. Aldrich, May 5, 1969; "Israel Pays Compensation Claimed for Men Injured on U.S.S. *Liberty,*" *Department of State Bulletin* 60, no. 1562 (June 2, 1969), p. 473.

277 *"evasive":* H. H. Stackhouse memo to Alfred L. Atherton, Jr., Jan. 12, 1971.

277 *"petulant":* Robert H. Neuman memo to J. J. Sisco, Oct. 9, 1969.

277 *"unresponsive attitude":* State Department telegram to the American Embassy in Tel Aviv, July 28, 1970.

277 *secretly offered:* Walworth Barbour letter to Alfred L. Atherton, Jr., Aug. 6, 1971.

277 *"The suggested sum":* H. H. Stackhouse memo to Alfred L. Atherton, Jr., Aug. 25, 1971.

277 *Lawmakers and the press:* Peter Constable draft memo to David Newsom, Aug. 20, 1979, Jack Anderson, "USS *Liberty:* Damages Have Never Been Paid," *The Washington Post,* July 17, 1977, p. B7.

277 *negotiations stalled again:* Harold H. Saunders draft memo to David Newsom, Aug. 12, 1980.

278 *By 1980:* Edmund Muskie telegram 315517 to the American Embassy in Tel Aviv, Nov. 26, 1980.

278 *"Since this ship":* William J. Small, "Probe Planned: Did Israel Intentionally Sink U.S. Ship?," *Seattle Times,* Sept. 28, 1980, p. A6.

278 *Israel offered:* Edmund Muskie telegram 331156 to the American Embassy in Tel Aviv, Dec. 15, 1980; Edmund Muskie telegram 334352 to the American Embassy in Tel Aviv, Dec. 18, 1980.

278 *"had finally closed the book":* Bernard Gwertzman, "Israeli Payment to Close the Book on '67 Attack on U.S. Navy Vessel," *New York Times,* Dec. 19, 1980, p. A1.

278 *"It was not":* Dean Rusk letter to Jim Ennes, Jr., Sept. 10, 1981.

278 *McGonagle sipped coffee:* William McGonagle interview with Tim Frank, Sept. 27, 1997.

278 *government offered:* Ibid.; William McGonagle letter to Mike Polston with completed questionaire, Dec. 12, 1994, Box 1, William Loren McGonagle Papers, 1947–99, HIA.

279 *"Command of a new ship":* "Skipper of USS *Liberty* Promoted to Captain," *Los Angeles Times,* Oct. 12, 1967, p. 25.

279 *Johnson presented:* "The Proceedings in Washington," *New York Times,* Feb. 2, 1968, p. 6; Max Frankel, "President Urges Patience on War," *New York Times,* March 13, 1968, p. 1; "Johnson Warns of 'Phony Peace,'" *New York Times,* March 21, 1968, p. 5; Nan Robertson, "Two Soldiers in Same Battle Get Medals of Honor in Rare Double Ceremony," *New York Times,* May 2, 1968, p. 5; Nan Robertson, "4 Men Awarded Medals of Honor," *New York Times,* May 15, 1968, p. 1.

279 *"Due to the nature":* Jim Cross memo to Lyndon Johnson, May 15, 1968, Box 17, White House Central Files, Medals-Awards, LBJL.

279 *The president instead visited:* Lyndon Johnson Daily Diary, June 11, 1968.

280 *"backhanded slap":* Thomas H. Moorer, "Memorandum: Attack on the USS *Liberty*—June 8, 1967," *Link* 30, no. 3, (July–August 1997), p. 3.

280　*"They had been trying"*: Findley, *They Dare to Speak Out*, p. 174.

280　*"I do not feel"*: William McGonagle letter to Phillip Tourney, Nov. 5, 1985.

280　*Handwritten notes:* Notes regarding the Medal of Honor presentations, Box 6, William Loren McGonagle Papers, 1947–99, HIA. Barnum and Marm held these ranks at the time the Medal of Honor was awarded.

281　*"When you"*: William McGonagle interview with Tim Frank, Sept. 27, 1997.

281　*"Despite continuous"*: William McGonagle Medal of Honor Ceremony Program, June 11, 1968, Box 6, William Loren McGonagle Papers, 1947–99, HIA.

281　*lowered his head:* "Liberty Skipper Gets Medal of Honor," *New York Times,* June 12, 1968, p. 4; Fred Farrar, "Honor Hero of Ship Hit in Mid-East War," *Chicago Tribune,* June 12, 1968, p. 8.

281　*The $162,608:* SECSTATE WASHDC msg. 262224Z, November 1980.

282　*The morning breeze:* James Harper, "Retiring 'Liberty,' But Mostly Her Men, Honored," *Virginian-Pilot,* June 15, 1968, p. 17; Meritorious Awards Presentation Program, June 14, 1968.

282　*the Navy awarded: Liberty* Citations, Box 6, William Loren McGonagle Papers, 1947–99, HIA.

283　*"The ship looked good"*: Harper, "Retiring 'Liberty,' But Mostly Her Men, Honored," p. 17.

283　*"What I have to say"*: Ibid.

283　*The men prepared:* Dave Lucas's journal; Richard Brooks interviews with author, Nov. 14, 2007, and April 6, 2008.

283　*The Pentagon dismantled:* Julie Alger, "A Review of the Technical Research Program, 1961–1969", pp. 132–34.

283　*In December 1970:* Stephanie L. Carr letter to author, Nov. 30, 2006.

284　*The few remaining officers:* Decommissioning of USS *Liberty* Program, June 28, 1968; "USS *Liberty* Decommissioned," *Hartford Courant,* June 29, 1968, p. 11C.

284　*Brooks departed last:* Richard Brooks interviews with author, Nov. 14, 2007, and April 6, 2008.

EPILOGUE

286 *The men were beaten:* Bernard Weinraub, "Pueblo Hearing: The Admirals Listen and Look Away," *New York Times*, Feb. 23, 1969, p. E7; Bernard Weinraub, "*Pueblo* Inquiry Is Told the Crew Yearned for Retaliation by U.S.," *New York Times*, Feb. 21, 1969, p. 14; Stuart Russell interview with author, Dec. 12, 2007.

286 *"incalculable":* House Committee on Armed Services, *Inquiry into the U.S.S.* Pueblo *and EC-121 Plane Incidents: Report of the Special Subcommittee on the U.S.S.* Pueblo, 91st Cong., 1st sess., July 28, 1969 (Washington, D.C.: U.S. Government Printing Office, 1969), p. 1674.

286 *In the more than 500 pages:* House Committee on Armed Services, *Inquiry into the U.S.S.* Pueblo *and EC-121 Plane Incidents: Hearings Before the Special Subcommittee on the U.S.S.* Pueblo, 91st Cong., 1st sess., March 4, 1969 (Washington, D.C.: U.S. Government Printing Office, 1969). The exchange between Moorer and Pike can be found on pages 686–87. Some witnesses were interviewed in executive session for reasons of national security. That testimony is not included in the published hearings.

286 *"If the lessons":* L. M. Bucher, "Remember the 'Liberty,'" *Washington Post*, May 18, 1980, p. BW5.

286 *When I interviewed Katzenbach:* Nicholas Katzenbach interview with author, April 19, 2007. Katzenbach described his sense of the president's logic: "His thinking on it was that the more generous they were about admitting a mistake and paying reparations—paying off the families—the easier it would be for the United States to ignore the incident."

287 *"We failed to let":* Lucius Battle interview outtake from the documentary *Dead in the Water,* Director Christopher Mitchell, Source Films for BBC, 2002.

287 *"Israel's leaders concluded":* George W. Ball and Douglas B. Ball, *The Passionate Attachment: America's Involvement with Israel, 1947 to the Present* (New York: W. W. Norton, 1992), p. 58.

287 *"national disgrace":* Thomas Brooks interview with author, Feb. 21, 2007.

287 *pilots refusing:* Greg Myre, "27 Israeli Reserve Pilots Say They Refuse to Bomb Civilians," *New York Times*, Sept. 25, 2003, p. A12.

ACKNOWLEDGMENTS

Writing a book is an arduous process that depends on the cooperation, support, and patience of many. I would first like to thank my father, John Scott, who served as an officer on the U.S.S. *Liberty* and never realized that this book would take as much out of him as it did me. I am equally grateful to his shipmates and their families, who welcomed me into their homes and shared with me some of the more painful memories of that tragic afternoon. I owe a special thanks to Jim Ennes, Jr., Lloyd and Ingrid Painter, Dave Lucas, Dave Lewis, Richard Kiepfer, Gary Brummett, Dennis Eikleberry, James Halman, Dale Larkins, Bryce Lockwood, Mac Watson, Patrick O'Malley, Richard Brooks, Ronald Kukal, Phillip Tourney, Pat Blue-Roushakes, Jack Beattie, and many more.

Many others shared invaluable insight into the Navy, State Department, White House, and intelligence community as well as provided me with important introductions. Along those lines, I would like to thank Paul Tobin, Jerome King, Jr., Roger Hall, Glenn Cella, Gerard Burke, and John Hadden. Gideon Kleiman proved an indispensable assistant in Israel, doggedly hunting down records, arranging interviews, and answering my constant queries. Closer to home, the Lyndon Baines Johnson Foundation graciously awarded me a Moody Grant to assist in my research. Regina Greenwell and the courteous staff at the Johnson Library made my trips to Texas a pleasure and tracked down answers to all my questions, both while in Austin and from afar.

I am indebted to Bob Giles and the Nieman Foundation for Journalism for the wonderful opportunity to spend a year at Harvard and work on this project. The foundation's incredible staff—as well as the terrific fellows I shared my year with—made Cambridge home. I am grateful to Chris Cousins for his great ideas and careful reading of the manuscript. I also want to offer a special thanks to Craig Welch, not only for his innumerable readings, suggestions, and edits, but also for his weekly—and sometimes daily—pep talks. Wendy Strothman and Dan O'Connell at the Strothman Agency in Boston believed in this project from the start, as did Bob Bender, my wise and patient editor at Simon & Schuster, who gambled on an untested, first-time writer.

Though welders cut down the *Liberty* for scrap decades ago, I know at times my family must have felt as though we all somehow sailed aboard it. I want to thank my mother, Sue Scott, and brother, John Scott, Jr., for the encouragement and readings over the years as I researched and wrote Dad's story. Most important is the thanks I owe my wife, Carmen Scott. She never wavered in her support, dedication, and patience as I traveled on research trips and spent countless weekends locked in an office at home even though I know it came at great sacrifice to her and our amazing daughter. Without her, this book never would have been finished.

INDEX